The Invention of the Beautiful Game

UNIVERSITY PRESS OF FLORIDA

Florida A&M University, Tallahassee
Florida Atlantic University, Boca Raton
Florida Gulf Coast University, Ft. Myers
Florida International University, Miami
Florida State University, Tallahassee
New College of Florida, Sarasota
University of Central Florida, Orlando
University of Florida, Gainesville
University of North Florida, Jacksonville
University of South Florida, Tampa
University of West Florida, Pensacola

THE INVENTION OF THE BEAUTIFUL GAME

Football and the Making of Modern Brazil

GREGG BOCKETTI

University Press of Florida
Gainesville · Tallahassee · Tampa · Boca Raton
Pensacola · Orlando · Miami · Jacksonville · Ft. Myers · Sarasota

Copyright 2016 by Gregg Bocketti
All rights reserved
Printed in the United States of America on acid-free paper

This book may be available in an electronic edition.

First cloth printing, 2016
First paperback printing, 2019

24 23 22 21 20 19   6 5 4 3 2 1

Library of Congress Cataloging-in-Publication Data

Names: Bocketti, Gregg, author.
Title: The invention of the beautiful game : football and the making of
   modern Brazil / Gregg Bocketti.
Description: Gainesville : University Press of Florida, [2016] | Includes
   bibliographical references and index.
Identifiers: LCCN 2015044262 | ISBN 9780813062556 (cloth : alk. paper)
ISBN 9780813064277 (pbk.)
Subjects: LCSH: Soccer—Brazil—History. | Soccer players—Brazil—History. |
   Brazil—Social life and customs. | Soccer—Social aspects—Brazil—History.
Classification: LCC GV944.B7 B63 2016 | DDC 796.3340981—dc23
LC record available at http://lccn.loc.gov/2015044262

The University Press of Florida is the scholarly publishing agency for the State University
System of Florida, comprising Florida A&M University, Florida Atlantic University,
Florida Gulf Coast University, Florida International University, Florida State University,
New College of Florida, University of Central Florida, University of Florida, University
of North Florida, University of South Florida, and University of West Florida.

University Press of Florida
2046 NE Waldo Road
Suite 2100
Gainesville, FL 32609
http://upress.ufl.edu

Contents

List of Figures vii

Acknowledgments ix

A Note on Translations and Names xiii

Introduction 1

1. Playing for the Nation: The Ideology of Brazilian Sports 17

2. Building and Rebuilding the Society of Football 60

3. Students and Masters: National Identity and International Football 117

4. Respectability, Emotion, and Gender in Brazilian Spectatorship 159

5. The Invention of the Beautiful Game 201

Epilogue: The Life of the Beautiful Game 243

Notes 259

Bibliography 291

Index 311

Figures

1.1. "Olympic Day" celebration, June 19, 1932 · 20
1.2. Fluminense Anniversary Program, July 21, 1916 · 27
1.3. Tenentes do Diabo parade float, 1920 · 41
1.4. Stadium of Fluminense Football Club, 1919 · 56
2.1. Fluminense Football Club and Club Athletico Paulistano, circa 1905 · 70
2.2. Fluminense Football Club, December 30, 1917 · 81
2.3. Andarahy Athletic Club, December 30, 1917 · 89
2.4. Football fans in Rio de Janeiro, May 31, 1914 · 105
3.1. Arthur Friedenreich, 1919 · 129
3.2. "Future Diplomacy," *A Leitura Para Todos*, July 1913 · 132
3.3. Club Athletico Paulistano players, 1925 · 136
3.4. Cover image of *Sport Illustrado*, July 20, 1938 · 153
4.1. Fluminense Football Club Women's Department of Physical Education, 1922 · 171
4.2. Cover image of *Tricolor*, February 1928 · 176
4.3. Football fans in Rio de Janeiro, July 4, 1926 · 184
4.4. Football fans in Rio de Janeiro, April 11, 1920 · 193
5.1. Paysandú Cricket Club vs. Botafogo Foot-ball Club, September 15, 1907 · 208
5.2. Botafogo Foot-ball Club vs. Fluminense Football Club, May 21, 1922 · 212
5.3. Leônidas da Silva, circa 1930 · 231
5.4. José Meurer Ripper and Domingos da Guia, July 28, 1929 · 236

Acknowledgments

In one form or another, I have been working on this book for fifteen years. I have learned a lot in that time, about history and about Brazil, and I am indebted to all of those who helped me along the way, for their advice, their assistance, and their patience. I am fortunate to have this opportunity to thank a few of them by name.

Tulane University is a wonderful place to learn, and I spent the better part of a decade there as a student, first in the Roger Thayer Stone Center for Latin American Studies and then in the Department of History. The university provided me with generous financial support throughout, and I am especially grateful for the award of the Paul and Elizabeth Selley Dissertation Year Fellowship, which helped me complete the research that became the heart of this book. I am also thankful to the U.S. Department of Education for its provision of a Foreign Language and Area Studies Fellowship, which allowed me to begin to learn Portuguese. Even more important were the people who guided me through my studies, both in the classroom and beyond it, especially Rosanne Adderley, George Bernstein, Suyapa Inglés, Colin MacLachlan, Guillermo Nañez, and Ralph Lee Woodward Jr. My wonderful friends and fellow students, William Connell, Richard Conway, Elizabeth Manley, and Niklas Robinson, encouraged me and helped me hone my ideas, and they were a big part of what made New Orleans my home.

Much of the research upon which the book is based I conducted in the archives of private sports clubs in Rio de Janeiro and São Paulo. The staff at the Fluminense Football Club, the Sociedade Esportiva Palmeiras, and the Club Athletico Paulistano have been especially helpful, and I am most grateful to Fluminense's Acervo Flu-Memória and Paulistano's Centro Pró-Memória for permission to use images from their collections to illustrate the book. The staff at the National Library of Brazil was always helpful and insightful. Alex Bellos, Aidan Hamilton, John Mills, and Leonardo Pereira pointed me in the right direction at the outset of my research. Daniel Marques de

Azevedo, Fabiano Pries Devide, Cristina Peters, Marilda Maia Rezende, and James Woodard have been great friends and research companions in working and living in Brazil.

I have had the great good fortune to work at Transylvania University, and I am grateful to the college and to the William R. Kenan Jr. Fund for Faculty and Student Enrichment for their support of my work on the project. I am lucky to work with dedicated and talented colleagues, and I appreciate the support of all of the faculty and staff at Transylvania. I am especially indebted to Katie Banks, who helped me to format images, among many other things; to Phil Walker, who moved mountains of books via interlibrary loan; and to the members of the history program, Melissa McEuen, Ken Slepyan, and Frank Russell, who have been unfailingly encouraging and generous as I have written and rewritten this book. I am also grateful to our students, who have helped me think through my ideas and helped make me both a better teacher and a better writer.

I have benefited greatly from the guidance and thoughtful questions of scholars working on Latin America. Molly Ball and Amy Chazkel helped me understand currency and economic issues related to my work. Teresa Meade and Barbara Weinstein have been thoughtful readers, and I am grateful for their encouragement, comments, and advice. I owe special thanks to Hendrik Kraay, whose comments on a draft of the manuscript have been invaluable to me, who has encouraged me at every turn, and who was the first to publish my scholarly work. I am grateful to the University of Calgary Press for permission to reproduce parts of that work, "Playing with National Identity: Brazil in International Football, 1900–1925," in *Negotiating Identities in Latin American Cultures*, ed. Hendrik Kraay (University of Calgary Press, 2007). I am also grateful to Cambridge University Press for its permission to reproduce parts of my article, "Italian Immigrants, Brazilian Football, and the Dilemma of National Identity," which appeared in its *Journal of Latin American Studies* 40, no. 2 (May 2008).

I am very grateful to Amy Gorelick for bringing me to the University Press of Florida, and to my editor at the press, Erika Stevens, who has been willing to answer every one of my many questions about the publication process and who has helped me through the final stages in completing the book. I am also grateful to the anonymous readers who took my work seriously and asked difficult and essential questions; the book is much better than it would have been without their insight.

Three families have made me feel like one of their own as I worked on this book, and I owe them special thanks. Carl and Winnie Brown; Narinder and Aruna Nath and Ranjan Nath; and Daniel and Mariella Castro opened their homes and their lives to me, and I was able to learn Portuguese, conduct research, and write among loved ones, which is one of the reasons it has taken fifteen years to complete the book—I haven't wanted the experience to end. Daniel Castro was my mentor since our days at Hartwick College. Without him, I would be doing something else with my life, something less thrilling and less fulfilling, and I will be forever grateful for his belief in me.

My own family has been my true north throughout these many years, providing me with much, much more than I can ever describe. I have been able to embrace the challenges of graduate school in Louisiana, of research in Brazil and Trinidad and England, of a life and work in Kentucky, because I have always known my mom and dad, Angela and Philip, and my best friends—my brothers Jon and Brian—are there in New York, inspiring me and ready to welcome me home. They planted the seeds of this book, at Spring Little League, in packs of baseball cards, and on the soccer field at Knickerbacker Park.

Finally, I can only hint at how grateful I am to Randi Ewing, for her insight, her sense of humor, her patience, and above all for her encouragement. She joined me on research trips, she helped me scan photos and talk through titles, and she read the book generously and critically, helping me to understand what I want to say and to make the book what I want it to be. She is my Ideal Reader.

A Note on Translations and Names

In Brazil's early football communities, many insisted that using the right word and correct language—English—for football terms was vitally important. At one time, officials even sought to mandate the preservation of terms like "offsides," "center forward," and "corner kick." In order to give the reader an idea of the importance Brazilians assigned to a specific sports terminology, in translations I have employed italics to indicate that a word was published in English in the original text.

Brazilian football players are often referred to by one name or a nickname, as in the case of Pelé (Edson Arantes do Nascimento). I have followed this practice. When I have been able to discover it, I have included the player's full name on the first occasion I mention him, except in well-known cases, as with the players discussed in the epilogue.

Introduction

According to tradition, Charles Miller introduced football to Brazil in 1894. The Brazilian-born Miller learned to play the game while attending boarding school in England. When he finished his studies, Miller returned home, disembarking at the port of Santos with a football in each hand, much to the surprise of his waiting father, who had expected him to be holding his diploma. Telling his charming and possibly apocryphal story years later, Miller recalled telling his father that he had completed his studies and was indeed holding his diploma. He "had graduated in football." Miller worried about his father's reaction, but, he said, his joke had broken the ice, and the homecoming was a happy one.[1] Charles Miller's enthusiasm was infectious, and the elder Miller was not the only one to be charmed. Miller recruited a few members of the English expatriate São Paulo Athletic Club to take up the game and then turned his attention to his Brazilian acquaintances, some of whom he convinced that playing football was an especially good form of physical education. Its popularity grew quickly from there.

A decade after Miller's return to Brazil, the magazine *Kosmos* commented that "*foot-ball* is the order of the day" in the country's leading cities, gaining "new and enthusiastic converts" and whole new clubs almost daily, and the educator José Veríssimo had begun to worry that enthusiasm for the game had become "a little exaggerated."[2] After another decade it had spread beyond the cities of the southeast and the coast, and a British traveler reported that it had become "a national pastime that attracts crowds in city, town, and village all over the Republic" and that "every town in Brazil has its football clubs and grounds."[3] According to the novelist and critic Lima Barreto, football had grown so popular that by the 1910s the residents of Rio de Janeiro discussed little else. Football filled newspaper columns, and it dominated conversations on streetcars and trains, in restaurants and homes, and even city council meetings, absorbing "all of the activities [of] ... almost every soul in the city." Barreto disliked the game, which he saw as a "spectacle of brutality," and in 1919 he helped found the Liga Contra Foot-ball (Anti-Football League), in the hopes of reversing football's growth.[4]

Of course the attempt failed, and football's popularity among Brazilians has become proverbial. Playwright Nelson Rodrigues famously called Brazil "the Fatherland in football boots" in the mid-twentieth century, and sociologist Janet Lever described Brazilians' "soccer madness" in the early-1980s, two of the many depictions that have helped sustain the idea of Brazilians' extraordinary love of the game.[5] In 2007 then-president of Brazil Luiz Inácio Lula da Silva described football as "a national passion" in accepting the invitation to host the 2014 World Cup, and the idea that Brazilians have a special affinity for the game was never more prevalent than in the marketing of the tournament and in much of coverage about it in the national and international media.[6]

According to Nelson Rodrigues and many others, Brazilians demand a very particular version of football, which is what makes it an essential part of Brazilian culture. This is *o jogo bonito*—"the beautiful game" of creativity and fantasy and joy—which ostensibly enacts Brazil's authentic identity, one rooted in the country's history of mixing cultures and peoples, among which the contributions of people of African descent are said to be especially important. Brazilians want to win at football but, according to this construct, they reject the functionalism of *futebol de resultados*, results-oriented football, which sits alongside *futebol força*, power football, as an object of their derision. Even more important than results is to win in a beautiful way, playing *futebol arte*, a game of poetry, not prose, in which the player is an artist and ideologue, not merely an athlete. Admirers assert that only o jogo bonito is truly Brazilian, and that other ways of playing are foreign to the Brazilian spirit. They argue that Brazilians have made the game their own, with their style of play and their football culture distilling what is Brazilian about Brazil.[7]

But it has not always been this way. Football in Brazil, and Brazilians' depictions of its meaning, began very differently. At the outset, those Brazilians who joined Charles Miller on the football field did not see the game as a means to show that Brazil was an inventive and richly diverse country.

The first Brazilians to play the game were wealthy and middle-class urbanites who saw football as a way to mark themselves as cosmopolitan and as a way to improve Brazil according to a European standard. This meant playing the way they believed Europeans played, in a measured, pragmatic, and, above all, disciplined manner; for them football was a science, not an art. This is one likely reason that Charles Miller's version of the sport's arrival has been preferred to others that have been put forward from time to time.[8] Miller's account resonates with the history of football as it came to be played in Brazil for a generation after 1894: dominated by urban middle- and upper-class white men, modeled on their selective reading of European football, and available to women, people of color, and working people largely on terms set by the men who were the first to join Miller on the field of play. These men, such as Antônio Prado Júnior and Arnaldo Guinle, scions of two of the wealthiest and most powerful families in Brazil at the turn of the century, called themselves "sportsmen," making sure to say the word in English, the language they used for all the terms of the game they called "foot-ball." More than just a love of sport, the name characterized an entire ethos, infused by Eurocentrism and social exclusivity, expressed in everything from the reasons they gave for playing the game, to the ways they organized their competitions, to their choice of opponents, to how they watched and played the game.

By the 1930s, within two generations of Charles Miller's return to São Paulo, influential journalists like Thomaz Mazzoni and Nelson Rodrigues' brother, Mário Filho, were arguing that the football of the sportsmen had given way to what they called a Brazilian version of the game. They argued that this game, which they called *futebol*, welcomed Brazilian men from all walks of life onto the playing field, and they pointed out that by the 1920s leading teams were fielding white and black players, workingmen as well as the well-to-do, athletes from big cities and small towns. Mazzoni, Filho, and like-minded commentators also argued that futebol was especially eloquent in displaying Brazil as a racial democracy, because the star players of the 1930s, such as Leônidas da Silva and Domingos da Guia, were Afro-Brazilian and working class, the kind of men who the sportsmen had been hesitant to include. Proponents of futebol rejected the Eurocentrism of the past, and they said that their countrymen played football in a particularly Brazilian way, a "Brazilian school" of football that had all the hallmarks of what is now called o jogo bonito. In the words of the player, coach, and critic Floriano Peixoto Corrêa, by the 1930s many Brazilians had become convinced that theirs was "a race especially chosen by the gods and goddesses of the leather ball" to dominate the game.⁹ They had made the game their own.

⚯

This book explains the changes in Brazilian football from the era of Charles Miller and the sportsmen to the consolidation of the ideas of the beautiful game and of Brazil's ownership of the game, the transition from "foot-ball" to "futebol." The period from the 1890s to the 1940s saw the transformation of Brazil's sporting life from a modest one, focused mainly on horseracing and water sports like crew and swimming, into an inescapable leviathan that included tennis, basketball, and other sports but was dominated by football. Rich and poor, white and black, men and women, intellectuals and the unlettered, native-born Brazilians and immigrants, people from cities and from the countryside, Northeasterners and Southerners, all seemed to embrace the game. It had its enemies, but—to the dismay of critics like Lima Barreto—they were fewer every year as football emerged as a national obsession.

The popular history of Brazilian football, as expressed, for example, in Mário Filho's extremely influential 1947 book *O negro no foot-ball brasileiro* (The black man in Brazilian foot-ball), has generally held that the transition saw football advance from antidemocratic and foreign beginnings to become ever more democratic and ever more Brazilian. It is an attractive story, one of progress and authenticity, a tradition of futebol's inevitable triumph. It is also susceptible to simplification. Dependent as it is on opposites—white/black, male/female, rich/poor, oligarchy/democracy, foreign/Brazilian—this progressive and nationalist tradition of Brazilian football misses quite a bit of the complexity of the story of the game in Brazil and therefore obscures some of the significance of football to the history of Brazil.

It misses, for example, the real and continuing influence of the sportsmen's clubs and their middle-class and wealthy directors. Those clubs and directors managed many of the changes Brazilian football underwent in the transition to futebol so that, even as the population of players grew and became more diverse, the ultimate power of Brazilian football never migrated very far from where Charles Miller and his partners had placed it. Usually discussed in terms of Brazil as a whole, the tradition tends to disregard regional difference and the continuing dominance of the southeast, especially Rio de Janeiro and São Paulo. Related to this, nationalist histories have often highlighted Rio de Janeiro's role at the expense of São Paulo because many of the Afro-Brazilian stars of the 1930s began their careers in the capital. This is especially telling of the choices nationalists made in constructing their story of football, not least because Brazilian football began in São Paulo and it was a club of the white elite of that city, the Club Athletico Paulistano, that first established Brazilians' international reputation as inventive and dynamic players when the club conducted a remarkably successful tour of Europe in 1925.

Nationalist history tends to downplay Brazilian football's persistently problematic relationship with foreign football, which is at times forgotten because of Brazilians' on-field success in international tournaments but which has if anything become more problematic as European club teams have recruited more and more Brazilian players at younger and younger ages, weakening the game in Brazil. And the nationalist story of the game has almost completely written women out of Brazilian football history, suggesting that they entered football only in the last two or three decades. The significant role of women fans in the early twentieth century has thus rarely even been mentioned, let alone explored. Given football's importance to Brazilian identity, this neglect has served to reinforce Brazilian women's marginalization from national history and one of Brazil's most important venues of national communion.

Therefore, this book also explains the omissions and distortions of nationalist history, which has had such influence on the popular memory of football in Brazil and which has had very real consequences for its performance and its organization. Mário Filho, Thomaz Mazzoni, and other nationalists in the 1920s and 1930s championed futebol as part of their attempt to "Brazilianize" Brazil, and they helped lead efforts aimed at reforming football along what seemed to them fairer, more inclusive, and more Brazilian lines. They attacked aspects of the football culture of the sportsmen that they disliked, and they helped change Brazilian football in important ways. But they also helped reinforce some of the legacies of the football of the sportsmen.

Nationalist reformers attacked the amateurism that Charles Miller and the sportsmen had insisted upon when they organized Brazil's first competitions, and they promoted professionalization as a way to make football more meritocratic and inclusive, hoping to afford greater opportunities for players of modest backgrounds to dedicate themselves to mastering the game. They called for clubs and representative teams like the national "select" team, or *seleção*, to recruit the best and most talented players, regardless of their race or class, in order to improve the quality of Brazilian teams and to make

Brazil more competitive in international competitions. And they supported efforts to diminish regional conflicts and to expand the administrative role of national bodies like the Confederação Brasileira de Desportos (CBD, National Sports Confederation, forerunner of the Confederação Brasileira de Futebol, the CBF, Brazilian football's governing body and the organizer of the national team).

Reformers focused especially on working to diminish some of the more obvious expressions of what they believed was the un-Brazilian and Eurocentric ethic of the sportsmen. For example, they demanded that Brazilian coaches replace European ones, and they insisted that immigrant athletes and organizations, such as São Paulo's Palestra Itália and Rio de Janeiro's Vasco da Gama, declare their loyalty to Brazil or suffer the consequences of nationalist anger. They also promoted the belief that their countrymen had created a Brazilian version of the game, that they had developed their own ways of watching and playing the game which were rooted in Brazil's true national identity, one characterized by creativity and feeling, and not "European" planning and rationality. The influential sociologist Gilberto Freyre called this version of the game a "Brazilianism" and, along with other influential interpreters of the meaning of Brazilian football, explained it as a consequence of the fusion of European and African cultures.[10] This was a game personified by players of African descent, though it could be played by Brazilian men of all types, a venue in which Brazilians could express their vibrant, poetic national identity.

The reformers' greatest accomplishment was arguably their invention and promulgation of a Brazilian football identity, which signaled their ideological commitment to rejecting the old ways of Charles Miller and the sportsmen and their promotion of futebol as a means of making Brazil more Brazilian. The idea of a Brazilian version of the game helped to transform the way Brazilians and foreigners came to think and talk about the game in Brazil, figuratively and also literally, through the invention of a new vocabulary for the game, trading "football" for "futebol," "game" for "*jogo*," "shot" for "*chute*," and dozens of other translations and neologisms. It helped convince the football public to make the kinds of changes for which reformers campaigned, from creating more powerful national institutions to opening up playing opportunities for nonwhite and working-class players to removing obvious examples of foreign influence in Brazilian football. Just as importantly, it helped obscure the fact that while much changed in the 1920s and 1930s, much did not. The sportsmen were not as exclusive, nor the reformers as transformative, as nationalist history suggests, and many of the legacies of the old ways—social and racial and regional disparities, and European domination of the business of international football—persisted despite the claims of nationalist activists in the 1920s and 1930s and many commentators since.

In order to understand the history of football in Brazil, it is necessary to understand the construction of this invented tradition of futebol.[11] Scholars have only recently begun to look closely and critically at this tradition, to look past the story of Brazilian football as told by the nationalists of the 1930s and the "new narrators" who have followed them and who have helped, as Antonio J. Soares says, "transform the oft-told history of futebol into a myth."[12] This book contributes to the work of scholars such as Soares, Denaldo Alchorne de Souza, and Roger Kittleson, who have begun to analyze the invention of the futebol tradition and its life since the 1930s.[13] These authors are among a small number of scholars who have begun to deepen our understanding of football and other sports in Latin America, looking beyond hopeful celebrations of sports' capacity to reveal "authentic" national identities. Sociologists and anthropologists Pablo Alabarces, Simoni Lahud Guedes, and Aldo Panfichi, among others, have been especially insightful in helping to reveal how Latin Americans use sports to define their nations and to build community, whether national, regional, or local. They have also paid attention to the inventions and narratives that Latin Americans use to make sports serve their purposes, showing some of the consequences of ideas about sports, both for sports themselves and beyond them.[14] Scholars of Brazilian and Latin American sport have paid relatively less attention to the late nineteenth and early twentieth centuries, the period I focus on here, aside from exceptional—and exceptionally important—works by historians including Brenda Elsey, Victor Andrade de Melo, and Leonardo Pereira.[15]

In this book, I trace the history of football inventions in Brazil to the beginning, to the 1890s and early twentieth century. In building early Brazilian football, Charles Miller and his partners made choices in how to depict their activities and justify their version of the game well before Gilberto Freyre and others began to build a new narrative in the 1920s and 1930s, as can be seen in Miller's story about the game's arrival in Brazil. The inventions of the sportsmen were largely displaced in the 1920s and 1930s, but they were very important to the early history of football in Brazil and in important ways their influence endured.

The book analyzes Brazilian ideas about the game between 1894 and 1941, and the choices Brazilians made about how to explain football during that period. It also analyzes the way those ideas shaped how the game functioned, for they had and have continued to have material consequences for football in Brazil.[16] For example, both the sportsmen and their later critics argued that their preferences about whether football should be amateur or professional grew out of their patriotic desire to improve Brazilian football and so that Brazil would get the most out of the game. Sportsmen argued that only amateurs played for the right reasons and benefited from it, drawing from the amateur tradition of private British schools that Miller and other early promoters transplanted to the first clubs in Brazil. They thereby justified their insistence upon amateurism and its limits on the participation of working-class Brazilians by a curious mix of nationalism and very carefully edited Eurocentrism. In the 1920s and 1930s, those who fought for professionalization claimed they worked to improve the game and to democratize it, since professionalization offered more opportunities for nonwhite and working-class players. But they also accepted the control that middle-class and elite clubs continued to exert, arguing that the clubs were transformed when they fielded nonwhite and working-class professionals even though those players, as employees, actually had less influence over club affairs than their amateur predecessors did. In short, both the defenders of amateurism and the promoters of professionalism crafted narratives that justified their choices in the administration of Brazilian football. The book analyzes the roots of these choices, the construction of these narratives, and their consequences.

Football was also important beyond the game's boundaries, and this book demonstrates that understanding the history of Brazilian football contributes to a deeper knowledge of Brazil as a whole in the late nineteenth and early twentieth centuries.[17] By the 1910s football was so popular that it was one of the few activities that seemed to include Brazilians of every type. It is thus unsurprising that politicians attempted to use it for their own benefit and to try to shape their communities and Brazil as a whole. It seemed able to serve as a touchstone of what it meant to be Brazilian during a critical era of debates over national identity and therefore attracted the attention of prominent cultural figures, with opponents like Lima Barreto warning of football's dangers and the poet Coelho Netto serving as a famous promoter of the game. With its local, regional, and national institutions—clubs and leagues and media—it was also a venue for social organization in which Brazilians debated and defined the roles men and women ought to play in modern Brazil. And it was an expanding business that offered economic opportunities to the players, administrators, media figures, and merchants who could exploit them.

Such connections made football more than a sport in Brazil, and understanding football and its complexities means understanding more than Brazil's sports history. The book complicates a common view of Brazil's First Republic (1889–1930) as an oligarchy of social and racial exclusion and reflexive Eurocentrism. Many of the sportsmen were exclusive, but they encouraged every Brazilian to play football and other sports, as long as it was in their own venues. They were Eurocentric, but, much more than simple imitators, they chose their Europe carefully and selectively, and they saw their Eurocentrism as a form of nationalism. Recognizing what they believed were Brazil's faults, and hoping to use the British game to help correct them, the sportsmen were not a placid and satisfied oligarchy. They did not always see Brazil clearly, and they certainly did not value all their countrymen equally, but they refused to fantasize about the country; this book thus complements the work of scholars who have reassessed elite views of popular culture and the possibilities for popular participation in civic life during the early twentieth century.[18]

In its examination of the popular narrative of football and its consequences, the book also evaluates the influential populist and nationalist movements that emerged in the 1920s and flourished in the 1930s. Many football reformers saw their work as coinciding with, and even part of, the "revolution" of Getúlio Vargas, the Rio Grande do Sul politician who took power by force in 1930 and ruled Brazil for fifteen years. The Vargas regime intervened in football in a variety of ways, including by promoting professionalization, providing government support to the seleção, and pressuring immigrant clubs to bury foreign identities. Rather than revolutionary, however, the regime's football activities were populist and authoritarian. It claimed to be helping transform Brazilian football, but it reinforced the roles of already-powerful actors and interests, for example by strengthening the elite-controlled CBD. Attention to football demonstrates that many of the nationalists of the 1920s and the 1930s were as concerned with impressing foreigners as were many of their predecessors, and it shows the extent to which Vargas-era populism was a way of "restructuring" Brazil's class, gender, and racial hierarchies rather than challenging them.[19]

This book demonstrates the nationalism of superficially Eurocentric sportsmen and the hierarchical thinking of the populist reformers of the 1930s, among other complexities, and the consequences of these ways of thinking, and it thus demonstrates the extent to which the history of the period from 1894 to the 1940s was characterized by constancy as much as change. Like the words themselves, the "futebol" of the 1930s and 1940s was not as different from the "foot-ball" of the 1890s as it sometimes seems, and as many champions of futebol have insisted. In order to underscore the complexities and inventions of Brazilian football, the book does not employ the chronological structure through which the history of Brazilian football is usually recounted. Each chapter that follows focuses on one aspect of the history of Brazilian football, one theme prevalent in the invented tradition of futebol. Each begins at the turn of the twentieth century and analyzes what changed and what did not change between that period and the late 1930s and early 1940s, focusing on the relationship between ideas and discourse and their consequences, and on how Brazilians narrated the choices they made as they organized their football lives.

Chapter 1 examines football's attractions to Miller and the well-to-do sportsmen who first took to the game, and to the reformers of the 1920s and 1930s who bent it to their uses. Like all of the chapters of this book, it draws heavily from the coverage of sports in the popular press, which grew rapidly in the late nineteenth and early twentieth centuries. Because it focuses on the ideology of sports, it also analyzes the discourse of educators and policymakers on the place of sports in Brazil. It shows that both sportsmen and reformers considered themselves part of larger movements to improve the country and its people. The sportsmen believed football would improve Brazilians' health and teach them to be good citizens, workers, and soldiers, their beliefs about football animated by the same impulse as that which gave rise to Brazil's First Republic in 1889 and to contemporaneous public health campaigns and urban renewal projects. Later reformers attacked the sportsmen, but they shared their predecessors' faith in football's power to build the nation. They viewed it as an important tool for fighting regionalism, and they continued to promote its importance to Brazilians' education, believing that football could teach Brazilians the discipline many of them seemed to lack. In this reformers echoed the sportsmen they criticized as well as their counterparts and partners in the Vargas regime. The chapter demonstrates that despite rhetorical and other apparent differences, Brazilian policymakers, educators, and other nation-builders from the 1890s to the 1940s shared a commitment to improvement and discipline, one revealed in an abiding ideology of football.

I address how this ideology shaped Brazilian decisions about how to organize football life in chapter 2. I analyze the character and function of football's institutions—its clubs, leagues, and media—by examining their public activities and their internal conversations, which is made possible by a close examination of the private archives of football clubs. The sportsmen organized the first teams, and they were the first sportswriters, which allowed them great influence over organized football, and they designed significant limits on the involvement of women, nonwhites, and workers, who sportsmen did not believe should participate fully in the game. None of these groups were ever fully incorporated into football, but talented nonwhite and working-class men were playing for the most important clubs as early as the 1910s, with the most obvious changes coming after the professionalization of Brazil's best leagues in 1933. Many of those who promoted the change framed it as a democratic victory against the exclusionary practices of the sportsmen, but neither the inclusion of nonwhite and working-class players in elite clubs nor professionalization meant that football had been transformed. Participation remained contingent on the will of middle-class and wealthy white administrators and journalists, whose influence was reinforced by the support of the Vargas government. The chapter demonstrates that the period was characterized by the renovation of elite privilege, even though popular memory has suggested the period as a whole, and football in particular, saw elite privilege eroded.

Chapter 3 focuses on international football, which Brazilians throughout the twentieth century saw as a proving ground of national worth. The sportsmen fielded select teams that advertised Brazil as white and cosmopolitan, sometimes to the detriment of the teams' technical quality, and were especially enthusiastic to demonstrate this to Europeans, whom the sportsmen considered the masters of the game and the arbiters of modernity. When Brazilian teams began to beat European ones in the 1910s and the seleção won its first international titles in 1919 and 1922, Brazilians became more confident in their own football and less likely to think of themselves as students. By the late-1920s reformers were demanding that talent be given greater weight in selecting representatives, and in the 1930s populists argued that the fact that many of the best players on the seleção were black or working class meant that football revealed a better and more just Brazil. The chapter demonstrates football's contributions to the nationalist movement of the

1920s and 1930s, but it also demonstrates that behind a veneer of inclusion lay many old tensions since administrators still took race, class, and region into account when building representative sides, and Brazilian nationalists in the 1930s continued to be highly sensitive to foreign opinion of Brazil. In promulgating Brazil's "new" identity in the international arena, and portraying the seleção as authentically Brazilian, football's narrators helped obscure these tensions, but they remained, to reemerge whenever the seleção failed to meet expectations.

In chapter 4 I examine the role that fans played in the history of Brazilian football because they have always been essential participants in the football spectacle. The sportsmen believed that spectators would be improved by watching gentlemen play football properly, and they encouraged the participation of fans whom they identified as the models of proper spectatorship, especially well-to-do white women. The chapter focuses on these women, drawing from the sports press and club archives and also from women's magazines like the *Revista Feminina* and the contemporary theater. Like many influential Brazilians, sportsmen believed emotional reserve was the key to respectability for football fans and for all modern women and men, but middle-class and wealthy women exploited the heterosocial space opened up by football spectatorship, and they challenged this belief.[20] Called *torcedoras*, twisted ones, many women fans were passionate about the game, and they crafted a model of respectability that encouraged fans to display emotion and zeal, a model that has gone unnoticed by historians. Reformers seized on the idea of fans' passionate involvement in the game and argued that it was a distinctive feature of Brazilian spectatorship. But they also joined the Vargas regime in objecting to the prospect of respectable women participating in the commercialized and mass football of the 1930s and 1940s, a perspective exemplified by the state's formal ban on women's football in 1941. The decline and the forgetting of the torcedoras indicates the character and limits of Brazilians' challenges to traditional gender norms in the early twentieth century and the nature of the reassertion of tradition during the Vargas years.

The last chapter focuses on Brazilians' ideas about how the game should be played, their debates about style, tactics, and strategy collected from such sources as match reports and coaching manuals. It demonstrates the sportsmen's struggle to train Brazilian footballers to play as they thought Europeans played and the widespread conviction that by the 1920s a Brazilian football style had begun to emerge. The chapter focuses on arguments about the meaning of the supposed "Brazilian" style, showing that critics and admirers alike relied heavily on ideas about race and nature in explaining it and that therefore Brazilian football arguments are useful for understanding Brazilian ideas about race and ethnicity in the twentieth century. Early republican improvers rejected strict racial determinism, for they believed that all Brazilian people could be improved according to carefully selected European standards, which in football meant teaching them a style built on teamwork and passing. Their successors in the 1920s and 1930s, however, adopted deterministic explanations to account for the success of footballers who played differently, who seemed to prefer to dribble the ball than pass it. They depicted the style as inherently Afro-Brazilian and its success as evidence of Brazil's racial enlightenment. The chapter shows that its champions' invention of a rhetoric of an authentically Brazilian football style obscured their choices and elisions, and demonstrates some of the limits of the racial democracy they claimed for Brazil, such as their insistence that Afro-Brazilian players still required the guidance of white coaches and administrators, regardless of their allegedly inherent talent for football.

The epilogue considers the life of the futebol tradition in the years since its invention in the 1930s. It examines a few key moments when Brazilians used it as a shared vernacular to discuss the meaning of Brazil and Brazilianness, moments drawn from Brazil's World Cup history because, as the saying goes, the nation measures its life with each four-year cycle of the tournament.[21] It begins in 1950, with Brazil's defeat in the final match of the first World Cup it hosted, prompting a painful reexamination of the Brazilian style and of Brazilian ideas about race. It discusses the triumphal years of 1958–70, when Brazil won three World Cups with teams that seemed to embody futebol but that could not assuage the doubts of the military that ruled Brazil from 1964 to 1985 and worried about the indiscipline futebol seemed to endorse. It examines Brazilian debates about the World Cup teams of 1982 and 1994, the former associated with the joyousness of futebol at its best, the latter unpopular because it seemed to play the futebol de resultados. Finally, it considers World Cup 2014, hosted by Brazil. Advertised as a homecoming for football and a celebration of futebol by organizers and in many of the extraordinary number of works released to coincide with the event, it also helped propel an ongoing protest movement that cast doubt on the value of football and the futebol tradition. The tournament broadcast the tradition's continuing importance to Brazilians' conversations about themselves and highlighted the importance of understanding its roots.

All of these chapters focus on questions of mentality and identity. That is, they focus on Brazilians' habits of thinking and why they thought about football as they did. They examine their differences of opinion about the game's meaning, the ways Brazilians expressed their views on football, and how those views shaped their activities, both within football and in using the game to shape the nation. In short, they examine Brazilians' use of football in thinking about and revealing their sense of themselves and their country over time, and they show that football was always much more than a game in Brazil. It was a means by which Brazilians organized their ideas about their nation and about the roles their countrymen and women should play in it, a vehicle for enacting those ideas, and a lexicon for imagining, expressing, and debating them.

As much as I would like to offer a comprehensive history of Brazilian football between the 1890s and the 1940s, the historical record does not allow for such an exhaustive portrait. It is possible to know more about the activities of the wealthy than the sporting life of poorer people, much more about the views of whites than nonwhites, much more about men than women. The most prominent of the early clubs, such as Fluminense in Rio de Janeiro and Paulistano in São Paulo, remain active today and preserve many documents related to their histories, such as club magazines and the minutes of directors' meetings, while many more modest clubs led brief lives and have left little imprint on the available record. The sports press, which grew quickly after football's arrival, lavished attention on the "big" clubs, while it rarely did more than mention the scores of games played by workingmen, students, or soldiers, all of whom had their own clubs and even leagues. When nonwhite players and fans and women enter the historical record, they often do so through the organizations of wealthy white men, as when black working-class professionals joined big clubs or when male sportswriters interpreted the meaning of women fans' interest in the game.

By the 1940s football was being played throughout the country, from Pará to Paraná, from the coast deep into the interior, but this book focuses on the two most important centers of football activity, Brazil's then-capital, Rio de Janeiro, and its most dynamic region, greater São Paulo. These two continue to dominate Brazilian football, so that while important teams and great players come from Belo Horizonte and Salvador de Bahia, the biggest clubs in Rio de Janeiro and São Paulo, such as Flamengo and Corinthians, gobble up many of the best players, the most championships, the most valuable sponsorships, and the most press attention. In the late nineteenth and early twentieth centuries, these cities possessed the largest football leagues, and, despite their constant feuding, they dominated the organization of football at the national level. The national team rarely included footballers who were not playing for a team in either Rio de Janeiro or São Paulo. For their part, Brazilians from outside Rio de Janeiro and São Paulo modeled their football lives on those in the two centers, which helps explain why there are eight different clubs called Fluminense, the newer seven inspired by the capital's first football club. In short, the history of football among Cariocas (residents of Rio de Janeiro) and Paulistas (residents of São Paulo) accounts for a great part of the history of Brazilian football. Still, the focus on Rio de Janeiro and São Paulo does have its limits. For example, they were among Brazil's most cosmopolitan cities, so that immigrant players and foreign coaches were more likely to play important roles in Rio de Janeiro and São Paulo than in, say, Belém in the far north or Cuiabá in the west. And they were among its wealthiest and most populated areas, which helped make the business of football more important there than in small cities and smaller towns.

As far as is possible within these constraints, the book examines football's enemies as well as its friends, and it considers the views and activities of players and fans; coaches and administrators; journalists, politicians, and businessmen; women and men; blacks and whites; rich and poor. As they struggled to define what it meant to be Brazilian and what Brazil should be, these Brazilians found in football an uncommonly useful vehicle for defining their goals and pursuing them. When they championed foot-ball, sportsmen were advocating for an entire way of life and a vision for Brazil modeled on their selective reading of what the game meant in Britain and Europe. Just as selective were the reformers who fought for futebol, who promoted a different Brazil defined by what they said was a rejection of Europe and an affirmation of Brazil's authentic qualities.

Today, when the discourse of those reformers dominates discussions of Brazilian football and the game is often depicted as something characteristically Brazilian, it is easy to miss the choices that both the sportsmen and their later critics made. In part because they told a romantic story of progress and authenticity, it is easy to accept the assertion of the inventors of futebol that it was completely different from foot-ball, that they were nationalists and the sportsmen were not. This book argues that the well-documented Eurocentrism of well-to-do Brazilians in the late nineteenth and early twentieth centuries ought to be understood as a purposeful and selective reading of Europe aimed at building the Brazilian nation. And it argues that the popular notion that futebol was an expression of Brazilians' authentic national identity obscures the lasting influence of the football culture invented by Charles Miller and his fellow sportsmen. When we understand the differences *and* the similarities between foot-ball and futebol, and why their similarities often go unnoticed, we better understand what changed and what did not during a critical period of Brazil's modern history. Understanding foot-ball and futebol, sportsmen and football reformers, we better understand the fundamental reasons for the game's original and continuing power in Brazil and its remarkable capacity to reveal Brazilians' visions of their country and their hopes for what it might be.

Playing for the Nation

The Ideology of Brazilian Sports

In Decree-Law 3199 of April 14, 1941, Getúlio Vargas established the Conselho Nacional de Desportos (CND, National Sports Council). Vargas had taken power in 1930, toppling the government of Brazil's First Republic (installed in 1889) and building a regime dedicated to centralization and state-sponsored development. This process culminated in 1937, when Vargas swept away the last vestiges of the republican system and established his Estado Novo, or New State. An explicitly authoritarian government, the Estado Novo aimed at destroying partisanship and regionalism, rationalizing public administration, and giving the nation a sense of common purpose under Vargas' paternalistic direction. The sports council was one part of this larger effort, tasked to reorganize and "discipline" sports administration, to promote amateur athletics, to supervise professional sports, to direct Brazil's participation in international competitions, and to oversee public investment in sports programs.

In organizing the CND, the Vargas state annexed sports to its nationalist project and asserted that previous governments had failed to understand sports' role in creating a greater Brazil. For decades Brazilian sports had been rent by administrative conflicts, for example, between promoters of amateur sports and professionalization and between partisans of Rio de Janeiro and São Paulo. Among other consequences, these conflicts had compromised Brazilian participation in international contests, most famously in the first two editions of the football World Cup. In 1930 regional disputes meant the national team was constituted almost exclusively by players drawn from the capital, and in 1934 the team did not include many of the country's best players because of a conflict over the installation of professional football the year before. At home, professional football monopolized public attention and scarce resources, allegedly leaving amateurs demoralized and underfunded, while professional leagues themselves required, according to the regime, "rigorous vigilance" in order to fight corruption and maintain them "within the principles of strict morality."[1]

Vargas and his allies had begun to address these problems soon after taking power in 1930, expressing concern about fractiousness among sports administrators, promoting physical education, and providing assistance to Brazilian athletes taking part in international contests. During the following decade, the state steadily expanded its role in sports, for example, by reviewing competition rules and player transfers; Vargas believed it was "necessary to coordinate and discipline" sports, especially football, because they promoted "the harmony of national consciousness."[2] The CND was the culmination of these efforts, a national solution to national—and seemingly intractable—problems, and it therefore possessed expansive powers to match its weighty responsibilities. In a hierarchical manner typical of the Vargas state, the CND organized confederations that oversaw every "sports" activity, from football to fencing, from basketball to chess. In turn, these confederations brought together federations that administered sports at the state level, federations that oversaw leagues organized at the municipal level, and leagues that brought together individual sports clubs, each and every one of which was obligated to participate in a scheme designed to provide Brazil a coordinated, effective, and nationalist sports bureaucracy that might overcome decades of disorganization, inefficiency, and disunity.

Having complained for years about private-sector sports administrators and their seeming unwillingness to cooperate with one another, the sportswriter Thomaz Mazzoni championed the initiative, insisting that the state must act because only it could guarantee that sport was what it should be, dedicated to "the service of the nation."[3] Members of the government extended the argument. In the words of João Alberto Lins de Barros of the Ministry of Education and Health, the state took an interest in sports because sports were a matter of national health and national well-being. They were one of the "pillars of the improvement of the race, improving the physical condition of the individual, making him capable of work, and necessary for the development of collective education and of collaborative spirit among youth." They could help keep youth away from criminality, developing their character both morally and physically. Echoing Lins de Barros' view of sports' role in promoting a "collaborative spirit," influential educator and eugenicist Fernando de Azevedo, who helped organize another Estado Novo project, the Escola Nacional de Educação Física e Desportos (National School of Physical Education and Sports) in 1939, argued that sports could bring the nation together. They were a "powerful force for national unity, an instrument for the consolidation of political union, whose base is established on the fundamental harmony of a developing people." Finally, Col. Mario Ary Pires said that because of the demands they placed on athletes, certain sports could "through the discipline of the stadium motivate soldiers to adopt battlefield discipline."[4] Sports could, in short, educate and improve Brazil and Brazilians, developing individuals and building the nation. The decree made this clear, situating the CND within the Ministry of Education and Health and stating explicitly that its overriding concern must be to "make sports into an ever more efficient process of physical and moral education for young people and a lofty expression of national culture and energy."[5]

The Vargas state depicted its actions as transformative, and in some ways they were. Among other changes, many of which echoed interventions taken by Vargas' populist counterparts in Mexico after its revolution and in Argentina under Juan Perón, the 1941 law centralized sports administration, which originally had been established at the local level and had remained mostly regional in scope into the 1930s.[6] It expanded the role of the national government in the administration and the promotion of sports. And it established formal conditions on participation in Brazilian sports. Women were banned from "sports incompatible with the conditions of their nature," which in practice meant the end of then-recent experiments in women's football. And it attempted to ensure that Brazilians would dominate Brazilian sports, the law allowing each professional team to field one foreign player and obligating foreign-born administrators and coaches to obtain formal CND permission to work in Brazil.[7]

The thinking behind these reforms was not, however, actually new. For example, Washington Luís Pereira de Sousa, the Paulista who Getúlio Vargas removed from the presidency, was a well-known supporter of sport and physical education and had done much to promote them during his tenure as governor of São Paulo and president of Brazil. Washington Luís' 1920 gubernatorial platform spoke both of man's "obligation to be strong" and the

FIGURE 1.1. "Olympic Day" celebration organized by the Confederação Brasileira Desportos, June 19, 1932, held at the stadium of the Fluminense Football Club. By permission of the Acervo Flu-Memória.

state's obligation to provide physical education, and it directly connected improvement to sport, arguing that "the creation of a sporting society has as much social value as the creation of a school." Further, contrary to the accusations that the Vargas movement would assert against him and his mostly Paulista supporters, Luís' platform did not speak in regional terms. Instead, it said that Luís' government would "fortify and, above all, Brazilianize the Brazilian," meaning, it seems, that through the promotion of sport and physical education, the government would train Paulistas to see themselves as Brazilians, better able to fulfill Brazil's needs as members of a national community.[8]

Washington Luís carried this commitment to Rio de Janeiro when he became president, for example, by appointing as mayor of the capital his fellow Paulista Antônio Prado Júnior, scion of one of Brazil's most powerful families and, as the longtime president of the Club Athletico Paulistano, one of the country's leading football figures. As mayor of Rio de Janeiro, Prado Júnior oversaw the 1928 reform of the capital's educational system, an important part of which was the mandate that all government schools provide physical education for their students. To lead the renovation as director of public instruction, Prado Júnior appointed Fernando de Azevedo, who would go on to work with the Vargas regime in the reorganization of sport and physical education in Brazil as a whole. Azevedo's work helped bridge what seemed to many to be opposed regimes; the 1928 Rio de Janeiro educational reform, in fact, served as a model for the rest of the country during the Vargas years.[9]

Across decades and the political divide, sport's promoters shared a vision of sports as a form of education, a means of building individual bodies and the nation, and as a way of bringing Brazilians together. This complicates claims made by the Vargas state and its allies that it was taking the country in a new, even revolutionary direction. But those claims were forceful and convincing enough that they had a great influence on accounts of Brazil in the 1930s and 1940s, including narratives of Brazilian football, to render the era as a period of nationalist, populist transformation overturning decades of elitist and Eurocentric mimicry. For example, historian Darién J. Davis states that in the 1930s, "As the state and more Brazilians from the popular and middle sectors became involved in the sport, soccer became Brazilianized as Brazilians eventually 'devoured' its foreign elements," which had dominated the game from its introduction to the country in 1894.[10]

There were significant changes in Brazilian sport in the 1930s, including a challenge to the participation of foreigners as players, coaches, and administrators. As the passages above suggest, though, promoters of sport and physical education in the Vargas regime had more in common with their predecessors in the First Republic than they were likely to admit. While they often insisted they were "Brazilianizing" Brazilian sport, their ideas about the reform of sports administration were partly inspired by central and southern European fascist models.[11] While they often spoke as populists and promoted racial integration, they also believed that working-class, nonwhite, and female athletes required the guidance of their social, cultural, and political betters. The hierarchical, gendered sports bureaucracy of the CND thus helped to reinforce the regime's efforts in taming workers and "restructuring patriarchy" in order to save it in the face of challenges to traditional gender roles in a modernizing Brazil.[12]

There was also more nationalism in the thinking of their First Republic forerunners than the nationalists of the 1930s acknowledged. It is true that for some wealthy devotees, football and other imported sports were part of what Jeffrey Needell calls elite Brazilians' "fantasy of civilization," in which they imagined for themselves cosmopolitan lives guided by European fashion, often ignoring the Brazilian reality before their eyes.[13] And in building Brazilian sport, they limited the participation of working people and people of color, their notions about building a modern Brazil, as José Murilo de Carvalho says, "allergic" to the idea that the majority of Brazilian people had the capacity to fully inhabit modern life.[14] It is also clear that many early enthusiasts hoped that football and other sports could help redeem the Brazilian people, that if Brazilians could learn to play sports in the proper way, they could help make Brazil a great nation. In this they shared the cautious optimism of Brazilian scientists and doctors who were heavily influenced by European determinist doctrines in doubting the character of their countrymen but who ultimately rejected the notion that the national character was fixed and inferior. Instead, certain Brazilian scientists and medical practitioners adapted foreign ideas to their projects of improving Brazilians and building a greater Brazil.[15] Some, like Fernando de Azevedo, made it explicitly clear that sports and physical education were vital to their work.

When they spoke of sports, all of these Brazilians—unapologetic Europhiles at the turn of the century, activist eugenicists in the 1910s and 1920s, and strident nationalists in the 1930s—spoke in terms of improvement, education, and training; of individual discipline and collective responsibility; of sports, and of football especially, as exceptionally productive in making Brazilians better workers, better soldiers, and better citizens. This chapter explores the meaning of sports to these commentators and activists during the period from football's arrival in Brazil in 1894 to the Vargas years, and it demonstrates the consistency of sports ideology throughout this period. This is sometimes missed because of the real changes of the 1930s and 1940s, such as administrative reform and professionalization, and because of the more obvious rhetorical differences that characterized the different generations; Vargas-era ideologues were more likely to make emphatic claims about patriotism and nationality than their predecessors had done. As the nationalism of Washington Luís and the discipline and hierarchy of the CND suggest, however, these years were characterized by constancy as much as change, something that the history of Brazilian football does much to reveal.[16]

Sport, Physical Education, and the Gospel of Progress

Brazilians played football and other sports because they enjoyed them. But the fun and excitement of sports can explain only so much about the reasons for their adoption by Brazilians or about the ways in which Brazilians pursued them. And they do little to explain the speed and intensity with which Brazilians embraced the sporting life, which left some contemporaries bewildered, in part because sports represented a significant challenge to old models of comportment for respectable men and women. In 1865 the British editor of Rio de Janeiro's *Anglo-Brazilian Times* complained of what seemed to him the absolute neglect of sport and exercise among middle- and upper-class Brazilians. He believed that these Brazilians had developed an aversion to physical exertion due to the devaluation of manual labor during the country's long experience of slavery. The "true Brazilian," he asserted, saw exercise as "degrading to himself and to his position of 'gentility' seeking to prove his aristocratic claims," and Brazilian youth were therefore willing to allow both mind and body "to degenerate and become emasculated through their indolence and contempt for usefulness." The writer bemoaned that Brazil's educated classes lacked both an interest in exercise and, more importantly, the work ethic that he believed physical exercise helped produce.[17]

Brazilian commentators shared the British writer's assessment of the faults of their well-to-do countrymen and noticed that the problem persisted as late as the 1880s. Looking back from 1905, social critic João do Rio noted that some Brazilians, especially working-class Afro-Brazilians, had exercised in the nineteenth century in the form of the martial art of capoeira. But wealthy Brazilians had disregarded all forms of exercise, he said, believing that capoeira, like physical labor, "was exclusively for the lower class."[18]

Alongside the common critique of capoeira's violence and its Afro-Brazilian roots, this social disdain helps to explain political attacks against the sport, which led to its formal criminalization in the Penal Code in 1890.[19] João do Rio explained that capoeira's critics "did not feel the necessity to develop their muscles" because they were interested in other pastimes. Instead of running and jumping or passing a ball, he said, they "dedicated themselves to the *sport* of writing bad verse."[20]

They aimed to become the *bacharel*, the degree holder who charmed nineteenth-century Brazilian high society and avoided the appearance of effort and perspiration at all costs. In the first edition of his influential *Educação Nacional*, in 1890, José Veríssimo attacked the bacharel, calling him a "man of letters, a poet, discussing philosophers with the great erudition that can be found in the card catalog, a dandy, a *poseur*, an orator, a lover, pretentious, a PhD since the sophomore year...." He considered physical exertion beneath himself and preferred games like billiards, cards, and roulette, which could be played in comfortable, smoke-filled parlors, to what Veríssimo considered more useful activities, such as running, gymnastics, and cricket. Like the British critic, Veríssimo said the bacharel was not only ridiculous but dangerous, for his was "the presumption of pretending to be a man," which was "the biggest factor in the moral indiscipline which is harming the country so much."[21]

In the second edition of the book, in 1906, however, Veríssimo noted that a change had come over the young men of São Paulo and Rio de Janeiro. Seemingly overnight, they had developed an "extraordinary taste for sports," which was so intense that he now worried that it was "a little exaggerated, without the planning and organization which contributes so much to its utility in the Anglo-Saxon countries." But they had made a start, and Veríssimo hoped that with guidance this start could be directed toward a broader change, more coherent, more useful, and carried to Brazil at large.[22] João do Rio noticed the change as well, stating that by the middle of the 1890s young men in the capital had completely rejected the pursuits that had interested their fathers and older brothers. With a dizzying speed and a zeal that struck him as almost pathological, in a dozen years they became consumed by and then discarded passions for bicycling, rowing, and other sports, before being taken by a "delirium" of shots, goals, and matches. In 1906 football was the latest obsession among young and fashionable Cariocas, through which they expressed their "fierce pleasure for life."[23]

Very quickly the model of the "true Brazilian" had radically changed, and, in what would have struck the mid-century British writer as heavily ironic, playing sports became proof that Brazilian men belonged in respectable society. No longer was it sufficient to play the part of bacharel, with his romantic pose and his awful poetry. By the middle of the first decade of the twentieth century, the bacharel had become a figure of derision, an "absurd statuette, without one single attribute to justify his arrogance," in the words of a critic in *Brasil Sport*. He wrote that "everyone is convinced" of the bacharel's worthlessness, and he demanded that Brazilians dedicate themselves to sport in order to become what Brazil required, "men of action."[24] Views of Brazilian women were changing as well, and by the twentieth century it was no longer enough that a respectable young woman in Brazil's major cities dress well, play the pianoforte, and remain cloistered among her family until she established her own household. Now the "static woman" was replaced by the ideal of the "active woman," one who took an interest in sport, dressed more freely, and felt more comfortable outside the bounds of home.[25]

Of course not every well-off Brazilian embraced the new model assigned her. And, even where changes seemed most obvious, tradition persisted, whether in the strength of accepted notions of sexual honor or, in sports, of women's exclusion from the football field.[26] Still, as Nicolau Sevcenko notes, the changes manifested by young sportsmen were obvious to contemporaries. Their shaved faces, relaxed clothes, and lithe manners were very different from the manicured beards, correct and form-fitting suits, and upright bearings of their older brothers and fathers. Even more shocking to contemporaries was the look and manner of sportswomen, whose short hair, comfortable dresses, social assertiveness, and dancing made many Brazilians uneasy. For many young, urban Brazilian men and women, Sevcenko says, sports represented a rejection of anything that felt artificial and restrictive in favor of instinct and "free physicality." This new outlook and the new gender dynamics it fostered took some time to develop; it did not emerge everywhere, but where it emerged it represented "a profound reconstruction of one's experience of life."[27]

João do Rio, José Veríssimo, and many others noticed that the change Sevcenko describes was already taking place as early as the century's first decade. João do Rio's explanation was that the winds of fashion had shifted, and, like weathervanes, wealthy Brazilians had transformed themselves from poets into athletes. Modern sports were fashionable, new to Brazil in the late nineteenth century, and this was important to the smart set in the country's leading cities. But there was more to Brazilians' enthusiasm for football and other sports than the posing of a few modish young men and women, as the comments by José Veríssimo and the *Brasil Sport* author suggest.

While these authors encouraged individual Brazilians to take up sports in order to improve their own moral and physical health, both also emphasized the collective benefits that sports offered. Veríssimo spoke of the need to confront the "indolence" and aristocratic pretensions that were hurting the country, and the *Brasil Sport* author identified himself with the "reformers" who took seriously sport's "social function" and its role in helping Brazilians fulfill their responsibilities in "the care of the social contract."[28] Sharing this outlook, many of the promoters of sport in the late nineteenth and early twentieth centuries were among the Brazilians who believed that their countrymen and their country required fundamental reform. The intellectual fathers of the republic were dissatisfied with Brazil's position in the world and the slowness of its development. In their view, the abolition of slavery in 1888 and the overthrow of the empire the next year were the first signals that Brazil was readying itself to take its rightful place among modern nations, but they were only a beginning. Much work was required.

In São Paulo, city leaders like Antônio da Silva Prado, the father of Antônio Prado Júnior and mayor between 1899 and 1911, commissioned the electrification of the city and the replacement of mule-led streetcars by electric ones, drainage projects to reclaim land and deal with disease, and the redevelopment of the city's water and sewage systems.[29] Under the leadership of Emilio Ribas of the city's sanitary service, São Paulo gained one of the most advanced public health systems in Latin America, and the nearby port of Santos was also improved in order to provide better service for the state's vital coffee industry.[30] Rio de Janeiro's leaders undertook a similar set of reforms, especially between 1902 and 1906 under mayor Francisco Pereira Passos. The capital began to be transformed during this period, exemplified in the modernization of the city center, where the cramp and dinge of hundreds of years of colonial and imperial commerce gave way to wide streets and monumental architecture designed to make Rio de Janeiro a reflection of Paris. Pereira Passos and other reformers also worked to extend streetcar lines to better service the growing city, to improve its port, and to deal with the city's well-earned reputation for disease through a mandatory vaccination program, organized by Oswaldo Cruz, and the improvement of the city's sanitation system, among other projects.[31] Finally, middle-class and

FIGURE 1.2. Football was an essential part of "high life" among the urban upper classes. Cover image, program of events celebrating the fourteenth anniversary of the founding of Fluminense, July 21, 1916. By permission of the Acervo Flu-Memória.

wealthy citizens complemented government activities: they constructed modern homes, subscribed donations for the development of cultural institutions, and promoted the expansion of education, which, as Brian Owensby says, middle-class Brazilians saw as "the gateway to everything."[32]

These reform projects were complicated by a variety of factors. The structure of the republican order, with its diffuse, state-centered politics, meant that few efforts were national in scope, in spite of the designs of some of the nation's leaders.[33] As important was "the force of tradition," which Carvalho identifies as a brake on the modernizing reforms of the republican era, especially the social preferences and prejudices of reformist leaders, which meant their efforts often favored forms over substance, cities over countryside, and the middle-class and the wealthy over working people.[34] Related to this was the fact that reformers, like Ribas and Cruz, and their intellectual partners, like Sílvio Romero and Euclides da Cunha, were heavily influenced by European theories of evolution and progress, which meant that their thinking vacillated between doubt and confidence as they designed Brazil's improvements. On one hand, judged by the teachings of Herbert Spencer and other European determinists, Brazil's lack of industry, its tropical climate, and especially its multiracial population indicated they ought to be pessimistic about Brazil's future. On the other hand, they regarded Brazil's size and resources as causes for almost unfettered optimism, especially if these could be paired with the promises offered by large-scale immigration and social reforms grounded in the teachings of modern eugenics.[35] Brazilian intellectuals and scientists rejected the idea that they should accept European teachings without adapting them to Brazilian reality, but reform movements were still often conflicted and controversial, both because reformers tended to be selective in applying their improvements and because even those most inclined to adapt imported ideas felt that Brazil's transformation must be guided by the knowledgeable and the responsible rather than left to the Brazilian people as a whole.

Thus, when planners contemplated infrastructure projects, they often disregarded the interests and the opinions of working-class Brazilians, for example, with the forced removal of working-class residents from Rio de Janeiro's refurbished downtown, the targeting of popular customs like capoeira by newly empowered police forces, and the application of modern medicine regardless of the views of working-class patients. For their part, working people and their allies defended themselves from the disregard and attentions of the reformers of First Republic Brazil. They maintained popular and, for their social betters, worryingly unmodern practices like samba and candomblé.[36] Feeling excluded from the republic, they built their own "republics" in Carnival clubs, mutual aid societies, and unions.[37] And they confronted their improvers and the state in the series of disturbances and riots that characterized the period. Most famously, in the "Vaccine Revolt" of 1904, working-class Cariocas challenged the modernizing project directly, both through resistance to mandatory vaccination against smallpox and through violence against other aspects of the reform movement, such as streetcar and electricity installations.[38]

These kinds of tensions affected promoters' efforts to convince Brazilians to take up sports as well. Like José Veríssimo and *Brasil Sport*, many of the earliest advocates of sports and physical education thought mainly about the middle and upper classes when they made their arguments, and the tension between reformers' drive for national improvement and their social prejudices persisted for many years. These tensions affected the way sports like football were organized and helped critics make their case against the value of sport. For example, as part of his withering criticism of the game, Lima Barreto described football as the cosmopolitan folly of Rio de Janeiro's well-to-do. He expected they would grow tired of their fad, and that football's popularity would diminish as quickly as it had grown.[39] He was mistaken, of course, in part because ideologues and promoters had succeeded in convincing Brazilians of the utility of football and other sports. They began before the turn of the twentieth century with the promotion of physical education.

When José Veríssimo published *Educação Nacional* in 1890, physical education was largely missing in Brazilian schools and Brazilian pedagogy. Imperial education prioritized literature, classical languages, and the law in order to produce a small class of lettered young men who would constitute the country's future elite. For the rest, few educational opportunities existed at all. The larger male population was afforded, at best, primary schooling aimed at providing simple literacy, while girls and young women were largely ignored. Moreover, the infrastructure of schooling matched these curricular and social priorities. A handful of good, well-appointed schools for the wealthy and middle class could count on well-trained teachers, while for the rest, school buildings were makeshift, teachers were poorly trained and poorly paid, and physical discipline was the norm. Republican reformers like Veríssimo undertook a broad effort to expand education for underserved groups, to improve school infrastructure and teacher training, and to introduce students to useful but understudied subjects, such as physical and applied sciences and social sciences.[40]

Physical education figured into their plans from early on, their way prepared by a handful of pedagogues in the years prior to 1889.[41] Especially influential was the ubiquitous intellectual and politician Rui Barbosa, who emphasized the importance of incorporating physical education in an 1882 survey of Brazilian education. Clearly influenced by contemporary evolutionist theory and the gospel of progress and especially reliant on Herbert Spencer, Barbosa insisted that "it is impossible to forge an industrious and productive nation without matching the hygienic education of the body to the cultivation of the spirit beginning with the very first school lessons." He asserted that to educate the mind and spirit without training the body, or vice versa, was "to create anomalies or monsters," and he stated that only proper schooling, which trained body and mind together, could allow Brazil to join the "virile nations" that were his constant models, such as England, France, and the United States.[42]

Republic-era reformers followed Barbosa both in emphasizing the importance of physical education and in justifying its adoption with arguments drawn from the teachings of Spencer and other theorists of social Darwinism and evolutionism. They often prefaced their calls for physical education by describing what they perceived as a crisis that threatened Brazil. For example, in his 1900 book *Gymnastica Infantil*, Eduardo Magalhães wrote, "It is not without running a great risk of the future humiliation and serious compromise of our race that we can continue to treat the physical education of Brazilian children with indifference, abandon, and contempt."[43] Similarly, Soares Dias asked educators, "What can we expect of a weak and physically underdeveloped people?" Anxious for Brazil's future, he answered that the country could only await "irresolution, cowardice, and disloyalty."[44] These educators worried that Brazilians were unhealthy, and they argued that individual infirmity constituted a collective problem. A nation of unhealthy individuals was unready for the "struggle for life" that faced all nations in the modern world, which made the incorporation of physical education into Brazilian schools a national and urgent necessity. In fact, many proponents of physical education and sport argued that Brazilians needed exercise and physical training more than other people because of the racial and ecological challenges they allegedly faced.[45]

A flurry of activity to promote physical education came during the early years of the republic, including its incorporation into the curricula of prominent schools, such as the capital's Ginásio Nacional, founded in 1890; its promulgation by public authorities in Rio de Janeiro and São Paulo as early as 1893; and the publication of a number of texts that spread the message more broadly, such as the works of Veríssimo and Magalhães and an 1890 thesis by Maria C. Gomes Ferrão aimed at physical education for girls.[46] One sign of these figures' success was the experience of the Englishman Charles W. Armstrong, who opened the Gymnasio Anglo-Brasileiro in São Paulo in 1899. Armstrong based the Gymnasio on the public school model that characterized Eton, Harrow, and other institutions serving England's middle class and wealthy, particularly their emphasis on sport and physical education. Guided by the school's predictable motto, the timeworn "mens sana in corpore sano" (a healthy mind in a healthy body), students took part in over two hours of obligatory physical education each day.[47] By 1908 Armstrong had enough students to oversee ten football teams in the school's intramural competition, and two years later he opened a sister institution in Rio de Janeiro.[48] As one Brazilian admirer stated at the time, the schools' attraction for Brazilians was their combination of intellectual and physical education, for "it is only thusly that we will obtain a generation of strong men, capable of fighting for life, with solid instruction and firm muscles as well, by means of a rational education, according to *good English methods*."[49]

With costly fees for day students and costlier ones for boarders, the Gymnasio Anglo-Brasileiro catered mainly to middle-class Paulistas and Cariocas, who were among those most dedicated to physical education during the republican era.[50] As Carmen Soares shows, they understood mass politics and modernization as challenges to their privileges, and they believed physical training could help their sons become the "new" men who could meet these challenges. However, although most reforms in the early years of the Republic were aimed at the urban middle- and upper-class boys, reformers were also concerned about working people, who they believed could be disciplined and improved through the provision of a physical education curriculum guided by the principles of eugenics. As Jorge de Souza told the Sixth Brazilian Congress of Medicine and Surgery in 1907, physical education must aim "to develop the qualities of dexterity, of agility, of gracefulness, and of strength, necessary for every class of society but indispensable for primary school students, especially those destined for manual labor."[51] Concerned with the health of all Brazilians because they were concerned with the fate of the nation as a whole, advocates like Souza saw physical education as an important means of pursuing the goals of the republic. They believed physical education would help Brazil in its pursuit of order and progress, and they set the stage for its eventual extension to all classes of women and men and all parts of the country in the 1920s and 1930s.

Citizens, Soldiers, Laborers, and Sport

Promoting physical education was not the same as promoting sport. Whereas the first implied the responsible direction of well-trained instructors, the latter could be pursued either thoughtfully or in an "unsystematic" way by anyone with the inclination and resources to do so, which was one reason why the pedagogue Carlos Sussekind de Mendonça published *O Sport está deseducando a mocidade brasileira* (Sport is miseducating Brazilian youth) in 1921. Mendonça insisted that Brazilians must take seriously the physical education of their young people, but he feared what he perceived to be an untutored mania for sports that many Brazilians developed during the first two decades of the twentieth century. This resulted, he said, in an improper academic education since an obsession with sports was leading many away from study, as well as misguided moral education, since many learned from sports to be hypercompetitive and violent. Mendonça claimed that Brazilians' unhealthy interest in sport was even failing to educate them physically because, rather than deliberate and "methodical," popular sports like football were "the aspect of physical education which is riotous and superficial although without doubt enticing; [students] lack any sense of how to connect this to the work already undertaken in earlier preparatory training." Worse, many of those interested in sports preferred to remain fans rather than play themselves.[52]

Mendonça therefore preferred martial drill and calisthenics to sports, and he partnered with Lima Barreto to found the Liga Contra Foot-ball in an attempt to convince Brazilians to abandon the country's most popular sport. The league was unsuccessful and short-lived, unable to reverse the tide of football's popularity, but Mendonça's preference for more orderly physical education was in fact the consensus view among Brazilian pedagogues. They installed calisthenics in most of the nation's publicly funded schools during the republican era, in spite of the success of the Gymnasio Anglo-Brasileiro and other private schools in developing curricula that incorporated team sports. Among other reasons, they made this choice because they believed that disorderly young people, particularly the children of the working class, required rote training and discipline rather than play if they were to benefit from physical education.[53] Still, Mendonça was one of the few who actively worked against sports. Instead, like Veríssimo and Magalhães, most saw sport as a valuable complement to formal physical education in the larger campaign to improve the Brazilian people.

Advocates of sport agreed, and they argued that Brazilians ought to play football and basketball, ought to run and swim and row in order to improve themselves and strengthen the nation. In fact, promoters depicted sport as a form of schooling in itself, and the metaphor was popular over the course of many years. In 1903 *A Gazeta de Notícias* called sport "a practical school of strength, of agility, of dexterity, and of health" that aimed at "the regeneration and the improvement of the human race."[54] Ten years later, *O Imparcial* called play "a school of initiative" that all children needed.[55] In 1915, in *Selecta*, Captain John called football "a school of energy, of discipline, of presence of mind," "a school of physical and moral development," "a genuine school of calm, of energy, and of resolute courage."[56] In 1920 *Sports* magazine called the game "a school of discipline," and in 1930 *Rio Sportivo* asserted that "well organized and directed, sports are a genuine school of individual and collective ethics."[57] When the Vargas regime placed the CND within the Ministry of Education and Health, it was following a long tradition.

These figures made a variety of claims about sports' capacity to improve those who pursued them, but their arguments and their rhetoric remained essentially consistent. From before the turn of the century and for at least a half century after, advocates depicted sports as one of the most effective tools available to Brazil in its drive for progress. First and foremost, advocates advertised the physical benefits they expected sport to provide, speaking with the confidence of expertise as they marshaled the minutiae of modern physical science to make their case. In an 1897 edition of *Semana Sportiva*, for example, a writer calling himself Watermann cited Herbert Spencer and the Portuguese hygienist Ricardo Jorge in support of his claim that rowing enlisted "all of the principal organs of the body and their respective parts, without a single negative side-effect," while Eduardo Magalhães cited the Frenchmen Eugène Bouchot and Armand Despres in recommending running to "young scrofula patients, with their restricted thoraxes, [who are] threatened by pulmonary disease."[58] Offering a different kind of evidence, "X" pointed to the example of the hale Englishmen and Germans resident in the capital in calling upon Brazilians to take up sports. He spoke of his admiration for the young Brazilians who viewed sports as a "religion" and said that in playing sports "this generation ... face to face with danger, generating muscular and moral energy, is already more beautiful, stronger, and more noble than mine ... today's boys are already as daring as men."[59] In a similar vein, the physician Alfredo Redondo wrote in *Sportman* that his experience of foreign countries had convinced him that "the progress of a nation is in direct relation to its advancement in *sport*." He assured readers that if they exercised and played sports, they would see their "bodies transformed—your shoulders will be wider, your chest will be fuller, you will have a solid physical and intellectual disposition, you will in short have life and health."[60]

These kinds of claims, often full of medical jargon and appeals to foreign authority, were especially common in the discourse of the turn of the century, for sports were new to Brazil, and some Brazilians required convincing. Leonardo Pereira shows that a few public figures worried that sport would bring not "strength and virility" but "degeneration." They were especially critical of sports that they saw as violent or that seemed to benefit one part of the body at the expense of holistic and even development, and a handful of hygienists and public health campaigners offered hesitant critiques and wondered whether to encourage their countrymen to play sports.[61]

By 1910 a broad consensus in favor of exercise and sport emerged to drown out questioning voices, but advocates did rehearse the arguments about sport's utility in building Brazilian bodies from time to time in order to defend sports from critics like Lima Barreto and Carlos Sussekind de Mendonça. As Captain John said of football in 1915, it still had "fierce adversaries." These critics feared "that it exhausts the player. That it is very violent and therefore offers no health benefits. That it does not develop but rather atrophies." John was one of the sport's proponents, but he understood the perspective of its critics, that football "can also atrophy all—muscles and character."[62] Even *Athletica*, the sports magazine founded by the poet and passionate football fan Coelho Netto in 1920, worried about the physical effects of playing sports, with Yantok wondering about the health of "*jockeys* with legs transformed into parentheses, *footballers* with legs the size of those of the Colossus of Rhodes, and rowers and rowing champions with arms like monkeys, [who] can only be suited to a teratological museum."[63] Hoping that Brazilians would develop their bodies methodically and according to the best teaching, *Athletica* published a regular column dedicated to eugenics, which highlighted, for example, Fernando de Azevedo's views on the benefits of athletics.[64]

Adopting a more optimistic tone, the editors of *Epoca Sportiva* made similar points in the magazine's inaugural edition in April 1919 about the importance of joining what it called "the miracle of *sport*" to the best scientific practices. They wrote that because of sports, Brazilians—once "a stunted race of pygmies, enervated by inertia"—had begun to "strain their muscles, feel their nerves and little by little resuscitate a holistic life." With sports, Brazil could look to the future with confidence:

> The legions of spectral figures who crawl painfully through Brazil ... must cede their place to a new and robust people, the people of a future Brazil who will realize, along with the benefits of prophylactic medicine, the miracle of *sport*. Those parasitic anemics, those swollen with Chagas disease, will disappear and of them only a vague and shadowy memory will remain, as with a nightmare that has passed. In their place will come a new generation, fit for life, exuding health, joining a civilized and educated spirit to the virile toughness of its musculature.[65]

Later that year, the promoters of sport found their muses, the members of the country's national team, which won the South American Championship in Rio de Janeiro. It was the first international tournament that Brazil hosted, and the first it won. Dozens of publications celebrated the victory with banner headlines, triumphant essays, and gaudy photographic spreads that equated the accomplishment of eleven Brazilians with the development of Brazil as a whole. The magazine *Brasil Illustrado* captured the mood when it stated that the football heroes had demonstrated the "great and effective physical and moral transformation that is developing among our youth," which owed a great deal to Brazilians' new passion for sport.[66]

This famous success gave sports advocates confidence and, by their lights, evidence to support their claims, but it did not mean that Brazil had fully realized the physical benefits sport had to offer, and they continued to make the case in later years, if less often. In 1930 in São Paulo, for example, the magazine *A Gazeta Esportiva*, which was normally concerned most with tactics, performances, and the politics of sport, recommended to its readers "a veritable hymn to the goddesses of Health and Nature," Ulysses Freire's book *Brasil Eugenico*.[67] Its Carioca counterpart, *Rio Sportivo*, regularly published pieces on physiology because, it said, the hygiene and physical education movements still had much to accomplish in Brazil.[68]

In 1930, the Confederação Brasileira de Desportos (CBD) appealed to the government of Washington Luís for financial support for Brazil's participation in the first world championship, held in Montevideo. *Rio Sportivo* was scandalized when the president informed the CBD that he was "completely uninterested in the Brazilian football delegation," and it complained that his failure to support the enterprise "jeopardizes the development of our nationality, making it more difficult to spread *sports*." It endorsed foreigners' observations that "Brazil is a vast hospital," and "in Brazil, everything is grand, except man," and it argued that the government failed to understand that Brazil was one of the "new countries, whose ethnicities are still in development." Such countries "must dedicate more attention to physical education, as it is one of the most efficient factors in the strengthening of a race, and the invigoration of a people." In order to assist and to cure the "thousands and thousands of enfeebled Brazilians who have physical deficiencies," the paper said, "first and foremost, we must spread health through the medium of *sports* and the orderly practice of physical exercise." The national government must take an active role in the promotion of physical health, which the paper said included the support of the country's national team, ostensibly due to the attention the team would attract by participating in the world championship.[69]

Despite the paper's claim, Washington Luís was indeed aware of the benefits of sport and physical education, and he had done much to promote them. There may have been any number of reasons for his "lamentable attitude" in 1930, such as the economic crisis facing the country at the time and the fact that, due to a dispute between the football authorities of Rio de Janeiro and São Paulo, the Brazilian national team was far from representative, constituted almost completely by Cariocas. But *Rio Sportivo* insisted that his government did not do enough and took the opportunity presented by the World Cup controversy to remind the Luís government of sports' physical benefits. "The spread of *sports* is the most patriotic and laudable enterprise," according to the paper, and "every government which contributes to this is worthy of praise and applause."[70] *Rio Sportivo* thus helped pave the way for the interventions of the Vargas government, which clearly understood this lesson and shared the paper's way of thinking.

Across decades and generations, advocates made another argument beyond their insistence on sport's benefits to Brazilians' physical health. They asserted that athletes would learn "moral" and "ethical" lessons, for the school of sport was a school both of health and, as the writers quoted above said, a school of "discipline," of "initiative," of "moral development," of "resolute courage," and of "individual and collective ethics." Again, what is striking is the durability of such assertions, such as the claim that sport would help to create the citizen. As James Woodard says of the political life of São Paulo during the First Republic, it was never enough to be born Brazilian in order to participate fully in public life. Rather, the era's "model citizen" was of a particular type, "literate, modern, and respectable, of middling or better means (but not idly rich), viriliously male, and (often, but not always) white," a set of categories that marginalized millions and helps to explain the era's extraordinarily low electoral participation, despite the relatively wide franchise established in the 1889 constitution.[71]

According to its advocates, sport could assist the Brazilian masses on their path to improvement and citizenship. The educator Paulo Lauret argued in *Rio Sportivo* in 1901 that the responsible citizen developed his soul, mind, and body, and in 1907 *Brasil Sport* asserted that the "absurd" bacharel was the antithesis of the "complete men" the country required, who could enter into and participate in the social contract, "scholars and citizens . . . [and] men of action."[72] And in 1917 *Illustração de S. Paulo* repeatedly used the term "citizen" to describe those who enrolled in a new, public program of sports and military exercises. It said they would prove that Brazilians "are not a degenerate and enfeebled people" and would "attest to the excellence of our climate and the vitality of our race."[73]

While these writers commented in a general way about their expectation that sports would help produce good citizens, *Athletica* was more explicit, explaining in 1920 that "the good *sportman*" accepted "the letter and the spirit of the rules" of the game he played. Those rules were analogous to the law itself, just as sports' authority figures, such as team captains and referees, were comparable to legitimate governing authorities. Accepting game rules won the athlete "the confidence and the admiration of his fellow citizens," just as accepting legal authority allowed the individual the opportunity "to be useful and to live happily." Sport thus helped create "*the social man*," especially if the athlete was part of a team:

> The boy learns his first lessons in civics when he joins an athletic *team*—there not only will he have the occasion to learn parliamentary procedure when he protests against breaches of protocol, but he will

also be initiated into the essence of democracy, in a real and vivid way, participating effectively in the team's management. He will have the experience of democratic engagement, when he loses his notion of his own individuality in the group with which he plays: this is the practice of democratic civics rather than simply a theoretical understanding of them.[74]

Sport helped to create the social man because it went beyond physical training to shape the athlete's personality. It trained him to accept legitimate authority and to consider himself "part of a social or political whole," working within the rules and with his team to accomplish something greater than himself. He thus became *"the citizen: loyal, brave, and generous."*[75]

When Vargas-era ideologues contended that playing team sports made Brazilians better citizens by building "the spirit of collaboration," they were drawing on timeworn arguments. The same was true of their claims that sports helped to produce good soldiers. Advocates were fond of the assertion, often attributed to the Duke of Wellington, that "the Battle of Waterloo was won on the playing fields of Eton and Harrow," with *O Malho* explaining as early as 1905 that sports cultivated the esprit de corps necessary to build military units, as well as the "spirit of discipline" and the "absolute obedience" required of the individual soldier.[76] Three years later, the sports administrator and publisher Alberto Silvares asserted that Japan's defeat of Russia in the countries' 1905 war owed to the "valor and strength" that Japanese soldiers had gained from practicing jiu-jitsu, and he cautioned that Brazil would suffer if it did not follow Japan and develop "the taste and love of *sport.*"[77] Many Brazilians also read about sport's ability to produce good soldiers from one of their favorite authors, Ernest Weber, the editor of the Parisian journal *L'Auto*, who called football "war, with its strategy and its tactics: a game of attack, retreat, and mock battles" in his 1905 rulebook, which was published in translation in Brazil in 1907 under the title *Sports athleticos*. The book went through nine Brazilian printings by 1910.[78]

World War I also helped motivate Brazilians to make the argument that sports were necessary, and to connect the promotion of sports to the creation of defenders of the nation. According to the *Correio da Manhã*, sport's "value" was proclaimed all over the world, but "the current war proves it."[79] *Brasil Illustrado* concurred, stating at the war's end that because of sport, England and the United States were able, "in a short time, to build armies from their healthy and vigorous youth which fell upon the Germanic hordes" and ended the conflict. The war convinced many that they lived in a dangerous and threatening world, leading them to argue that Brazil must pay closer attention to military preparation, physical fitness, and other forms of improvement if the country were to survive and flourish. *Brasil Illustrado* explained the role sports would play, asserting that "the desire to win sporting contests will train the will for the struggle for life; audacity in a dangerous play will translate later into civic courage on the field of battle."[80]

Among those who forged the connection between war and sport were the Liga da Defesa Nacional (National Defense League) and the Liga Nacionalista de São Paulo (Nationalist League of São Paulo), which were founded during the war years. Both promoted sports and physical education and forged relationships with sports organizations in their larger projects of strengthening Brazil by promoting patriotism, military preparedness, and civic engagement. In the capital, the Liga da Defesa Nacional encouraged sports clubs to offer military training because, Coelho Netto said in the "Civic Commandments" he wrote for the league and published in *Athletica*, the true Brazilian "loves the Fatherland above all things and works with us to make it greater."[81] The leading ideologue of the Liga Nacionalista was Antônio Sampaio Dória, who oversaw the expansion of physical education, including military exercises, in Paulista schools in 1920 while serving in the administration of then-governor Washington Luís.[82] The league appealed directly to its allies among the sports public, for example, in working with the Federação Olympica Paulista (Paulista Olympic Federation) to stage a sports festival in 1918 to benefit its educational work.[83]

Others shared the nationalist fervor of the war years. Before Brazil's entry into the war, sports clubs in the capital hosted athletics events to promote the war efforts of the Western powers and to raise money to support the activities of the Red Cross among the armies of those states.[84] After Brazil declared war on Germany in October 1917, the CBD acted, in its words, "in concert with the patriotic orientation of the government" when it directed all leagues and federations affiliated to it to exclude all German immigrant clubs from participation for the war's duration.[85] One Carioca writer captured the spirit of these administrators and advocates when he commented on the decision by a Flamengo player, Sidney Pullen, to enlist in the British army in 1918. He said that the popular Pullen left behind many friends in the Brazilian capital "who are here missing him, pulling for him to score many '*goals*' against the 'Huns' and to return soon, covered in glory, to the land of his birth."[86] Pullen did return to Brazil and to the playing field, winning championships with Flamengo in 1920 and 1921.

In São Paulo, where the Palestra Itália club hosted a match to benefit the Italian war effort, the Escola de Gymnastica e Educação Physica da Força Publica (Public Defense Forces School of Gymnastics and Physical Education) opened its doors to citizens who wanted "to prepare themselves for national defense, fortifying their bodies and beginning to learn those military principles required of the good soldier." According to the *Illustração de S. Paulo*, at the school the Paulista would enter into "a temple of athleticism, to strengthen his muscles, to acquire agility, to undertake, in short, the *training* necessary if he wants to employ the physical energy he possesses." It assured its readers that because of this, if Brazil sent soldiers to war, "the S. Paulo contingent will prove that we are not a broken and degenerated people." Rather, it would prove "the excellence of our climate and the vitality of our race, our soldiers well trained, first by sports and now by military training," and the magazine called on every municipality and every state to follow São Paulo's lead so that Brazil would be a nation of good, modern soldiers.[87]

Brazilians continued to pair sports and soldiering in the succeeding decades, and to claim that the former helped prepare the latter. In 1920 in *Athletica*, Anselmo Ribas quoted approvingly Pierre de Coubterin's statement that sports do not make young men more aggressive, but that in the event of war they provide armies with soldiers who are prepared, men who, because of sports, "are more decisive and more rapid in taking initiative than they were." Ribas explained that for "the man who is familiar with sport war is nothing more than a great game, a game of violent and decisive attacks."[88] Football and other sports clubs maintained shooting and military training programs that they had begun during the war years and continued to cultivate the relationships they had established with military and civil defense authorities into the 1930s. This prepared them for the opportunities and challenges of the Vargas years, with, for example, Rio de Janeiro clubs like Fluminense and Vasco da Gama hosting government rallies and a "Sports Battalion" taking up arms against Vargas in São Paulo's Constitutionalist Rebellion in 1932.[89] It was thus no surprise when the *Jornal dos Sports* referred to the members of the Brazilian national team as "our soldiers of sport" in reporting on their participation in the 1938 World Cup.[90]

Many advocates linked sport to national defense because they believed it instilled in those who played the discipline required of good soldiers. They

FIGURE 1.3. Float in the Tenentes do Diabo Carnival parade, 1920, depicting a Fluminense player as a chariot driver. The float flattered the club's self-image, a chariot driver the central image in the set of stained glass windows in Fluminense's ballroom, and it alluded to ideologues' view that football prepared Brazilians for military service. By permission of the Acervo Flu-Memória.

pointed to athletic discipline in recommending sports in the making of good workers as well. They argued that sports would help to cultivate the health and the habits required for productive and modern farming and industry so that Brazil could fulfill its potential. In writing to promote physical education in *A Eschola* in 1900, for example, Soares Dias drew the connection between physical training and the ability to both defend the country and work productively. Soares Dias asked his readers to think of the typical unhealthy Brazilian, who was "poorly developed and anemic, weak and prematurely weakened by inertia, by the neglect of physical education." This Brazilian, the author said, might, "in a noble outburst of patriotism, take up arms to defend the Fatherland abroad," but "he cannot." The poor figure might also "feel in his soul the flame of imagination, the ferment of genius, and cannot undertake industrious work upon whose execution his reputation might depend, because his body cannot endure the difficulties of his labor." Lacking the discipline and improvement offered by physical education, he must join another "debased, anemic, and atrophied generation."[91]

But if he were educated physically, whether through basic calisthenics or in sports, the Brazilian could be redeemed. He could be part of a new generation of workers, "laborers whose physical, intellectual, and moral vigor unites them to the great destiny which is certain to await us in the not-distant future."[92] Similarly, Tell stated in *Brasil Sport* in 1907 that sport was for all Brazilians, from those interested in sailing, shooting, and car racing, which required considerable amounts of time and money, to those who preferred football, "which the laborer can play with a minimum expense of time and money." All were participants in "this campaign which we are pleased to call patriotic," of spreading an interest in sport among Brazilians, patriotic because it helped guarantee "the future of our nationality."[93]

The perspective that Soares Dias and Tell outlined helps explain why some Brazilian labor leaders were suspicious of organized sports in the early twentieth century. They resented the social exclusivity of the sportsmen, and they also worried that employers would attempt to use sports to discipline or co-opt their workers. As an example, they could point to Rio de Janeiro's Companhia Progresso Industrial do Brasil, which offered its patronage to the Bangú Athletic Club soon after the firm's British employees founded it in 1904. Together company and club helped pioneer a new category of laborer in Brazil, the "worker-player." Helping to advertise the company and build company pride among his fellow employees on the football field, the worker-player received lighter work duties and other benefits, and other companies adopted the model in the ensuing years.[94]

These activities annoyed labor activists, such as a writer in the anarchist *A Voz do Trabalhador*, who in 1914 compared a depressingly quiet anarchist educational center—it was "completely empty" when he visited it—to the football field erected by a match factory in the same vicinity, "full of excitement." The writer explained the lesson of this contrast by quoting a municipal intendant who had said that "while the people play, they don't conspire."[95] It seemed that sport could be an opiate for the masses, and this writer and other labor leaders therefore worked against its spread in the early years of the century. Neither the prejudices of the well-to-do nor the concern of labor leaders kept workers from sports, however. By the 1910 decade labor activists were beginning to grudgingly accept sports' undeniable popularity, and Communists even proposed the organization of a league exclusively for unionized workers in order to protect them from capitalist patrons.[96] Meanwhile, middle-class advocates of sport continued to make the case that participation in sports made for better workers.

For example, *Brasil Illustrado* asserted that Brazil's 1919 South American Championship victory might have "a weighty international effect" because it would prove to potentially dubious foreigners "the degree of our capacity for work." These foreigners knew, as Brazilians had come to learn, that "discipline in *sport* will mean discipline in work," and the victory would therefore advertise Brazil's progress.[97] A decade later, Faustino Esposel enumerated for the readers of *Rio Sportivo* a variety of benefits that sports offered, arguing that they "awake energy, initiative, [and] will," and that they "develop vital qualities in the individual, who will subject himself, when necessary, to self-denial and sacrifice." Their benefits extended to the workplace, because they "cultivate discipline, solidarity, and the division of labor." Esposel pointed out that sports could develop individuals' understanding of their particular roles in group work, which was one reason to prefer sports to simple physical training, but he argued that this and other benefits could not be gained simply by playing games. Rather, echoing the rhetoric that made labor activists wary of sports earlier in the century, he insisted that sports must be "regulated" and "well organized," by well-educated experts like himself, of course.[98]

Fernando de Azevedo argued that physical education and sport were more necessary than ever in the Brazil of the 1930s. In his *A Evolução do Esporte no Brasil*, published in 1930, Azevedo outlined his views on education reform and argued that policymakers must promote athletics both inside and outside the school setting, for example, by building parks and playgrounds in Brazil's rapidly developing cities. Nostalgic for a Brazil that his predecessors had never thought existed, Azevedo worried that as Brazil urbanized and industrialized, the country was losing the "natural culture" of the hale and hearty countryside. He worried that young, urban Brazilians "stiff with indolence and amusements, began to degenerate into weakness; their work habits were disfigured by idleness; their honest ways threatened and replaced by moral laxity, which could not help but be reflected in their level of physical energy." The consequences were "degrading and prejudicial," both for individuals and for "the healthy and natural evolution of the race." Brazil might begin to industrialize, it might build factories and railways and adopt the automobile, but in doing so it was losing the physical activity which would prepare Brazil to reach its economic potential, and Brazilians therefore continued to require sports. In sports, Brazilians found what they had lost, "physical activity discarded or diminished," and they would find what they needed—sports "shaking society from its torpor, in an intense pulse of life, [and] preparing the movement for an athletic rebirth." Azevedo believed this renaissance produced effects far beyond the playing field, reviving Brazilians' physical and moral strength and their capacity for productive labor so that the benefits of modern living would not be accompanied by the loss of the benefits of traditional ways of life.[99]

Many forms of exercise could make Brazilians stronger, more flexible, or increase their stamina. Calisthenics and marching could inculcate the discipline that physical educators and sports advocates were especially eager to promote. Many different sports promoted competitiveness, and various team sports might develop players' sense of cooperation. As João do Rio noted, at the time of football's arrival, Brazilians were already engaging in a variety of sporting activities, including rowing, biking, and even capoeira, despite the legal prohibition placed upon it. During the early twentieth century, Brazilians also experimented with competitive swimming and water polo, target shooting and boxing, tennis, basketball, and volleyball, and even baseball and other novelties, such as "aero-ball," while a handful of well-to-do Brazilians embraced cars and airplanes as sporting pursuits.[100] Proponents of sport argued about the relative merits of all of these pursuits and asked, as Rictus put it in *Sportman* in 1912, "Which *sport* is best, and which best suits us?"[101]

The answers were seemingly endless, and new sports were constantly being announced and promoted by their advocates. For example, Rictus argued that Brazilians should choose swimming because of its capacity to develop the body in a proportionate and uniform manner, while in 1920 Flavio Vieira called water polo "the best of sports." Brazil was, he said, "a marvelously maritime country," and Brazilians ought to play water polo because an American researcher, Philip Hawk of the University of Pennsylvania, claimed to have proven that, more than any other sport, it produced the greatest positive health effects in its participants.[102] Despite these arguments and many others like them, football, of course, won the most followers in Brazil, quickly overshadowing those sports Brazilians had played before 1894 and maintaining its dominance to the present day. There were a number of reasons for this.

Football is a modern sport, with codified laws instead of improvised rules, precise and defined time and space requirements, and clear outcomes that can be tracked in official records. Rational, standardized, specialized, quantified, recorded—football and other modern sports appealed to the sensibilities of the improvers of the late nineteenth and early twentieth centuries.[103]

These improvers were repelled by traditional pastimes such as capoeira and bullfighting because they either missed or rejected their structure and meaning; because they associated the activities with African and Iberian influences that they were, at best, doubtful about; and because these pastimes were often too violent for their tastes. Echoing arguments made throughout Latin America in the late nineteenth century, the Brazilian Council of State said in 1877 that bullfights were "spectacles that are contrary to the enlightenment of the current century and to principles of modern civilization."[104] Although Brazilians sometimes described football, without regret, as "the violent game," most objected to any sport that they found too physical and too rough, which explains their rejection of rugby, especially its "American" version (i.e., American football), which Captain John called "an exaggerated form" in 1915.[105]

There was a small basketball league in Rio de Janeiro in the 1910s, but the game never became broadly popular in the early twentieth century, likely in part because Brazilians adopted sports during the country's "English century," and football was the most popular sport in England and among resident Englishmen in Brazil during the period.[106] Brazilians were interested in volleyball and field hockey, but they saw them as women's sports; hockey was, according to *O Imparcial*, "more delicate and more 'chic' than '*foot-ball*,'" and therefore better suited to women than men.[107] Also working against basketball, volleyball, and field hockey as well as crew, which was one of the most popular sports in Brazil before the arrival of football, was that those sports required more equipment and, in the case of basketball and volleyball, which Brazilians seem to have always played indoors during this period, the use of expensively constructed venues. They were therefore more costly to play than what Tell called "modest *foot-ball*."[108]

Finally, swimming, cycling, and "respectable" martial arts like boxing generally lacked the crucial element of teamwork, which was one reason that *O Malho* said in 1905 that "of all the *sports* available to our youth ... *foot-ball* really is the most beautiful and the most complete." The paper mentioned the game's physical benefits, but, though it stated that "the argument for *foot-ball*, already victorious for some time, dispenses with debate," it suggested that it was worth "insisting upon speaking of its precious moral qualities, which each player acquires." Among these, the paper mentioned discipline, obedience, decisiveness, courage, stoicism in the face of danger and misfortune, and initiative, "which the game instills through its unexpected reversals." Finally, it stressed "the admirable spirit of solidarity and self-denial which it demands of players," and stated that Brazilians should celebrate the popularity of "this rugged and stimulating exercise" among their countrymen.[109]

In a 1906 piece, São Paulo's *Sportman* mentioned football's ability to promote physical health, saying it "possesses the best qualities for the proper function of our bodily organs." But it said football was "our preferred *sport*" for another reason. It was football's influence on the player's moral character, and especially its contribution to the development of a sense of "solidarity" and teamwork that made it so valuable, and this was a constant refrain among the game's promoters in Brazil.[110] As the *Correio da Manhã* stated in 1910, "solidarity and self-sacrifice" were the "primordial qualities of the foot-baller."[111]

Brazilians perceived clear connections between the reasons to play the game and the way it should be played, and at least until the end of the 1910 decade, Brazilian tacticians stressed the importance of teamwork to the successful football team. As I show in chapter 5, in the 1920s and especially the 1930s, some conceived of an alternative approach to the game, one that allowed for more individuality and creativity—an approach they called "Brazilian." But even then many of the sport's most vocal and influential advocates continued to insist on the central importance of teamwork to football. For example, the journalist Mário Filho, who was one of the chief promoters of the "Brazilian" style, also identified with the hierarchical and centralizing Vargas state, which helps to explain his insistence that even the best player must be obedient and consider himself "a part of a machine."[112] Other sports might require teamwork, but, Brazilians argued, football was best at developing it, which was a crucial aspect of what made it important for improving Brazilians both as individuals and as members of the nation. Football would make Brazilians healthier and stronger, and it would make Brazil a nation of good citizens who understood their place in the polity, of good soldiers who could defend the Fatherland, and of good workers who fulfilled their roles in building a stronger Brazil.

Sport for the Nation, Nationalists for Sport

The nationalism that ran through the justifications of the early advocates of football and other sports has sometimes been missed by historians, and it was dismissed by contemporaries like Lima Barreto. Barreto rejected the notion that sportsmen were nationalists and questioned whether football could contribute to the strength, vitality, and unity of the nation. His view was that football's true "social function" was that it sowed "discord at the heart of our national life."[113] He argued that football produced men who believed they were part of a "race elected by God, due to the abilities of their feet" but who were "by all accounts intellectually mediocre," while their clubs were little more than "dancing circles." Nor did football bring Brazilians together. Rather, the pretensions of middle-class and wealthy sportsmen exacerbated social differences, and competition set clubs against one another, meaning that football "created a foolish division among Brazilians."[114]

Barreto could certainly offer examples to prove his points. The advocates of sport were often as obvious in their dissatisfaction with Brazil as they were explicit in their reliance on foreign teachings in making their case, appealing especially to European authority as the incontestable proof of the value of sports. When they spoke dismissively of their fellow Brazilians, as did *Brasil Illustrado* when it called Brazilians the "heirs, in part, of the blood of Jéca Tatú," Monteiro Lobato's archetype of the coarse country dweller, it was likely they would offend some of their countrymen.[115] Moreover, since many leading sports clubs in Brazil were as much venues for the social functions of the fashionable and chic as athletic centers, the advocacy and the practice of sports exhibited a divisive set of social and racial biases that worked against the notion that they could bring Brazilians together.

Team sports like football further divided Brazilians because of the same inherent competitiveness that appealed to many of their advocates. *O Estado de S. Paulo* noted in 1916 that many Brazilians became so devoted to their clubs that they became "intransigent [and] implacable" in their allegiances, and their "clubism" often made football matches into real conflicts "with all of the dangers characteristic of battle."[116] Also, in part because Brazilian sports lacked an effective national administration before the mid-1930s, they were plagued by and exacerbated longstanding regional rivalries, especially between loyalists of Rio de Janeiro and São Paulo.

Still, in spite of the criticisms of enemies like Barreto and in spite of evidence that sports alienated Brazilians from one another, advocates consistently insisted that they acted in the national interest. Physical educators, from José Veríssimo in the late nineteenth century to Fernando de Azevedo in the 1920s and 1930s, helped justify the biases that annoyed Lima Barreto by claiming that the physical improvement of the Brazilian masses must be managed and guided by experts. Labor leaders were suspicious of the motives of employers who patronized sport, but those which did so, such as Bangú's Companhia Progresso Industrial, claimed they served their workers and the nation as much as themselves. They believed that in promoting sports among their employees, they acted to promote their workers' health and their morale and to build a sense of community that bound workers to one another and the firm, making Brazilian workers better able to meet the challenges of the modern economy.[117] Finally, political figures such as Washington Luís claimed the right to use sport to lead Brazilians to a better future, helping to make them better citizens and better soldiers, and more "Brazilian" Brazilians.

Advocates saw no contradiction between, on one hand, admitting their discontent with Brazil as they found it and their admiration for Europe and, on the other, their confidence in Brazil's future if it could take advantage of the "miracle of *sport*." To them it was obvious that to follow European teaching, in sport and in many other things, was the only choice for Brazilians if they hoped to forge a great nation. They might cite the role of sports in the making of Englishmen or Americans in justifying their enthusiasm and might call for Brazilian schools to be modeled on Eton and Harrow, Harvard and Yale. But they did so selectively, choosing foreign examples very carefully rather than simply mimicking foreign practices. They looked abroad in the hopes that by following foreign examples Brazil would gain the benefits that sport seemed to provide those who had already embraced it. As he watched Brazilians play sports, Afranio Hiroz said in 1915, "at times, I rejoice: I foresee a Brazil of tomorrow, sending a victorious *team* to Yale or Harvard."[118] Following foreigners and playing their sports was not, then, the choice of pessimists or the disloyal, but of optimists and nationalists. In fact, by 1920 *Athletica* was rejecting the notion that football should even be considered foreign at all. It was "as Brazilian as it was English," nationalized, as it were, in great part because Brazilians understood its advantages.[119]

The CBD summarized the views of many in its institutional report for 1918. The report noted that it might be that in the past only "the idle rich" were interested in sport, seeking diversion in their easy lives. But in modern society, "all" had come to understand that sport was more than a simple amusement. It fulfilled a "great" and "generous" social role, making participants stronger and healthier, more disciplined and more dependable, and even more intelligent and more perceptive. This was why Brazilians should play sports and why they should encourage their countrymen to do the same; athletes took on a deep responsibility to the nation when they committed themselves to sport, for in improving themselves they improved the whole country. According to the CBD, "the ultimate aspiration of sport is to create *healthy*, *upright*, and *educated* men and to offer them to the Fatherland." As sport was a school of physical, moral, and intellectual improvement, its pursuit and its promotion were obviously and indisputably patriotic endeavors.[120]

The advocates of sport became especially likely to depict their work as patriotic as the vocabulary of patriotism and nationalism proliferated in Brazil during the war years. For example, they acknowledged that regional rivalries did affect sports, most obviously in the almost constant bickering between Paulistas and Cariocas over the organization of national teams. But they did not accept that sports contributed to these rivalries, instead arguing that sports helped resolved them. *Epoca Sportiva* argued in 1919 that part of the "noble mission" of sport was its "promotion of the more perfect union of the country's regions."[121] When teams from different parts of the country played against one another, they had the opportunity to learn about their fellow Brazilians, and if sports leaders could come together to resolve their differences, they could provide civic leaders with an edifying example. Thus, for example, Coelho Netto's attempt to reconcile warring Carioca and Paulista bodies in 1919 was about more than sports; it was a "patriotic mission" and "elevated and patriotic experiment," according to the *Jornal do Brasil*.[122]

Similarly, when they called for government to provide support for football and other sports, advocates used explicitly national and nationalist arguments. In 1920 the head of the national Olympic committee, Sen. Fernando Mendes de Almeida, requested government funds to finance the Brazilian delegation to the Antwerp Olympics. According to *Athletica*, the government must fulfill the request because Brazil's representatives would disabuse Europeans of the idea that the Brazilian was a savage, "a half-breed with a bow and arrow, plumed like a feather duster, who goes to war to hunt prisoners," the fate of which was ritual sacrifice. Participation in the event, which the paper called "this contest of races, this famous trial of strength and physical beauty," was a point of national pride and an opportunity to advertise Brazil at its best rather than as foreigners might imagine it to be. Properly supported by their government, Brazilian athletes would demonstrate to an ill-informed and skeptical Europe that the Brazilian was a citizen of the modern world; a refusal to support these athletes would constitute a failure of patriotism on the part of public authorities.[123]

Though they hesitated to provide the support Almeida requested, authorities were more amenable to a proposal made by federal deputy J. E. Macedo Soares in June 1921, in which the deputy, also president of the CBD, proposed that federal tax law be reformed to allow a customs exemption for foreign-produced sporting goods. In a larger proposal that he presented the same year, Macedo Soares sketched a permanent role for the national government in the promotion of national sport, including the provision of financial assistance, the administration of national competitions, and even the creation of a league for professional athletes. He explained that the federal government must acknowledge "the noble value of the great and constructive activities of the sports organization ... in favor of physical education and Brazilian youth" and therefore must offer its patronage.[124] National leaders were not ready to take such an assertive stance, but they did accept the tax proposal, which was adopted in late 1921. Balls, uniforms, and goal frames for football; gymnastics apparatus and mats; tennis rackets and nets; rowing sculls and oars; and many other items were exempted from customs duties.[125] As far as sports advocates were concerned, this was the least the authorities could do, for they saw themselves as engaged in patriotic work that deserved public support. As Sans Peur argued in *O Imparcial* in 1921, "in all the advanced countries government takes an interest in *sport*" because it knows that "it is in *sport* that the boy develops himself and finds the courage to face life, properly preparing himself for any emergency that might befall the country."[126]

The role that sports advocates conceived for themselves and the devices they employed to promote their vision of the nation were apparent in a number of episodes like these. They were especially apparent in the works of the Fluminense Football Club, one of the country's most prominent sports organizations. Fluminense rarely missed the opportunity to advertise its nationalist credentials, and it was especially active during the war. Among its wartime activities, Fluminense was in 1915 one of the first sports organizations to hold events to raise money for the Red Cross, and in 1916 it convinced the Ministry of War to appoint a military instructor to train its members in rifle shooting and other forms of military preparedness.[127] In 1917 Fluminense's representatives were integral in convincing the CBD to turn against German sports organizations in Brazil, and in that year it formally requested that its own German members withdraw from the club.[128]

Fluminense set up the country's first Boy Scout troop, in 1916, which, it said, was "a great undertaking on behalf not only of the physical but also of the civic education and development of our youth."[129] Among its other benefits, scouting would promote a sense of national community among Brazilian boys, each one of whom would be taught that all scouts were "his brothers, regardless of their social classes," and when the club president and secretary, Arnaldo Guinle and Mário Pollo, respectively, published a scouting manual to spur the movement, they enlisted the prominent poets, nationalists, and sports advocates Olavo Bilac and Coelho Netto to introduce the volume.[130] Other sports clubs formed their own troops because they saw scouting as "an important contributor to the physical and moral culture of a people," according to O Echo. Fluminense continued to lead the way, and its own scouting effort did not peak until ten years later, when it counted 389 members.[131]

Fluminense was as guilty of "clubism" as any of its peers, and, despite the lessons it taught its scouts, it was a central actor in the construction of Brazilian sports as socially and racially exclusive. But the club saw itself as acting in the national interest, which was never more apparent than when it built Brazil's first sports stadium, in 1918. Fluminense and its supporters portrayed the construction of the stadium as an effort of extraordinary patriotism and national responsibility in which the club took on a project that would benefit all Brazilians and announce Brazil as a modern and enlightened nation. In their judgment, Fluminense was therefore justified in appealing for governmental support of the project, and they saw critics as misguided at best, and at worst antisporting and even unpatriotic.

Fluminense announced its plan to build the stadium in October 1917, with the aim of completing it in time to host the third edition of the South American Championship, which was to take place in Rio de Janeiro in 1918. Supporters immediately defined it as a patriotic endeavor. *A Notícia*, for example, noted its relief, for it had feared Brazil would need to host the championship without a proper venue. Argentina and Uruguay had already hosted previous editions of the tournament in their own national stadiums, potentially leaving Brazil in "a situation of deplorable inferiority" in comparison to its neighbors. The newspaper was grateful to Fluminense, for its "brilliant initiative ... will save us from the fiasco" and "lend a great service to our country."[132] Due to the 1918 influenza pandemic, the tournament was postponed until May 1919, but the games did take place in Fluminense's new stadium, the first a 6–0 victory for Brazil against Chile, star forward Arthur Friedenreich leading the way with a hat trick. Six matches later, when Friedenreich scored the winning goal against Uruguay in extra time in the final, the stadium was the site for what enthusiasts called a nationalist triumph, one that announced Brazilian football's coming of age and indicated the progress of the country as a whole. Contemporaries made national heroes of Friedenreich and the team's other stars, such as Corinthians' Neco (Manuel Nunes) and Fluminense's own Marcos de Mendonça.[133]

Casting the stadium project as a nationalist effort was important because building the stadium was not easy or uncontroversial. The *Revista de Theatro e Sport* noticed early on that Fluminense faced a "lack of space and accommodations" at the club's grounds in the well-settled and desirable Laranjeiras neighborhood.[134] Building the stadium required the club to expand its footprint, and it acquired several pieces of private property on the Alvaro Chaves and Guanabara roads, which collectively cost almost 520 *contos de réis*.[135] Stadium plans also required the club to obtain parts of the Roso and Retiro da Guanabara roads that ran along the club property, which meant Fluminense needed to obtain the support of city and national authorities. Two other matters involved the government as well: the club's application to the federally controlled Banco do Brasil for a large loan of 2,000 contos de réis to pay for construction and the prospect that the stadium would be built right up to the property line that the club shared with the Guanabara Palace, then overseen by the country's historic preservation office, the Patrimonio Nacional.[136] Without government support, in short, Fluminense would not have the space, the financing, or the permissions necessary to complete its plans.

Christopher Gaffney calls the sports stadium in Latin America a "quasi-public" space that helps shape the social landscapes of the region's cities, with their influence extending beyond the private clubs that have used and sometimes built and controlled them.[137] The direct involvement of the city and federal governments made Fluminense's stadium quasi-public both figuratively and literally from the very beginning; it also made the stadium a matter for both public comment and public controversy. Mayor Amaro Cavalcanti hesitated to support the project when the club requested pieces of public property in late 1917, before eventually following the recommendation of his director of Public Works in approving the request.[138] Not all administrators were as amenable. In early August 1918 a director of the Patrimonio Nacional informed his superior, Minister of the Treasury Antônio Carlos Ribeiro de Andrada, of what the *Correio da Manhã* characterized as "various inconveniences" that the stadium would cause the Guanabara Palace, especially its effects on neighborhood roads. Club documents also speak of palace administrators' concerns that club expansion would "disturb the palace's tranquility."[139] *O Imparcial* alleged that the complaint had to do as much with the palace majordomo's dislike of the club as with practical concerns or questions of aesthetics or respectability, but Ribeiro de Andrada briefly backed the complaint. Had the complaint been sustained, Fluminense would have been obligated to reconsider its plans, and the matter drew the attention of the press.[140]

Another indication that Fluminense would not have everything its own way came early on in the construction process, when *A Noite* publicized the intrusion of the stadium site onto the Roso Road. It complained the stadium was "a monster rising up in the middle of the road!" It implied corruption in the government's willingness to cede the land required for the stadium, noting that the decision-making process was opaque, Fluminense having obtained the cession "from God knows whom." It called the entire project "absurd," "scandalous," and "immoral." And, finally, like the Patrimonio Nacional director, it reminded readers that this "monster" also threatened to compromise Brazil's reputation, for it would confront every distinguished visitor that the country lodged in the Guanabara Palace.[141]

Its defenders argued that Fluminense was acting in the national interest. In the view of most commentators, the stadium was an important and worthwhile investment that would distinguish both the club and the entire country. *O Imparcial* rejected the complaints of the Patrimonio Nacional, calling the complainant "some insignificant sub-director," and it called on the minister of the treasury to reverse his position so that his "illustrious name" would not be connected to a "most revolting injustice." It argued that the stadium would not mar the reputation or appearance of the palace but rather would help it to impress foreign dignitaries "because these men recognize the value of sport in their own countries," especially its role in "preparing men strong of body and of character, capable of perseverance." In the stadium, foreign dignitaries would see that Brazil, too, realized its value. Far from embarrassing Brazil, the stadium was "a work that can only bring honor to us Brazilians."[142]

The *Correio da Manhã* made similar arguments, noting that "it causes amazement, if not disbelief, the news that someone of good sense could think of impugning a project destined to give the country the most beautiful monument of its type in South America!" Like *O Imparcial*, the *Correio* argued the stadium would impress foreign visitors, serving as a second "palace" alongside the Guanabara as it hosted the foreign football teams that would come to compete in the South American Championship and in other contests. For Brazilians, the stadium was a "coliseum in which a people until very recently battered and debilitated will continue to build its physique."[143] Finally, "a group of *sportsmen*" wrote to *A Noite* to defend the project and especially Fluminense. They wrote that Fluminense aimed only to "give to Brazil a dignified venue in which to receive foreigners in the great football tournaments," that it did so "without consideration of the sacrifices involved," and that the cession it had obtained from the city was justly awarded, "by no means a favor."[144]

All of these defenders also made another point that helped Fluminense's public case. All asserted that governments all over the world encouraged their peoples' sporting habits and often offered significant assistance in the building of sports communities and infrastructure. *O Imparcial* noticed the "money and official support" that modern governments provided;[145] the "sportsmen" noticed that in other countries, including Brazil's South American neighbors, governments not only supported stadium construction but built the facilities themselves;[146] and the *Correio da Manhã* reminded the national government that in its public platform the Wenceslau Brás administration had stated its aim "to stimulate the moral, civic, and physical education of the people whose destinies it directs." It therefore must support the stadium project, "a dedicated and patriotic initiative."[147] The *Revista de Theatro e Sport* complimented Brás when it learned that he had offered his support to the stadium plans, suggesting that he understood that financial concerns were less important in this instance than they usually were because Brazil's hosting the tournament meant "the name of Brazil is in play."[148] The *Gazeta de Notícias* noted that Brazilians could now be confident that their government had finally become "intensely" interested in sport, as it should be. It called upon the authorities to "follow the example of the leaders of Argentina and Uruguay," who had paid for stadium construction with public money, which "guarantees these countries the great esteem of *sportsmen*."[149]

Ultimately, government support came through the cession of the portions of the Roso and Guanabara roads that the project required, the approval of Fluminense's loan request to the Banco do Brasil, and the public encouragement offered the club by government figures, including the president and the ministers of transportation and the navy. When navy minister Adm. Alexandrino de Alencar visited the construction site in September 1918, he called the stadium a "coliseum" and noted that it demonstrated "much work, much strength, and, above all, much patriotism."[150] Although critics thought even this support was too much, for advocates it seemed far too little, "nothing or almost nothing," in the words of the *Correio da Manhã*, which made the complaints and difficulties that Fluminense faced even more galling.[151] While government dithered and critics complained, O Imparcial said, a private club "does not hesitate in giving Brazil a plaza of sports which will do it honor," taking on "a gigantic work which fills all *sportsmen* with the most justified pride."[152] Though it would be built by Fluminense, the stadium would belong to all of Brazil. It would be the site for the country's heroes to prove their mettle, to test themselves against foreign opponents, and to advertise Brazil as a modern and accomplished nation. Significantly, in the media discourse that surrounded these debates, writers slipped easily between "they" and "we," between Fluminense and Brazil, as they built their case in support of the project. Fluminense benefited from their willingness to conflate the two.

Of course, it was Fluminense that built the stadium and that would benefit most from its construction. It would, according to member Octavio da Rocha Miranda, make Fluminense "the leading Club of South America and one of the leaders of its type in the world."[153] Admission income provided the club with resources for future projects, and possession of the stadium guaranteed it a means to moral and political influence in the ensuing years. Fluminense's players had an excellent new field to play on. Members enjoyed special seating in covered grandstands and private access into the new clubhouse, which was built contiguously to the stadium and inaugurated in 1920. And in the stadium they had their own "grand amphitheater" where members attended performances of Verdi's *Aida* and Gluck's *Orfeo ed Euridice* in 1920.[154]

To design the new stadium and clubhouse, Fluminense hired Hypolito Pujol, then a professor at São Paulo's Escola Politécnica. Pujol had worked with the family of club president Arnaldo Guinle before, designing its eponymous building in São Paulo. The Guinle building and other Pujol designs, such as his redesign of the Banco do Brasil's Centro Cultural in São Paulo, are emblematic of the era's mix of art nouveau and neoclassical, and Pujol brought the same sensibility to the stadium project. Pujol's design flattered Fluminense members' sense that they were engaged in as much a moral endeavor as a sporting one, the finished stadium featuring Greek columns and neoclassical flourishes. As the *Jornal do Brasil* described it, "the superb edifice of our stadium, in its magnificent lines and its Hellenic architecture, offers to all a grandiose notion of its capacities."[155] The clubhouse, still in use today, continues the theme, housing a library, a dining room, and a ballroom—an ornate affair with carved balconies, in-laid mirrors, and a parquet

FIGURE 1.4. Fluminense's stadium during the South American Championship, 1919. The Guanabara Palace is the domed structure that can be seen on the right. By permission of the Acervo Fluminória.

floor. Three enormous windows of stained glass imported from France dominate the ballroom, which, like paintings in the corners of the room, depict Greco-Roman scenes, tunic-clad dancers, and a discus thrower flanking a helmeted soldier who rides a chariot led by two white horses. The *Gazeta de Notícias* pointed out that "a stadium is simply an example of a modern adaptation of ancient inventions for the needs of the twentieth century," and the design of Fluminense's stadium and clubhouse showed that club members took the comparison literally.[156]

Club documents show that Fluminense saw the stadium as a work of social and cultural significance, and saw constructing it as a patriotic initiative. The club's annual report for 1918 stated that the stadium "secures not only Fluminense's greatness, but also guarantees, in an elevated way, civilization itself in the Capital of the Republic."[157] Secretary Mário Pollo elaborated on Fluminense's view of its work on the stadium in a manuscript history of the club in 1923. He wrote that the construction of the stadium was a "patriotic task" and that, in completing it, "the national blood demonstrates it is capable of gathering the energy for great accomplishments which, before now, local commentators had suggested was the privilege of foreigners in the other part of America." In 1922, when Brazil required an even larger venue in order to stage events related to the country's centenary celebrations, Fluminense expanded the stadium and hosted a variety of events. "Fluminense," Pollo wrote, "assumed responsibilities which rightly pertained to the government." The fact that the club had made "sacrifices on behalf of our Brazil" was "absolutely clear."[158]

The patriotic sentiment did not diminish with the completion of the stadium or after thirty thousand fans celebrated Brazil's victory in the 1919 South American Championship. The stadium continued to be the capital's premier sports venue for some time and hosted political and patriotic events for many years. For example, when the Belgian monarchs Albert and Elisabeth visited Rio de Janeiro in 1920, Albert's Brazilian hosts acknowledged his reputation as an avid sportsman and organized a parade of thousands of athletes in his honor at Fluminense's stadium.[159] The visit was a triumph for Brazilian diplomacy and its postwar strategy of improving the country's international position by focusing on its reputation, for Albert was a hero owing to his leadership during the war, and his presence seemed to ratify Brazil's emergence among rising nations. As Sueann Caulfield says, the visit also served policymakers' domestic purposes, for the couple combined "cosmopolitan modernity with a firmly patriarchal conception of honor and nationhood," which Brazilian statesmen envisioned for their own country.[160] When one of the principal public events of the visit highlighted the role of sports in building that Brazil and took place at Fluminense's stadium, Albert and Elisabeth's hosts validated Fluminense and other promoters of sports and their claim to the nationalist mantle.

In the first half of the twentieth century, the nationalistic discourse that surrounded the construction of the Fluminense stadium was revived whenever organizers contemplated erecting other stadiums, such as Vasco da Gama's São Januário, built in 1926, the São Paulo stadium at Pacaembu, built in 1938, and—biggest of all—the Maracanã, begun in 1948 and completed in 1950. As the early leaders of the campaign to construct the Pacaembu stadium said in asking for the support of the Liga Nacionalista in the early-1920s, the stadium would help make Brazilians "a stronger race, hardier and more energetic." It would make São Paulo, already a large city, a great one, allowing its citizens to assist Brazil in attaining its "lofty destiny." In short, a stadium would be a sports and civic monument in which Paulistas and Brazilians could improve themselves, come together, and prove their progress and their worth.[161]

⁖

Like others who encouraged Brazilians to play sports and those who sought to bring physical education into Brazilian schools, the builders of these stadiums characterized their work as patriotic and themselves as nationalists. Carlos Sussekind de Mendonça might claim that sport was hurting Brazilian youth, and Lima Barreto might reject the idea that sport brought Brazilians together, but the proponents of sport made exactly the opposite arguments. They began to make the case for sport's contributions to the nation even before the turn of the twentieth century, arguing that sports were an invaluable means to improve Brazilians' health; that sports helped make Brazilians good citizens, good soldiers, and good workers; and that sports helped to "Brazilianize" Brazilians, binding them to the country and to one another through their shared experience of sports. The relationship between nationalism and sports became more and more intimate during the 1910s and 1920s. The war played an important role, giving sports' advocates evidence to illustrate the value of sports and physical education, and the leaders of the maturing nationalist movement picked up the argument, claiming sports as part of their platform. Aside from the critiques of Mendonça and Barreto, few voices were raised in doubt.

The Vargas state built on the connection forged in the early twentieth century and formalized the relationship between nationalist doctrine and national sports in the 1930s and 1940s, culminating in the creation of the Conselho Nacional de Desportos. While the regime's activities were more extensive and more durable than those of predecessor governments, the character of its activities and the thinking behind them was rooted in decades of work by physical educators and sports promoters during the First Republic. Thus, imitating the organizers of the parade to honor Albert and Elisabeth in 1920, Vargas-era diplomats helped arrange an exhibition football match at the Fluminense stadium between sides selected to represent Rio de Janeiro and São Paulo to honor the British princes Edward and George when they visited Brazil in 1931. Fluminense's leaders had demonstrated in the previous decades their ability to cultivate political support and their perception of the club in nationalist terms, and they would have been gratified to read in *O Jornal* that, in hosting the event, the club had "prevailed, on behalf of national *sports*."[162]

The next year Fluminense opened its doors to tens of thousands who came to celebrate the second anniversary of the Vargas revolution. The club clearly appreciated the benefits of the relationship and made Vargas an honorary president in 1934.[163] The 1932 event was only one of many political rallies that the Vargas movement organized at sports venues, and Vasco da Gama's São Januário was a particular favorite of the regime throughout the 1930s and 1940s.[164] With their electric lights, capacity to host thousands, and media infrastructure, stadiums were attractive for many reasons. Using them, the regime also advertised the connection it sought to make between government, nationalism, and sport. All of the Vargas state's activities to promote sports were premised on the idea that playing sports was an important way to improve Brazil and an important way for proud Brazilians to demonstrate their nationalist feeling. The regime and its supporters asserted that they understood this better than their predecessors. However, like the stadiums that were used by Vargas but were built before he came to power, nationalist arguments on behalf of sport were made at the very beginning, even before 1900. When Vargas used football stadiums for political purposes and when he promoted sports in Brazil, he followed patterns set years before.

Building and Rebuilding the Society of Football

There was a time, the writer A.C. noted in 1931, when many of the football players who turned out for leading clubs in Brazil, Argentina, and elsewhere on the continent were foreigners. He cited the Buenos Aires club Alumni, which in 1910 fielded ten Britons in its first team, including the six brothers Brown. Most Brazilian teams of that era were not so heavily foreign, but there were ethnic clubs, like Germania and Charles Miller's largely British São Paulo Athletic, and there were Englishmen and other foreigners in the "big" clubs of São Paulo, Rio de Janeiro, and elsewhere in the decades after 1894. A.C. noticed that times had changed by 1931. In his view, Brazilians, like their South American neighbors, had assimilated the game, honing their own style and improving football "with the virtues innate to the race and its temperament." A.C. believed Brazilians had made football their own and said that clubs now preferred to recruit Brazilians, who understood this "Brazilian" game, rather than the foreigners they had once sought out. So far had this shift gone, he said, that if a British player were to turn out for a Brazilian team in 1931, he "would be as out of place among us as a polar bear in Tierra del Fuego."[1]

In terms of the British presence in Brazilian football, the change did seem remarkable. Where British teams like São Paulo Athletic and the Scottish Wanderers, Paysandú and Rio Cricket had played at the highest levels of competitive football into the late-1910s, by 1930 no British club competed. Where individual British athletes like Charles Miller and Sidney Pullen had led their teams to great victories in Brazil's best leagues, no Briton even played. And where British coaches, such as John Hamilton and Charles Williams, had trained leading Brazilian teams, only Harry Welfare, coach of Rio de Janeiro's Vasco da Gama, remained. Other foreigners, such as the Rio de Janeiro league's American administrator Fred Brown and Flamengo's Hungarian coach Dori Kürschner, still found work in Brazilian football, but it did seem that A.C. was correct, that the time of a truly Brazilian football had arrived by the 1930s.

However, while some of the most obvious indications of "foreign" football had disappeared by 1930, not everyone would have agreed with A.C.'s observation that football in Brazil had become a Brazilian game. This was never more apparent than when A.C.'s own publication, the *Jornal dos Sports*, complained that foreigners were rampant in Brazilian football only three months after A.C.'s confident announcement of their remarkable absence. In late August 1931 the paper launched a broadside against the coach Amílcar Barbuy and the players Armando Del Debbio, Rato (José Castelli), and Henrique Serafini, denouncing them as foreigners and calling them "renegades" and "ingrates."[2] These men, all Paulistas by birth and upbringing, had gone to Italy to work as professional footballers. The Italian league, reorganized under Fascist direction in 1926, had banned all foreigners from participation, but it allowed an exception for *rimpatriati*, children of the Italian diaspora, like Del Debbio, Rato, and Serafini, whom the regime considered authentic Italians regardless of their places of birth. There was even room in the Italian national team for some of these players, including the four Argentines and one Brazilian, Filó (Amphilogio Guarisi), who helped Italy win the World Cup in 1934.

These were not the first South Americans to "move with the ball" to Europe, and of course they would not be the last. But there were so many to leave for Italy after the Fascist reforms of the late-1920s—sixty from Argentina, thirty-two from Uruguay, and twenty-six from Brazil in the period between 1929 and 1943—that it felt like an "exodus" to *O Estado de S. Paulo*, and a "caravan," long and with no end in sight, to Buenos Aires' *La Cancha*.[3] Angry and disappointed, *La Cancha*'s Alberto Arena advised the Argentine emigrants to "say, 'goodbye!' to the hearts of all your country's fans!"[4] For its part, the Brazilian paper called the players who had left São Paulo "pseudo Paulistas," who had only pretended to be Brazilian.[5]

While at first most Brazilian commentators were more sympathetic, admitting that the players had been offered an attractive opportunity, they thought again when Barbuy, Del Debbio, Rato, and Serafini were quoted by the Italian Olympic Committee's *Il Littoriale* as rejecting their Brazilian roots. According to *Il Littoriale*, they stated, "We do not accept the false and hypocritical expression Italo-Brazilian. We are Italians!"[6] Del Debbio was quoted as saying that the idea that they were Brazilian was a "joke" [*droga*] and that they were "Italians, arch-Italians." Less excitedly, Barbuy stated, "We are all Italians and we are proud to offer to the fatherland a synthesis of [Italian] emigration to Brazil, demonstrating that our parents have forgotten neither the language nor the customs of the land of their birth."[7]

With the news arriving during a period of rising xenophobia, many Brazilians reacted indignantly, and the debate over the loyalty of the migrants played out in the press, both because it was one of the principal venues for building Brazil's football society and because the scandal made for good copy.[8] The *Jornal dos Sports* labeled the players not only ingrates and renegades but also "mercenaries" who had "cynically turned against the Fatherland," and it offered the threatening promise that "our public, which so long tired out its hands applauding these renegades, will have those hands ready to receive them, if, some day, they have the audacity to return to our great land."[9] The players' friends in São Paulo were more patient, and three weeks after receiving the news of the interview, *A Gazeta* was happy to report that it had received a telegram from the four in which they denied they had made the offensive remarks.[10] Regardless, the controversy simmered on, implicating the entire Italian community of São Paulo, in the form of attacks on one of its leading institutions, the Palestra Itália club. Several of the migrants had played for the club, and the *Folha da Manhã* suggested that the club chose "not to pose the minimum resistance" to the players' departure, allegedly because of Italian chauvinism.[11] This was untrue. Club directors opposed the players fiercely when they decided to move to Italy and had taken the lead in having the players banned from the city league.[12] But the damage had been done, and the club suffered from persistent suspicions about its loyalty for years to come.

The movement of these players to Italy and Brazilians' reaction to it show that defining nationality was not as simple a proposition as A.C. had implied. As Brazilians argued about whether these migrants were Italians or Brazilians or Italo-Brazilians, and about what this meant for them and for Brazil, they could look back on over three decades of football in the country, during which figures like A.C. had attempted to draw distinctions between those who belonged in football and those who did not. In spite of their attempts,

Brazilian football was always characterized by the kind of doubt that surfaced when the erstwhile Paulistas claimed Italian citizenship. For example, Charles Miller was born in São Paulo but was educated in England, played football for the British expatriate São Paulo Athletic Club, and even served as British consul for a time. Sidney Pullen was born in England, played for the British club Paysandú, and fought for the United Kingdom in World War I, but he also played for Flamengo and represented Brazil on the seleção on five occasions.

And it was not only Britons who frustrated easy categorization. One of the conspicuous features of Brazilian football, from the beginning and into the 1940s, was the participation of clubs drawn from the country's expatriate communities. Like immigrant clubs in Buenos Aires and Santiago, Chile, clubs like São Paulo's Palestra Itália and Rio de Janeiro's Vasco da Gama served immigrants as venues for civic engagement, allowing them to protect and promote immigrant identities while also helping them to participate more fully in the life of their new South American homes.[13] Brazilians tended to accept and even encourage the participation of such clubs, but when Italian professional teams began signing Brazilian players, observers realized that a lack of clear definitions about the identity of Brazilian football might injure it. While some were proud of their countrymen and their success across the Atlantic, others—especially those inspired by the forthright nationalism they shared with the Getúlio Vargas regime—bristled with the pride of injured patriots.

The migration of the Paulistas to Italy also intensified debates about another marker of belonging, the distinction between amateurs and professionals. The organizers of Brazil's first football leagues enshrined amateurism as their ideal and an absolute requirement for participation, establishing a variety of mechanisms to guard against any hint of professionalization. Ostensibly amateurs, Del Debbio, Rato, and Serafini moved to Italy in order to play football as professionals, and that prompted one of the chief criticisms made by *O Estado de S. Paulo*, which said, "they have lost any notion of self-respect, and have become salesmen of their own talents."[14] But the paper also realized that this was only a symptom of a broader problem, for in the 1910s and 1920s Brazilian football had come to be characterized by what contemporaries called "false amateurism" and "masked professionalism." That is, while many administrators, coaches, players, journalists, and fans claimed that Brazilian football was amateur, most clubs paid their players. At first they paid small amounts for good performances, goals, and victories—little more than tips, which is what these payments were called. By the 1930s most footballers at the highest level were amateurs in name only. The informality of the arrangement, however, meant that very few were paid very much, and clubs lacked the means to keep hold of their players. Italians' appetite for Brazilian footballers—*A Gazeta* called the 1931 episode "the first spoonful"—demonstrated the unsustainability of this system.[15]

The Italian episode, in short, demonstrated the muddiness of notions of belonging and of national and other kinds of football identity in Brazil. At a moment when Brazilians were refashioning the laws of citizenship and making citizenship rights more difficult to enjoy, when national football had seemed to have matured and shed some of the uncertainties of the past, football's complexities and its vulnerabilities stood revealed.[16] In response, critics demanded that immigrants declare their loyalties, and they also redoubled their ongoing efforts to professionalize football, in the hopes that formal contracts and higher wages would hinder the emigration of players wanted by foreign clubs. Like their counterparts in Buenos Aires who reacted to the loss of Argentine players in much the same way, Paulistas and Cariocas successfully enacted the reform in the aftermath of the Italian episode, formally professionalizing the country's leading leagues in 1933.

This chapter examines the ways that Brazilians in São Paulo and Rio de Janeiro arranged their football lives between 1894 and the early-1940s, focusing on the ideas and actions of the middle- and upper-class men who were the first to play the game in Brazil, whose roles as pioneers and whose resources afforded them persistent influence over the character of Brazilian football. It demonstrates that in the formative years, roughly from 1894 to 1914, these Brazilians modeled their football on a particular version of sports they found in Europe: fiercely amateur and socially exclusive, and in decline. First in Britain and then elsewhere, this model was losing out to an increasingly popular and commercialized version of the game by the time Brazilians adopted it. But the decision gave Brazilian organizers a crucial tool for policing entry into their fledgling leagues, and they buttressed that decision with other actions aimed at making organized Brazilian football an exclusive pastime branded as British and more generally European, such as recruiting British players and coaches and purchasing equipment from European vendors.

They also broadcast foreign terminology, such as "foot-ball" and "sportsman," and the values they associated with it, through their control of the sports press, which grew very rapidly in the early twentieth century. The press became one of the most important vehicles for the promotion of football and for the defense of middle- and upper-class privileges. Alongside clubs and leagues and local and national governments, the football press was a critical institution in the construction of football in Brazil; it was vital in establishing the sportsmen's interpretation of "British" amateur football as the only acceptable form of football in Brazil.

Yet by the 1930s, as A.C. noted, some of the most obvious expressions of the sportsmen's commitment to the British identity of football had eroded. Brazilians recruited fewer foreign players, invented neologisms to replace foreign words, and produced their own equipment. The popular history of Brazilian football, narrated by influential journalists like Thomaz Mazzoni and Mário Filho, depicts this erosion of Anglocentric football as a nationalization of the game and its democratization, exemplified by the abandonment of amateurism for professionalism. However, like the sportsmen of the turn of the century, who had been selective in adapting British customs to Brazil, their successors in the 1920s and 1930s adapted the nationalism and populism of the 1920s and 1930s to their purposes. They joined nationalists in attacking Del Debbio, Rato, and Serafini by banning them from local leagues, and they joined with populists in working for the game's professionalization. But they also confirmed their own prerogatives to run football and explain the meaning of the game so that the social hierarchy that had characterized the era of the sportsmen persisted—and was even reinforced—because of the actions of nationalist reformers. By the 1940s organized Brazilian football changed in important ways, but it also carried the hallmarks of the game organized four decades earlier.

Building the Society of Football

Many early advocates saw modern sport as an especially useful means of improving Brazil, a way to develop the physical health of Brazilians and to cultivate in Brazilians the habits of republican citizenship, of productive labor, and of national service. This does not mean, however, that they believed that all Brazilians should play sports in the same manner. Rather, many believed that the pursuit of sports should be determined according to each Brazilian's gender, race, class, work, and education. Many Brazilian women and men were convinced, for example, that football was inappropriate for women, and influential physical educators believed that working-class students ought to practice calisthenics and other rote forms of physical training geared toward their prospects for future work. Meanwhile, middle- and upper-class boys played football and other team sports at schools like the Colégio Pedro II and Gymnasio Anglo-Brasileiro. José Veríssimo's concern that all Brazilians pursue sports according to a proper "method and system" helped establish the principle that it was not enough for Brazilians to play sports; they must do so correctly, and this required organization and guidance, preferably from physical educators like himself.[17]

This hierarchical thinking helped shape decisions about how to organize Brazilian football, as did the way middle-class and wealthy Brazilians practiced sports before 1894. Before football's arrival, middle- and upper-class Brazilians swam, skated, practiced gymnastics, attended horse races, and raced against one another on foot, on bicycles, and in racing sculls. Although working-class people participated in these events as jockeys, as fans, as bettors, and occasionally as athletes, wealthier Brazilians dominated sports because they were the founders and administrators of the organizations that arranged them.[18] They organized clubs, such as São Paulo's Jockey Club and its Tietê rowing club and Rio de Janeiro's Derby Club and Flamengo, which was a rowing club before it adopted football. These clubs launched the first formal competitions in Brazil; they acquired and improved the first dedicated sports grounds, such as São Paulo's important Velodrome; and they worked with the first generation of sports journalists who wrote for general audiences and in genre publications, like *O Sportman*, published in Rio de Janeiro in the 1880s.

At a time when late-imperial and republican authorities were attacking working-class pastimes like capoeira and cockfighting, these institutions made nineteenth and early-twentieth-century Brazilian sports socially exclusive. Clubs and the leagues they established were private organizations, and they used informal and formal means to obtain close control over Brazilian sports. They were self-selecting, relatively expensive to join, and decided their own rules, and thereby justified keeping out social undesirables such as workingmen and women and people of color. For example, in 1906 Rio de Janeiro's amateur rowing league banned the participation of all barbers because barbers seemed uniquely positioned to receive money for their athletic talents in the form of tips at work.[19] Although the logic is not unassailable, its aim is clear since it not only excluded a particular group of potential competitors but also communicated the social preferences of the league's member clubs: most barbers were from modest backgrounds, and many were men of color.

Through decisions like this, middle- and upper-class Brazilians attempted to make organized sports into a venue for maintaining their privileges in a Brazil that was changing in worrying ways, especially after the establishment of the republic in 1889. The challenge to social distinctions came from many directions. It came in the abolition of slavery, one of the old regime's last formal provisions against equality, in 1888. It came in the form of proponents' justifications for the establishment of the republic, many of them rendered in rhetorics of inclusion and democracy. It came in the form of working-class reactions to threats against traditional social economies, such as the millenarian Canudos movement in 1890s Bahia and the 1904 Vaccine Revolt in Rio de Janeiro.[20] And it came in the form of massive European migration, which promised to provide the country with industrious labor but also brought the hazard of laborers familiar with the dangerous ideas of Europe's mass politics, which helped bolster the Brazilian labor movement.[21]

Whether reacting against change or demanding it, such episodes dismayed middle- and upper-class Brazilians, such as the coffee planters of São Paulo and their urban, middle-class allies. They had hoped the republic would bring peace and modernity, order and progress, but this did not mean that they were any more trusting of the masses than the rivals they replaced.[22] Middle- and upper-class republicans possessed a variety of instruments to confront the challenges they faced from below. Among those instruments, Leonardo Pereira says, they hoped to use sports, and, more precisely, sports organizations, "to restore the [social] distinctions whose clarity, to their eyes, had been lost during the first years of the new regime."[23] Reflecting the complexity of Brazilian sports ideology, on one hand, they argued that all Brazilians should play sports while, on the other, they insisted that their participation should follow orderly and hierarchical patterns appropriate to Brazil.

The fathers of Brazilian football followed their predecessors in horseracing and crew in using the game's institutions to balance inclusion and exclusivity. Membership in football clubs was self-selecting, with many leading clubs considering new members only if they were sponsored by existing ones, and all of them required payments in the form of initiation fees and monthly dues. The clubs in turn established control over the leagues in which they competed and determined which new clubs could join them. São Paulo Athletic, Mackenzie College, Internacional, Germania, and Paulistano—all either expatriate clubs or clubs of the Brazilian middle and upper classes—formed the country's first league in 1901, the Liga Paulista de Foot-ball. The Liga Metropolitana de Football was the capital's first league, founded in 1905 and formed by the clubs of the Brazilian upper classes (Fluminense, America, Botafogo, and Football Athletic) and expatriate organizations (Bangú, and, later in the first year, Paysandú and Rio Cricket). The leaders of these clubs and their leagues also formed parent bodies to govern Brazilian football and Brazilian sport as a whole. Cariocas founded the Federação Brasileira de Esportes (Brazilian Sports Federation) in 1914, which later became the Confederação Brasileira de Desportos (CBD), and Paulistas formed the Federação Brasileira de Football (Brazilian Football Federation) in 1915; regional rivalry was among the only issues that divided the football elite in the first two decades after the game's arrival in Brazil.

Joining a club required an initiation fee and monthly dues, which, for middle-class clubs in the years before 1910, were usually around ten mil-réis and five mil-réis, respectively.[24] These clubs passed on payments to their leagues, with the Rio de Janeiro league requiring that each club pay thirty mil-réis each year in 1905 and the more established São Paulo league charging two hundred mil-réis as an initiation fee and sixty mil-réis annually in 1906.[25] Circa 1912 membership in the fashionable Fluminense and Botafogo clubs came at a price of twenty-five mil-réis initially and eight mil-réis each month. By then, league costs in Rio de Janeiro had risen toward those charged in São Paulo, despite the fact that the rapid inflation for which the First Republic is well known did not accelerate in earnest until the late-1910s. Each club paid the Liga Metropolitana a one-time initiation fee of one hundred mil-réis, one mil-réis for each member registered to play in league competition, and 10 percent of the income they raised from attendance.[26]

Inflation helps account for the fact that Botafogo had raised its initiation fee to thirty mil-réis and its monthly dues to ten mil-réis by the middle of the next decade. Similarly, monthly dues for members of Fluminense had more than doubled, to twenty mil-réis. The rise in the club's initiation fee, though, outpaced inflation, to a remarkable two hundred mil-réis, eight times the amount it had been in 1912.[27] Clubs also charged spectators to watch their teams play. Fluminense charged one mil-réis for general admission and two mil-réis for a seat in the grandstand for ordinary league matches in 1905, with higher prices for more important games. At the beginning of the 1920 decade, even the least expensive ticket to a Rio de Janeiro league game was one mil-réis, while a seat in the grandstand cost three mil-réis, and a numbered chair, six.[28]

In themselves, these fees did not block participation since the average urban laborer, for example, made between three and five mil-réis per day between 1890 and 1915, after which inflation meant rising wages, to more than seven mil-réis per day in 1920, more than nine in 1925, and more than eleven in 1930. But real wages did not rise, they fell, so that in the worst years of the mid-1920s workers were making less than a third of what workers had made in 1890 in real terms, which meant that the prices of rent and food could easily overwhelm the earnings of working adults.[29]

For workers struggling to get by, even the superficially affordable costs of joining a middle-class club would have seemed a challenge, were they invited to join by the sportsmen who ran the organizations, which of course they were not. Moreover, there was more to consider than the cost of initiation and dues. Besides needing free time to practice and money to travel to games, players had to dress the part, and the gear required for official matches could be quite expensive. For example, in 1921, a year in which the average Paulista laborer was making a little over seven mil-réis per day, at the Mappin department store a pair of football socks cost 9 mil-réis and a jersey cost 10. The cheapest pair of cleats the store sold was 175 mil-réis, with the "best" pair costing 280. Even with a 10 percent discount for those who belonged to clubs, such material was unaffordable for many footballers.[30]

Although football can be played cheaply enough, playing organized, competitive football in Brazil in the early twentieth century was not easy to afford, in part because middle-class and wealthy sportsmen designed it that way and in part out of necessity. Regional and national bodies organized matches between state select teams and Brazil's competition against foreigners, and they hired coaches to train them. Leagues had to pay the expenses of administrators and referees and, eventually, had to work with public authorities to police football grounds once the game became so popular that matches attracted tens of thousands of spectators.

Most important were the responsibilities fulfilled by clubs, the fundamental institutions of organized football. Clubs had to acquire playing fields, and they had to obtain goal frames and balls, at a minimum. Clubs with the financial resources to do so also erected grandstands, clubhouses, and, eventually, stadiums; they arranged transportation and meals for players on game days; and they helped players improve their performances by hiring coaches and

FIGURE 2.1. Before a match between Fluminense and the Club Athletico Paulistano, circa 1905. Antônio Prado Júnior is standing in front of the railing, fourth from left in the boater hat, with a mustache. By permission of the Club Athletico Paulistano.

physical trainers. Purchases and appointments served as quotidian means that the clubs of the middle class and the wealthy used to distinguish themselves from their working-class counterparts, both in an aesthetic sense and in a competitive one. That is, those with financial means could dress sharply, play with better balls on better fields, and hire more accomplished coaches, thereby helping to establish social and cultural hierarchy in Brazilian football and reinforcing it against the challenges presented by a sport with few laws and fewer essential items.

Middle- and upper-class clubs revealed their tastes and indicated their financial strength by turning to Europe when they needed to buy equipment or hire coaches. For example, the three most prominent clubs in Rio de Janeiro, Fluminense, Botafogo, and Flamengo, ordered their football gear directly from Britain even though British suppliers were not always able to satisfy their demands and even after the equipment became available on the local market. In 1903 Fluminense changed its colors from its original charcoal and white to the now-familiar green, red, and white after its London supplier, a Mr. Piggott, informed the club of his inability to locate gray uniform material.[31] This did not stop the club from placing large orders for British-made equipment, which included a lawnmower and an irrigation device. A large order in 1905 consisted of sixty each of ties, hat-ribbons, hats, socks, and jerseys as well as seventy-two handkerchiefs and thirty-six blazers, the price for all of which was 1 conto and 642 mil-réis.[32] Early on, the lack of local providers may have dictated clubs' decisions to seek this kind of equipment in Britain, but by 1907 the Bangú club was having its jerseys made locally, and local stores, like Rio de Janeiro's Casa Colombo, were selling balls and pumps as early as 1908.[33]

Still, leading Carioca clubs continued to send to Britain for their equipment. For example, Flamengo indicated the particular tastes of the clubs of the well-to-do when it added football to its roster of activities in 1911. Making sure the team dressed properly when it took the field in the club's first match, on May 3, 1912, directors made "an immediate order to Europe for all of the material for *football*" as soon as the decision to play the game was made. Clearly proud of the accomplishment, President Edmundo de Azurém Furtado informed a club assembly that the team "appeared on the pitch perfectly uniformed" in Flamengo red and black.[34] For its part, Botafogo was still ordering sports equipment from Great Britain in 1917, despite the difficulties created by the war.[35]

While big clubs like Fluminense, Botafogo, and Flamengo sent to Britain for custom uniforms and what they believed were the best balls and other equipment, other clubs had to settle for either Brazilian-made goods or items available in local shops. Brazilian merchants responded swiftly to the opportunities that Brazilians' new taste in football offered in the early twentieth century, and their advertisements suggest that it was not only the wealthiest athletes who wanted English-made football equipment. There was Au Petit Paris, which stated in 1907 that its footballs, boxing gloves, and other items were "Genuine English Articles, Imported Directly," and Casa 'Sportman,' which in a 1913 advertisement mentioned that its jerseys, balls, pumps, and cleats came from London. As late as 1921 Mappin Stores still promised customers "English Products at Advantageous Prices."[36] Casa Clark, Casa Colombo, Casa Fuchs, and others followed along in the same way, always announcing the obvious quality of their products with the statement that their products were English.

At the end of 1921 the national government gave its support to this business when it adopted the CBD's proposal for the exemption from tax of imported sporting goods, but even here there was a suggestion of the social hierarchy of Brazilian football. Nine years earlier, Flamengo president Azurém Furtado had noted that Flamengo's directors had been able to convince the Ministry of the Treasury to exempt the club's purchase of its first football gear from regular customs duties.[37] A club of middle-class and wealthy sportsmen, Flamengo possessed useful political connections. More modest clubs, with fewer financial resources, continued to pay higher prices for almost a decade longer, and even then they only received the tax exemption if they participated in leagues recognized by the CBD.[38]

Wealthier clubs also used their resources to hire professional coaches and trainers. The Paulistano club was the first to do so, hiring the Scot John Hamilton on a three-month contract in 1907. Hamilton had had a successful career as a professional player in Scotland and England, and in 1907 was a coach at London's Fulham.[39] Few clubs in Brazil had the contacts or the financial means to make this kind of arrangement. Fluminense was one of these, and it hired Charles Williams as coach in 1911. *O Jornal do Commercio* called this "welcome news," and, echoing the Anglophilia of many in Brazilian football, said that Williams, "like the majority of English *sportsmen*, is honest, open, and lacking any prejudice that could make him unfriendly."[40] Williams was a former professional and was a successful coach in Scotland and Wales and managed the Danish national team before moving to Brazil. During his long career there, he coached Fluminense, America, Botafogo, and Flamengo in Rio de Janeiro and Corinthians in São Paulo. When he left, Fluminense hired another Briton, J. H. Quincey-Taylor, who served as coach and masseur between 1914 and 1918.[41]

Fluminense employed a professional coach continuously after 1911, which helped ensure its ongoing influence in the sporting life of the capital. It won eight Rio de Janeiro championships between 1906 and 1919, including three years in succession in 1917, 1918, and 1919, five more titles than any other club. In the years when Fluminense did not win, other clubs of the middle class and wealthy did so, and no club outside the elite won the Carioca championship before 1923. The wealthier clubs of São Paulo enjoyed similar success, with Paulistano winning eight city titles between 1902 and 1921, four more than the second most successful club, Charles Miller's São Paulo Athletic.

One reason for the success of these clubs was that they were able to field experienced expatriate players, such as Sidney Pullen and Harry Welfare. Welfare, who had played for Liverpool and other clubs in England, joined Fluminense soon after moving to Brazil in 1913. He led Fluminense's line as center-forward for over ten years, earning the nickname "the Tank" on his way to scoring more than 160 goals and winning four city championships while also helping the club to dominate Rio de Janeiro's basketball league, which was formed in 1919 and which Fluminense won every year from 1920 to 1927. Welfare was remarkably popular, one fan saying he was "worshipped almost like a god" and that he was the "Emperor of Attack" in a poem published in 1915.[42] He also represented the city of Rio de Janeiro, including in massively important games against Paulista select teams and two teams visiting from England, and he went on to a long career as a coach and administrator in Rio de Janeiro after his playing days.[43] Fluminense and clubs like it had the connections to cultivate relationships with players like Welfare, and they were able to offer first-class facilities, professional training, and other inducements that might attract skilled athletes like him. For example, Fluminense club members helped Welfare find work in Rio de Janeiro, and one of them, the owner and director of the Gymnasio Anglo-Brasileiro, Charles Armstrong, hired Welfare to teach English. Quincey-Taylor was still making contacts with potential employers on Welfare's behalf four years after his arrival.[44]

Harry Welfare was an extraordinary footballer, and these were extraordinary circumstances—an accomplished player moving to Brazil in the prime of his playing career. However, Welfare's experience and the ability of clubs like Fluminense and Paulistano to recruit experienced coaches like John Hamilton, Charles Williams, and J. H. Quincey-Taylor suggest the variety of their resources as they took the lead in organizing Brazilian football. Moreover, as in Welfare's case, sports clubs offered members much more than football. Many clubs that fielded football teams also participated in other sports, such as rowing and basketball; they hosted intramural competitions; and they provided members with tennis courts, swimming pools, skating rinks, and other facilities for the pursuit of their athletic interests. Even the most modest of these organizations were also as much social clubs as athletic ones, and the clubs of the working class and the clubs of the wealthy offered members and their guests a variety of activities, from picnics to gourmet dinners, from parties to formal dances, from modest libraries to opera performances. Football was the central part of an expansive social life for many urban Brazilians in the early twentieth century, and the club was the principal venue for it.

The clubs of the middle class and wealthy provided expensive and sometimes elaborate entertainments, which helped make the football lifestyle fashionable and chic, and made a football match about much more than football. Elite clubs helped cultivate a sense of belonging among their members and fans, selling items like jackets, sweaters, and pins so that they could advertise their allegiances to their football cliques.[45] Society magazines like Rio de Janeiro's *Careta* and São Paulo's *A Vida Moderna* covered the arrival of fans at club grounds, with photographs of well-heeled and fashionable fans often the extent of their coverage. After the match, players and other members and their guests retired to well-appointed clubhouses to dine, listen to music, and dance. Especially important matches were followed by elegant banquets and formal dances, for which players exchanged their uniforms for tuxedos and demonstrated they could waltz or foxtrot as well as they could dribble, pass, and shoot.

In recruiting members, club administrators thus had reason to think about more than football. They were responsible for providing and maintaining infrastructure for the pursuit of a variety of interests, which meant that a potential member's financial situation was a necessary consideration. Perhaps more importantly, they were also building new social venues, and a candidate's reputation mattered—often as much as his athletic prowess, especially since many club members did not play sports. Together these factors helped limit membership in leading clubs in spite of the accessibility of the game itself. Thus, Fluminense's 1920 club registry lists members drawn from a narrow range of professions. Businessmen, bankers, lawyers, engineers, and public servants predominated among approximately 2,500 full members, and this was the pattern for most leading clubs. Depending on their particular character and their location, the clubs of the middle class and wealthy also drew from two other categories in selecting members—university students and military officers. Botafogo, for instance, had a reputation as the club of the capital's younger sort, and many members in the early twentieth century were students.[46]

Amateurism and the Defense of Privilege

In principle and in practice, dues and rules allowed middle-class and wealthy organizers to shape clubs to their liking and, because these clubs dominated the administration of Brazil's leading football leagues and its governing bodies, to define organized Brazilian football according to their tastes. Sportsmen also ensured themselves influence even outside their own clubs by using league bureaucracies to set conditions on participation in competitive football, conditions that they justified by asserting they followed English practice. In its inaugural statutes in 1905, Rio de Janeiro's Liga Metropolitana de Football announced that it would follow English practice literally to the letter. It stated that its laws would be, specifically and uniquely, those of the English Football Association, and, further, that the league would use "English terms," like "*offside, foul, goal, penalty*, etc." As late as 1913 the league was still insisting upon both provisions, and reminded clubs that it expected them to play their matches on grounds which "conform to the rules of the Foot-ball Association."[47]

However, the Football Association had administered the transition to professional football even before the game arrived in Brazil, in 1885. Brazilians did not follow suit until 1933, instead insisting that Brazilian football should be exclusively amateur. Here social bias seems to have trumped cultural affinity, as the sportsmen, like their counterparts in medicine, education, and philosophy, chose selectively in adapting European models to Brazil. In fact, although they chose not to follow the experience of the Football Association on this question, Brazilian sportsmen did follow an English model in building their football on a foundation of amateurism, and the choice is revealing. By the time of the game's introduction to Brazil, the amateur tradition in England was most closely identified with the public schools of the middle and upper classes and the great universities and the graduates of those institutions, such as the members of the aristocratic Old Etonian and Corinthian clubs. These clubs resisted the establishment of professionalism in England and eventually organized the Amateur Football Defence Foundation to rival the Football Association in 1907.

J. A. Mangan has shown that these schools and clubs promoted a genteel "games ethic," an ideology that saw modern sport as a school of gentlemanly values, of selflessness and teamwork, of honest ambition and leadership. They insisted that sport could deliver on its promise only if it were pursued correctly, by amateurs. The amateur played because he loved sport and sought to improve himself and make himself more useful to his community and his country. In contrast, those who accepted payment undermined the entire sporting project. They might become physically fit, they might demonstrate leadership, they might work together in a team, but ultimately they benefited only themselves because their priority was personal enrichment. Moreover, they were much more likely than were amateurs to betray the spirit of the game they played so that—whereas amateurs could be trusted to demonstrate respect for competitors, the referee, and fans—professionals' greed made them prone to cheating and any number of other violations.[48]

Brazilian sportsmen were quite familiar with this ethic and these champions of amateurism. Charles Miller attended an English public school, Bannister Court in Southampton, where he played cricket, football, and other sports. His cousin and fellow leader of São Paulo Athletic, William Fox Rule, was also an alumnus of Bannister Court, and many of the founders and early members of Fluminense had been educated in private schools in England or on the continent. The tradition of sending sons to Britain continued beyond the turn of the century, and schools like the Gymnasio Anglo-Brasileiro and American-run Mackenzie College brought the public school and university model to Brazil. Alongside Brazilian pedagogues of Anglo-American physical education, these schools trained some of Brazil's first sportsmen in the ideology of amateur sport.

Brazilian sportsmen reinforced their commitment to this games ethic by cultivating relationships with English amateur sport and especially with the Corinthian Football Club, which was one of the leading defenders of English amateur football and one of the best football clubs in the world in the late nineteenth and early twentieth centuries. Charles Miller had played with the Corinthians occasionally while living in England, and he helped organize two visits by the club to Brazil, in 1910 and 1913. These visits, described in detail in the next chapter, were part of what an early historian of the English club called its "missionary" work abroad, promoting its version of football, gentlemanly and unequivocally amateur, among those who had not yet accepted professionalism.[49] The Corinthians were pleased that Brazilians seemed committed to amateurism, and their Brazilian hosts were gratified by the approval of their guests.

Middle-class and wealthy Brazilian sportsmen in the first two decades of the twentieth century were Anglocentric and, more generally, Eurocentric. But they chose their England and their Europe carefully. Unlike the Football Association and the vast majority of Englishmen and increasing numbers of continental Europeans who played and watched the game, they were committed to amateurism as the best and only acceptable way of pursuing an interest in football. Like the Old Etonians and Corinthians in England, they pointed to an ideologically substantive games ethic to justify their resolution. Like those English aristocrats who were their friends and their models, their commitment also seems to have been motivated by social preferences.

Administrators demonstrated this when they turned from establishing amateurism to enforcing it. When middle-class and wealthy Brazilians and their expatriate friends first started playing football, they could be confident that they would dominate football institutions and competitions since they had the resources to field the best teams. They knew the game better than working-class athletes, they were friendly with those from whom they could lease private and public urban space for playing fields, and they could afford the free time to practice the game and the money to hire coaches to train them. When talented working-class athletes did emerge, the sportsmen turned to amateurism, among other means, to preserve their hegemony.

This was most obvious in Rio de Janeiro, where administrators formally excluded nonwhite athletes from participation in the city league in 1907. In May of that year, the directors of the Liga Metropolitana informed its clubs that the league would no longer accept applications from "people of color" to be registered as amateurs, which meant that they were barred from participating in the league. The next month they revisited and revised the decision, now stating their intention that the league would refuse registration to athletes who "performed or have performed" certain kinds of work, the specific nature of which they left conveniently undefined.[50]

Sportsmen were not unanimous in supporting rules and exclusions based on race and occupation. Writing in São Paulo's *Sportman* magazine in 1906, M. Marcello made the popular argument that "sports organizations tend to improve the physical health of nations, accompanied *pari passu* by improvements in their intellectual and moral culture." He argued that it was widely accepted in Brazil that the benefits provided by sports "are not the privilege of certain classes, but are rather the common wealth of all respectable and civilized men," and he therefore complained that Brazil's sports clubs had become "simply recreation centers for the privileged," excluding workers from membership and cynically using amateur rules to exclude them from competition. He reminded the sportsmen that the republic was founded on the principle of "the absolute abolition of every privilege of caste, of religion, of profession" and asserted that they should match the republic's civic equality with their own promotion of equality in sports. It was especially important that they do so, Marcello argued, because workers "have a greater need for well-designed physical and moral education."[51]

Marcello understood the social bias at work in the application of amateur rules by middle-class and wealthy sportsmen, and in their selective reading of European example. He accepted that some Brazilians might prefer amateur to professional sports, though he rejected that the distinction was a moral one, admitting only that "it makes sense to distinguish *sport* from *profession*." Further, he agreed with the sportsmen that Brazil should follow European examples, but, he claimed, most Europeans "do not make any kind of social class distinctions" in organizing their competitions. Perhaps anticipating sportsmen's objections, he asserted that Brazilians were "unjustified" in choosing to follow the examples of English aristocrats not only because of the social prejudices they displayed, which were inappropriate to republican Brazil, but also because their sporting lives were in decline—"decadent," according to Marcello.[52]

A few Cariocas made similar arguments when they learned of the Liga Metropolitana's decision to exclude people of color. Botafogo club director Alfredo Chaves called the measure a "truly odious choice" and argued that it was "contrary to every democratic and rational principle." He insisted that color should have nothing to do with football and that it was certainly "not a sufficient motive for exclusion from our company." The league "should consider only the behavior of those who apply for registration."[53] The members of the Bangú Athletic Club threatened to bolt from the league if the decision stood. Bangú, the club founded in 1903 out of the Progresso Industrial textile plant in northern Rio de Janeiro, was led by British directors and was one of the founding members of the Liga Metropolitana. The fact of Bangú's British leadership on and off the playing field helped earn the club's involvement in the largely middle-class and wealthy new league, despite its connection to industry and despite the fact that it drew players from the plant's variety of employees, workers as well as managers, white and nonwhite.[54] This may have had to do with the significant distance between the Bangú neighborhood and the rest of Rio de Janeiro, with a camaraderie borne of the industrial experience, or with company owners' insistence that sponsorship would be available only if the club were to bring all of their employees together. Whatever the reasons for Bangú's inclusiveness, the league's 1907 policy was in conflict with the club's character, and Bangú threatened to withdraw rather than accept the sportsmen's stance.[55] That threat is almost certainly the reason that league administrators reconsidered the policy of a formal ban on the participation of nonwhite athletes.

The reversal did not, however, indicate that most sportsmen had been convinced that football should be organized according to the "democratic principles" that Alfredo Chaves championed. First, administrators exchanged one kind of bias for another, judging footballers by the kind of work they did rather than the color of their skin. Second, as Marcello noticed, the attitudes that produced exclusive policies were very common among middle- and upper-class sportsmen in the early twentieth century, and these sportsmen were slow to change their minds. In 1907 Botafogo director Cruz Santos responded directly to Chaves' objection, speaking for many when he defended the league's racial policy and giving voice to a common defense of the social disparities of the ostensibly democratic republic. Cruz Santos argued that the democracy implicit in the republican project need not apply to the activities of football clubs, which were, according to him, private organizations unconnected to political questions. The attempt to "confuse" political and sporting issues was, he said, "an invalid point of view." Cruz Santos argued that the success of sports organizations depended upon "bonds of camaraderie and friendship," which were strongest between men of the same color since differences in color "almost always indicate people of different classes." Administrators' decision to exclude people of color indicated their awareness that race and class were strongly related in early-twentieth-century Brazil, and it demonstrated their awareness of the racial and class preferences of the middle- and upper-class sportsmen who had appointed them. The exclusion, according to Cruz Santos, would be "quite reasonable" and "in the interest of the *Sport*."[56]

In the next decade, social distinctions continued to formally condition participation in Rio de Janeiro's most important league. In 1912, for example, a league directive instructed clubs to field only players who were students, military officers, or who possessed postsecondary educational degrees.[57] In August 1915, with rare candor, the author and administrator Alberto Silvares explained the thinking behind such policies in a piece published in *Sports*, a well-read magazine that he managed. Silvares was an influential figure in Brazilian football, serving as the president of the Villa Isabel club and second secretary of the Rio de Janeiro league in addition to running *Sports*, in the pages of which he adopted the pseudonym "Joffre," after the French hero of the Marne.[58] In the August 1915 piece, Silvares announced his "campaign," which amounted to a defense of football's social distinctions. Silvares identified himself with the chic and cosmopolitan members of the clubs of the well-to-do and complained about the burden that egalitarians expected sportsmen to bear in order to play the game:

> We attend an Academy, we belong among high society, we get a shave at the Naval Salon, we eat at the Rotisserie, we attend literary

conferences, we take *five o'clock* tea; but when we decide to play *sport* we go to Icarahy, a distinguished club affiliated to the 3rd Division of the Liga Metropolitana, where we are obliged to play against a worker, a machinist, a mailman, a mechanic, a chauffeur, and others who have nothing to do with the milieu in which we live. In this case playing *sport* is turned into a punishment or a sacrifice, but not a diversion.[59]

Silvares did not object to the idea that workers should play sports, and he said that he hoped they would learn to play football. But he did reject the idea that the "illustrious boys" of the leading clubs should be forced to play against and socialize with their social inferiors, who had the temerity to believe, according to Silvares, who wrote in dialect, "on the field we equal."[60]

As far as Silvares was concerned, this was clearly ridiculous. Football was "a violent *sport*" that required "education first and foremost," and he warned that it would suffer if well-to-do sportsmen were forced to choose between the game and their social preferences. Sportsmen would hesitate before playing against footballers who "lacked even the rudiments of an education," and they would certainly never dream of bringing "their respectable sisters" to the grounds of the city's poorer clubs. Silvares dismissed the claims of those who "idolized equality," who failed to understand that football "is a *sport* which can only be played among people with the same upbringing and the same level of culture," and he therefore recommended that the league organize divisions according to social class and exclude working-class players from participation in the first division.[61]

Although criticized for his obvious bias and his arrogance, Alberto Silvares represented a view common among middle-class and wealthy sportsmen, demonstrated the next year when the league formalized exclusivity in its statutes for 1916.[62] As before, sportsmen used amateurism as means of both organizing and justifying discriminatory policies. The league now explicitly refused to register as amateurs "those who gain their means of subsistence from any manner of manual labor, included among these those individuals who depend entirely upon their physical resources, and not from their intellects." Manual laborers were thus officially banned from the capital's leading league, and that was not all. Following the rowing league's earlier prohibition on barbers, the Liga Metropolitana also excluded "servants [and] employees (called clerks) of dry and wet goods shops, groceries or markets, ice-cream parlors, bars, cafés, taverns, [and] restaurants [and] those whose profession permits the receipt of tips." In case these prohibitions did not produce the

FIGURE 2.2. Fluminense first team, December 30, 1917. Harry Welfare is on the far left. Marcos de Mendonça, the paragon of the sportsman, is in the center, holding the ball. By permission of the Acervo Flu-Memória.

kind of football sportsmen preferred, the league reserved the right to judge each athlete applying for registration and the right to exclude "those whose job or profession the Superior Council judges to be beneath the moral and social level required by amateur sport."[63]

The next year, the CBD endorsed the Liga Metropolitana's approach. By then the CBD could claim to speak for all of Brazil, since Paulistas had recognized the Rio de Janeiro–based body and dissolved its only serious rival for the leadership of Brazilian sports, their Federação Brasileira de Football. The CBD's 1917 law established amateurism as a nonnegotiable requirement for participation in Brazilian sports, and institutionalized socially discriminatory rules for the registration of athletes as amateurs. It directed the administrators of Brazilian sports leagues to refuse to allow the participation of athletes paid for their play, and, further, to refuse amateur status to those "who in any sport will have an advantage over the rest because of the performance of their profession, which serves as a physical preparation for the practice of this sport."[64] Like the Liga Metropolitana, the CBD thus clearly defined amateurism as about much more than financial gain and vindicated the league's decision to ban physical laborers. Laborers might use the physical fitness they acquired in the completion of their work when they entered the playing field, and they could therefore justifiably be refused registration as amateurs. The CBD also made explicit its view that "moral and social" distinctions should be taken into consideration in deciding who should play, and it refused to grant amateur status to illiterate athletes, thereby excluding the majority of Brazilians from the competitions of organized sport.[65] Lest sportsmen worry that the CBD's particular interpretation of amateurism might limit their prerogatives, the 1917 law concluded by noting that these rules, which must be "rigorously observed" by all sports leagues in Brazil, were minimum requirements; leagues were "able to demand more rigorous stipulations" as they saw fit.[66]

The CBD followed the guidelines set down in 1917 until the professionalization of Brazilian football in 1933, revising them only to further restrict its definition of amateurism, for example, by refusing amateur status to professional coaches and physical educators and to any athlete accused of "crimes that reveal a corrupt or perverse character" and those "guilty of dishonest acts."[67] That the CBD insisted on such a clear defense of the exclusive amateur ethic is unsurprising, given that it was sportsmen like Alberto Silvares who organized and controlled the CBD and the most important leagues. Álvaro Zamith, for example, was head of the Liga Metropolitana before he became the CBD's first president in 1915. He was succeeded as league president by Joaquim Antônio de Souza Ribeiro, who at that time was serving his third term as president of the Botafogo club, and who oversaw the writing of the league's 1916 statutes according to Silvares' recommendations.

In 1917, when the CBD enacted its restrictive amateur law, the president of the organization was Arnaldo Guinle, whose tenure lasted from 1916 to 1920 and who was at that time also president of Fluminense. Guinle also led the reorganization of Rio de Janeiro football in 1924 and took charge of the successor organization to the Liga Metropolitana, the Associação Metropolitana de Esportes Athleticos (AMEA, Metropolitan Athletic Sports Association), over which he presided until 1928. Helping Guinle maintain Fluminense's influence were leaders like Oswaldo Gomes, one of the club's best players in the 1910s, who was president of the league between 1919 and 1921 and of the CBD between 1922 and 1924. The pattern was much the same in São Paulo. The organizations of the Brazilian middle and upper classes, such as Palmeiras, Internacional, and Paulistano, and middle-class expatriate clubs like Germania and São Paulo Athletic exercised control over the city's leagues and controlled its representation at the national level. Coming together in their own clubs and making sure those clubs worked together in leagues and governing bodies, sportsmen like Alberto Silvares, Joaquim Souza Ribeiro, and Arnaldo Guinle left little to chance. They used the organizations of Brazilian football to shape it according to their own preferences, which usually meant discrimination in favor of the white and the well-to-do.

The sportsmen also understood the importance of shaping the narrative of Brazilian football. They insisted on preserving both English laws and English terms, and they imprinted their preferences—especially for amateurism—on the pages of the country's sports media, which grew quickly alongside football and helped to legitimize the influence of middle-class and wealthy sportsmen and their sports ethic. There are several reasons that Brazil's earliest sportswriters and editors may have contributed to this process. The clubs of the sportsmen were dominant in competition until at least the middle of the 1910 decade, which helps explain reporters' interest in their teams. There were also significant differences in literacy rates among wealthier and working-class Brazilians throughout the late nineteenth century and the first half of the twentieth century, which meant that the middle class and wealthy constituted the greater part of likely readers. Added to this, while daily newspapers like the *Correio Paulistano* in São Paulo and the *Jornal do Commercio* in Rio de Janeiro covered football early on, by the first decade of the twentieth century the sports press also included sometimes expensive specialty magazines, such as *Sportman* and *Revista Sportiva*, indulgences not every sports fan could afford.[68]

Close personal connections between the organizations of the middle class and wealthy and the media that covered them were also clearly important, especially in the formative years, as was the case with Alberto Silvares and with Mário Cardim, who was even more influential. As a young law student in 1899, Cardim, the son of a federal judge, played football for the Internacional club and also began working as a reporter for *O Estado de S. Paulo*, then the most important newspaper in Brazil's second largest city. In 1900 he helped to found the Club Athletico Paulistano, which immediately became one of Brazil's leading sports clubs, in part because another of the founders was Antônio Prado Júnior, a member of one of the wealthiest and most influential families in the state. Cardim did his part for Paulistano and the other clubs of the sportsmen, making *O Estado* Paulistano's unofficial gazette as he moved from reporting to editing to becoming the dean of Paulista sportswriters in the early twentieth century.

Cardim helped guard Paulista football from the threat of social leveling by making sure *O Estado* covered the clubs of the middle class and wealthy more fully than modest clubs. He insisted on amateurism but attacked working-class violators while ignoring violations committed by wealthier figures and clubs. And he carried the ethic of middle-class and wealthy sportsmen beyond the city of São Paulo, helping to organize leagues elsewhere in the state, making contacts with like-minded figures elsewhere in Brazil, and helping to organize the Associação de Chronistas Esportivas (ACE, Association of Sports Journalists) in 1917.[69] In 1906 Cardim published *O Guia de Football*, which brought together statutes and advice about proper football practice, including, for example, a piece on the "Physical and moral qualities of *football* players," based closely on the work of the popular French writer Ernest Weber, who was a vocal champion of amateurism.[70]

In the first two decades after football's introduction to Brazil, most sportswriters and editors depicted the sport much as Cardim did, and though most were not as conspicuously connected to particular clubs as were Cardim and Silvares, neither were these figures unique. Paulistano's Carioca counterpart, Fluminense, could count on the early and continuing support of Coelho Netto, the widely read and widely respected poet and public intellectual, whose support *Epocha Sportiva* called "Brazilian *foot-ball*'s biggest victory" in 1919.[71] The next year he founded the magazine *Athletica*, which promoted the sportsman's view of ethical football and called for the game's "moralization" during a period when it was becoming more popular but was also, according to *Athletica*, "in decline."[72]

It was not the quality of Brazilian football that was in decline in 1920—Brazil won its first South American Championship in 1919, an event widely celebrated as announcing Brazilian football's coming of age. From the point of view of middle-class and wealthy sportsmen, however, there were things to be concerned about in the late-1910s, especially two phenomena that many commentators suggested were closely connected: increasing numbers of talented working-class players and clubs, and breaches of football etiquette, such as violent play and violations of amateur rules. The sports press played a vital role in determining the meaning of such changes, real and perceived, and in assigning blame for transgressions. In doing so, they followed a pattern set by Mário Cardim and other early sportswriters who, as André Ribeiro says, depicted two types of Brazilian footballers, "boys from good families," like Coelho Netto's sons, Emmanuel, Georges, Paulo, and João, all of whom played for Fluminense, and "poor kids from the suburbs." The former were gentlemen, honorable, and chic, "illustrious boys," as Alberto

Silvares called them; the latter, when they were covered at all, were "coarse, incapable of following the rules of fair play, often ridiculed by journalists," who characterized them as possessing little skill and less tactical awareness.[73] As Silvares said, they were lacking even the "the rudiments of an education," and it allegedly showed in their football.

The press stressed the importance of education as a marker of belonging in Brazil's football culture by joining administrators in using English terms. A few early primers on football for the Brazilian market included translations. The Brazilian edition of Ernest Weber's rulebook, first published in 1907, included *arbitro* (referee), *golpe de canto* (corner kick), and *golpe de reparação* (penalty kick), and the *Guia Sportiva para 1912*, published in Porto Alegre, Rio Grande do Sul, offered many of the same terms as well as *ponta-pé inicial* (kick-off) and *fóra do jogo* (offside), among others.[74] But it would take years for such terms to be preferred in football leagues and the sports press. Instead, administrators and editors preferred English terms, even if the writers sometimes acknowledged the reading public by including Portuguese-language definitions, as when O. T. de Oliveira defined the "Full-back" as the "Player who is close to the *goal*" in 1912.[75] Going further, the 1916 *Guia Brasileira de Football Associação*, which drew heavily from Mário Cardim's 1906 guide, even offered an English primer so its readers could learn the correct way to pronounce football terms, introducing the English word, its pronunciation, and its meaning:

    Back   bek   He who plays behind; the 2nd line[76]

When the commentator João do Rio wrote about his visit to Fluminense to watch a match in 1905, he took special notice of young trendsetters who set themselves apart by speaking English. They were, he said, "girls in pretty dresses" and well-dressed "gentleman *sportsmen*," all of whom "watch the game with a knowing air, speaking English. . . . Even when they speak Portuguese, for every six of our words there are three British ones. *All right!*"[77] Sportswriters catered to the tastes of these men and women, regardless of their own language ability, the limits of which are indicated by numerous examples of misspellings and misuse of English terms in the contemporary sports press.[78]

More important than accuracy, it seems, was to demonstrate one's awareness of the expectations of those who dominated organized football, and the press assisted administrators in making sure Brazilians knew what those expectations were. The popular magazine *Careta* noticed this and mentioned sports language in lampooning Brazil's "new grammar" in 1908. *Careta* named "foot-ball" and "jockey" (and up-to-date, smart, and whiskey and soda), alongside French, German, and Italian terms as examples of "language vices" that threatened good Brazilian Portuguese.[79] G. J. Bruce noticed the ubiquity of English terms in Brazil in the next decade, calling it "an amusing feature of football in Brazil." But he also saw that it might be significant, suggesting that "if there is going to be a universal language, English leads for the honour, and British sports, especially football, will help to secure it."[80]

Language helped Brazilian sportsmen advertise their preferences and determine which of their countrymen possessed the social and cultural attributes to participate in their sporting life, and their influence extended beyond football. For example, a society magazine called *O Off Side* appeared in São Paulo in 1916, and in 1920 M.F. published an open letter to his daughter in Porto Alegre's *Correio do Povo* in which he offered his best wishes on her sixteenth birthday, hoping "that you never go *off-side* in life, dribbling around all of its difficulties, shooting on target at the *goal* of happiness, winning all of your *matchs* [sic] by high *scores*."[81] Alongside administrators, these writers helped to shape Brazilian football according to the tastes, and for the benefit, of the middle class and wealthy. When news about football shared space with coverage about the arts in publications like the *Jornal de Theatro e Sport* and the vocabulary of the game was identified with the social life of the well-to-do, the written word helped to reinforce the effects of selective membership policies, club dues, and amateur rules on who might participate in organized Brazilian football. To the dismay of sportsmen committed to exclusive football, though, none of these tools was permanently effective, and their task became more difficult in the 1910s and 1920s.

Lost Allies and New Rivals in the 1910s and 1920s

In 1913 São Paulo Athletic retired from league competition. Popular memory suggests that the club withdrew because of the worrying social drift of the league, but it is also clear that twenty years after Charles Miller introduced the game to Brazil the club was finding it increasingly difficult to remain competitive while also fielding only players who were British or of British descent.[82] Having won the city league for the fourth time in 1911, winning seven of its nine matches, in 1912 São Paulo Athletic won only three, drawing once and losing seven times, and placing sixth among seven teams.

In order to replace São Paulo Athletic, the Liga Paulista organized a small tournament for four aspiring clubs, which was won by Sport Club Corinthians Paulista. But winning the tournament was not enough. Administrators demanded more, sharing the view of *O Comercio de S. Paulo*, which stated that "the simple elimination match will not be sufficient... [because] even if one is a perfect player, this is not enough to be a *sportman*." According to the paper, "it is necessary to match one's sporting education with a social one: lacking the latter kills sport and ruins clubs."[83] This meant that joining the city's premier league would be especially difficult for Corinthians, despite the team's success and despite the club having been named for English aristocrats, because it was a working-class club founded by five laborers in the Bom Retiro suburb in 1910, and wealthy sportsmen assumed that its members lacked the proper social education.

Ambitious leaders understood the challenge, and in 1912 and 1913 they set about proving the club's respectability. They purged some of the club's rougher elements, courted patronage from men of wealth and in politics, and eventually even relocated to a more dignified address. In short, according to Plínio Labriola Negreiros, Corinthians attempted to transform itself from a "neighborhood club" and a "sporting association for humble people" into "a city club" with pretenses to elite status, for example, traveling to away games only in the first-class train car.[84]

Still, rather than accept Corinthians when it won the tournament to replace São Paulo Athletic, the city's most important clubs—Paulistano, Mackenzie, and Palmeiras—founded an entirely new league, the Associação Paulista de Esportes Athleticos (APEA, Paulista Athletic Sports Association), which Corinthians was not invited to join. Because of the elite clubs' popularity and the resources they controlled, the APEA almost immediately eclipsed the Liga Paulista as São Paulo's most important league. Corinthians and other more modest clubs were left behind. The clubs of the sportsmen offered Corinthians the possibility of entry into the new league only if it recognized their authority by, among other things, accepting a financially and competitively bruising one-year withdrawal from all organized football; among other consequences, this would mean Corinthians would lose some of its best players to clubs that could offer them playing time. Eventually, in 1917, Corinthians did obtain entry to the new league, but it "was almost unrecognizable" from the club organized by workingmen in 1910.[85]

Reinforcing the notion that Corinthians suffered from the social biases of middle-class and wealthy sportsmen is the fact that several clubs with dubious football credentials gained entry into the APEA before it did. In 1914 three clubs joined the new league, Ypiranga, Scottish Wanderers, and São Bento. Ypiranga was a well-established, traditional club and had played in the city's leading league as early as 1910, but Wanderers and São Bento were organized only in 1913 and 1914, respectively. What they did possess, though, was the right social profile to justify their admission. Wanderers was British, and São Bento had been organized by an instructor at the prestigious Ginásio São Bento, of which most members were alumni. Two years later two more clubs joined the APEA: Santos, which was not even from the city itself, and the club of the city's Italian expatriate community, the Societá Sportiva Palestra Itália.

Palestra Itália gained entry to the first division of the new league quite easily, after only one season of indifferent and irregularly organized play, compared to Corinthians' several years of proving its football merit. It included many working-class members and even fielded players who had played previously for Corinthians, like Bianco Spartaco Gambini, but its directors were middle class, like the leaders who had emerged to transform Corinthians into a "respectable" club. The difference seems to have been rooted in national and ethnic questions, Palestra Itália benefiting from the same kind of thinking that meant the easy admission of the Scottish Wanderers, despite its lack of talent; the Britons won only four matches in two years of competitive football, in 1914 and 1915. The Italian was not the model sportsman in early-twentieth-century Brazil, but in the eyes of wealthy Brazilians, he was an acceptable one, especially as compared with nonwhite and working-class players. Palestra Itália almost certainly benefited from that distinction, at Corinthians' expense.

Carioca sportsmen took similar measures to check the erosion of their privileges. For example, in 1914 and 1915 the Paysandú and Rio Cricket clubs, respectively, ought to have been relegated from the first division following their last-place finishes in the league. Instead, the leading clubs attempted to save the British organizations by changing competition rules to help the clubs remain in the top tier. Like São Paulo Athletic, both of these clubs preferred to field only Britons, and they suffered when some of their best players left Brazil to fight for Britain in World War I. Paysandú chose not to accept their friends' intervention and shuttered its football operations permanently. Rio Cricket accepted the assistance but unexpectedly lost a specially invented elimination match to the winner of the second division, Andarahy, a working-class club from the city's north side that was affiliated with a local factory. Rather than accept playing in the second-class league,

FIGURE 2.3. First team of the Andarahy Athletic Club, December 30, 1917. Andarahy joined the Carioca first division in 1916. By permission of the Acervo Flu-Memória.

Rio Cricket withdrew from competitive football, but even then the generosity of Anglophile sportsmen softened the blow, for Rio Cricket's best players joined Botafogo and therefore remained in the first division.[86]

If one reason that early-twentieth-century sportsmen built football clubs was to make them bastions of privilege in a changing Brazil, the impulse to defend those privileges would have become especially acute in the middle of the 1910 decade. The withdrawal from competitive football of expatriate clubs like São Paulo Athletic, Paysandú, Rio Cricket, and Germania (in 1916) meant the loss of partners who had helped to design and defend the restrictions of early Brazilian football. At the same time came the emergence of Brazilian clubs of questionable respectability, like Corinthians and Andarahy, and expatriate clubs whose social credentials were not nearly as strong as the British organizations' had been, such as Palestra Itália and its

Portuguese counterparts, Portuguesa in São Paulo and Vasco da Gama in Rio de Janeiro.

This period was also characterized by a more conflicted social and political atmosphere that demonstrated that the republic's promises of modernity would indeed mean a challenge to the privileges of the sportsmen and their classes. The 1910s witnessed spasms of social and political conflict, beginning with the Revolt of the Lash (1910), when sailors rose against the Brazilian navy's habitual use of corporal punishment, and the Contestado War (1912–16), a conflict in the states of Santa Catarina and Paraná fueled by the dislocations brought about by economic development and colored by a popular messianism that echoed the more famous Canudos episode. The brief 1914 conflict called the Juazeiro Sedition, in which the elite of Ceará attempted to resist a challenge to their power by the government of President Hermes da Fonseca, was another in a long line of examples of the regionalist sentiment that troubled the republic as it had troubled the empire.

Meanwhile, São Paulo, Rio de Janeiro, and other cities saw the consequences of a more confident and aggressive labor movement in the 1910s, most famously when the general strike of July 1917 paralyzed the Paulista capital and sympathy strikes took place as far away as Porto Alegre. The next year, a textile workers' strike in greater Rio de Janeiro presented a potentially greater threat as anarchist activists hoped to use the strike to launch an insurrection against the central government. The revolution did not materialize, but these actions were part of a sustained movement of laborers and their allies that represented a challenge to the socioeconomic and political power of the republican order and that helped set the stage for the similarly turbulent 1920s.

Political and business leaders responded to the movement in various ways, making concessions in certain instances and using force to end disturbances in others. They were usually inclined to defend the status quo, adopting an approach similar to that taken by their counterparts in organized football. In a rare but telling instance of the harmony of purpose among political, business, and football leaders, in October 1919 the members of the Paulistano club asserted their support for the city's business interests during a strike by the employees of the São Paulo Tramway, Light & Power Company. Paulistano's footballers volunteered to work as conductors, helping the company keep its streetcars running and, according to its general manager, W. N. Walmsley, offering "the first public indication" of support the company received in the dispute. The footballers were some of the city's most popular public figures, and law, medical, and technical school students followed their example, serving as volunteer conductors, motormen, and switchmen. Walmsley believed Paulistano's help accounted for the press paying closer attention to the strike and ultimately turning against the workers. The strike failed, and Walmsley "naturally" took the opportunity to fire four hundred employees he identified as troublemakers.[87]

The episode serves as a useful reminder that Brazil's football history did not unfold in a vacuum of goals, games, and leagues. Paulistano's reasons for assisting Light are not revealed in club documents, but in a public letter the medical students who volunteered alongside the players claimed they were impartial in the labor dispute. However, they also asserted their support for public authorities and alleged that honorable Paulista workers had been misled by anarchists and other "disturbers of the social order."[88] Given the great influence wielded in the club by its longtime president, Antônio Prado Júnior, it is probable that many club members would have agreed. Prado's father, Antônio da Silva Prado, was a successful businessman and prominent conservative politician, serving as mayor of São Paulo from 1899 to 1911, during which time he oversaw the modernization of the city's infrastructure, including the expansion of its electrical grid and streetcar lines by Light. His son followed him into business and into politics, serving in the state legislature from 1922 to 1926, when Washington Luís appointed him mayor of Rio de Janeiro.

Prior to becoming the mayor of Rio de Janeiro, Prado Júnior's foremost role in public life was as Paulistano president, a position that family resources had helped him secure. Prado Júnior was one of the club's founders and quickly emerged as its dominant figure, in part because he could offer the club access to the family-owned Velodrome. First-class facilities—at the Velodrome until 1915, and at large, modern new grounds in the tony Jardim América neighborhood, inaugurated in 1917—helped establish Paulistano as the club of the city elite and one of the leading sports organizations of Brazil. Under Prado Júnior's leadership, Paulistano built a dominant football side and pursued a fierce commitment to protecting amateurism and elite privilege in Paulista football. Such was its commitment that it withdrew from football in 1929 rather than accept the decline of amateurism and the erosion of elite privilege, even though, unlike São Paulo Athletic in 1913, Paulistano was still fielding a very competitive side in the late-1920s. The Light incident in 1919 points to Paulistano's social and political outlook and, understood in the context of the club's struggle to defend its version of football, it suggests that the club saw a correlation between social, political, and sports questions in a changing Brazil.

The meaning of Paulistano's perspective and choices is accentuated by a comparison to the activities of its closest peer in Brazilian football during the early twentieth century. Fluminense worked in many of the same ways and toward the same goals as Paulistano, but it was much more willing than Paulistano to adapt to the circumstances of the 1910s and 1920s. Fluminense took a leading role in organizing Rio de Janeiro's first football competitions and in shaping early Brazilian football as a domain of middle-class and wealthy hegemony, but this became increasingly difficult in the 1910s as it lost partners like Paysandú and faced their replacement by clubs like Andarahy. Fluminense's appeals to patriotism and for public support as it built its stadium in 1919 suggest its leaders' awareness of changing circumstances and the necessity of adapting their approach if the club were to maintain its influence. This would become even clearer in the late-1920s and early-1930s, when Fluminense made its peace with the decline of amateurism and played an important part in bringing professional football to Brazil.

However, neither its pursuit of the stadium project nor its later support for professionalization ought to be understood as democratic or even populist endeavors. Rather, in their own ways these actions can be seen as Fluminense's reactions against threats to its position. Opening a stadium that could seat twenty-five thousand paying fans offered club directors the prospect of a renewable resource of prestige and finance to help manage their negotiation of changes in the Brazilian game. Fluminense was not the first Brazilian club to make plans to build a stadium. As early as 1916 Alberto Silvares' Villa Isabel was working with Rio de Janeiro's Municipal Council to build a "Brazilian Stadium" on public land on Boulevard 28 de Setembro on the city's working-class north side.[89] Two years later another northern club, São Christovão, floated a plan to build a stadium in the public Praça Marechal Deodoro, and Arnaldo Guinle, who was president of both Fluminense and the CBD, met with Wenceslau Brás, the country's president, and city mayor Amaro Cavalcanti in order to obtain their support for the project. Over the objections of the city's director of public works, Brás and Cavalcanti offered their support for the plan, and the *Gazeta de Notícias* was reporting the stadium would be erected in São Christovão as late as April 1918.[90]

But, instead of Villa Isabel or São Christovão, it was Fluminense that built Brazil's first stadium, on its grounds in the city's affluent south. That Fluminense benefited from its social position at the expense of more humble clubs is indicated by *A Noite*'s annoyance at the club's ability to obtain government concessions and by a *Gazeta* story in April 1918 reporting that unnamed "sportsmen" objected to São Christovão's plan and preferred that Fluminense build the stadium. When the time came for the CBD to make a final decision on which project to support, it considered only two formal plans, from Fluminense and Flamengo. There may have been practical reasons for this, as Fluminense and Flamengo possessed financial resources that clubs like Villa Isabel and São Christovão lacked, and Fluminense was in the midst of a building campaign. Flamengo and Fluminense were also two of the most powerful clubs in Brazil, working together to shape football to their own preferences as much as they competed against one another. And both clubs' grounds were situated in the south of the city, the zone of middle-class and wealthy residence. The CBD voted to accept Fluminense's plans, and awarded it the right to host the South American Championship in June 1918.[91]

Construction began shortly thereafter, but Fluminense still had to resolve several problems, including logistical concerns and public relations issues as well as financial difficulties. Fluminense and its supporters reacted to these challenges by calling on their friends in government and by appealing to Brazilians' sense of patriotism. The club also took concrete steps that reshaped it in more than a physical sense. In 1910 Fluminense had 297 members. Two years later it had 398. The number continued to rise in the ensuing years, first surpassing the 1,000 mark in 1917, when the club had 1,224 members. In 1918 alone, however, the club added 1,478 new members, for a total of 2,808. Although club records do not explain why so many sought admission, and why so many applications were accepted, it is probable that the rise in membership was related to the club's physical expansion, of which the stadium was the central part. After all, loans had to be repaid. Some members seem to have become concerned about the burgeoning size of the club, and in 1919 Fluminense established a limit on the number of full members it would allow, at 2,500. This did not halt its growth, though, and by the early-1920s there were over 3,000 members.[92] Fluminense was no longer an intimate club. With a large and modern stadium and a fast-growing membership roster, it was losing some of its original characteristics while gaining access to the kind of resources that would allow it to flourish as Brazilian football became both more popular and more commercialized.[93]

Another aspect of Fluminense's transformation was related to Guinle's role, which in some ways paralleled that of Antônio Prado Júnior at

Paulistano. In the minutes of meetings of the club Directorate and General Assembly, in club histories, and in the contemporary media, Arnaldo Guinle appears as a hero, a tireless worker for club and country. According to Mário Pollo, Guinle's vision for the club was "a construction program of such proportions which in the moment seemed to more than a few a dream, a marvelous but impossible vision." But the doubters were proved wrong, for under Guinle's leadership Fluminense seemed "directed by magical forces," and "over the ashes of the rubbish of old and small things were erected modern and monumental edifices," as the "limited perspective" of previous administrations was followed by the Guinle regime's "ample view and aspirations to responsibility."[94]

It was not only Guinle's work that brought him such esteem and the power that came along with it. The Guinle family was heavily involved in a variety of development projects in Brazil's major cities, most significantly in its operation of the docks at the coffee economy's port of Santos and most famously in the construction of the Copacabana Palace hotel in Rio de Janeiro. The family's relationship with Fluminense began early, when two of Arnaldo's brothers, Guilherme and Carlos, joined the club in the first decade of the century. In 1905 family patriarch Eduardo turned patron by purchasing the club's grounds in Laranjeiras and then financing and building its first grandstand.[95] Probably not coincidentally, that same year Guilherme Guinle became vice president. Guilherme became president in late 1912, succeeding his brother Carlos, who returned to the position in 1913.

Finally, Arnaldo became president in 1916, and he remained in office until mid-1931, returning to the role in 1943 and serving until 1946. Prior to Arnaldo Guinle's tenure, club presidents had usually served for between one and two years, and his tenure is still the longest that Fluminense has ever had. In 1917 he had briefly championed São Christovão's proposal to build the stadium, but by 1918 he was leading Fluminense's project and its press to have its work ratified by government authorities and the CBD, of which he was president. He also personally guaranteed the repayment of the loan that the club took from the Banco do Brasil to finance the stadium, and he supplemented the loan with twenty-five contos de réis of his own money.[96]

Arnaldo Guinle made the building of the stadium as much a personal project as a club goal, and its success seems to have helped him secure an unprecedented amount of power at Fluminense. He oversaw the club's expansion, he was president when it began surreptitiously to compensate players for their performances, and he worked as Fluminense's representative in the final movement to professionalize Carioca football in 1933. In 1926 the Guinle family also strengthened Fluminense's position by evicting Flamengo from Guinle-owned property on the Guanabara Road.[97] Like Antônio Prado Júnior, Arnaldo Guinle was a prominent example of a type of football leader that became increasingly significant as football changed in the 1910s and 1920s: powerful, wealthy, and conspicuously active in private and public settings. Guinle was comfortable enough with mass culture that he sponsored popular samba musicians in the 1920s, and, unlike Prado, Guinle was willing to adjust to football's changes.[98] This is not to say he embraced them.

In 1923 and 1924 Guinle helped to engineer the reorganization of Carioca football through the founding of the new AMEA to replace the old Liga Metropolitana. This reinforced the position of Fluminense, Flamengo, Botafogo, and America—the quartet of the big clubs of the capital—and defended them against the threat posed by the rise of the Club de Regatas Vasco da Gama. Like Corinthians in São Paulo, Vasco da Gama was eventually accepted by the older and more powerful clubs; like Corinthians, this acceptance did not come until those clubs had impressed upon Vasco da Gama that it would be accepted on their terms, and that acceptance did not mean equality.

Founded as a rowing club by middle-class Portuguese immigrants in 1898, Vasco da Gama began fielding a football team only in 1916. The club was used to a certain amount of success in rowing, having won the city championship for the fourth time in 1914, but it had to begin its football life in the Liga Metropolitana's third division. Ambitious to make up for lost time, Vasco recruited talented footballers wherever it could find them, and quickly began to rise through the divisions. It achieved promotion to the top competition in 1922 and won it at the first opportunity the next year, with a team including working-class black players who were widely suspected of being false amateurs, such as goalkeeper Nélson da Conceição and forward Bolão (Claudionor Corrêa).[99] Their coach was the Uruguayan Ramón Platero, who had previously worked for both Fluminense and Flamengo.

The big clubs saw the danger of Vasco da Gama's approach—Botafogo, for example, had finished last among the eight teams in 1923, behind socially inferior clubs such as São Christovão, Andarahy, and Bangú. After a failed attempt to reform the Liga Metropolitana in a way that would guarantee their control over league policy, the four abandoned the league and founded the AMEA. With Arnaldo Guinle as its first president and quickly recognized as a member organization by the CBD, the president of which was Oscar Costa, another member of Fluminense, the AMEA almost immediately eclipsed the old league as Rio de Janeiro's most popular, while reigning champions Vasco da Gama remained in the declining Liga Metropolitana.[100]

One of the reasons that Vasco da Gama did not immediately join the new league was because the big clubs designed it to guarantee themselves an outsized voice, for example, guaranteeing founding members the right to decide which matches would take place on Sundays, when attendance—and therefore gate revenue—was highest.[101] More importantly, the traditional clubs established their defenses against the recruitment policies of Vasco da Gama and other clubs like it, enacting strict rules in favor of amateurism and against social leveling. The league required all players to provide information about their past and current employment status and established the league's right to investigate the accuracy of the information, and it also refused to register players who were either manual laborers or illiterate.[102] Thus, when Vasco applied for entry to the new league in time for the 1925 season, the league refused to accept the application unless the club would accede to the demand that it drop twelve players on the grounds that each of them had a "dubious profession."[103] The charge was not without merit, though Vasco da Gama was far from the only club that paid its players. But Vasco's sins were intolerable. It was successful, it was new to football, and many of its players were working class and men of color. The big clubs used their new league to remind Vasco da Gama that it might be successful, but it was not yet big.

Vasco da Gama refused to be bullied. It hired a teacher to help its players meet literacy requirements, and club members who owned businesses provided them with easy employment. The quality of these players, and their popularity among the Carioca public, did the rest, and Vasco joined the AMEA in 1925, finishing third to Flamengo and Fluminense. This was a watershed moment in the destruction of racial barriers in Brazilian football, and it contributed to the sense that professional football must come. Still, the traditional clubs were not content to accept defeat easily. As a condition of its admittance to the AMEA, they forced Vasco da Gama to accept another rule aimed at guarding the gates of first-class football, a requirement that every club must play at a ground that met specific standards, an elaboration of a 1913 ruling that required clubs to possess "enclosed grounds, with dimensions in accord with the laws of the Foot-ball Association," and a medical post.[104] Now the AMEA added demands for at least three dressing rooms, including bathrooms, one for each team and one for the referee and his fellow officials, and for a scoreboard.[105] Because it did not possess such a ground, in 1925 and 1926 Vasco da Gama played on Andarahy's field, which meant a lesser advantage in "home" matches and less revenue from gate receipts.

When the Portuguese community came together to help the club build the São Januário stadium, the country's largest and most modern when it opened in 1927, it seemed that Vasco da Gama had gotten the last laugh. But it ought not be missed that, as in the case of Corinthians in São Paulo a decade before, the big clubs had enforced a measure of discipline on the club. When Vasco da Gama, its members, and its supporters expended their resources in order to obtain entry into first-class football, they demonstrated that, at its highest levels, Brazilian football was still dominated by the well-to-do. The vast majority of football clubs could never hope to undertake a project like the construction of the stadium, or to even marshal the resources to reach the first division's minimum standard. As false amateurism became more common in the late-1920s, they could not hold on to their most talented players when wealthier clubs came calling with bags of cash.

In spite of their demands on those they deemed their social inferiors, the clubs of the middle class and wealthy often allowed themselves the prerogative of applying the rules they designed selectively, as in the case of the attempts to save Rio Cricket and Paysandú and the difficulties faced by Corinthians. Big clubs also broke convention in recruiting players for their own teams, as when Fluminense fielded Carlos Alberto, who joined from the America club in 1914. At America, Carlos Alberto had played in the second team, calling little attention to the fact that he was mulatto. Turning out for Fluminense was a different proposition, and he therefore covered his face and hair with rice powder to hide the fact. But in the closed world of Carioca football, it was impossible for Carlos Alberto to pass as white. When he played against his old club, America's fans refused to ignore the deception, and chanted "Pó-de-arroz!" (rice powder) in an attempt to embarrass both Carlos Alberto and Fluminense. Fans of other clubs adopted the epithet as a way, Mário Filho said, of pointing out Fluminense's desire "to be more than others, more chic, more elegant, more aristocratic."[106]

Faced with the challenge represented by Vasco da Gama and other clubs willing to bend or break competition rules, middle- and upper-class clubs were willing to go further than breaches of etiquette in order to remain competitive, which was made very clear by the player Floriano Peixoto Corrêa, who joined Fluminense in 1924. Floriano began playing football in his home state of Minas Gerais before going on to play for a series of teams in south and southeastern Brazil, including the army team that played in the Liga de Esportes do Exercito (Army Sports League), Rio Grande do Sul's select team, and several club teams, including wealthy ones like Grêmio Foot-ball Porto Alegrense, Santos, Atlético Mineiro, and, in Rio de Janeiro, Fluminense and America. In his invaluable *Grandezas e Miserias do Nosso Futebol*, published in 1933, Floriano launched a broadside against what he saw as the fiction of amateur football in Brazil, alleging that throughout his career he had been paid to play the game, and that he knew payments to players were commonplace among the leading clubs.

Floriano told his readers that Fluminense was especially eager to provide for his comfort and to help him craft the right personality so that he could take his place among the members of the club and their peers. Club members helped him obtain his discharge from the army, invited him to live at Fluminense's clubhouse, and gave him money for his expenses. Later, members provided him with lodging in a "mansion" and made a luxury car available to him, and they even provided him with fashionable clothes. With the help of the club, Floriano could play both football and the part of the aristocratic sportsman, despite his humble beginnings. In his words, "I was able to enjoy the life of a capitalist, in spite of having no capital."[107]

With Floriano in the side, Fluminense won the inaugural competition of the AMEA league, and it finished second in two of the next three years. Floriano succeeded so well that he was chosen to represent the federal capital in the annual championship between state select teams each year between 1925 and 1928, and he played for Brazil in the 1925 South American Championship. He left Fluminense to play for America in 1928, and won the city championship again, but not before he had been paid not only by Fluminense but by the AMEA and CBD to play in their select teams, and not before America had given him a significant sum to do so. Almost immediately, Fluminense, its fans, and its allies turned on him, accusing him of being a professional and even a cheat, charges that dogged him during the next two years before he left Rio de Janeiro in frustration. As long as he fought for the club's colors, Fluminense was content to accept Floriano as a sportsman. When he did not, accusations began to fly. Fluminense directed few accusations at its rival club; America's social standing and its long participation in Rio de Janeiro football kept the controversy from boiling over, and so the player suffered, and America and Fluminense moved on.

Professionalization, Populism, and the Press

Like Vasco da Gama, Floriano was not content to accept the lot assigned him by Fluminense and America. Leaving Rio de Janeiro in 1932, he moved first to São Paulo, where he played for Santos, and then home to Minas Gerais. There he played for Atletico Mineiro until 1936, when he became the club's coach. Floriano also sought to expose the hypocrisies of his former friends and campaigned for the formal professionalization of Brazilian football. His 1933 book was a memoir and tactical manual but also an accusation and call to action. In the book's preface, his ally in the professionalization movement, the journalist Paulo Várzea, said Floriano was a "laborer of the ball" who had been "sacrificed to a degrading era." For his part, Floriano used the book to detail how football had "distorted" his life and to call for its transformation.[108]

Although he suffered, Floriano's willingness to draw attention to the missteps of Fluminense and other wealthy clubs helped to demonstrate that false amateurism made those clubs vulnerable. False amateurism afforded less affluent players the opportunity to hone their skills, which meant there were greater numbers of players like Nélson, Bolão, and Floriano every year, whose abilities warranted their inclusion in first-class competitions. False amateurism also allowed smaller clubs willing to recruit those players to rise in the football hierarchy, as was the case with Vasco da Gama, regardless of its late interest in football or its members' athletic abilities. Other clubs could try to do the same, and some did, such as Bonsuccesso in Rio de Janeiro and Portuguesa in São Paulo, though almost never with as much success as Vasco da Gama. The lack of legal contracts in the informal environment of false amateurism also meant that clubs had difficulty in controlling the players they were paying, and players took advantage of their liberty to move from club to club, whether within Brazil like Floriano or abroad like the Italian Paulistas. Finally, a lack of elite consensus on how to deal with these problems, some experimenting with false amateurism and others implacably opposed, amplified the challenges faced by big clubs and elite administrators.

Almost until the last moment, most big clubs fought against formal professionalization. In 1930 the CBD introduced a transfer tax and passed the Apprentice Law. The tax was a payment of between one hundred and two hundred mil-réis each time a club recruited a player already registered by a rival. The Apprentice Law, a version of which had been used in Rio Grande do Sul as early as 1917, required any player who transferred from one club to another to wait a full year before he could play for his new team.[109] These rules could not stop clubs from paying their players, but the CBD and its supporters hoped that, by making masked professionalism a more expensive business, they would discourage clubs from using their financial resources to strengthen their teams.

Still, by the time the CBD enacted these measures, it was clear that amateurism, real or feigned, had become impossible, a fact exemplified by Paulistano's withdrawal from competitive football before the Apprentice Law was even enacted. As early as 1924 the club began to complain that the APEA was failing to defend amateurism, and began to discuss the prospect of forming another new league that would be more rigorous than the APEA in enforcing amateur rules. It followed through in 1927 by organizing the short-lived Liga de Amadores de Futebol (LAF, League of Football Amateurs). Unlike the APEA a decade before, the LAF failed to attract leading clubs, so while Corinthians, Palestra Itália, and other popular sides remained with the APEA, Paulistano was left to play against declining and small clubs, such as Germania, Antarctica, and Britannia. Paulistano's traditionalists felt they had only one option left to them. They withdrew the club from competitive football before the beginning of the 1930 season, and the LAF collapsed. Club members who were unwilling to abandon football left the club to organize a new one, the São Paulo Futebol Clube, which quickly and successfully adapted to the new reality. Fielding Paulistano players, including its idol, Arthur Friedenreich, São Paulo finished second in the city league in 1930 and won the championship the next year. It helped bring about the professionalization of Paulista football in 1933, and it has been one of São Paulo's biggest clubs since its founding.[110]

Many of the leaders of the professionalization movement depicted its adoption as transformative, even "revolutionary," as Paulo Várzea said, and historians have continued to depict it in this manner since.[111] Aspects of the process certainly suggest as much, not least of which was Paulistano's decision to close its football section, since this meant the loss of Brazilian football's most successful team and the club most committed to defending amateurism. Activists argued that professionalization was a matter of challenging powerful figures and clubs that resisted formal professionalization while bending amateur rules to the breaking point. Writing in the *Folha da Manhã* in 1931, for example, R. Castello argued that clubs expected their "false" amateurs to dedicate their lives to the game, and to play for pride and glory, but "Glory doesn't fill the belly." Meanwhile, he said, club directors, who he called "football magnates," lived on profits earned by selling tickets to watch these players.[112]

Further, the Getúlio Vargas government helped make the case for professionalization, and the case that professionalization was a populist measure, framing it as a question of protecting footballers as laborers. From an ideological point of view, the Vargas regime seems to have preferred amateur athletics.[113] But the regime began working to rationalize and regulate professional football in the early-1930s, well before tasking the Conselho Nacional de Desportos with oversight of professional football.[114] Another indication that professionalization meant momentous change was that by the end of the 1930s, Botafogo and Flamengo, always among Rio de Janeiro's most aristocratic clubs, were fielding black working-class professionals; Brazilian football did seem to have been transformed.

Besides populist, campaigners characterized their activity as nationalist, a matter of strengthening and protecting Brazilian football. When Del Debbio, Rato, Serafini, and other Brazilian-born players moved to Italy to play football professionally in 1931, some critics questioned the players' patriotism, but others, like *A Gazeta*, stated that the loss of the players was one of "the results of false amateurism." Even if Brazilian clubs paid their "amateurs" substantial sums, the clubs possessed no legal right to stop their players from moving because the system lacked formal contracts and so "can do nothing to avoid this loss for our football."[115] The players themselves helped make the case. Attilio De Maria challenged the morality of false amateurism and explained his decision to move to Italy as partially to do with his desire to "live honestly," while Ministrinho (Pedro Sernagiotto), one of São Paulo's most popular players, echoed Castello when he stated that, in the colors of Palestra Itália, "I played for love and glory," but "times are tough" and he could no longer play for love and glory alone. Similarly, Serafini asserted that his move to Italy had nothing to do with patriotism and that he left Brazil with a heavy heart. He said, "I would remain in Brazil for much less than I will receive in Italy. To continue playing for my club was my dream."[116]

Advocates could thus assert that professionalization was a nationalist measure, defending Brazilian football from foreign threats, and the argument became only stronger. Even Fluminense lost a player, Fernando Giudicelli, to the Italians, and it was not only Italians who moved. Though less often than white players, Afro-Brazilian footballers received contracts to play abroad as well. Vasco da Gama's goalkeeper, Jaguaré Bezerra de Vasconcelos, and midfielder, Fausto dos Santos, joined Barcelona during the team's tour of Spain in 1931, and in 1933 Leônidas da Silva and Domingos da Guia both moved to Montevideo to play for Uruguayan clubs. When Fausto, Leônidas, and Domingos all came back to Rio de Janeiro, to Vasco da Gama, when Carioca football professionalized, advocates' assertion that professionalization was a nationalist reform seemed that much stronger.

The idea that the changes to Brazilian football in the 1920s and 1930s should be understood as populist and nationalist measures extended beyond the argument between defenders of amateurism and the advocates of professionalism. For example, in 1938 the CBD mooted hiring Flamengo coach Dori Kürschner to help coach the seleção at the World Cup. Some argued that Kürschner's perspective would be especially useful, given his familiarity with both European and Brazilian football, but this did not stop others from launching what the *Jornal dos Sports* called "repeated and violent attacks" against him as a foreigner.[117] Kürschner survived the nativists' hostility, but he played little role in preparing the seleção for the world championship, and the job was taken over by the Brazilian Adhemar Pimenta. In part because of nationalist feeling, foreigners were becoming more rare in Brazilian football, if not quite as rare as polar bears in Tierra del Fuego.

When nationalists did identify "foreigners," as they believed they did within São Paulo's Italian immigrant community, bureaucratic defensiveness, popular antipathy, and, ultimately, state action helped to resolve the problem, or at least to demonstrate that many Brazilians refused to tolerate outward signs of divided loyalties. First Paulista authorities banned the footballers who transferred to Italy. Then Palestra Itália, the club many of the migrants played for, suffered repeated attacks from journalists and fans, and the assaults were more than figurative. In 1934 the club was one of several that refused to allow its players to play in the World Cup for the seleção due to the kinds of administrative disputes that had plagued Brazilian football throughout the period. Ignoring those disputes, critics alleged that the club was among those "most responsible for the poor performance of our team at the World Championship" because it had refused to allow its players to join the national side.[118]

Angered by the club's intransigence and the seleção's defeat in its first and only match, a crowd gathered at the club's grounds to give "vivas" to Brazil and to protest against the club. Then some in the crowd began to throw rocks at the club's headquarters before attempting to force their way into the building. They were prevented from doing so by the police. In order to protect against further disturbances, the authorities decided to provide security to the premises of both the club and the home of its president, Dante Delmanto. Finally, protestors staged the "burial" of Palestra Itália, which entailed a candlelight funeral march and the delivery of a garbage dumpster carrying flowers in the shape of a coffin to the headquarters of the APEA. The crowd finished by stoning the league's headquarters as well, prompting another intervention by the police.[119]

The Paulista crowd was not alone, as fans in Rio de Janeiro staged similar protests at the offices of the CBD, the Liga Carioca, and Vasco da Gama, another club that refused to allow its players to play for Brazil in 1934.[120] Although we cannot know exactly what these protestors had in mind, it is apparent that some, at least, were attacking what they saw as immigrant clubs' disloyalty to Brazil. In the words of a writer in the *Folha da Manhã*, "When there was a campaign for the formation of our team, the papers began to insinuate that the attitude of the Palestra president was due to a question of patriotism . . . Italian patriotism, a question of '*Italianitá*.'" The writer was convinced that the critics had been correct, that the directors of Palestra Itália had been motivated by Italian patriotism, and he asserted that their decision in 1934 was the latest evidence of their divided loyalties, of a piece with their stance when the club's players left for Italy, which, he alleged, they either tolerated or encouraged.[121] Although this was untrue, suspicions about the allegiances of immigrant athletes and organizations persisted into the 1940s.

It is important to understand these suspicions and attacks within the larger context of nativism and xenophobia that characterized the 1930s, one consequence of which was intervention by the Vargas regime to redefine citizenship and to reform immigration policy. The 1934 constitution established immigration quotas and obligated the national government "to guarantee the ethnic integration and physical and civic capacity of the immigrant," and these were accompanied by other measures, such as an April 1938 law facilitating the deportation of foreigners and another the same month which limited immigrants' political rights.[122] As Jeffrey Lesser shows, the regime and its allies were adamant about enforcing immigrant assimilation and tended to "define an authentic Brazilian culture by denying the viability of supposedly foreign elements."[123]

The regime took the same approach in dealing with foreigners in sports. The 1941 law that established the CND set limits on the participation of foreigners and, when Brazil entered the war on the side of the Allies in 1942, the regime attempted to settle the question of immigrant football identity once and for all. In September 1942 the CND ordered immigrant organizations to "nationalize" themselves in a formal manner by, for example, producing all internal communications in Portuguese. Under government pressure, Palestra Itália became Palmeiras, and its namesake in Belo Horizonte became Cruzeiro, among other name changes.[124] Such changes did not mean that the organizations or their members automatically abandoned their immigrant identities, and, in fact, these organizations retain hints of their ethnic roots today. But the experience of Palestra Itália highlights the increasing difficulty that those considered "foreign" faced in Brazilian football in the 1920s and 1930s, as those who considered themselves populists and nationalists sought to change the way the game functioned in Brazil.

Sportswriters were essential to this process. André Ribeiro calls journalists "the masters of the spectacle," not only because they interpreted what was happening on the field and in the clubs for the reading public but also because of their direct interventions in football administration, which became especially frequent and impactful in the 1920s and 1930s. Mário Cardim and others were active in football clubs and organizations in the earliest years, and sportswriters' influence persisted throughout the decades. For example, Floriano called Max Valentim, of the capital's *O Imparcial*, "the leader of the country's football revolution" for his work to bring about professionalization, and he cited others, including Mário Filho and Thomaz Mazzoni, as vital to the movement as well.[125] They worked not only in print but also behind the scenes to bring about professionalization and other changes, among other activities, by serving as agents helping club administrators to recruit and negotiate terms with "amateurs" in the years before 1933.[126] Just as importantly, they characterized those changes as populist and nationalist measures that transformed Brazilian football for the better.

The football press grew rapidly between 1894 and the 1930s. From short capsules attached to a newspaper's society section or in small sports sections that gathered football together with horseracing, cycling, boxing, and cricket, football coverage grew to occupy a full page and more in broadsheet dailies, some of which launched editions dedicated specifically to sports, which were dominated by football coverage (*O Imparcial* and *A Gazeta* were especially successful with such initiatives, launched in 1921 and 1929, respectively). Every kind of magazine covered it, from general interest titles like *A Leitura Para Todos* and *Brasil Illustrado* to women's publications like the *Revista Feminina*, to a plethora of sports magazines, including, to name just a

FIGURE 2.4. Fans arriving at a match between Fluminense and the Rio Cricket and Athletic Association, May 31, 1914. Such images were common fare in the early sports press. By permission of the Acervo Flu-Memória.

few, *Vida Sportiva* (first published in 1902), *Sportman* (later *A Vida Moderna*, 1906), *Auto-Sport* (1912), and *Athletica* (1920). The reading public's appetite for the game was such that football coverage filled most of the columns of successful sports dailies, the first of which was *Rio Sportivo* in 1926; the best-known, the *Jornal dos Sports* (1931). Finally, Brazilian radio covered football from almost the beginning of its existence, in the 1920s, and live broadcasts of game coverage and programs of football commentary were essential to radio programming by the mid-1930s.[127]

The character of the sports press changed as it grew. Early on, columnists covering football wrote almost as much, and as often, about fans and postmatch parties as about the game itself. They took note of which fashionable women and men attended matches, and what they wore, what they ate, and what music they danced to at postmatch parties. Football coverage in society magazines like *Careta* and *Cigarra* was often simply a collection of photographs of women fans arriving at a match, and the *Jornal de Theatro e Sport*, which enjoyed a publishing run of over ten years beginning in 1914, depicted football as a natural fit with the arts. This kind of sports journalism suited readers (and sometimes skeptical editors) who were unfamiliar with the niceties of the game, some of whom were often interested in football mainly as a way to demonstrate their cosmopolitan credentials.[128]

But even as the *Jornal de Theatro e Sport* published its first editions, the Brazilian football press was beginning to change, becoming more and more focused on the game. Longer and more detailed match reports, with fewer notes on fans and more focus on the playing field; increasing attention to tactics and formations; and constant comment on football administration, including player movements, directors' decisions, and infrastructure development, characterized the new kind of football journalism. This was in part a natural consequence of the growing popularity of the game as readers became more familiar with its laws, clubs proliferated, and tournaments became larger and more competitive. It was also a purposeful decision on the part of football writers, as *A Cigarra Sportiva* stated in its second edition, in June 1917. An offshoot of São Paulo's successful *A Cigarra*, *A Cigarra Sportiva* rejected the kind of sports journalism that had predominated in earlier years. It rejected the kind of journalism that focused on fans rather than players and social lives rather than sporting ones, "football" writing that was often little more than a series of statements about women fans: "Miss A. is pretty, Miss B. a delight, and Miss X. a paradise of temptations." The magazine dismissed the idea that such comments had anything to do with sports, and it informed its readers that it would "leave these charming subjects for the other *Cigarra*."[129]

In the late-1910s and early-1920s, many journalists adopted this perspective, abandoning what they depicted as frivolous subjects and dedicating themselves to covering sports in a professional manner, exemplified by their formation of trade organizations, such as ACE, founded in 1916, which aimed to establish best practices, among other tasks.[130] Connected to this, many saw themselves as making their writing—and, they argued, football itself—more accessible and more "Brazilian." A key step in this effort was the movement to "nationalize" football language.

In the first two decades after 1894, many organizations and journalists used the English terminology of the game, though few formally committed to preserving it in the manner of the Liga Metropolitana in 1905. But their preference could not resist the consequences of the social diffusion of the game because as the game's popularity advanced rapidly and haphazardly, it was played not only by those who spoke or understood English but also by the many Brazilians who did not. As early as 1909 Bangú discarded English terminology in its internal records, exchanging the exotic "match" for "*partida*," for instance.[131] Other Brazilians pronounced English terms in their own ways, either because of mispronunciation or conscious adaptation. In 1915 Rio de Janeiro's *Sports* magazine lampooned working-class Brazilians who modeled themselves on fashionable sportsmen, imagining them using "official English terms" but mangling them, "center-forward" becoming "*centri-frôe*"; "kick," "*krique*"; "ground," "*grunde*"; and "referee," "*rifiri*."[132] Similarly, writing in *Vida Sportiva* in 1918, Paulo de Magalhães portrayed a black working-class fan pronouncing "free kick" as "*fri-crique*" and "football" as "*futibó*."[133] Though meaning to ridicule, these authors were not far off in presenting the way that Brazilians were adapting sports terminology in the 1910s. The *Imparcial* newspaper published a regular column entitled "Shootando" in the mid-1910s, making a Portuguese gerund from the English "shoot"; spelled differently—*chutando*, from "*chutar*"—the word continues to be Brazilians' preferred way of talking about shooting a football.[134] And it is worth noting that, despite Magalhães' condescension, spoken aloud, "*futibó*" sounds a lot like "futebol."

The emergence of new football terminology was also an ideological choice, an expression of sportswriters' nationalism, which was especially prevalent in the late-1910s and early-1920s. Echoing *Careta*'s earlier complaint about the "new grammar" of foreign words imported into Brazilian vocabulary, for example, Arcy Tenorio D'Albuquerque wrote in 1920 that he worried that Brazilian sportsmen were contributing to the decay of the Portuguese language and Brazilian culture. He reminded his readers that "the decadence of a people is demonstrated by the decline of its language," and he asked Brazilians to renounce "the barbarianisms" of foreign terms, for example, by substituting "*estadio*" for the foreign "stadium." He also committed *Athletica* to the cause, announcing that "we will use DESPORTE or ESPORTE, but never again *sport*."[135]

D'Albuquerque framed reporters' choices about vocabulary as a question of patriotism, and many writers agreed. Alcides D'Arcanchy considered it "unpatriotic" to use foreign words like "football," and argued, in print and during a public lecture at the National Library in 1918, that Brazilians ought to call the game "ballipodo."[136] The *Jornal do Theatro e Sport* adopted *ballipodo* in 1918 and within a year spoke confidently of the term as "almost victorious" over its foreign competitor.[137] Unfortunately for D'Arcanchy, the innovation did not win a broad following, and the periodical eventually returned to the original English term. Other writers offered other suggestions, from "pólo inglez" (English polo) to "pébol."[138] They complained of the foreignness of "football," and like D'Albuquerque and D'Arcanchy, worried about the effects of Brazilians' insistence on retaining English terms. As "A Carioca player" wrote in *Vida Sportiva* in 1919, "the inexplicable use of foreign words" would injure "our language, degenerating it and enfeebling it in its development and in its progressive course toward the greatness of the fatherland."[139]

Despite the preference of a handful of traditionalists, football language did change. At least as early as 1918 Brazilian writers were using futebol, and the term had become widely adopted by 1921.[140] When São Paulo's *Sports* magazine adopted the new spelling in 1920, it proudly announced, "We have nationalized!"[141] The next year the magazine published a comprehensive dictionary, which it called "Nationalized Football Terms," prepared by ACE, in hopes of spreading knowledge and regularizing use of Brazilian terminology. The organization recommended replacing "foul" with "*falta*," "corner kick" with "*escanteio*," "draw" with "*empate*," "goal" with "*méta*," and "match" with "*jogo*"—a few of the dozens of terms it offered, many of which are still in use today.[142]

Finally, the fourth edition of the *Guia Brasileira de Football Associação*, published in São Paulo in the mid-1920s, omitted previous versions' section on the proper pronunciation of English words. The editors explained, "We have judged it to be expedient to substitute English terms for others from our language," and they linked their choice to the popularization of the game as well as their own pride in Brazil and its football. They wrote of "Brasil—colossus of America—country of great and innumerable possibilities" and claimed that football and other sports would allow Brazilians to realize those possibilities. They saw the guide as "a book designed essentially for Brazilian players," though, of course, previous editions had been aimed at the same audience. What had changed was Brazilians' abilities and Brazilians' pride in their own football culture, and so, to ensure the book was "practical and modern," the editors abandoned English terminology, and noted that they relied as much on rules adopted by the APEA and the CBD as they did on the offsides chart prepared by the English Football Association.[143]

José Sergio Leite Lopes emphasizes the connection between sportswriters' commitment to "nationalizing" football vocabulary and their work to popularize the game, both in how they wrote and in their work to eliminate race and class barriers, which included their fight for professionalization. The writers of the 1920s and 1930s, he says, opposed the "unconscious snobbery of [earlier] journalists," and they rejected English terms in favor of "the terms of contemporary language, from the point of view of a larger public." Like many commentators, Lopes draws attention especially to the influence of Mário Filho, who he says "practically invented the genre of sports journalism in Brazil at the beginning of the 30s." As a sportswriter and editor at several Rio de Janeiro newspapers, including *O Globo* and the *Jornal dos Sports*, which he purchased in 1936, Filho battled the pretensions and exclusivity of aristocratic sportsmen and journalists and promoted a populist vision of what football in Brazil could be, namely "a sporting activity which contributed to the mixing of classes."[144]

Filho's writing matched his political aims. On one hand, he wrote as a populist, using Brazilian football terms and breaking the formality that had characterized Brazilian football writing in the past. As his brother, the playwright Nelson Rodrigues, described his writing,

> In a half page, Mário Filho demolished the good taste which until then had been used in popular journalism. At the same time, he laid the foundation for our language. And not only this: he gave a new view of football and the star player, a lyrical turn, dramatic and humorous, which no one employed before. He created a spiritual connection between football and the fan. Mário Filho made the reader intimate with the facts. And, as his reporting went on, he enriched the vocabulary of the sports section with the most informal slang.[145]

The novelist José Lins do Rego, who was a regular contributor to the *Jornal dos Sports*, shared Filho's approach. He insisted that the sportswriter employ only popular diction, only speak to his readers in their own language, and so "Nothing of the Academy" should enter his vocabulary.[146] When sports journalism developed to include radio coverage, many commentators adapted the popular style to the new medium. For example, Nicolau Tuma, the "Machine-gun Speaker," spoke up to 250 words each minute as he broadcast game coverage in São Paulo, and Erik Cerqueira, who hosted a call-in talk show in the capital in the late-1930s, employed a conversational and inclusive style of the type recommended by Lins do Rego.[147]

On the other hand, Filho, Lins do Rego, and other commentators stressed football's great national importance by discussing the game in heroic terms. In the words of Cesar Gordon and Ronaldo Helal, Filho's "sporting chronicles described football matches in epic proportions, not merely as sporting contests but as events where noble human values were at stake," and he lionized footballers as national heroes.[148] Filho lionized, even "deified" successful footballers, especially black players like Domingos da Guia and Leônidas da Silva, who he depicted as the exemplary representatives of Brazil's popular classes.[149] In short, Mário Filho and others who wrote and spoke in this vein, such as Lins do Rego and Thomaz Mazzoni, portrayed football as at once intimate and grand, but they saw no contradiction. Rather, they claimed that the game belonged to and involved every Brazilian, and because of this it was part of a great national project. Just as their predecessors' condescension was rarely "unconscious," the journalists of the 1920s and 1930s made purposeful choices in what terms to use and how to write and speak about football, and they understood themselves as popularizing and nationalizing both journalism and football itself.

Football's Persistent Hierarchies

It is essential, however, to acknowledge the limits of the changes journalists and other reformers were willing to promote. Though they often depicted themselves, and often have been remembered, as transforming both their writing and football itself, many influential journalists were committed to maintaining some of the most important features of football as it had been played and organized in Brazil since 1894. As Joseph Arbena points out, one suggestion of this is that many of the "nationalized" football terms adopted by Brazilian and other Latin American writers preserve a linguistic record of the earlier desire to preserve foreign terminology, hinting at the writers' unwillingness to transform the game in a radical way.[150] In Brazil, "futebol" is the most obvious example of this record, but not the only one; "gol" (goal), "craque" (from the English "crack," a star player) and "escrete" (from "scratch," a term for a football eleven) are others.[151]

Mário Cardim, for example, was active in the nationalist campaigns of the late-1910s and 1920s. He helped to form the Federação Brasileira de Football in 1915, and he worked to "Brazilianize" football terminology through his work with ACE in São Paulo and as an editor of *Sports* magazine.[152] It also seems that Cardim did not waver in his dedication to helping middle-class and wealthy sportsmen maintain their privileged position in Paulista football through his work as an administrator in the Liga Paulista and the Paulistano club, for example, by recommending the expulsion of working-class clubs suspected of false amateurism and recommending literacy and other tests to guard against encroachment from below.[153] Nationalism did not belong only to populists, as Fluminense's patriotic claims during the debates over its stadium indicate.

Nor did professionalization imply radical reform or a commitment to football democracy. It was wealthy and powerful sports administrators who played the leading roles in the final transition to professional football. Floriano wrote that journalists like Paulo Várzea were at the forefront of the fight for professionalization. But he also noted that in the final move to adopt professionalism, these journalists were joined by the leaders of some of the country's most prominent clubs, including São Paulo's Luiz de Barros and the president of Fluminense, Oscar Costa. He also cited the participation of directors of Rio de Janeiro's America, Bangú, and Vasco da Gama and São Paulo's Palestra Itália, Corinthians, and São Bento. Although some of these had grown from more modest roots than Fluminense and São Paulo, clubs like Vasco da Gama and Corinthians had worked hard to join the clubs of the middle class and wealthy, and they were all among the most powerful football organizations in Brazil by the early-1930s. Among elite clubs, only Botafogo of Rio de Janeiro hesitated to adopt professionalism, even though it too had its own "laborers of the ball" and had been "one of the first to practice masked professionalism in Rio," according to Floriano.[154]

Most of these leaders and their clubs had resisted professionalization into the early-1930s, for example, by supporting the CBD's Apprentice Law. The possibility of intervention by the Vargas regime and the threat of losing players to professional clubs in Italy and elsewhere, especially, seem to have done what appeals from reformers could not do alone, and once Fluminense, Flamengo, São Paulo, and other important clubs committed to professionalization the transition occurred in short order. In 1932 and 1933, these clubs embraced the argument that the only way to "moralize" the game was to bring payment out into the open. Now, they agreed, legally binding contracts and proper administrative oversight could ensure that all clubs played fairly and by the same set of rules, and that players were rewarded properly for their performances.

As with the earlier Apprentice Law, professionalization also strengthened big clubs at the expense of both their humbler rivals and players. The clubs of the middle class and wealthy could afford the cost of transfer fees and could outspend most of their rivals because they possessed resources that others did not, including large and profitable venues. They joined Fluminense and Vasco da Gama in building their own stadiums, and the 1930s saw the opening of a spate of new and reconditioned grounds. São Paulo remodeled the Chácara da Floresta stadium in time for the 1930 season, and Palestra Itália opened its stadium at the Parque Antártica in 1933, joining Corinthians, which had opened the Parque São Jorge stadium in 1928. In Rio de Janeiro, Botafogo expanded and reconditioned its stadium on General Severiano Street in 1937, and Flamengo inaugurated a new stadium in Gávea in 1938. Seating thousands of paying customers, these venues brought wealthy clubs the revenue needed to keep their best players and recruit new ones. Thus, it was not the big clubs that joined Botafogo in its rearguard effort to defend amateurism in the mid-1930s but rather smaller ones, whose leaders knew that they could not hope to remain competitive in fully professionalized football leagues. As Fluminense president Oscar Costa admitted, professionalization would mean the end of many small clubs.[155]

Meanwhile, like the Apprentice Law before it, professionalization allowed the wealthy to tighten their grip on their own clubs by cutting down on player movement and by distinguishing between club members and players. Those who joined a club as paying members retained the privileges that membership had always proffered, including voting rights and the use of club facilities. Those who joined as athletes became club employees who were paid for their work as football players and not necessarily entitled to membership or to participate in club activities, and the difficulty of movement from one club to another deepened their dependence on the good will of their employers.[156]

The ill-starred professional career of the midfielder Fausto dos Santos illustrates the point. Fausto had emerged as a star in the mid-1920s with Bangú before moving to Vasco da Gama and then abroad to Barcelona and other foreign clubs during the era of false amateurism. When Brazilian football professionalized, he came home to Rio de Janeiro, playing for Vasco da Gama before transferring to Flamengo in 1936, one of several popular Afro-Brazilians the club signed as it began to renovate its image and traded its traditional aristocratic profile for a populist image that helped it become the country's most popular team. By 1936 Fausto was beginning to break down physically due to complications from tuberculosis, and club coach Dori Kürschner demanded he play as a defender. Still acting as players had during the era of masked professionalism, Fausto refused and looked to move to another club, but Flamengo refused to negotiate his release, leaving Fausto little choice other than to beg forgiveness. He wrote a public letter of apology in which he said he was "enthusiastic and absolutely ready to defend the glorious colors of the most beloved club in Brazil" and to accept Kürschner's orders, whom he addressed formally and called an "extraordinary coach." Although Kürschner and Flamengo accepted his apology, Fausto never returned to the field, and he died before the 1939 season began, only thirty-five years old.[157]

Some club members and administrators may have rejected elitist notions. But the suddenness of leading clubs' conversion to professionalization along with actions they took to limit the professional players' agency and participation in club life indicates that the shift should not be seen as a moral stand or an assertion of democratic principles. Big clubs' adoption of professional football is better understood as the latest way they found to defend their position of influence and authority. By managing the transition from amateur to professional football, the leaders of powerful clubs ensured that they would continue to enjoy important privileges as Brazilian football became more socially inclusive. They shared an outlook and approach with their counterparts in government, who, under Vargas' leadership, enacted concrete changes in reforming the way Brazilians worked, engaged in politics, and managed Brazilian art while reinforcing essential aspects of the country's race, class, and gender hierarchies—just as previous generations of Brazilian reformers had done.[158]

In fact, state authorities helped elite administrators maintain their control over Brazilian football. Working through the CBD, which it took control of in 1936, and later through the CND, the Vargas government helped to resolve disputes between rival governing bodies that grew out of the debate over professionalization, it registered and enforced player contracts, it supported stadium construction, and it expanded state support for teams organized to represent Brazil in international competitions. Although its allies depicted these actions as necessary and populist, each of them helped strengthen the big clubs and their organizations. The bodies lost some of their autonomy to the state, and they lost some of their prerogatives in dealing with players because of professionalization, but in many ways they were actually stronger by the 1940s than they were in the 1920s and 1930s. In the case of the regime's enforcement of player contracts, for example, the support the regime offered professional footballers was like the protections and expanded benefits it offered all Brazilian citizens, contingent on engagement with the state and its institutions and on their acceptance of its view of the roles they should play in society.[159] For professional footballers, protection and regular pay were available, but only within the centralized, hierarchical system sponsored by the state: the player was hired by a club made legitimate by its affiliation with official leagues, the CBD, and the CND. That is, the populist regime confirmed elite administrators as football's proper authorities and communicated to players that their claim to football citizenship depended on accepting their subordinate role in football society.

Getúlio Vargas' populist image is complicated by his compromises and work with industrialists and other powerful figures and interests, and he could seem like the "Father of the Poor" or the "Mother of the Rich," depending on where one stood and to whom one listened.[160] In a similar manner, the rendering of professionalization and other changes in the 1920s and 1930s as parts of a populist (even democratic) and nationalist football transformation obscured the persistence of traditional hierarchies. That narrative depended in large part on the intervention of populist sportswriters who interpreted those changes and who, like Mário Cardim before them, forged close relationships with powerful administrators and political leaders. An obvious example was the journalist Lourival Fontes, a member of Brazil's corporatist Integralist movement who served Vargas as propaganda minister between 1934 and 1942 and helped lead the physical education department of the Ministry of Education and Health. Fontes helped guide the state's intervention in football administration and was the state's appointee to lead the Brazilian delegation to the World Cup in Italy in 1934.[161]

More influential within football, and in shaping football memory according to the story of populist and nationalist transformation, were Thomaz Mazzoni and Mário Filho. Mazzoni, the longtime sports editor of *A Gazeta* and *A Gazeta Esportiva*, published several volumes on Brazilian football, including an important 1950 history that narrated the game's becoming more and more Brazilian, much to his satisfaction as a committed nationalist. He also worked closely with the CBD and promoted the official views of the Vargas regime in São Paulo, a city where neither were very popular in the 1930s and 1940s.[162] In Rio de Janeiro, Filho received support from the leaders of Flamengo and Fluminense, including Arnaldo Guinle, when he purchased the *Jornal dos Sports* in 1936. The writers had their differences, Mazzoni's "conservative" style contrasting with Filho's popular language, but both were firmly committed to essential aspects of the ideology of the Vargas movement.[163]

Both writers insisted that Brazilian football open up to include working-class and nonwhite players more fully, and both believed that racial and social inclusion was one of the most important things that distinguished Brazilian football as Brazilian. With its claim of Brazilian difference, this view corresponded closely with the nationalism of the Vargas regime. It also corroborated the regime's claim of building an inclusive Brazil. For example, Mazzoni called on the press to dedicate more attention to the "little clubs" so that those outside the best leagues would feel they were part of the football culture, and he justified the state's intervention in football as a measure of discipline and nationalism.[164] In Filho's telling, Brazilian football was both "interclassist" and multiracial. In his extremely influential 1947 book *O negro no foot-ball brasileiro*, which he based on his own reporting and conversations with contemporaries rather than on documentary sources, Filho narrated a version of the history of Brazilian football that suited the ideologies of the Vargas regime.[165] He argued that, by the 1930s, "in football there was not even the merest shadow of racism."[166]

Seeing Brazilian football as democratic and inclusive, Filho missed or ignored the reality that traditional hierarchies and traditional exclusions persisted in the 1930s and after, and the narrative he, Mazzoni, and other like-minded writers helped construct has remained influential in the popular memory of Brazilian football, just as the image of Getúlio Vargas as the Father of the Poor has continued to inform common views of his regime. In fact, these writers not only sometimes ignored the persistence of traditional hierarchies in their writing but also reinforced them on the page and beyond it.[167] For example, José Lins do Rego took on several roles in football administration, as a member of both the board of directors of Flamengo and the CND and as secretary-general of the CBD. Regardless of Lins do Rego's sense that he contributed to contributed to the game's social diffusion (he was also a founder of an important fan club), Flamengo still privileged wealthy, white administrators in the 1930s and 1940s, as Fausto learned. Flamengo administrators embraced the popularity to be gained by hiring Afro-Brazilian footballers but were also quick to censure Fausto and other "rebellious" players in order to teach them their responsibilities a professionals, and the club relied on leading sportswriters to endorse its actions.[168]

Finally, like the Vargas regime, both Thomaz Mazzoni and Mário Filho viewed discipline as indispensable, the crucial means by which Brazil's variety of races, classes, and regions would be brought together. Discipline was one of the key and persistent themes of *A Gazeta* under Mazzoni and of both the *Jornal dos Sports* and *O Globo* under Filho's editorship, guiding coverage not only of football politics but also of football styles, which I examine more closely in chapter 5. Mazzoni and Filho championed stars like Fausto dos Santos and Leônidas da Silva, but they also were quick to criticize them for alleged acts of indiscipline and to call for intervention to correct the problem by figures of authority. Years before the Vargas regime acted to create the CND, for example, Mazzoni argued that Brazilian football required "the power of the authoritarian voice, which has never existed in our sport, which has never known deference, and in which neither responsibility, nor harmony, nor order exists."[169] For his part, Filho argued that Leônidas became a truly great player in the late-1930s only when he learned restraint to go along with what Filho suggested was inborn talent. The writer called this his "disciplined phase," and when his discipline seemed to lapse, Filho supported Flamengo's decision to sell Leônidas to São Paulo in 1942.[170]

Filho and Mazzoni were two of the most important and influential football figures of the 1930s, and they saw the compatibility between nationalism and hierarchy. They and their allies railed against the exclusivity and preferences of the football of the turn of the century, and they saw themselves as helping to transform football into a more inclusive and more Brazilian game. Their narrative was a powerful and romantic one, and it obscured the persistence of important aspects of football as it was first played in Brazil. Football organizations—powerful clubs and their leagues, governing bodies and the state, and the media—oversaw and enacted real changes, like professionalization, the lessening of the participation of foreigners, and the popularization of sports writing. But they also limited the extent of those changes by cooperating to resist challenges from individual players and smaller clubs and by depicting the changes in Brazilian football as more extensive than they were. In spite of claims to the contrary, the challenges of the 1910s, 1920s, and 1930s did not overturn the hierarchical structure of organized Brazilian football. It had to be reformed and restructured, but football hierarchy persisted, in some ways even stronger than before.

Students and Masters

National Identity and International Football

It was not long after learning how to play football that Brazilians began to look for opponents beyond their own borders, eager that Brazil should participate in international competition. Sportsmen organized Brazil's first national team, the seleção, in 1914, one hundred years before the country hosted the whole football world in the 2014 World Cup. And their participation in international football began even before then, as club teams and city select sides hosted visitors from as close by as Uruguay and as far away as South Africa. During the first part of the twentieth century, they also sent teams abroad to compete in South America as well as in France, Switzerland, Portugal, Spain, Italy, and Yugoslavia.

Some commentators saw testing and improving the quality of Brazilian football as the chief attraction of international contests, which is why they tended to be most enthusiastic about games against English and other British teams. These matches allowed Brazilians to learn from the sport's creators and acknowledged masters and attracted enormous attention, with extensive media coverage matched only by the huge crowds that attended the contests. Writing during the critical years between 1910 and 1914, when Brazilian football administration was taking shape, bringing with it a more intentional approach to participation in international football, commentators asserted that visiting English players "ought to serve well as a model for our '*footballers*,'"[1] and that "the profit that we will have ought to be extraordinary, if our *foot-ballers* pay close attention to the [Englishmen's] play and if they are disposed to imitate them."[2]

International contests were, though, about more than training. Many Brazilians also saw them as opportunities to craft and express their individual, group, and, ultimately, national identities, for they allowed for the possibility of careful planning and deep meaning. Organizers of international matches and tournaments were able to control when and against whom Brazilians would play as well as which players would represent the nation. Writers interpreted the action and results of the playing field, using the occasion of matches between eleven carefully chosen men and a particular group of foreigners in order to make assertions about the character and destiny of the nation as a whole. Finally, players and fans drew their own conclusions about these games, extraordinary opportunities for the invention and public performance of nationality.

At the time they entered the international arena, in the first decade of the twentieth century, Brazilians accepted the notion that Europeans were football's masters. The organizers of Brazil's participation in international football—the same sportsmen who dominated the country's domestic leagues—remained convinced of European football superiority into the 1920s and strained to demonstrate that the game's Brazilian pupils followed their teachers' lessons. In assembling representative teams, they presented an image of Brazil that corresponded as closely as possible to their ideal footballer, who was in turn modeled on an idealized version of the European athlete: male, wealthy, white, cultured, and amateur. With few exceptions, Brazilians who did not meet this ideal, whether female, working class, nonwhite, or clearly parochial, were confined to roles as spectators to the feats of acceptable representatives of the nation. Competition was a secondary concern. More important was the opportunity to broadcast an ideal version of the nation playing the modern sport, serving to improve Brazil's image abroad and communicate edifying messages to watching Brazilians, of all races, classes, and regions.

Because they usually ended in expected but honorable defeat, matches against Europeans in the first two decades of the twentieth century bolstered the Brazilian game's European cast. However, Brazil's best footballers became better at the game over the years and by the 1920s began regularly to defeat the old masters at their own game. The more likely international victories seemed to be, the more strident became the voices of critics who demanded that Brazil be represented by its best players, regardless of their backgrounds.

Nationalist and populist critics went further, calling for a national team that was not only highly skilled but one that also included whites and blacks, working-class players and wealthy ones, and players from various parts of the country. They argued that such a seleção would indicate that Brazilians had discarded Eurocentrism for nationalism, exclusivity for inclusion, and privilege for democracy. They used international football to assert that they and their partners in government, the arts, and industry had transformed Brazil into a more just, more inclusive, more *Brazilian* country.

Participating in international football involved Brazilians in debates about the meaning and character of the nation, and it echoed Brazil's broader international experience in the late nineteenth and early twentieth centuries. Statesmen and soldiers, businessmen and artists wrestled with the problems and challenges of Brazil's engagement with the world. They argued about the modern-day implications of the Portuguese inheritance, Britain's nineteenth-century preeminence, the country's connections with its Latin American neighbors, the foreign policy impact of Brazil's large immigrant communities, the economic and military rise of the United States, and the meaning of nationalism in an international setting. Over the long term, from the explicit Eurocentrism of the empire to the conflicted nationalism of the Getúlio Vargas years, Brazil's commercial ties, its diplomatic commitments, and its cultural orientation moved toward the New World and away from the Old. Though hesitant and contested, the movement away from Europe occurred because the world changed, because Brazilians came to believe it more likely to serve national interests, and because they decided that Brazil's traditional European orientation was not authentically Brazilian.[3]

Reinforcing conclusions they drew from negotiations over international commerce, their experience in the League of Nations, and their participation in international exhibitions, in international matches Brazilians engaged with the foreign football they idolized, testing themselves against real opponents rather than imaginary ones. This meant the toppling of the idols, and by the late-1930s only a few Brazilians still thought Europeans the masters of sport. Because of Brazilian victories against foreign opponents, most became convinced that Brazil was home to the "kings of football." Some things changed and some did not, with, on one hand, the seleção including increasing numbers of black and working-class players in the 1930s and, on the other, Brazilian involvement in international football remaining in the hands of administrators who were always men, always well off, and almost always white. More than any concrete change, international football was important because it helped transform Brazilian views about what the game said about Brazil.

A Corinthian Ethos

Brazilians' experience with what they called international football began before the turn of the twentieth century. At first, matches between Brazilians and resident expatriates were described as "international" matches, with media reports describing local clubs as "national" and "English," for example, and matches between select teams made up of native-born and expatriate stars as "Brazil [versus] England."[4] Such matches were often given special attention by the early sports press, as they offered tests of Brazil's football development and of the national loyalties of administrators, players, and fans. Matches against visiting teams were even more important, whether they came to play football, as when a South African team visited São Paulo in 1906, or whether they were in the country for other reasons, like British sailors who sometimes took on Brazilians while on shore leave.[5]

Brazilians gave greater or lesser attention to matches against foreigners depending on a number of concerns. First, much depended upon the opponents. Europeans, especially Britons, garnered much more attention in the early years than South American opponents. Second, matches involving the seleção, which purported to field footballers who could claim to truly represent Brazil, fired the imagination. The first such match is generally accepted to have been against the English Exeter City Football Club in 1914, which Brazil won 2–1. Finally, the venue was important; official tournaments, such as the South American Championship and the World Cup, were much more important than "friendly" matches, and games played abroad—especially in Europe—carried more weight than those that took place at home. Of course, this rubric would evolve over time from the first informal matches between "Brazilians" and "Englishmen." But the attitudes and experience of the early years did much to define how Brazilians thought about international football matches into the 1940s.

The most important of Brazil's early experiences of international competition was with the Corinthian Football Club between 1910 and 1914. Brazilians had participated in a handful of international matches before 1910, but the experience with the English Corinthians was crucial, especially because it helped define an ideal to which Brazilian organizers aspired in the years to come. Indeed, it would be difficult to find, in that or in any other period, a group of athletes who more closely filled the profile preferred by Brazilian sportsmen than these English footballers, whose club was fiercely devoted to amateurism. Almost as important, club members were solid members of the English upper class. Many were graduates of the universities of Cambridge and Oxford, gentlemen whose wealth and education meant they could afford and understand the value of amateur athletics. Brazilians' interaction with the polished, well-to-do Corinthians helped sportsmen press their case that football properly understood and pursued was a game of white gentlemen and amateurs. When working-class or nonwhite players took up the game, they must abide by rules set down by European authorities like the Corinthians and must model their behavior on the comportment of their social betters. The proof that the sportsmen were right, and were rightly building Brazilian football, was apparent for all to see, for the great Corinthians were willing to come to Brazil.

Despite the restrictions the club placed on membership, the Corinthians were widely regarded as one of the best, most skilled football teams in the world in the period before World War I. However, after 1907 and the breakdown of its relationship with the Football Association and its affiliated clubs, which left the Corinthians marginalized at home, the club began to look outside Britain for opponents and to promote its views in "missionary" tours.[6] The Corinthians' travels eventually took them to Brazil, where the club conducted tours in 1910 and 1913. The tours proved so popular that another was organized for 1914, but war intervened at the moment the team reached Brazil, and the travelers returned to Britain before they played a match.

On each trip to Brazil the Corinthians visited Rio de Janeiro and São Paulo, staying two weeks and playing three matches in each city. The Corinthians' fame preceded them and the Brazilians extended them a warm welcome. According to one of the Englishmen, "We had a magnificent reception everywhere. No team could possibly have been treated better, and the people there couldn't do too much for us."[7] On the first tour, the Englishmen won all of their matches handily. They almost repeated the feat three years later, when they drew once and lost once, winning the balance of their matches. The pattern was set in the very first match, on August 24, 1910, when Fluminense, one of the organizers of the tour, took the lead against the visitors within two minutes of kick-off. This was the hosts' one shining moment, for, according to *Campo e Sport*, Corinthians took the ball at the ensuing restart and began "to dominate the game completely, pressing their attack deep into the Fluminense half." Within minutes the game was tied, with S. H. Day scoring the first goal in an eventual hat trick, and by the half the score was 7–1 to the visitors. Fluminense had a handful of opportunities in the second half, but the pattern persisted, and the match ended 10–1.[8]

This was the Corinthians' largest margin of victory, but few matches were really competitive during the first tour. Brazilians expected their teams to lose, and the single victory against the Englishmen in 1913 was greeted with joy but also with "widespread surprise at the result."[9] Still, Brazilians were no less enthusiastic for the lack of parity. The matches of the Corinthians were extremely well attended, both in the media and in the grandstands. At that first match in 1910, Fluminense's ground "was too small to hold the Carioca multitude, which wanted to witness the exploits of the famous English game."[10] Similarly large crowds greeted them in São Paulo, where the excitement of the event left a lasting impression in the name of the Sport Club Corinthians Paulista. And the Englishmen's popularity did not diminish in the three years between tours. In 1913 each of their matches drew between six thousand and ten thousand spectators, according to one estimate.[11]

In attempting to understand the Corinthians' popularity, it is worth remembering early-twentieth-century Brazilians' press for improvement and their many reform projects, from public health campaigns to electrification programs, from educational initiatives to telegraph construction in the country's most remote areas, many of which carried republican faith in expertise into the realm of public policy. Like republican social and political reformers, Brazilian sportsmen usually associated skill and expertise with Europe and Europeans, and in the Corinthians they found a perfect model, one that brought together polished skill, modern education, and just the right social and cultural qualities. Learning from the Corinthians' example, Brazilians could apply the lessons of order and progress to the football field, itself a staging area for the more fundamental remaking of Brazil that some sportsmen expected a proper football education would engender.[12]

Brazilians' enthusiastic reception also extended beyond the football grounds of Rio de Janeiro and São Paulo. In 1910 Cariocas took the Corinthians on a driving tour of the city, on a trip up the Corcovado Mountain, and on a boating excursion in Guanabara Bay. To honor the Englishmen, the Brazilians also hosted a "soirée" as well as a farewell banquet including Yorkshire ham and "European" fruit.[13] Similarly, in São Paulo, the young Englishmen received special treatment far from the football fields. Their farewell banquet in 1910 was an extravagant affair, the menu including even "Coeur de filet de boeuf à la Corinthian."[14] In 1913 they received tangible proof of Brazilians' admiration, when the Associação Paulista de Esportes Athleticos gave them a variety of "lavish presents, as mementos of their visit to S. Paulo," including jeweled tiepins, cufflinks, and gold and platinum watch chains; the English vice-consul in São Paulo, Charles Miller, the father of Brazilian football himself, distributed the gifts.[15]

The Paulistas, like the Cariocas, felt honored by the visit of the Corinthians. Each tour was an important event in the life of the city, a highlight not only of the sporting season but also of the social life of the sportsmen and women who entertained the Englishmen. During each visit a handful of Brazilians had the opportunity to play against some of the best footballers in the world, and thousands watched them play. And football was only part of the attraction. Press accounts of the Corinthians' activities usually cited their connections to Britain's great universities and always emphasized their amateur status. They were the "distinguished young Corinthians," and they dedicated themselves to the same amateur, patrician ideal as did their Brazilian hosts.[16] As one Corinthian noted with satisfaction, Brazilian sportsmen had "set their faces sternly against professionalism in any shape or form."[17]

The Corinthians' exclusivity had served to isolate them in the world of English football. In Brazil, it helped make them respected opponents and honored guests. They were invited to Brazil and hosted in Rio de Janeiro by aristocratic Fluminense, whose members went to great lengths to impress their guests. Beyond honoring the Corinthians with parties and banquets, entertaining them with sightseeing trips, and hosting the matches in Rio de Janeiro, in 1910 Fluminense paid half the cost of the team's passage from Britain and organized its hotel accommodations.[18] In São Paulo, the team was hosted by the Liga Paulista in 1910 and by the APEA in 1913. The leading parts there were taken by Paulistano and São Paulo Athletic, clubs that shared with Fluminense both a social profile and an obvious deference to the travelers.

Many other Brazilians attended the matches of the Corinthians as well, like the young Afro-Brazilian spectator who ran on to the field and kicked one of the Englishmen "in the correct place with his bare foot" after a referee's decision had gone against the local team.[19] But many of the spectators at the matches of the Corinthians were quite well-heeled, as *A Notícia* noticed:

> If anyone still doubted that *foot-ball* is the *sport* of fashion, the favorite *sport* of our fine and elegant society, yesterday afternoon would be enough to demonstrate this truth.

> The curious observer who situated himself at Fluminense's main gate, at 3:30 in the afternoon, would have seen an intermittent parade of the prettiest *girls*, the most distinguished gentlemen, some wearing circumspect dress-coats and others, bright and happy suits; he would have seen a parade of senators, deputies, diplomats, representatives of high commerce and high administration, [and] he would have seen the continual arrival of automobiles and coaches carrying the distinguished families of our society.[20]

Inside the gate, the observer would also have noticed the similarities between the two sets of players on the field. Like the Corinthians themselves, their Brazilian opponents were almost exclusively white and wealthy.

On the field, in the grandstand, in tuxedoed ballrooms, a visit by the Corinthians was an event for the Brazilian elite, who used each visit to portray Brazil as a nation in its own self-image, with a patrician, amateur sports ethic and a culture of European refinement. The Corinthians were judges to whom Brazilian sportsmen could appeal for validation, and it is no accident that the English diplomat Ernest Hambloch noticed that "the enthusiastic Brazilians made almost a national occasion of the first match."[21] To many Brazilians, it was exactly that, which explains the horror of many Brazilians at the suggestion by the *Brazilian Review*, a local English-language newspaper, that some Paulista spectators had booed the Corinthians. According to a writer in the *Jornal do Commercio*, there may have been boos and hisses, but they could not be attributed to the city at large, much less its "best elements." Instead, any indiscretions were the fault of "a few dozen little-educated and perhaps illiterate individuals."[22] With relief, one imagines, his newspaper was able to publish the Corinthians' letter of thanks to their Paulista hosts two days later, proving that Brazilians had indeed demonstrated themselves and their nation worthy of Corinthian friendship.[23]

The experience with the Corinthians established a model for Brazil's early participation in international competition. In the period before 1920, Brazilian organizers approached international football as a venue for making friends and promoting their ideal of Brazil. They ensured that their representatives were amateur and, as far as possible, patrician and cosmopolitan, and they hoped their counterparts would do the same. They expected that both sides in an international encounter would devote themselves to the most gentlemanly behavior, for competitiveness was less important than respectability and decorum, and Brazilian commentators were quick to draw attention to positive examples of this kind of sportsmanship. For example, during a match between Brazilians and Argentines in Buenos Aires in September 1914, the Brazilian referee awarded a goal to the hosts, not having noticed an infraction by one of their players. However, the Argentine players refused to accept the goal. They went on to lose the match but won the respect of their Brazilian guests, with a writer in *A Leitura Para Todos* praising their "fidelity" to the demands of sportsmanship.[24] Finally, organizers staged banquets and receptions for players, administrators, and a handful of guests in order to diminish on-field rivalries and to emphasize the exclusivity of their football culture, with its Corinthian remove and refinement.

Unfortunately, international football did not always provide this kind of experience, as Brazilians learned when another English team, the professional club Exeter City, visited in 1914. Brazilians were sure that they could learn from the visitors, and Exeter City's three matches were very well attended, between six thousand and twelve thousand spectators turning out for the final match between the Englishmen and a team including both Paulistas and Cariocas, the first seleção.[25] While some enjoyed the experience, reporting that the first match was "a true festival of '*sport*'" and "full of phases of sensation and beauty," most were disappointed because the Englishmen played aggressively, even violently—mainly because, Brazilians said, they realized they were not skilled enough to win otherwise.[26]

There were hints of the problem in the first match, against a team of expatriate Britons, but according to critics, Exeter City's character was truly revealed when it faced Brazilian teams. *O Paiz* said that against a Carioca select team the Englishmen revealed they were "brutes, absolute brutes." Every time a Brazilian approached the Exeter City goal, the paper reported, he fell victim to violent fouls, often by the Englishmen's "scoundrel" of a center half. The Cariocas were lucky not to end the day in the hospital, and the Brazilians enjoyed little protection from the referee, who whistled for fouls only "from time to time," most likely because each time he did call a foul the Englishmen crowded round him to complain. Exeter City won the game, 5–3. Still, according to *O Paiz*, the victory was won dishonorably, and it refused even to give the names of most of the Englishmen. Only one, the center forward William Hunter, "deserved" to have his name printed in the paper, for only he had demonstrated the "loyal, correct, and dignified manner" necessary to represent England abroad. The rest embarrassed themselves, England, and football.²⁷ Among others, *O Imparcial* joined in the critique, stating that Exeter City did not play a game that could even be called "true association."²⁸

Brazilians had, in fact, criticized the Corinthians' own rough play, but critics were sure these were occasional lapses, much different from what seemed like the purposeful adoption of violence by Exeter City. In reality, there may or may not have been a great deal of difference between the way that Corinthians and Exeter City played, but Brazilians criticized Exeter City in much more forceful terms than they did the Corinthians. The Corinthians could be forgiven their missteps for, despite them, they were amateurs and "distinguished young men," and on the field they were "masterful, faithful observers of the most minute rules of the wholesome *sport*, and slaves to the most rigorous *training*."²⁹ Exeter City lacked Corinthians' polish and, even more important, their amateurism.

Many commentators argued that Brazil's 2–0 victory over Exeter City was more important than Cariocas' defeat of the Corinthians in 1913. The match was especially violent, and Exeter City was to blame, the Englishmen leaving at least one Brazilian player seriously injured but unable to avoid defeat despite their "brutality."³⁰ According to the *Correio da Manhã*, it was impossible to give readers a sense of the emotion of the enormous crowd that carried the Brazilians off the field in triumph and unleashed "deafening screams, wild gestures, [and] dancing, moved momentarily to a veritable outburst of madness."³¹ The *Jornal do Brasil* called the victory "the most beautiful gilded page in the history of sport in our country," in part because the adversaries were English, and in part because the match had seen Brazil "united, in the symbolic union of Rio and S. Paulo for the formation of a legitimate national *team*." Even more important, the paper said, the victory was significant precisely because the Englishmen were professionals, a point other commentators made sure to emphasize.³²

Sportsmen assumed Exeter City's professionalism explained its faults. Two years later, during the South American Championship of 1916, Brazilian representatives met amateurs who seemed to have the same failings. The Brazilians did not fare well in the new tournament, drawing once and losing twice. However, according to Francisco Pereira Lima Filho, writing in the immediate aftermath of the tournament, the Brazilians were the real victors because they had not resorted to the rough tactics of the Chileans and Uruguayans, to whom they lost. The members of the seleção had maintained the proper demeanor and had thus identified Brazil with the highest sporting values. Lima Filho summarized the views of many:

Honor, then, to our countrymen! The *score* of matches does not always express the valor of the adversaries: victories can afterward be discredited as defeats, but chivalry during the match, courtesy, the good, the true, calm, rational and intelligent game, without violence, with energy, the force of determination, with all of this together, finally, in the qualities which our patricians implanted in Buenos Aires and which were rewarded with moral victory in all of the matches, this impressed because it is not the work of chance, this endures because it is not the fruit of materialism, this elevates, honors, dignifies and glorifies not only our *foot-ballers* but all of us, Brazilians, because it is the reflex of our culture, the expression of our character, the essence of our race.[33]

Brazilians had gone to Argentina to play three football matches. But because they were playing in an international arena, they had the responsibility of representing Brazil; victory was a secondary concern.

Brazilians also criticized their own countrymen when they did not live up to that ethic, at least to a point. As in the episode concerning fans' treatment of the Corinthians, commentators admitted that some might be guilty but did not accept that these could be members of Brazil's better classes. The offenders were ignorant, perhaps illiterate, in the same class as the "horde of urchins" who booed a referee during a match against a visiting Italian team in 1914. Such activities were "absolutely condemnable," according to one writer, and had no place in Brazilian football, but true sportsmen were not to blame.[34]

Another controversy, and another opportunity for sportsmen to defend their ideal, came during the South American Championship of 1919. One of the stars of the tournament was the Uruguayan Isabelino Gradín. He was one of the tournament's best, most skilled players, and he was black. Uruguay was the only South American country against which Brazilians played that consistently fielded players of African descent during these early years. Gradín, for example, had played in the 1916 edition of the tournament. However, the 1919 championship was held in Rio de Janeiro. Brazilian sports fans had a closer look at the Uruguayan team, and many did not like what they saw. During the tournament, Brazilian newspapers attacked the Uruguayans for their inclusion of Gradín, for example, by satirizing him in cartoons.[35] Black Cariocas adopted Gradín as a favorite, even though he was a foreigner, but the Carioca media ignored them, instead asserting that black and white Brazilians agreed that black players should not participate in international contests. According to *O Imparcial*, "the black man in Brazil does not want to be black" and therefore did not believe black men should represent the nation.[36]

Regardless of their views, Gradín's Brazilian fans did not control the selection of representative teams or the organization of international contests. This was the prerogative of Brazilians like Epitácio Pessoa, the country's president and a member of the Confederação Brasileira Desportos. Under Pessoa's direction, the federal government financed the participation of the CBD team for the 1921 South American Championship on the condition that the members of the seleção be "rigorously white."[37] Like Pessoa, the middle-class and wealthy Brazilians who oversaw the country's participation in international competitions sought, as far as possible, to ensure that representative players reflected their white, patrician vision of the nation.

They recruited players like Marcos Carneiro de Mendonça, a goalkeeper who played for America and Fluminense in Rio de Janeiro, represented the city in national and international competitions, and became first-choice goalkeeper of the seleção during the 1910 decade (see fig. 2.2). Before his premature retirement in 1919, which came about because he was repelled by the social leveling that had begun to characterize Brazilian football, Marcos stood as the embodiment of the refinement and elegance Brazilian sportsmen sought to portray in international venues. Tall, handsome, well educated, and wealthy, he had a highly successful football career. He was champion of Rio de Janeiro on four occasions, while in international football, among many highlights, he represented Brazil against the Corinthians, defeated Exeter City, won the Roca Cup against Argentina in 1914, and helped lead Brazil to its first South American Championship triumph in 1919. Perhaps more importantly, as Leonardo Pereira puts it, contemporaries considered him a "true symbol of elegance." "Representative of a distinguished and healthy youth," Pereira writes, "Marcos Mendonça was, for football's defenders, the perfect image of the glory of sport in Brazil."[38]

While Marcos embodied sportsmen's ideal during the first decades of the twentieth century, there was one consistent exception to the general rule. His name was Arthur Friedenreich. Friedenreich was the son of a German father and Afro-Brazilian mother. Despite the fact that he was not "rigorously white," as early as 1912 Friedenreich was called to play in international contests. He eventually became a fixture in the representative side of São Paulo as well as the national team, for which he played as late as 1930. He was immensely skillful—without doubt one of the best Brazilian footballers of

FIGURE 3.1. Arthur Friedenreich in 1919, the year he led Brazil to victory in the South American Championship. By permission of the Club Athletico Paulistano.

his era. But it was not only Friedenreich's skill that made him acceptable to the sportsmen. In many respects, he was one of their own. He was a member of the São Paulo social and cultural elite, starting his career with Sport Club Germania, the club of his German roots, and later moving to Paulistano, one of the country's most aristocratic and exclusive institutions. Moreover, Friedenreich seems to have shared the sportsman's ethic that favored educated, wealthy Europeans. In Mário Filho's telling, which echoed the assertion *O Imparcial* had made about Afro-Brazilians in 1919, Friedenreich "had a German father, [and] did not want to be mulatto." Elite administrators and organizers accepted the image he sought to project: he was "neither white nor mulatto, colorless, above these things."[39]

Friedenreich was exactly the type of person of color traditionally accepted by Brazilian elites, many of whom rejected strict interpretations of racial determinism in favor of the promise of cultural whitening and looked to an individual's health, education, and class in judging his worth.[40] An exception could be made for Friedenreich. He was a man of color, but he possessed great athletic skill and seemed to support sportsmen's vision of Brazilian national identity. Moreover, given his success and his refined manner, he may have seemed an exemplar of Brazilian elites' insistence upon the ameliorative possibilities of social and cultural improvement, the possibilities of the regeneration of the Brazilian "race." In these early years, Brazilian sportsmen were not prepared to go further. The closer that episodes of international competition came to their particular view of what Brazil should be and how the ideal nation would interact with the world, the happier the experience, as with the Corinthians tours and the visit to "loyal" Argentina in 1914. When some aspect of the preferred ethos was violated, they leveled criticisms and stoked controversies. The rough play of Exeter City's team, the catcalls of poorer Brazilian spectators, the presence of a black player in the Uruguayan side: these were out of place in football and unacceptable in international contests.

Nationalist Internationalists

Together the administrators, coaches, players, journalists, and fans who embraced the sportsmen's ideal helped to restrict the constitution of the national side and the character of Brazil's experience of international football well into the 1920s. Sportsmen were competitive, but they were often more concerned with presenting a proper advertisement for their nation than they were with victory, one that effaced the differences between Brazil and sportsmen's selective idea of Europe. Even during this period, though, Brazilians hinted at a more competitive sense of nationalism, for example, when a boy ran onto the field and kicked one of the Corinthians and when sections of a Paulista crowd booed them. By the 1930s the cosmopolitan amity of the sportsmen was largely left behind.

One way to understand the character of this shift is to consider the evolution of Brazilian foreign affairs during the three decades after the republic's founding in 1889. When Brazilian sportsmen were cultivating a relationship with the Corinthians, Brazil was still in the track of its "English century," the period of "British preëminence in Brazil," which began even before the country obtained its political independence in 1822.[41] The Corinthians were prized friends because they were great footballers, because they were gentlemen, because they were amateurs, and also because they were English. Great Britain enjoyed extraordinary diplomatic and economic power in Brazil during its first century of independence, pressuring Brazil to abolish the slave trade, shaping Brazil's approach to the fate of Uruguay, and serving as Brazil's most important trading partner, while Britons developed Brazilian infrastructure and invested in mining, manufacturing, and agriculture. There were few major economic endeavors in Brazil in the nineteenth and early twentieth centuries in which some British actor did not take a hand.[42] British activity helped amplify Britain's considerable prestige among Brazilians, including not only sportsmen but also those interested in philosophy, science, education, and fashion.[43]

The sportsmen's understanding of international football also echoed the way in which imperial and republican statesmen approached diplomacy. Eugênio Vargas Garcia writes that republican statesmen understood international relations as interactions "among friends," and they assigned sentiments usually understood as individual and personal, such as "gratitude, regret, courtesy, envy, jealousy, and betrayal," to relationships between states. They worried about appearances and especially about Brazil's reputation among the Great Powers, whose good opinion they hoped to win. Therefore, according to Garcia, they "overvalued" symbol and ceremony, and their diplomacy was "dominated by courtesy, protocols of cordiality, florid rhetoric, form over substance, [and] speech as the standard of and basis for action."[44]

Like Brazil's diplomats, sportsmen saw football as a way to cultivate foreign friends, and they made distinctions between them, especially between Europeans and South Americans, for diplomats and sportsmen alike were

FIGURE 3.2. "Future Diplomacy," *A Leitura Para Todos*, July 1913. In the caption, the player tells the attendant at the Ministry of External Affairs, "As it has been proven that international '*foot-ballers*' contribute more to strengthening of the bonds of friendship between nations than do diplomats, I've come to offer my humble . . . feet to diplomacy!" By permission of the Archive of the National Library Foundation—Brazil.

convinced of the importance of Europe but ambivalent about their continental neighbors. Like diplomats, sportsmen approached the international arena as an opportunity to obtain recognition and prestige, for Brazil and themselves. And they adopted a very similar vocabulary, of amity, gentlemanliness, gratitude, and loyalty, heavily invested in the notion that maintaining proper etiquette was one of the most important responsibilities of the representatives of the nation.

But Brazilians also bristled at the extent of European and, especially, British power in the country, and the British century was littered with controversies, over British intervention in the slave trade, Britain's privileged commercial position, and the extent of the British presence in vital areas of the economy.[45] Officials wrung their hands, and the public complained, so much so that, at the height of the slave trade disputes in 1842, British minister Hamilton Hamilton noted an "uncompromising aversion" among Brazilians toward England.[46] The Briton emerged as a trope for the snob, the insular, and the bully, the butt of innumerable jokes in the nineteenth century, one part of a rhetoric of umbrage available to critics of European pretensions during the nineteenth century and in the twentieth, as European diplomatic, economic, and cultural influence declined and Brazilian policy, economy, and identity shifted toward the Americas.[47] When Brazilians criticized Exeter City as bullying and brutish, they employed a well-worn vocabulary for disparaging English prestige and English character.

The shift in perspective among Brazilian diplomats, from Europe to America, began before the arrival of football in Brazil, a sign of which was the republic's abrupt departure from what one historian calls the empire's "systematic opposition to inter-American initiatives" by its participation in the First International Conference of American States, held in Washington, D.C. in 1890.[48] Ultimately, the shift included the decline of British financial influence and participation in the Brazilian economy, to be replaced by the rising power of the United States and greater openness among Brazilian policymakers to cooperation with the country's neighbors. When Argentine president Julio Roca and the Baron of Rio Branco, Brazil's longtime minister of foreign relations, dedicated trophies in 1914 and 1916 for football competitions between Brazil and Argentina and Uruguay, respectively, they were promoting this shift in Brazilian diplomacy. And the diplomats found partners among the players, administrators, and fans of football. It was during the second half of the 1910s that Brazilians began to cultivate a South American football identity as venues like the South American Championship took on greater significance in Brazilian minds and Brazilians began to see similarities between their football and the football of their neighbors.

Brazilian statesmen became increasingly committed to Pan-Americanism after 1889, but the change came hesitantly because they worried about the damage Brazil's reputation might suffer if the nation were to be understood as simply another Latin American country, freighted as was the region's reputation with notions of instability, unreliability, and underdevelopment.[49] Diplomats cultivated a closer relationship with the United States as a means of lessening the possible negative impact of a turn away from their old partners. Even after the Great War, when European investment and commerce declined precipitously, they also maintained ties with European states by, for example, committing to participation in the League of Nations.

Ironically, Brazil's involvement in the League reinforced the shift from Europe to America. Already aware of the decline of European economic and diplomatic influence in Brazil and in the Americas, Brazilian statesmen had little patience for European insularity and their own lack of influence. This was highlighted when the League admitted Germany over Brazilian objections in 1926, leading to Brazil's exit two years later.[50] Brazilian football contributed to this process during the 1910s and 1920s, when Brazilians became more familiar with European football as it was rather than as they imagined it to be, and this led to a decline in the prestige of Europe and European football in Brazil.

In fact, the apogee of elite achievement—the successful European tour of the Club Athletico Paulistano in 1925—was a major turning point in Brazil's experience of international football. During the tour Paulistano's footballers achieved extraordinary success against some of Europe's best athletes, and on European soil. In Brazil their exploits were cast in national terms, and the Paulistas were treated as national heroes upon their return. Paulistano was one of Brazil's most elite, most Eurocentric sports clubs, and it mounted an unprecedented challenge to Brazilian notions of European sports supremacy. Its accomplishments also served to undermine the old elitist paradigm of Brazilian sports, proving the ordinariness of European athletes and demonstrating the emerging excellence of Brazilian players, and it contributed to Brazilians' greater openness to the idea of an American identity for Brazil.

During the first three decades of the twentieth century, Paulistano's success on the playing field was only matched by its great influence in the administration of Paulista and Brazilian football. While star players like Arthur Friedenreich and Rubens Salles brought the club championships, Antônio

Prado Júnior and Mário Cardim fought to defend amateurism and elite privilege. In the mid-1920s this was still the case, but Paulistano was becoming increasingly isolated as its friends withdrew from football and its rivals more and more frequently paid players and recruited nonwhites and other undesirables. Ultimately, Prado Júnior and his allies abandoned football, but before then, in an expression of their commitment to the old ways, in 1925 they organized a tour of Europe, the first foray of its type by a Brazilian team, and one the most significant ever undertaken by Brazilians.

Tour organizers had originally hoped to arrange matches in England, France, Switzerland, Belgium, Italy, Spain, and Portugal.[51] Paulistano could not realize those grand ambitions, but the club still played ten matches over the course of forty-three days in France, Switzerland, and Portugal. Alongside Paulistano regulars like Friedenreich, Júlio Kuntz Filho, and Bartholomeu Gugani, organizers recruited several reinforcements, including players from Flamengo in Rio de Janeiro and Ypiranga and Santos in São Paulo. Most of the players were solid members of the Brazilian middle- and upper-classes: the team included businessmen, state bureaucrats, and a number of students from leading schools, such as the American Mackenzie College, even a medical doctor and an accountant. The party also included two administrators, two sportswriters, and, in keeping with the tradition of aristocratic Brazilian football, several of the players' family members.[52]

They played against club teams, select teams representing several cities and regions, and the national teams of France, Switzerland, and Portugal. The attention these games garnered in Europe matched the importance assigned them by the club and its supporters. Thousands attended the matches, and among the spectators were Jules Rimet, the French president of the Fédération Internationale de Football Association (FIFA); Luiz Martins de Souza Dantas, the Brazilian ambassador to France; and even Pedro Henrique of Orléans-Braganza, heir to the vacated throne of Brazil. The matches garnered significant press attention in each locale, as Europeans wondered about and commented on the progress of South American football. It is also worth noting that, in a reversal that pleased Brazilians enormously, the tourists were treated as special guests, honored by formal banquets, a reception at the Université de Bordeaux, and regular champagne toasts to their football and their sportsmanship.[53]

To the surprise of many, the players performed extraordinarily well, dazzling their hosts with attractive, attacking play, and finished the tour with the impressive record of nine victories and one defeat in ten matches. European

FIGURE 3.3. Paulistano players and other club members during their voyage to France aboard the *Zeelandia*, 1925. Friedenreich is holding the guitar in the second to last row. Filó, who went on to play for Lazio and the Italian national team, is seated in the second row, holding the child. By permission of the Club Athletico Paulistano.

sportswriters said that Paulistano possessed the power of an automobile, worked with the narrow precision of a wristwatch, and, flattering the club's self-image, offered the "most beautiful example of education, candor, gentility and dignity" yet seen on European playing fields.[54] Writing after Paulistano defeated the French national side 7–2 in the tour's first match, one French commentator said the Brazilians played "the famous Latin game, which might be ours if we possessed as much technique as the visitors," and another crowned them "les rois du football," the kings of football, a name which followed the team throughout the tour and back to Brazil.[55] For these writers, and others like them in France, Switzerland, and Portugal, it seemed that the students had become the masters. They had proven themselves on European playing fields.

Echoing the cheers of expatriate Brazilians living in Europe, Paulistano's performances and results had a profound effect in Brazil. According to *O*

Estado de S. Paulo, the news of the first victory was met by great popular enthusiasm. At the grounds of the club, outside the offices of the newspaper, in the stands at a football match, in the city's cinemas, and elsewhere, upon learning the result Paulistas cheered the victory, the players, and their hosts "with clamorous joy" and "warm vivas."[56] Other victories were celebrated in a similar manner.

In fact, Brazilian interest in and responses to the tour illustrated how widely the notion extended that sportsmen from São Paulo and Rio de Janeiro were justified in claiming leadership in the organization and representation of Brazilian football. In São Paulo, the team's practices on the eve of its departure attracted large crowds and a film crew.[57] As they made their way up the Brazilian coast and into the Atlantic on board the *Zeelandia*, which flew the Paulistano flag, the travelers discovered that support for their endeavor extended far beyond the city. In Santos, Rio de Janeiro, and Salvador, local delegations met the travelers and organized parties and dances in their honor, and cheering crowds saw them off. In contrast, according to journalist Mário Vespaziano de Macedo, who accompanied the team to Europe, the mild response they received in Recife struck some as demonstrating an "unspeakable lack of civility and even a lack of patriotism," putting the more common and enthusiastic response of Brazilians in other places into relief and reminding the travelers that they were not only members of a club but Brazilians, leaving the country "in order to represent it abroad."[58] According to *O Estado de S. Paulo*, the tour was "a patriotic initiative," and the travelers accepted the role they had been assigned, for example, by carrying and distributing in Europe photographs, tracts, and films publicizing Brazil.[59]

When they returned, Brazilians treated the players as conquering heroes at each stage of their journey. For example, in Rio de Janeiro, fans boarded launches to meet the arriving ship and flooded the dockside and Rio Branco Avenue, and President Arthur Bernardes received the players at the Catete Palace. In São Paulo, dozens of sports clubs sent representatives to join city officials and thousands of fans to meet the party at the Luz train station, and the Associação de Chronistas Esportivos organized a torchlight procession to honor the "modern *bandeirantes*" of Paulistano.[60] Meanwhile, the club's headquarters received hundreds of telegrams and letters of congratulations and encouragement from other clubs, journalists, politicians, and individual citizens. Finally, the city of São Paulo erected a monument to commemorate the tour near the club's headquarters in the Jardim América neighborhood, which still stands as a reminder of the significance some contemporaries invested in it. In fact, according to President Antônio Prado Júnior, the response was so generous that it caused members temporarily to desist from their intention of withdrawing from the city football league.[61]

Of course, Brazilian pride in the tour was strengthened immensely by the excellent results obtained by Paulistano. Its victories were not Brazilians' first against European opposition, but the tour marked the first time a Brazilian team traveled to Europe to play, and, as often as not, commentators referred to the club's victories as victories for Brazil as a whole.[62] *O Estado de S. Paulo* explained that for many Brazilians the tour was about more than football:

> To glorify, with all the prestige of "kings of football," is not an expression of mere sporting enthusiasm, since, with all the importance that sport undoubtedly has with civilized people, the triumphs produced by our brave countrymen in the countries of the Old World assume a character still more significant, exposing the goodness of our land to the eyes of people perhaps distracted or indifferent or deliberately skeptical of the racial capacities of a distant and relatively ignored nation. No one will be able, in good reason and sound conscience, to dispute the moral value of the deeds performed by the young Paulistas in Europe, and it is from there that is born the splendid unity of enthusiasm that today seizes all spirits, in São Paulo, motivated by the arrival of Paulistano.[63]

The "moral value" of Paulistano's accomplishments was a well-developed theme. The tour seemed to prove the worth of the Brazilian nation, and it was especially important because it demonstrated it to a European audience. Coelho Netto confidently noted that, because of Paulistano, Europeans would finally come to know "the value of the South American colossus," while a Carioca writer said that the team's success was "a grand advertisement for our country abroad" because it left Europeans with the knowledge that "there exists on the other side of the Atlantic a great and strong country," one that was until then "almost unknown."[64] At home, Brazilians came together, unified to celebrate the deeds of their countrymen amid "unanimous popular joy," something that could not be missed in the glowing coverage of the players' exploits and the adoring receptions they received as they made their way home after the tour.[65]

The 1925 tour, then, was assigned even greater significance than past accomplishments, transcending football and sport. It was a "baptism for Brazilian youth," in the words of *O Estado de S. Paulo*, a "consecration" of

Brazilian worth, more significant because it took place in Europe.[66] In the view of many, the tour signaled that Brazilians need no longer look to Europe for leadership or instruction, at least in football. According to Rio de Janeiro's São Christovão club, Paulistano had accomplished more than win a few matches; it had proven the "incontestable superiority of Brazilian *football* over that of other nations."[67]

Perhaps even more telling, the *Jornal do Commercio* writer Benjamin Costallat took an aggressive tone as he bristled at a reference in the French press to the Paulistano footballers as "little Brazilians." The French writer was probably referring to the players' physical appearance; in addition to their generally small stature, several were quite young, no more than eighteen years old. But this is not how Costallat read the remark. Brazilians were small, he wrote, only because their country was so large. And he regarded the "little Brazilians" as superior to their French hosts:

> Little Brazilians, yes, but little Brazilians who always have more moral elegance than you; little Brazilians who will never boo a fallen adversary; little Brazilians who on the day that you come here will teach you how to practice the old obligations of hospitality; little Brazilians who will teach you many things, including how to be educated and to play 'foot-ball.' ... Thus, I agree—we are 'little Brazilians.' ... And the 'little Brazilians' will always be at your service, whenever you are disposed to be thrashed![68]

This was quite a different perspective to the affable demeanor Brazilians had displayed toward European football in years prior. Costallat called for nothing less than a radical reevaluation of the relative value of Brazilian and European sports.

The Paulistano tour was, then, a watershed event that accelerated the process away from Eurocentrism in Brazilian football. It demonstrated Brazilian football's quality in comparison to European football, and, more importantly, it eroded Eurocentric attitudes and altered discourse about the proper and the permissible in Brazilian football. That is, one of the things that Paulistano accomplished was the destabilization of its own paradigm. If Europeans were so easily and comprehensively beaten by the Paulistas, how could they be the best models and opponents for Brazil's athletes? If Brazilians, white and black, rich and poor, could demonstrate that they were as good at football as Paulistano's players, what could keep the unwanted off first-class playing fields? Why should they not represent Brazil?

This is not to say that either the tour or Brazilians' responses to it overturned the exclusivity or the selective Eurocentrism of the sportsmen. Rather, reaction to Paulistano's exploits exacerbated the tension in Brazilian football between Eurocentrism and nationalism. It seems to have taken European approval to convince many Brazilians of their countrymen's abilities, and Brazilian periodicals made sure to tell their readers about Europeans' opinions about Paulistano.[69] Brazilians had sought the approval of Europeans in measuring their own progress for a long time; the articulation of Brazilian nationalism in 1925 depended almost as much on European judgment. Moreover, while it was represented on European playing fields by Paulistano, Brazil was still identified with the old model of the wealthy, white cosmopolitan—the sportsman. Like those nationalists who modeled the 1922 Modern Art Week in São Paulo on modernism honed in France and those middle- and upper-class Latin Americans who took European cues in accepting tango, rumba, and other forms of music and dance associated with the popular classes in their own countries, the members of the Club Athletico Paulistano and their supporters imported some of their reasons for football nationalism from Europe, the same place they had found the game and their justification for playing it.[70]

Antônio Prado Júnior and Paulistano's other leaders temporarily renewed Brazilians' focus on Europe and their belief that only comparison to European sport could give Brazilians a true test of the worth of their football and their culture. But, largely in spite of themselves, they also helped alter Brazilians' attitudes toward Europe, toward international football, and toward Brazil's identity within it. They helped breed a new kind of football nationalism, one less dependent on either Brazilian sportsmen or their European peers, and one that helped usher in concrete changes, including the expansion of opportunities for working-class and nonwhite players in domestic and international contests.

South American Masters

Such changes came incrementally and unevenly during the second half of the 1920s and in the 1930s, when competition between Brazilian and foreign teams became more and more common. During these years, Brazilians played against European and South American club sides and national teams, and participated in official international tournaments, including the Roca and Rio Branco cups and the three world championship tournaments of 1930, 1934, and 1938.

Brazilians continued to pay special attention to the reality and the myth of European sport in the late-1920s and 1930s, and one important indication of shifting attitudes was a change in Brazilian opinion about British football. Although Paulistano had not been able to travel to Britain in 1925, one writer claimed that the Brazilians would have "astonished the masters of '*association*' in London itself."[71] By the end of the decade Brazilians got their opportunity to measure themselves against British players, when Motherwell, from Scotland, and Chelsea, from England, visited Brazil. As in years past, Brazilians were enthusiastic about the visit of British teams, and large crowds watched the two professional teams play in Rio de Janeiro and São Paulo.[72] The visitors failed to impress, neither winning a match on Brazilian soil. When Motherwell visited in 1928, it drew once and lost once, the latter by the embarrassing score of 5–0. A year later Chelsea lost two of its five matches, drawing the rest. Brazilians were especially "disappointed" by the Englishmen, because, according to *O Globo*, "Chelsea did not produce as lofty a game as its fame announced." Not only did Chelsea not win, not only did it not play particularly well, but, the paper said, the English team was "visibly inferior to ours."[73]

This should not have been terribly surprising since the sides fielded by the hosts were select teams including Brazil's best players, while neither Motherwell nor Chelsea figured among Britain's leading clubs at the time of their visits. However, according to British ambassador Christopher Steel, this did not stop Brazilians from overvaluing the results. Commenting on the Chelsea visit, Steel irritably reported to his superiors that spectators, playing conditions, and referees worked against the visitors and made results in favor of home sides "a foregone conclusion." With his typical dismissiveness about Brazilians, he wrote that among them "such events are not looked upon as purely 'sporting,' and are made national questions. . . . The Brazilian crowd, who are quite incapable of appreciating the situation, claim as a nation to have beaten England, and the articles in the press follow this tone, with a consequent loss of British prestige out of all proportion to the importance of the occasion." Therefore, expressing a view that was becoming increasingly common among British diplomats around the world, Steel recommended that "further such visits should be discouraged" by British authorities.[74] The Chelsea tour was the last by a British side until the Arsenal and Southampton clubs organized visits in 1948, but the performances of Motherwell and Chelsea meant a decline in Brazilian respect for British football and, according to Steel, Britain itself.

British football suffered more criticism later in 1929 and in 1930, when Brazilians learned that the Football Association had chosen not to send an English side to participate in the first world championship, held in 1930 in Uruguay. Unaffiliated with FIFA, the English body refused to participate in the first World Cup, just as it had refused to participate in football at the Olympics. The English objected to FIFA's willingness to allow professionals to participate in international football, but, even though Brazilians continued to insist on amateurism at home and abroad, they rejected English arguments. According to Thomaz Mazzoni's *A Gazeta Esportiva*, "Old Albion does not want to subject itself to a confrontation with the possibilities of a disaster." The paper asserted that the English were "still masters" of the game they had invented. What had changed was that there were no longer "disciples to learn."[75]

Especially ready to leave lessons behind were South Americans, particularly Argentines, Uruguayans, and Brazilians, who Mazzoni called "the modern masters of football."[76] Like Brazilians, Argentine and Uruguayan footballers demonstrated the excellence of their football time and again during the 1920s and 1930s. In 1925, the year of Paulistano's continental tour, two clubs from the neighboring republics staged their own visits to Europe and achieved almost as much success. The Buenos Aires club Boca Juniors won six of nine matches during a trip to Spain that, according to one historian, helped launch "Argentine sporting nationalism."[77] Montevideo's Nacional also toured Europe and preceded Paulistano to France by a few weeks. The Uruguayans also visited Spain and won four of seven matches, losing only once.[78] Among national teams, the Argentine *selección* took second place in the 1928 Olympics and in the World Cup two years later. Uruguay enjoyed a period of unrivaled success on the international stage, winning both of those tournaments and the 1924 Olympic tournament before them. Importantly, the 1924 and 1928 Olympics took place in Europe, in Paris and Amsterdam, respectively; like the Paulistano, Boca Juniors, and Nacional tours, success against Europeans in Europe only amplified the significance of these victories.

These were only a few of the many accomplishments of South American club and national teams against European opponents during the 1920s and

1930s as they consistently defeated their erstwhile teachers. The confidence stoked by such victories was deepened by Europeans' increasing admiration for South American football, which was demonstrated, for example, through their attempts to recruit Argentines, Brazilians, and Uruguayans to play in Europe as professionals. While some critics challenged the recruits' patriotism, others took pride in their accomplishments, including South Americans' contribution to Italy's 1934 World Cup victory. The editor of the *Jornal dos Sports* argued, "If the Italians or the Spaniards (victors over the English national team) come looking for reinforcements in Brazil, it is because, undoubtedly, they recognize and accept the superiority of our game." A month before he launched a nationalist attack against the football migrants from São Paulo, the editor boasted that Lazio's nickname was "Brasilazio" and that its coach, Amílcar Barbuy, was Brazilian. Surely this was evidence enough that Brazilian football had left school days behind.[79]

By 1930 Brazilians had discarded the awe they had exhibited in the past in discussing European athletes. They were willing to critique the shortcomings of their opponents, from the discipline of the Italian Torino club when it visited in 1929 to the technique of the United States national team in 1930.[80] And they were willing to call into question the sportsmanship of Englishmen and other Europeans who refused invitations to participate in the World Cup tournament.

This helps explain Brazilians' subdued response when Rio de Janeiro's Vasco da Gama became the second Brazilian team to play in Europe in 1931. Vasco da Gama visited Spain and Portugal in June and July of that year and achieved some excellent results, including a 4–2 victory over a Portuguese select team, but Brazilian commentators seem to have been largely unmoved by its success. The tour received only a fraction of the attention accorded Paulistano's travels only six years before, when the merest hint of matches in Europe caused a major stir in Brazilian football circles. There are many possible reasons for this, including social differences between Paulistano and Vasco da Gama and organizational difficulties faced by the Carioca club. It also seems that by 1931 many Brazilians had begun to think of matches and victories against Europeans as unremarkable events. Tellingly, when it came to assigning blame for the fights and disturbances that marred a few of Vasco da Gama's matches, Brazilians tempered their criticisms of the Brazilian players involved, even though some of them were Afro-Brazilians from working-class backgrounds. As Mazzoni explained in *A Gazeta*, Brazilians ought to avoid condemning the Vascaínos since, "among the majority of the foreign clubs that have visited us recently, some have comported themselves worse than has Vasco in Portugal."[81]

One consequence of Brazilians' success in international competition was their greater willingness to rethink notions of what it meant to be Brazilian on the football field. They revised their ideas about European, South American, and Brazilian football, about how to play, and about who should play—in short, they changed their view of what it meant to represent Brazil. This can be seen most clearly by examining the seleção in the second half of the 1920s and in the 1930s, when working-class, nonwhite, and other former undesirables took to the field to represent the country in increasing numbers.

A glance at the team sheets of the seleção begins to tell the story. Fewer players came from traditional aristocratic sides, such as Fluminense and Flamengo in Rio de Janeiro and Paulistano in São Paulo, and more came from smaller and more modest clubs, like the Corinthians, Palestra Itália, and Vasco da Gama. Among these, many were the children of immigrants, including the Italo-Brazilians Filó, De Maria, Del Debbio, and Serafini, who went on to play professionally in Italy. Another type was represented by Floriano Peixoto Corrêa, the former soldier. Before his fall from grace, accused of accepting bribes from opposing teams, Floriano played for the seleção several times, representative not only of Brazil but also of a changing sporting ethos in which a humble background was no longer grounds for exclusion.[82] The most obvious sign of change came when players of African descent began to represent Brazil more frequently, including on the largest stage, in the World Cup.

One of the last great obstacles to this shift—though in one sense a spur toward it—was the effect of the intense regionalism that characterized Brazil in the early twentieth century. Regional rivalry, especially between Rio de Janeiro and São Paulo, spilled over into football and plagued attempts at building "national" football and truly representative national teams. For example, though in 1916 Paulista leaders had dissolved their Federação Brasileira de Football and recognized the authority of the Rio de Janeiro–based CBD, regional tensions wrecked Brazilians' first attempt at organizing an interstate competition, called the Ioduran Cup. The competition was meant to pit the winners of the city leagues of Rio de Janeiro and São Paulo against one another, but the match was played only once, in 1918, when Paulistano defeated Fluminense 3–2 at Botafogo's ground in the capital. Fluminense expected a rematch in August 1919, after the teams won their respective championships again, but Paulistano did not participate, perhaps because the 1918 match was marred by what Fluminense called "acts of indiscipline."[83] Fluminense claimed victory and the cup on the grounds of Paulistano's alleged forfeit, but the Paulista club refused to part with the trophy, which it argued it had won permanent possession of in 1918. The argument was eventually resolved amicably, with the trophy deposited at the Ipiranga museum in São Paulo and the CBD overseeing the organization of a new interstate competition for 1920, which Paulistano won against Fluminense and a team representing Rio Grande do Sul, Grêmio Esportivo Brasil de Pelotas.

The argument between the great aristocratic sides of São Paulo and Rio de Janeiro, normally quite friendly, was worrying because it was part of a larger and longer pattern of rivalry between the two cities. For example, in 1919 Paulista and Carioca administrators argued about the organization of the seleção for that year's South American Championship, and the Paulistas threatened to refuse to allow their players to participate before they were convinced to relent by Coelho Netto and other public figures.[84] Regionalism had thus threatened to prevent Brazil's first great international triumph. The resolution of the dispute made the triumph doubly satisfying, for it meant Brazilians could cheer a team that included Fluminense's Marcos and Agostinho Fortes Filho and Paulistano's Friedenreich and Sérgio Pereira Pires. But then the Ioduran Cup controversy was followed by a match between Rio de Janeiro and São Paulo select sides in July 1920 that ended amid accusations of bad sportsmanship and rough play, with *Rio Jornal* describing the game as "Capoeira in action" because of the alleged violent tactics of the Paulistas.[85] It seemed the feud would never end.

In 1922 the CBD organized another kind of national competition, the Campeonato Brasileiro de Football (Brazilian Football Championship), the country's only national tournament before 1959. This was an elimination tournament pitting select teams representing the states of Brazil and the federal capital against one another. In spite of its national scope, the final match almost always saw Cariocas taking on Paulistas, and the tournament often ended as other competitions between the rivals had. In the final match of the 1927 edition of the tournament, regionalism brought Brazilian football to the breaking point and initiated an intensely conflicted decade.

The immediate cause of controversy in 1927 was referee Ary Amarante's decision to award a penalty to Rio de Janeiro for handball against the Paulista

Bianco. Led by Amílcar Barbuy, who was the team's captain, the Paulistas protested against the decision. Then, Amarante said, since the Paulistas refused to listen to him,

> I directed myself to the *captain* of the *team* Mr. Amílcar Balbury [*sic*], making him see that his players refused to permit [the game's restart], to which he retorted, with a certain insolence: "*The penalty-kick will not be taken.*" ... The players, then, took discourteous and indelicate attitudes, uttering base slang words.[86]

Faced with the players' intransigence, Amarante appealed first to administrators and then to civil authorities. The president of Brazil, Washington Luís, was in attendance, and he personally ordered his fellow Paulistas to continue with the match.[87] The team responded by abandoning the field, leading the match to be suspended immediately after Oswaldo Gomes had converted the penalty kick, scoring into the empty net. Rio de Janeiro won the match 2–1, and thus the championship.

Journalists in Rio de Janeiro denounced the Paulistas for their lack of discipline and sportsmanship, with *A Noite*, for example, calling their behavior "the most distressing occurrence in sports history."[88] But they were not alone. Authorities in Rio de Janeiro and in São Paulo joined in a chorus of general condemnation, and punishment came swiftly, in the form of immediate suspensions for eight players identified as troublemakers by the CBD and the APEA.[89] Santos Football Club sacked Feitiço (Luiz Mattoso) and Tuffy Nejeun for their part in the incidents, an act that *O Globo* lauded as honoring the club's "glorious traditions."[90] And the CBD expelled these two and two others, Palestra Itália's Amílcar and Pepe (Pedro Rizzetti), from Brazilian football and suspended a fifth, Corinthians' Pedro Grané, for one year.[91]

However, the Paulista players did not humbly accept these criticisms and punishments as they had not accepted Amarante's decision in the penalty incident. Feitiço is alleged to have responded to Washington Luís' order by saying, "Tell the president that he runs the country. In the Paulista seleção, we're in charge."[92] They continued to defend themselves after tempers had cooled, rejecting the idea that they were poor sportsmen in an open letter to the football public published six days after the game. They defended their actions as a logical response to what they saw as the referee's partisanship, and explained his decision as the latest in a long history of wrongs suffered by Paulista athletes at the hands of Cariocas. In their words, "All S. Paulo is familiar with the repeated injustices we have suffered on the fields of Rio." They depicted themselves as patriots who had finally reached the end of their tolerance of maltreatment and who had acted to defend their honor and the honor of the city and state they represented. They justified their rejection of Amarante's authority as an honest reflection of their own disparagement of the sportsmanship of the referee, their opponents, and tournament organizers—the same aspersion with which they found themselves confronted.[93]

Feitiço, Amílcar, and the rest of the Paulista select team were making arguments that would have been familiar to the football public, and they had reason to hope that their fellow Paulistas, at least, would come to their defense. But they were faced with an implacable and, more importantly, unified set of antagonists in the form of all of the leading administrators of regional and national football—and the president of Brazil. Their position was unsustainable if they hoped to continue to play organized football, and they therefore changed tack. A day after the publication of their "manifesto" against Carioca partisanship, they released a letter in which they began to retreat, stating that their original letter was meant to explain their actions, not to challenge the authority of football administrators. Hoping for leniency, they eventually accepted that they had misstepped and apologized for their actions.[94] Administrators did reduce the punishments they had originally decided upon; as far as they were concerned, the important point had been made: regardless of what he might like to believe, Feitiço and his teammates were not in charge of Brazilian football, even on the playing field.

When Paulista fans rioted the next month because a planned rematch of the Paulista and Carioca select teams did not take place, the cooperation of administrators from the rival cities against challenges to their authority seemed even more imperative.[95] But their cooperation did not last. The most famous example of Carioca/Paulista rivalry came in 1930, when the team Brazil sent to the first World Cup was far from representative. The CBD saw itself as the proper authority in the international arena, but the leaders of the APEA demanded a significant role in the organization of the seleção. Accusations of a lack of patriotism flew back and forth from one city to the other, ending with the Paulistas deciding to withdraw completely from participation in the project. The CBD therefore drew players almost exclusively from the capital city; it was a "Carioca representative side" and "a mediocre Carioca squad," in the words of Paulista critics, with only two players from outside the city, Poly (Policarpo Ribeiro de Oliveira), from the Americano club in Campos de Goytacazes in Rio de Janeiro state, and Santos' Araken

Patusca.[96] Moreover, despite the calls of many, the Washington Luís government refused to provide financial support for the enterprise. Regardless of its reasons for doing so, in the view of *Rio Sportivo*, the government had "prejudiced the development of our nationality, and made more difficult the diffusion of sports."[97]

Despite these difficulties, Brazilians (especially Cariocas) were excited by the prospect of the world championship, and expectations of a successful tournament were quite high. Once the tournament began, even Paulistas remained interested despite the absence of their players, with *A Gazeta* reporting on the "multitude" that gathered outside its offices to follow the opening match by telegraph.[98] In Rio de Janeiro, a massive crowd gathered to celebrate the side at its departure, representing, according to *Rio Sportivo*, "the voice of all Brazil." Fans met at the city dockside "with hearts pulsing in unison, communicating the same sentiment, driven by the same ideal: the rise of the nation."[99]

The fans' clear favorite was Fausto dos Santos, the Vasco da Gama midfielder, who was lifted on to the shoulders of the adoring crowd. He became quite emotional, telling a reporter, "I have never felt as Brazilian as I feel today." He went on, "I will take to Uruguay the memory of this manifestation, which will give me animus and resolve. . . . I will know how to fight as Brazilians have always done when they are called to defend their standard."[100] In fact, the team performed poorly when measured against expectations, defeating Bolivia but losing to Yugoslavia and failing to progress beyond the initial group stage. Commentators agreed that Fausto was the only player who played up to the new standard Brazilians demanded of their football.

And this was one of the remarkable things about the 1930 episode: while most of the team was light-skinned and well-to-do, Fausto was Afro-Brazilian and working class. He was the favorite not only of the popular classes but also of sports journalists, a group that had done so much to promote exclusivist football in the past. Following an amazed Uruguayan observer, they called him the "Maravilha Negra," the Black Marvel, and they dispensed harsh criticism to players who in the past would have received only praise. *A Gazeta* called the side "mediocre" and Fausto its "one notable player"; the less said about the rest of the team, the better.[101] *Rio Sportivo* called him "incomparable," and it was willing to address the defects of the rest of the team. According to the paper, Fausto was the leader of the team's "poor faction," players who were willing to fight for Brazil. The others, "rich" players like team captain Preguinho (João Coelho Netto), Coelho Netto's son, seemed more interested in tourism than football.¹⁰² Poly had admitted as much before the tournament began, telling the press, "I want to go to Montevideo not only to play football, but also to enjoy the delicacies of the cabarets, the tangos and the 'muchachas.'"¹⁰³ According to Fausto, once on the field, Poly and others were "fearful" in the face of opponents, dandies who lacked toughness and were not dedicated enough to give their all for Brazil. The press agreed with him. *Rio Sportivo* published his criticism under the title "Fausto Is Right!" and *A Gazeta* republished it without comment.¹⁰⁴

Fractured by regional rivalry and rent by tensions of class and race, the seleção suffered through the 1930 World Cup. In 1931 and again in 1932, however, the team won the Rio Branco Cup against world champion Uruguay. Brazil won the first match, held in Rio de Janeiro, 2–0, and the second, in Montevideo, 2–1. Defeating the world champions at their home ground was an impressive feat, and Brazilians assigned the 1932 victory great meaning. The *Jornal dos Sports* argued that "the Brazilian delegation that went to Montevideo provided a better advertisement for Brazil than all of the ambassadors and ministers that we have sent to the neighboring country."¹⁰⁵ It helped organize an enormous welcome for the returning heroes, including a delegation of one hundred members of the capital's Special Police, public speeches from sports and political leaders, a formal parade, and a meeting with Getúlio Vargas.¹⁰⁶ Thomaz Mazzoni called the team a "revelation" and its win a "miracle," Brazil's most important ever.¹⁰⁷ A decade later, Mário Filho published an entire volume on the match, in the preface of which José Lins do Rego called the victory the "biggest achievement in [Brazil's] sporting life."¹⁰⁸

Geography alone does not account for this reaction, especially given that Uruguay fielded seven of its world champions in 1931 but only four in 1932. For its part, Brazil in 1931 fielded four survivors of the World Cup, and six players from big clubs of the capital, including the captain, Botafogo's Nilo Murtinho Braga, who scored both goals. It also included three Paulistas, though not Fausto, who had signed to play professionally for Barcelona after Vasco da Gama's 1931 tour of Spain. In 1932 the seleção was an entirely Carioca side, and regional discord was only one problem the team faced. The team's preparations were thrown into disarray when several players declared a "strike," the nominal amateurs refusing to play unless administrators met their demands for better pay and other concessions, and CBD president Renato Pacheco reacted by threatening to resign.¹⁰⁹ Players and organizers reached a compromise, but the cost of the victory was high. The team's two star players, Domingos da Guia and Leônidas da Silva, who scored both goals, signed professional contracts with Montevideo teams, Nacional and Peñarol, respectively.

Commentators looked past these difficulties. What they saw in the 1932 team was proof of a new Brazilian football that succeeded because in certain ways it was more inclusive than previous versions of the seleção. Lins do Rego called it "a portrait of a social democracy, in which Paulinho, son of an important family, joined with the black Leônidas, the mulatto Oscarino, and the white Martim."[110] Even more important, they said, the team demonstrated the essential role Afro-Brazilians would play in building a better Brazil and a better Brazilian football. Mário Filho said the team was "full of blacks," and indeed no previous seleção had included as many players of African descent, as Oscarino Costa Silva, Gradim (Francisco de Souza Ferreira), and Jarbas Baptista joined Domingos and Leônidas in the side.[111] Narrating the event as a victory for Brazil's racial democracy, nationalists echoed the rhetoric of Thomaz Mazzoni, who said it "definitively consecrated" the new generation of Afro-Brazilian stars, even if several of them had only joined the seleção in 1932.[112]

Rather than diminishing the value of the victory, the controversy over the 1932 seleção seems to have made it more useful to critics who argued that Brazil's national team must be transformed to match what they believed was Brazil's authentic national identity, one embodied by Afro-Brazilian and working-class players from Rio de Janeiro. One of the effects of regional discord was that it meant the absence of Paulista players, who were mostly white and often the sons of immigrants, whose patriotism many doubted. And it meant more room for Cariocas, the best of whom in the 1930s were working-class players of color. This helped populist critics of the idea of a national team that was aristocratic, white, and cosmopolitan rebrand the seleção—and the country it represented—as the happy result of Brazil's emerging racial and social democracy and a newfound faith in the value of Afro-Brazilian culture, which they argued was most fully realized in Rio de Janeiro.[113] The seleção need not be truly representative of Brazil; what mattered was that it advertise the Brazil that organizers and media narrators, and their partners in government, hoped to portray.

The 1934 World Cup team included white and black players, both Paulistas and Cariocas, but it did not reproduce the form of the 1932 seleção—its participation was limited to a 3–1 loss to Spain in the first round. This time the controversy over the recent installation of professional football meant that the CBD could not call on all of the country's footballers, and the team it cobbled together was not well regarded. Even before it left for Italy, reporters noticed the team was very unpopular and that fans expected its "inevitable failure."[114] Still, the moment served the aims of national critics, for they used it to call for the intervention of the Vargas state so that Brazil would not be embarrassed again by the failures of insufficiently patriotic administrators.[115] They were especially willing to blame Palestra Itália and Vasco da Gama, two of the clubs that refused to release their players for the competition, allegedly because of their lack of loyalty to Brazil. Although they were not the only clubs to refuse to cooperate, the immigrant clubs suffered violent attacks by disappointed fans as Brazil's poor showing became nationalists' ammunition against their enemies.

Four years later, professional football firmly implanted and the Vargas government having enforced a measure of discipline on club and league administrators, Brazil's successful World Cup campaign seemed to prove the reformers right. The seleção defeated Poland 6–5 after extra time in the opening round. Next the Brazilians faced Czechoslovakia, drawing 1–1 at the first attempt and winning 2–1 in the match replay. They lost only at the semifinal stage, to the Italian side, in a match that many Brazilians alleged had been unfairly officiated. In their last match, the Brazilians claimed third place by defeating Sweden, 4–2. As with previous tournaments, there was controversy in 1938, as Brazilians argued over whether Flamengo's Hungarian coach Dori Kürschner should be invited to help train the team and over whether the right players were being selected.[116] Also several well-to-do players seemed more interested in sampling French night life than in working for the team, much to the chagrin of the coach, Adhemar Pimenta. At first the CBD indulged the players, but the press and the team sided with Pimenta, and the privileges of wealthy players were worn further away.[117]

Compared to previous experience, though, the problems of managing the seleção in 1938 were minor. Administrators were able to bring together a team that included white and black players, well-to-do and working-class players, players drawn from both Rio de Janeiro and São Paulo, players from big, traditional clubs and smaller ones, and even players who claimed immigrant identities, such as Niginho (Leonídio Fantoni), who had been one of those who migrated to play professionally in Italy earlier in the decade. Early pessimism gave way to confidence that Brazil was sending a strong team to the tournament and that Brazilians could expect excellent results. Many, in fact, expected Brazil to become champion. The *Jornal dos Sports* published the opinion of a variety of European sportswriters and coaches who suggested Brazil might very well be a finalist in the tournament.[118] *Sport Illustrado* confidently asserted that Brazil was "recognized as the best in the world, whether in the technique of its members or in the personal qualities of its players."[119] Even the conservative *O Estado de S. Paulo*, which had been consistently critical of the seleção in the 1930s, acknowledged that the team "did not leave a bad impression" and that it was probably Brazil's strongest possible side, a true seleção.[120]

Instead of regionalist attacks or concerns about how the players might look in tuxedoes, the tournament was accompanied by a fairly uninterrupted discourse of pride about the seleção and its football accomplishments. Commentators celebrated the nation's representatives, but they were also aggressive in challenging European sportsmanship. Indeed, in Brazil the major controversy of 1938 was over the seleção's treatment at the hands of its opponents and the referees. Both the *Jornal dos Sports* and *O Estado de S. Paulo* said that the Polish and Czechoslovak sides relied on their strength and size rather than speed, agility, or technique, and they complained bitterly about Czechoslovakia's "brutality."[121] Tournament referees shared the blame for this, Brazilians said, because they were "partisan and dishonest" and failed to protect Brazilian players from Czechoslovak violence.[122]

There was worse to come. In the semifinal match, the Swiss referee awarded Italy a penalty kick that the reigning champions converted, helping them to a one-goal victory. Brazilians claimed that the penalty was incorrectly awarded, but there were few who suggested this was simply a mistake. Instead, Brazilian players and administrators in France and fans and journalists back home drew weighty conclusions about the decision and the result, Getúlio Vargas noting that the loss produced "deep disillusionment and grief in the public spirit," as if the loss were a "national disaster."[123] Many Brazilians saw prejudice and even conspiracy in the referee's decision. The Broadway theater in Rio de Janeiro showed a film that replayed thirty-two times in succession the sequence that led to the foul call, apparently so that Cariocas could make sure of the justice of their outrage.[124]

While the Brazilian delegation lodged an official protest with FIFA, others called into question the sportsmanship, the honesty, and the integrity of individual referees and the governing body itself. Team captain Martim Mércio da Silveira, a Botafogo player, stated quite plainly that "all" European referees had set themselves "against the triumphs of South American football."[125] More charitably, *O Estado de S. Paulo* reminded its readers that

FIGURE 3.4. The front cover of *Sport Illustrado*, July 20, 1938, depicting a clash between Walter de Souza Goulart and Silvio Piola during Brazil's match against Italy the World Cup semifinal in Marseille, France, on June 16, 1938. The caption mentions Walter's "indisputable class, courage, and determination" in winning the ball. By permission of the Acervo Flu-Memória.

there was more to Brazil's defeat than the penalty decision. But it did say that "certain European elements" were guilty of an "inexplicable and unsporting envy" of Brazilian and other South American footballers and that this came out in the poor performances of tournament officials.[126] The *Jornal dos Sports* stated confidently that in a "fair competition" the Brazilians would have won the match and the tournament.[127] With anger undimmed in the following days, the paper suggested that Brazil should consider withdrawing from FIFA, perhaps immediately through a refusal to play in the third-place game.[128]

Disillusioned by "ambitious and Machiavellian Europe," many Brazilians became even more confident of the moral and technical qualities of their footballers. According to *Sport Illustrado* and *O Estado de S. Paulo*, Brazilian players' "exemplary conduct" and "sporting spirit" in the face of unfairness would stand as a lesson for their old teachers, just as their obvious technical abilities would cast a shadow on the Italians' victory.[129] In fact, regardless of their defeat by the eventual champions, the members of the seleção were treated as victors upon their return to Brazil. In *O Estado de S. Paulo*, Apoxy wrote of the "crushing victories that Brazil well deserved" but did not gain because of European jealousy.[130] In Rio de Janeiro, the *Jornal dos Sports* helped organize a massive rally to "consecrate" football's "uncrowned champions," and, in an echo of the greatest success of the 1920s, hailed the Brazilians as "the kings of *foot-ball*."[131]

An important aspect of this intense nationalism was that it helped reinforce the idea that Brazil was represented best by working-class and nonwhite players, an important facet of the football tradition that Mário Filho and other writers were promoting during the 1930s. José Lins do Rego "discovered" a passion for football because of the performances of the seleção in 1938, and Gilberto Freyre said that the tournament demonstrated the importance of Brazilian football because in it the nation's footballers offered proof that "being a Brazilian is being a mulatto."[132] Leônidas, especially, shone in the tournament, during which he shared Brazil's team captaincy with Martim. He was the tournament's leading goal scorer, netting seven, and he collected plaudits from Europeans and Brazilians alike. Europeans admitted their anxiety at facing him on the field, while at home he dominated media coverage, with enormous photographs, interviews, and stories about his accomplishments overwhelming attention to other players.[133] According to *Sport Illustrado*, Leônidas became the "idol of millions of Brazilians" during

June 1938, and he was carried in triumph at each stop along the team's long return journey to Rio de Janeiro through Brazil.¹³⁴

Leônidas was a new kind of football idol. He was black, working-class, and professional, and yet many celebrated him as the best Brazil had to offer. José Sergio Leite Lopes argues that Leônidas and other Afro-Brazilians players were "exemplary products of the transition between two different eras in the history of Brazilian football."¹³⁵ If Marcos de Mendonça exemplified the original vision of Brazilian football identity, and players like Arthur Friedenreich and Floriano Peixoto Corrêa were transitional figures, the success and participation in domestic and, especially, international football of players like Fausto dos Santos and Leônidas da Silva seemed to represent the passing of the time of white, amateur, exclusive football, and the coming of a multiracial, inclusive football, at least in the seleção.

Still, it is also important to remember, as the previous chapter demonstrated, that wealthy and well-connected white men continued to control Brazil's participation in international football. They were the administrators who selected the players, the coaches who fielded the teams, and the media figures who took the lead in defining success, so the participation of any individual player remained contingent on their good will, just as it did in the context of club football. As Mário Filho said in justifying coach Flávio Costa's decision to drop Leônidas and several other players from the seleção in 1945, "A player is only a part of a machine. The part can be replaced."¹³⁶ For Filho and Costa and the many other influential figures for whom they spoke, individuals were relatively unimportant in the international context; what mattered was Brazil.

Because it suited the purposes of competition and nationalist ideology, the ways Brazilians talked about international football changed between 1900 and 1940, as did the symbols of the nation. The celebrations of the 1938 seleção were capped by a visit with Getúlio Vargas, who made sure to have his photograph taken with Leônidas (published in the *Jornal dos Sports*), another of many examples of Vargas' awareness of football's utility. Unlike Washington Luís, Vargas provided direct financial support for the seleção throughout his tenure as part of the regime's broader policy of rationalizing football and, ultimately, taking control of football organizations. It also promoted direct contacts with the seleção, as in the case of Lourival Fontes' leadership of the delegation to the 1934 World Cup. Vargas' daughter Alzira served as "godmother" of the 1938 team.[137]

Like the regime's other interventions in Brazilian sports, these actions should be understood in the context of its attempts to manage Brazilian culture to brand Brazil with its populist, nationalist, and hierarchical vision of what the country should be. In spite of a façade of confidence and unity, however, there were serious disagreements within the Vargas coalition and in Brazil at large in the 1930s and 1940s about what it meant, and ought to mean, to be Brazilian. Culture warriors viewed the international arena as a particularly testing and consequential domain because, as Daryle Williams shows, they saw debate over what constituted "export quality" culture as an opportunity to obtain the regime's sanction for their view of Brazilianness.[138] What brought disputing camps together was their shared nationalism, as the First Republic–era shift from Europe to America intensified further, to a pursuit of an independent foreign policy.

But the regime's claims that it pursued an independent foreign policy driven principally by nationalism cannot be taken at face value. Vargas-era foreign policy was inconsistent and flexible, allowing for public insistence on independence in some moments and cultivation of friendships with Germany and the United States in others because policymakers believed that Brazil did not possess the resources or expertise to insist upon autonomy if they were to advance its industrialization. Prioritizing development, they pursued all avenues open to them—independent and interdependent, German and American—until the war closed all but the American one.[139]

Tension and conflict characterized Brazil's foreign affairs during the Vargas era. Its nationalism was palpable and influential but never as coherent as it seemed, and in its way the regime helped impress these traits on Brazil's participation in international football as well, annexing football administration, sponsoring the seleção's matches against foreigners, and endorsing a new kind of Brazilian football ambassador. Vargas, his regime, and allies like Gilberto Freyre, Thomaz Mazzoni, and Mário Filho depicted futebol as a kind of "export quality" culture in its own right, a success because it was the creation of multiethnic and socially democratic Brazil, celebrated especially for its embodiment in Afro-Brazilians like Leônidas.

The regime helped also to strengthen the hierarchies of the sport, especially through creation of the Conselho Nacional de Desportos and its patronage of the CBD, both of which reinforced the roles of the administrators of big clubs like Fluminense, Flamengo, and São Paulo. Even as they allowed and at times promoted the inclusion of socially marginalized athletes, these leaders also limited the extent of change to Brazil's experience of international football. Persistent regionalism meant the seleção continued to be drawn from a handful of clubs in Rio de Janeiro and São Paulo. Managerial roles tended to be reserved for white and light-skinned men. And, although World War II meant the breakdown of international football, Brazilians forged ever-closer links with Europe, beginning with Brazil's hosting of the first World Cup after the war.

It is clear that by the late-1930s some Brazilians had changed their attitudes about international football and had begun to change the way Brazil interacted with it. In the past sportsmen had defined success to mean honorable participation by respectable representatives, their respectability derived mainly from the color of their skins and their class status. They hoped to use football to make cordial contacts with friendly nations, aiming to advertise Brazil as modern and cosmopolitan. A more assertive and aggressive nationalism had emerged by the 1930s, and populist reformers were more expectant than their predecessors that international footballers would demonstrate the superiority of Brazilian football over foreign rivals.

Still, it is important to note that the transition began with nationalist sportsmen, exemplified in the experience of the Club Athletico Paulistano in 1925, and that populist reformers were just as concerned about the image broadcast by those who would represent Brazil as were their predecessors. Like the sportsmen, the populists of the 1930s argued that the nation's proper representatives could be identified by their color and their class, as when critics argued that the "poor faction" led by Fausto dos Santos was Brazil's true seleção in 1930. International football remained a proving ground for Brazilian worth; what changed was how Brazilians measured it.

On one hand, the consequences of this change were concrete. As organizers attempted to obtain victory, talented working-class and nonwhite players found increasing opportunities to represent their clubs, cities, and country in international competition. On the other were more pervasive consequences for Brazilians' sense of their country's place in the world. Social and geographic biases persisted and the seleção never truly became what reformers claimed it to be, socially and racially democratic and an authentic reflection of all of Brazil, but the on-field accomplishments of representative players in the 1910s, 1920s, and 1930s led many Brazilians to reevaluate the merits of foreign and national football and, through football, the country itself. They believed they saw a European football plagued by decadence and even corruption, and they became more comfortable in claiming the sport as their own and using it to proclaim Brazil's emergence as a better country, ready to take its rightful place on the world stage.

Respectability, Emotion, and Gender in Brazilian Spectatorship

In *Soccer Madness*, Janet Lever describes the lives of Brazilian football fans and the fierce loyalty and zeal that many Brazilian men, and some women, display on behalf of the teams they support. Since the book's publication in 1983, Brazilian fans' passion for football has become only more widely known, if not better understood. World Cup audiences are familiar with broadcasters' frequent depictions of Brazilian fans as a multiethnic microcosm of the country, bedecked in the yellow, blue, and green of the national side, dancing and singing as their heroes play samba soccer on the field below. In Brazil, fans play a prominent role as members of *torcidas organizadas* like the Gaviões da Fiel (Hawks of the Faithful, followers of Sport Club Corinthians Paulista) and the Raça Rubro-Negra (Red and Black Nation, supporters of the Club de Regatas do Flamengo). These organizations gather thousands of fans to cheer on their chosen teams, to defend the teams' honor in song and sometimes with fists, and to cajole administrators and players when their commitment to the cause is considered suspect. Far from seeing themselves as mere supporters of their clubs, the members of the torcidas organizadas claim a vital role in the football spectacle, in the outcome of individual matches, and in the destinies of their clubs.

It was fans' passion for and commitment to a private sports club—to which they rarely belonged—that Lever sought to explain when she interviewed dozens of Cariocas three decades ago. It is fans' passion that teams like Corinthians and Flamengo hope for and sometimes fear. It is the passion of the Brazilians who have traveled as far as away as Japan, Germany, and South Africa to make Carnival in the grandstands of World Cup stadiums that broadcasters have highlighted in telling the story of Brazilian football. Of course, Brazilians are not the only passionate fans. European football's *ultras*, fans of American college sports, and, in Latin America, Cuban baseball's debaters and the members of *barras bravas* fan clubs in Argentina, Peru, and elsewhere all display passions for the teams they love as intense, as joyful, and at times as dangerous as those of Brazilian football fans.[1]

Brazilians fans' passion for football is not unique, but it is and has been remarkable and remarked upon in part because the narrators of the futebol tradition have often linked it with depictions of Brazil as a place of festival and vibrant color, of immense size and outsized personality, of intensity and danger. The popular and often celebrated image of passionate Brazilian football fans, though, contrasts with the kind of spectatorship that Brazilian football's founders promoted. The sportsmen of the late nineteenth and early twentieth centuries rejected the idea that anything like a typically Brazilian kind of spectatorship should exist. After all, they hoped that by playing and watching football Brazilians would become more like the sportsmen's cultural heroes, especially respectable, upper-class Englishmen like the Corinthians. Moreover, they preached that proper spectatorship was measured, not passionate. Fans ought to be enthusiastic but should avoid overt displays of emotion. They should avoid partisanship, and they were to never, ever boo.

Sportsmen crafted this model on what they believed were the best examples across the Atlantic as well as on their interpretations of the ideologies of improvement in Brazil, especially the promotion of hygiene by public health officials, physical educators, and political figures. Like those who promoted public works and "hygienic" marriage, sportsmen hoped to inculcate a more measured, more rational attitude among Brazilians, who they believed too often allowed their passions to run unchecked. They often explained the failing as a result of Brazilian ethnicity, especially the influence of allegedly inherent qualities of Latin and African peoples, and, as Sueann Caulfield and others have shown, they worried especially about the consequences of Brazilian passion for the honor and morality of Brazilian women.[2] Although they were often vexed by football fans who did not conform to their rules of etiquette, sportsmen's sustained attempts to enforce those rules indicate their commitment to using football as part of a larger civilizing project.

Sportsmen thus communicated both social and cultural preferences when they talked about how fans should participate in football. While Janet Lever found that fans came from all walks of Brazilian life, and while many popular images of Brazilian fans celebrate the country's ethnic and racial diversity, early-twentieth-century sportsmen expected that true fans would be white and middle and upper class while working-class and nonwhite spectators would either follow their social betters' lead or be excluded from football grounds. And both men and women attended football matches during the early twentieth century; in fact, sportsmen sought specifically to encourage the participation of women fans. Most of Lever's informants in the 1980s were men, as were most of those she judged to be "strong" fans; knowledge of football, she argued, was vital to Brazilian men's sense of themselves as men. Lever argued that most Brazilian women were at most "weak" fans, usually drawn into the culture of football through a brother, partner, or male friend.[3]

Things have changed since the early 1980s, and more Brazilian women are involved in football as both fans and as players. The recent successes obtained by the *seleção feminina*, the women's national team, including a second-place finish at the 2007 World Cup in China, attest to that fact. Still, the typical Brazilian football fan is male, and the vast majority of those who participate in the torcidas organizadas are men. Many of the women who do participate as spectators are still assigned traditional roles of the kind that Lever described, and the Brazilian and international media often characterize them not as sports fans but as sex objects, football versions of the Carnival queens and beach beauties so often featured in popular depictions of Brazil.[4]

Brazilian sportsmen would have been horrified to encounter stereotypes of the country's football fans as intensely passionate partisans whose murky social and ethnic character is moored only to their Brazilianness and who lack the ethical tutelage of cosmopolitan social betters. And yet the stereotypical image of Brazilian football fans is deeply rooted in the football culture of the late nineteenth and early twentieth centuries. In spite of the aims of leading sportsmen, Brazilian fans refused to behave as they should. They were often fiercely partisan, passionately supporting their favorite players and clubs. They booed and cheered and even "invaded" the field of play. Elite observers tended to blame nonwhite and working-class men for such behavior, but it is clear that whites, the wealthy, and women were as likely to be passionate and partisan as were blacks, working people, and men.

Men and women; white and nonwhite; wealthy, middle class, and working class—fans became passionately involved in Brazilian football. Early on, sportsmen balked at what they understood as inappropriate ways of watching football, but if passionate fans were otherwise respectable, if they were wealthy, white, or female, administrators and commentators generally indulged their involvement in the game. In the 1920s and 1930s, writers like Mário Filho and Thomaz Mazzoni began to celebrate fans' passionate involvement and used it to cultivate the notion that Brazilians had made the game their own. Depicting Brazilian fans as integral to futebol, they encouraged them to form fan clubs, which were the forerunners of the torcidas organizadas, in which their passion could be disciplined and channeled to positive ends in support of their favorite clubs.

Such writers and the administrators who they partnered in building futebol tended to understate or ignore the crucial role of the wealthy and white women fans, the torcedoras, who were among the most celebrated of the fans of early Brazilian football and who were vital in making passion respectable in Brazilian football circles. Neither the torcedoras' wealth nor their race nor their gender matched the idea that futebol was rooted in urban, working-class, Afro-Brazilian, male culture. Nor did they fit into the vision of the Getúlio Vargas regime, which attempted to marginalize women's participation in football. Given their importance, the absence of the torcedoras from the history of Brazilian football as it is usually recounted reveals a great deal about both the choices of the inventors of futebol and Brazilian ideas about the performance of gender in the twentieth century.

Respectable Spectatorship and the Ideal

Beginning before the turn of the twentieth century, organizers and ideologues sought to train footballers to display proper etiquette and to adopt the proper playing style, the etiquette and the style drawn from what sportsmen took to be best European practices. Similarly, they attempted to train Brazilians in the kind of conduct they expected of spectators. They did not encourage spectators to be passive, attending football matches only to witness the accomplishments of athletes on the field of play. Instead, football leaders asserted that spectators helped build football in Brazil by encouraging players and by contributing financially to support club operations. Further, the presence of knowledgeable and interested fans made football matches into more than games. Matches also became social events for clubs and their members, and, more importantly, they were opportunities for community and nation building, opportunities to spread among Brazilians the modernity that sportsmen believed football embodied.

Because fans were participants in their own right, football's leaders expected them to take seriously the tasks of learning the game and of enjoying it in the proper manner. Just as athletes were expected to hone their skills and to demonstrate the moral qualities of the sportsman, so too were fans expected to learn the rules and customs of the game and to behave as sportsmen and women. Spectators ought to comport themselves, in short, as gentlemen and ladies, and football organizers attempted to provide the education, encouragement, and penalties required to create the right kind of football fans.

In 1934 the *Jornal dos Sports* printed an official statement from the Liga Carioca de Basketball that encapsulated what administrators expected of sports fans. The league called fans "important partners in sporting events," and it called on them to "show your enthusiasm, give initiative to your favorites, respect your adversaries, as all respect and admire you." Echoing statements made by many sports ideologues over the previous four decades, it emphasized the importance of fans' self-discipline, and it ended by asserting that the way fans acted reflected both on themselves and on the country as a whole. It called on fans to "show yourselves for what you are, responsible members of a vibrant, happy, enthusiastic, and well-educated people."[5]

Like the basketball league, football organizations sometimes issued their own directives concerning proper fan behavior, including formal regulations, in order to assist in educating the sports public. The directors of several clubs reminded fans of their responsibilities by mounting signs in their grandstands that read, "Booing Is Expressly Forbidden."[6] In 1907 Fluminense issued a brochure to club members, stating that "disagreeable comments" directed at players, referees, or other spectators would be punished by sacking.[7] A few years later, in 1918, Rio de Janeiro's Liga Metropolitana tried its hand at educating the football public, distributing to its clubs the advice of leading sportswriter João de Carvalho, who wrote about proper football and proper spectatorship for many years in important publications like *Vida Sportiva* and *Athletica*.[8] In a more punitive mood, in 1922 it announced plans to fine individual fans for the use of insulting language and other proscribed behaviors.[9]

For its part, the Bangú Athletic Club, the largely working-class club from the capital's northern suburbs, issued rules for fan behavior in 1920, demonstrating that, like São Paulo's Corinthians, modest clubs with pretensions to playing in the leagues of the elite were well aware that their participation depended on constantly proving their respectability to the clubs of the middle class and wealthy. Not only must the clubs' players abide by rules set down by administrators and the clubs provide facilities sportsmen expected respectable clubs to possess. So too must club members and fans look and behave as sportsmen expected them to do. Bangú informed its members that administrators would not tolerate loud or obscene speech, and that "members who are not dressed decently will not be permitted to watch first-class games."[10]

Administrators who sought to educate fans also turned to their usual, and willing, allies in the sports press for assistance. Newspapers and magazines often addressed spectator etiquette, noting missteps and making sure to compliment the public when it displayed what one writer called the "courtesy and chivalry" required of all participants at sporting events.[11] According to Stuzenegger, writing in Rio de Janeiro's *Vida Sportiva* in 1919, "composure" and "impartiality" ought to be the watchwords of the football fan.[12] Fans ought to display generosity, fairness, and discipline, demonstrating respect for their own side, the opposition, and the referee. They should recognize good play regardless of their own loyalties, applauding a bit of skill or a fine team move whether it was performed by the members of the home team or the visiting side. And they ought to avoid revealing any disappointments, never criticizing either the players or the referee. As the *Jornal dos Sports* reminded its readers in 1938, the fan "ought to be more" than a fan; he must be a "sportsman."[13]

Early commentators were often more interested in the appearance and conduct of spectators than they were any action on the playing field, as seen, for example, in a 1910 *A Notícia* report that described "the most pretty *girls* [and] the most distinguished gentlemen" who attended one match, the kind of fans who graced the grandstands of elite clubs like Paulistano and Fluminense.[14] As they were expected to do by football's ideologues, these spectators cheered on both teams, demonstrating special regard for teams visiting from other cities or from abroad. The rapturous receptions afforded to the English Corinthians in 1910 and 1913 and the two Italian teams that visited São Paulo in 1914 exemplified sportsmen's expectations of Brazilian fans' education. Similarly, when a Portuguese side visited São Paulo in 1913, fans saluted their guests with warm applause during a match against Paulistano. At its end, they took to the field to congratulate the victorious visitors and carried them in triumph to the grandstand, where they received a bronze trophy from the Brazilian minister of agriculture, Pedro de Toledo.[15]

These spectators were as much part of the spectacle and the experience of the match as the players themselves, and because of this football ideologues were also careful to make distinctions among them. On one hand, sportsmen relied on middle-class and wealthy fans to help them promote their football ethic, including its European cast, for example, by dressing in the latest European fashions, learning the English terms for the game, and even cheering in English, shouting, "Hip, hip, hurrah!" when teams took to the field.[16] On the other hand, before the first large stadiums were built in the 1910s and 1920s, working-class and nonwhite fans rarely appeared either in the grandstand or in media notices. They had to content themselves with seats on the grassy areas and hills surrounding football fields because the limited seating that was available was either too expensive for working-class budgets or reserved for club members and their guests. As clubs built larger and larger venues, working-class fans were welcomed in as paying guests, but still they had limited access to the best seats. Prices and club rules that favored members and friends made sure of that.

When working people were mentioned in the press, it was often because a writer sought to identify them as the guilty parties when some point of etiquette was breached, or to complain about what he perceived to be a lack of discipline among certain classes of sports fans. For example, when *The Times of Brazil* alleged that Brazilian fans booed the Corinthians in 1910, Brazilian writers leaped to the defense of local fans, admitting that poor and poorly educated fans might have acted improperly but insisting that Brazilian sportsmen were models of proper comportment. Later, one Paulista commentator was surprised enough that a working-class black spectator at a match in 1922 did not meet his expectations that he wrote that the fan "understood Football as well as a white person."[17]

The Vital Role of Women Fans

Even more than their expectations about how fans' class or race would affect their behavior, football's leaders in the early twentieth century demonstrated their notion of proper spectatorship by their inclusion of women in their football lives. The participation of women, especially wealthy white women, as fans and in other ways accomplished two of the sportsmen's most important goals. First, women popularized the game. In spite of the fact that few of them played, it is clear that from at least as early as the 1900 decade, women embraced football, attracting many Brazilians who might otherwise have taken no interest in the sport or questioned its respectability. Second, women's participation deepened the relationship that sportsmen hoped to cultivate between players and fans as partners in building the right kind of football, seemingly without threatening sportsmen's leading role. Women fans seemed much more reliable than potentially unruly men or working-class and nonwhite fans who might like to play the game themselves and in their own ways. They therefore provided sportsmen with an ideal group of spectators, emissaries of the chic and paragons of respectability and willing to promote the game according to sportsmen's vision. Or so the sportsmen thought.

Football and other sports clubs provided women with a number of opportunities to play sports, though they almost always discouraged women from playing football. Women never became full members of the leading football clubs, and there is little evidence that they played the game in an organized or sustained way before 1940. In that year, in response to a letter from citizen José Fuzeira to Getúlio Vargas, the regime initiated an inquiry into the activities of a handful of newly formed women's teams in the suburbs of Rio de Janeiro. Those who organized, played for, and supported teams like Casino do Realengo and Sport Club Brasileiro had little chance to build women's football before Vargas acted to formally prohibit women from playing the game as part of Decree-Law 3199 in 1941; the ban endured until 1975. It is important to emphasize that the Estado Novo did not innovate in gendering football as a masculine pastime in Brazil. Rather, it formalized a historic feature of Brazilian sport and attacked the relative novelty of women playing the game in an organized way before it could spread. In so doing, the regime reinforced the popular view that football was inappropriate for women as well as its own insistence that citizens' health choices were a government concern.[18]

There is evidence that women played football formally and informally before 1940, but it is scant. Most historians cite a June 1921 match between residents of the Cantareira and Tremembé neighborhoods of São Paulo as the first official women's game, a unique event organized to celebrate the Feast of St. Peter and considered at the time more a curiosity than the beginning of a new phase in Brazil's football history.[19] Commentators depicted other matches in a similar manner. For example, when the *Jornal dos Sports* reported on a match organized by the second-division Brasil club in Rio de

Janeiro in 1931, the paper was at once interested in the novelty, dubious of the femininity of the players, and disdainful of their awkward play.[20]

I have located two examples of more sustained efforts by women footballers in the 1920s, but these seem to have been exceptional cases. ABC Football Club, in Natal in Rio Grande do Norte, fielded a "*team* feminino" in 1920.[21] Three years later Sport Club Feminino Vasco da Gama formed in Rio de Janeiro.[22] The brief media reports that introduced the teams to the public suggest they were active and well organized, with photographs demonstrating that Vasco da Gama's players, at least, were perfectly familiar with the game. Both teams looked the part as well, with ABC's well-uniformed players wearing caps and jerseys very similar to those of their male counterparts but with skirts rather than shorts completing their attire, and the Vasco da Gama women wearing uniform black and the stocking-style caps then popular among many footballers. Some opted for long, baggy t-shirts and full, knee-length shorts while others wore long, belted dresses.

The existence of these teams is remarkable and Vasco da Gama's activity is especially interesting given that almost all of the evidence of women's football in the early twentieth century demonstrates that it was never sponsored by clubs competitive in the best men's leagues. Here, however, was a women's team officially affiliated with the 1923 champion of the Rio de Janeiro city league. One wonders whether Vasco da Gama's conflicted relationship with the big clubs of Carioca football, which seems to have been largely due to paying nonwhite players in an ostensibly amateur league, might also have owed something to its similarly provocative promotion of football among women. It is worth noting that several among these Vascaínas were women of color.

Still, in neither case is it clear that the women were part of larger efforts, and without more evidence we must assume that ABC and Vasco da Gama played intramural football rather than as part of organized leagues. It is also difficult to know how long the teams endured. It is most likely that, if they continued to play for long, these women played the sport informally, like other women of the period before 1940. Paschoal Totisone Toti Jr., for example, recalled in 1921 that in his youth he had organized "games in which our girl friends played too." He explained, "We never had enough [boys] to field a full squad, and so we did what was done all over Europe during the war; we substituted women for men."[23] Similarly, in *Sportman* magazine in 1906 another writer imagined an irate mother who could not enforce her edict that football not be played in the house. As "d[ona] Genoveva" complained, not only "Juquito" played the game; "Fifito, Dócas, Cácá, the servants, and even the girls, all took *kickes* [*sic*]."²⁴

In the gendering of sport in Brazil, though, most agreed that football was inappropriate for women. In fact, some believed that women should never play sports. For example, in a 1921 interview, the poet Helena Duarte de Azevedo stated that, although she loved sport and she and her friends were sports fans, women should not play. She argued that women who played sports were "exhibitionists" and suggested that the respectable woman's proper role was "to be intelligent, to write poetry, to write for the newspapers, to have her portrait in all the magazines, to take part in all that is chic, [and] to triumph in politics."²⁵ In a similar vein, the writer Magnolia published a broadside against feminism in the pages of *Vida Sportiva* in 1918. Ambivalent about the role of women in 1910s Brazil, the magazine also published Elza G. Do Nascimento's direct rebuttal in a succeeding issue, and in the same magazine another writer called participation in athletics "the physical obligation of the modern woman."²⁶

In spite of critical voices, this view was the more common among Brazilian commentators in first half of the twentieth century. It was perhaps best articulated by the *Revista Feminina* (1914–36), the important Paulista periodical aimed at middle-class women that promoted Catholic feminism.²⁷ The *Revista* regularly covered football and other sports and issued regular calls for Brazilian women to pursue "physical culture." This included simple stretching and exercises but also sports as well because, the magazine argued, "one cannot deny that sport, pursued rationally and without excesses, represents an optimal factor in women's physical development."²⁸ The *Revista*'s position echoed throughout Brazil. As Fluminense's *Tricolor* magazine said, "Women need *sport*!"²⁹

Like boys and men, girls and women were advised to play sports in order to improve their health. But, whereas men played sports to develop their competitive instincts and toughen themselves for the "struggle for life," ideologues believed women should have other priorities. For women, sports were important because they were potential mothers. According to *Tricolor*, "In each adolescent girl is the promise of a woman; in each woman the promise of a baby"; each woman, the magazine said, "above all other missions, has a noble mission that God has devised for her: to be a Mother!"³⁰ Others recommended sports because they would help make women beautiful, because, said *Revista Feminina*, "beauty can only coexist with health, with vigor, and with strength."³¹ Another writer asserted, "In order to be healthy, beautiful, and strong, women have the physical and moral obligation to undertake physical culture."[32] Like other aspects of the ideology of sports in Brazil, these views survived the First Republic—for example, in the *Revista Educação Physica*, which promoted women's athletics in the 1930s and 1940s by asserting that sport would make the Brazilian woman "beautiful, maternal, and feminine."[33] A feminist rationale for women's sports went almost unheard.[34]

These being her goals, the sportswoman should not pursue football because, as one 1911 newspaper article put it, "*foot-ball* was too violent for her constitution."[35] A series of pieces published by the *Revista Feminina* in the mid-1920s showed the durability of this proposition. The sport was too rough, too violent for women, since "women's organic and muscular constitution [is] more delicate than men's."[36] Citing European experts, the magazine asserted that "the majority of doctors and hygienists condemn football" and that it "ought not be allowed to become an object of interest or a sporting passion for women."[37] "Happily," the magazine reported, in Brazil women avoided "violent" sports like football, preferring instead "delicate *sports*, like tennis, dance, and Ping-Pong," which were "more moderate and more . . . feminine."[38] In short, advocates generally agreed that women should focus on their physical well-being and play sports by which they could improve personal and natal health and cultivate their appearance. They also agreed that football might very well prejudice those ends, and women should avoid it.

Women did find many ways to participate in the gendered context of early-twentieth-century Brazilian sports. Beside the activities the *Revista Feminina* mentioned, they also played field hockey, basketball, and volleyball; participated in track and field events; and swam for pleasure and in competition. It is difficult to comment more than anecdotally on these women, but it does seem that in Brazil women came to sports later than did men.[39] Writing in the mid-1910s, one English traveler noted that "until very recent years athletic exercises for girls were strictly tabooed, and those that to-day dare to take part in outdoor games are the 'anglicised' girls, or the foreigners only."[40] The writer understated Brazilian women's pursuit of sports, but he did correctly highlight the importance of immigrant communities and European influences, and Brazilians shared his hope that women would do more to tend to their physical health and take up sports.

Most women athletes pursued their interests by participating in football and other sports clubs founded and run by men. There were rare women's sports clubs, and some schools included physical education and sports for women at an early date, but the most active groups of female athletes were in the ostensibly male preserve of football clubs. Although women were denied full club membership, they enjoyed many of the privileges of membership when male family members joined certain clubs. Generally, they could not vote on club business and could not visit certain areas of the clubs. But they were invited to attend football matches and they were always present at the cultural and social events organized by the clubs, such as musical performances, parties and formal dinners, and roller skating nights. Their access to football clubs allowed them the use of facilities such as playing fields, gymnasiums, swimming pools, and tennis courts.

Though often informal, women's sports could be quite well organized, as they were at Fluminense, which became a leading venue for women's athletics. As early as 1916, the club's annual report called a newly laid field for basketball, croquet, and peteca (a Brazilian game, like badminton, in which the shuttlecock is struck with the hand instead of a racquet), the "Women's field."[41] Two years later the club opened a "women's section," which became the Department of Women's Physical Education, and which the club claimed was the first of its kind in Brazil.[42] In the beginning the department had a male director and within a short period had 175 members. They attended gymnastics and swimming classes and played volleyball and tennis.[43] The club later recruited a female director, and the department had between 121 and 214 members in the period between 1918 and 1935.[44] The most popular sport was volleyball, with as many as six teams competing in intramural tournaments.[45] Another popular activity was gymnastics, and classes drew 50 students on average in two separate calendar years in the 1930s.[46] Members also participated in track and field events and pursued other interests, such as gathering each Thursday for a sewing circle.[47]

Club photographs show that most of the members who played volleyball and others sports were young women, probably between thirteen and twenty-five years old. But, as the department secretary, Maria Luiza Fernandes, reported in 1934, membership was drawn from across the generations, and members were "girls in the care of their babysitters, young ladies, young mothers and less young grandmas, all searching for physical experiences, health, and the perfection of their figures."[48] This dedication attested to the concern for women's health among club members and their families as well as their confidence that sports were among the best means improve it. Thus, like the *Revista Feminina*, the club's *Tricolor* magazine, published in the

FIGURE 4.1. Participants in a program organized by Fluminense's Women's Department of Physical Education, 1922. By permission of the Acervo Flu-Memória.

late-1920s and early-1930s, regularly offered pieces on women's sports and "physical culture." In the view of Magdala da Gama Oliveira, "indolence" had infected Brazil's women. To cure the condition, sport was the best antidote.[49]

Fluminense claimed it was "the *club 'leader'* of South America" in terms of developing sports opportunities for women, and it is unlikely that many football clubs offered women the options available at Fluminense.[50] But most clubs seem to have made arrangements for women's participation, which helped make the clubs more than simple venues for the organization of football sides. Football clubs provided women and men opportunities to play sports like tennis, volleyball, basketball, and gymnastics, making them comprehensive sports institutions. They also became venues for entire families, with mothers and fathers, sisters and brothers, daughters and sons following relatives interested in football into the clubs to pursue their own interests. As such, football clubs provided one of the vital heterosocial spaces that Caulfield describes as having emerged in early-twentieth-century Brazil, venues that allowed respectable women to enter into a larger society, away from the colonial and imperial cloisters of home and church but still safe among family and peers.[51]

By opening their doors to women and men with various sports, social, and cultural interests, Brazilian football clubs helped make increasing numbers of women and men advocates of sport and of football. Moreover, leaders specifically welcomed women into football itself, especially as fans. As early as 1907, Paulistano's coach, John Hamilton, noticed the popularity of the game among Brazilian women and remarked upon their knowledge of the rules of the game and the avid interest they took in their clubs.[52] Club administrators recognized their enthusiasm and encouraged women's participation by providing them with free admission. While by the 1920s the price of the best seats could reach as high as six mil-réis and general admission to football grounds usually cost at least one mil-réis, women fans usually entered gratis, and middle- and upper-class women took the very best places at midfield.[53] In São Paulo in 1927 the Associação Paulista de Esportes Athleticos followed the longstanding practice of many Brazilian clubs and adopted the policy of free admission for women for all of its matches.[54] So frequent was women's attendance that the directors of the Botafogo club were convinced that the financial difficulties the club faced in 1919 owed in part to members' usual practice of attending matches accompanied by "two or more senhoras," who took expensive grandstand seats but did not pay for admission.[55] Still, the directors do not seem to have taken any particular action to curtail the practice.

Well-to-do women fans, called torcedoras, were ubiquitous in the media of the period. Some publications, such as *Revista Feminina*, *Vida Sportiva*, and *Sport Illustrado*, afforded women's sports significant attention, but it was as fans that women received the most constant and intense consideration. Before 1920 it was rare that a match report did not begin with notice of the size and character of the crowd, and many writers mentioned the torcedoras, football's "feminine element." The number of these notices and the space they were given declined over time, but they were never far from the sports pages. In the first two decades of the twentieth century, it was even common to cite the names of many of the individual women who attended matches, and these lists sometimes took more room in reports than descriptions of the games themselves. Sports periodicals and general-interest publications dedicated significant space to news about and the views of the torcedoras, especially to their opinions of individual players and to their appearance. Some even took the approach of the popular Carioca magazine *A Careta*, and dispensed with the football altogether, preferring to fill what it labeled "football" coverage with photographs of fashionable women arriving at matches (see fig. 2.4). Meanwhile, the early media ignored most male fans, usually mentioning them only in the most vague way—in estimating the size of the crowd or its collective conduct—or when their presence was remarkable, such as when a government official or diplomatic visitor attended a match.

Organizers' and journalists' commitment to the participation of women as fans was part of their larger effort to promote football and its benefits throughout Brazilian society, even if they did not encourage women to play the game themselves. As the *Diario de Notícias* suggested in 1911, promoters hoped that attendance at football matches would inspire Brazilian women to take up sports themselves, "following the example of the blonde '*misses*,'" the English, German, and other foreign women whose cultures were more encouraging of women's sports.[56] The aim here was to introduce Brazilian women to the importance of modern ideas about physical health and of their responsibilities not only to themselves and their families but to the nation, and advocates of women's sports often employed nationalist arguments.

For example, when the *Revista Feminina* reported on the activities of women rowers in Natal in 1923, it complimented them for their part in helping Brazilians "wake themselves from the lethargic sleepwalking that had characterized their bodies." These women were contributing to the "reinvigoration of the race" and participating in a "beautiful and patriotic movement," especially because by improving their physical health they would be better able to fulfill the mission of the Brazilian woman, the "mission of fecund maternity."[57] Fluminense's Oliveira made the same point later in the decade, asking, "how will we obtain the perfect citizen, if his mother, while a girl, did not strengthen herself through *sport*, conscientiously pursued?"[58] As Silvana Vilodre Goellner shows, physical educators during the 1930s and 1940s built on the connection forged by writers such as these between women's sport and national progress, focusing especially on the Brazilian woman's role as a "civic mother."[59]

The torcedoras also promoted football itself, helping to stoke the interest of their social peers and to establish the game's legitimacy. Just as striking as the amount of attention the media afforded torcedoras is writers' consistent vocabulary in describing them. Commentators tended to echo a sportswriter who said in 1907 that wealthy women fans "always" gave "a smart and elegant tone to the grandstands," and another, ten years later, who made the assertion that women fans were vital in "elevating" football matches "with all the grace and charm of our gentle countrywomen."[60] Another typical report focused on the torcedoras' fashionable clothes, "their many-colored 'toilettes'" and "their peculiar grace, which gave a 'chic' note to the brilliant sporting festival."[61] Elegance, style, grace, gentility—these terms were unfailingly applied to the torcedoras, as sportswriters made sure not only to compliment the fans' appearance but also to note that they lent their sophistication to the game itself.

These Brazilian women served the same role as the women who Warren Goldstein and Louis A. Pérez describe as having promoted the popularity of baseball in the nineteenth century in the United States and Cuba, respectively. Goldstein shows that in the United States promoters thought of women fans as especially able to attest to the game's respectability and "legitimacy." They were also "agents of control," bringing what one commentator called "their magic sway" to the task of training male ballplayers to their responsibilities as gentlemen.[62] The example of the United States convinced many Cubans of baseball's value, and Pérez writes that Cuban women played a key role as well because they "further ennobled baseball in the eyes of Cubans, who interpreted the *afición* of women for the game as yet one more confirmation of the gentility and refinement of baseball."[63]

Similarly, the middle- and upper-class white women who became the torcedoras attested to football's value during the critical years after its introduction to the country in 1894, when the game was new and its respectability uncertain. As they were the arbiters of fashion and of morality, women's attendance at matches and their zeal for the game helped make football a touchstone for what was modern and chic. Contemporaries also believed that their attendance raised the moral tone of the football event, adding their refinement to players' exertions. Their presence helped defend "the violent English game" from the critiques of those who might think it was too physically demanding for upstanding young Brazilians to play. The torcedoras were the ideal football spectators and perfect models for the rest of the football public. They were modern, fashionable, and respectable, interested, but with the proper amount of reserve, which they demonstrated by staying off the playing field.

Football organizers and the sports media also found ways for the torcedoras to compete in their own right. Following a popular Brazilian trend, football clubs and media sponsored contests that judged the most beautiful, the most dedicated, or the "queen" among torcedoras. Fluminense administered one of these competitions, a beauty contest between club torcedoras that lasted for six months in 1927 and 1928. Competitors' photographs appeared on the cover and in the pages of the club magazine, which also provided pen portraits of the candidates, with jewelry and other prizes for those receiving the most votes from readers. The winner, Zilda Faria, had already won contests as the "Princess of Fluminense F.C." and the "Queen of the Torcedoras" in a competition between women representing all of the capital's leading clubs (see fig. 4.2).[64] Paulistano organized a similar contest in 1928, won by Maria Prado Aranha, a member of the ruling Prado family, who received a gold brooch and the title "Queen of Paulistano."[65] Contests were also administered by other clubs and by sports magazines, such as Rio de Janeiro's *Sport Illustrado*, which in 1928 ran a contest to discover Flamengo's most devoted torcedora.[66]

Despite a rhetoric of meritocracy, these contests defined an ideal torcedora who reflected the social preferences of sports leaders quite closely.[67] The great majority of the contestants and all of the winners were middle class or wealthy and white, with modern tastes but without the more threatening traits of modernity. The contests rarely gave voters more information than the woman's place of birth and generic statements about her beauty, her intelligence, and her love for her club, establishing the ideal torcedora as a reflection of the selective modernity preferred by the sportsmen. Such contests and the media focus on torcedoras' appearance affirmed the gendered roles assigned to men as players and women as the audience that witnessed their exploits. The fact that torcedoras were sometimes called club "mascots" reinforces the fact that women not the leading actors of Brazilian football.[68] As Anatol Rosenfeld has written, the presence of well-to-do young torcedoras, "the flower of feminine youth," allowed male players "a kind of physical rhetoric, incomparably more effective to the exploration of their masculinity than a verbal one."[69]

Alongside other reasons, courting and the performance of heterosexual gender roles also contributed to sportsmen's eagerness to welcome certain women into football, and the connection between football and courting (along with football and war, and football and citizenship, and football and work) was a consistent feature of sports discourse in the early twentieth century. This included the use of football as a metaphor for romance and vice versa, and the privileging of football as a site for the pursuit of romantic interests. Most commentators seem to have been sympathetic to the connection, though some were certainly annoyed. Unimpressed with the credentials of

FIGURE 4.2. The front cover of *Tricolor*, featuring Zilda Faria, winner of Fluminense's contest to find the "queen" of its torcedoras, February 1928. By permission of the Acervo Flu-Memória.

sportswomen, the editor of the new *A Cigarra Sportiva* stated in 1917 that his periodical would not report on the torcedoras. He argued that many women fans did not "love *sport* for *sport's* sake. What they like are the boys who play *sport*."[70] Another Paulista, A. G. Filho, recalled in 1928 that ulterior motives for attending football matches in the early years were just as likely to belong to young men, who attended matches not because they were particularly interested in football but because they were attracted by the presence of the torcedoras.[71]

Literature and the arts were especially active in developing the connection between football and romance and in incorporating the torcedoras into football. Demonstrating the mutual affection of football and arts enthusiasts, clubs hosted literary readings and theater evenings; artists played the game, as when the Escola de Bellas Artes fielded a team in Rio de Janeiro's Campeonato Academico; and football enjoyed the intense support of prominent intellectuals and writers like Olavo Bilac and Coelho Netto. The *Jornal do Theatro e Sport* was purposeful in pairing arts and athletic interests, and other sports periodicals regularly published stories and poems that built the connection between football and romance: romance, like football, was a competition, players were lovers, and a love match was a goal scored or a game won.[72]

Such saccharine discourse is especially apparent, for example, in a handful of plays from 1920s. The federal police of Rio de Janeiro required that playwrights submit their works for approval of the public censor before they could be enacted on Carioca stages, and Brazil's National Archives preserve many of these plays, which probably would not have been preserved if the decision had been made based only on their literary merits. A number of these plays forged the football–romance relationship, with titles such as "Off-Side," "FLÁ-FLU!" "As Torcedoras," and "America 'Versus' Fluminense."[73]

In 1925's "FLÁ-FLU!" Cupid informs the Three Graces that in modern Brazil the game of love is played not with arrows but with "*shoots*," that is, shots. Faced with their confusion, he explains, "It's the game of kicks / To a leather ball!" The god and goddesses go on to promote a love match between a young Brazilian woman and a young Englishman in spite of the tensions that sprang from their being supporters of the title's rivals Flamengo and Fluminense.[74] Similarly, in "America 'Versus' Fluminense," from 1928, young lovers come together in spite of their families' opposing loyalties. The match is forged among those who love "the beautiful British *sport*," "in which it is valor that earns victory." Love is a game to win, and, because the lovers belong to the right clubs—the chic and well-heeled America and Fluminense, both of which were, impossibly, "always invincible," in the words of the play—it is not surprising that love achieves its victory.[75]

The theme is most fully developed in "As Torcedoras," a 1927 play by Luiz Iglesias and M. Paradella. The play begins with an oration by two older women about their love of football:

> What a pretty day
> To go enjoy
> A hard-fought *foot-ball match*!
> The ball comes here
> The ball goes there . . .
> It makes us tremble, tremble with excitement!
> What a great feeling!
> And so, cheer
> Cheer! . . .
>
> We only think of cheering
> Until the sun goes down!
> FOOT-BALL!

For the playwrights, much of the attraction of the game was the emotion it stoked. Their torcedoras were taken with passion for the game. Taken, too, by both football and love, were the play's protagonists, Margarida and her sister Rosa. As Margarida insists to her father as she asks for permission to attend a match, "If you only knew how much I like to see those dandies messing around with the ball . . . I'm so happy when I go to watch *foot-ball*!"

The play's action develops around the insistence of the women's stepmother, Regina, that they will not attend the match, especially not in the company of two sportsmen, Bibino and Marzullo. As is the pattern in these plays, the young people come together through their shared love of football, aided in this instance by the trickster servant Marvino, and, after a series of struggles, they realize their aspirations in love and football. Marvino informs the women's father, Mauricio, that finally winning over their mother was like "playing *foot-ball* here in the house," with the result, "one to zero against Dona Regina!" As in the other plays, in "As Torcedoras" the young triumph over the old, modernity triumphs over tradition, and football is articulated as a respectable pastime for all Brazilians. As Eriberto José Lessa de Moura points out, the play demonstrates that the authors were aware that "for women football was neither an unknown sport nor strange to their world of leisure."[76]

Like much of the evidence of women's roles in First Republic football, these plays were produced by men. But there is evidence of the voices of sportswomen and the torcedoras. For example, several popular sports publications provided torcedoras venues to share their views, printing interviews with individual fans as well as messages from fans to their favorite players and teams.

These women were intensely interested in football as a sport and as a culture, and they helped to cultivate the connection between football and courting. *Sport Illustrado* carried a regular section, "Messages," in which torcedoras placed personal advertisements and messages for players and other men they had seen or met at football events. "Indiscreet" counseled Jullien to take care; he risked losing the interest of a possible admirer because "she is not happy about some of the news she's received about you." "The girl on 19th Street" encouraged the player Dino to learn to dance, the better to "to score ... the heart of the queen of the white-and-black fans [i.e., fans of Botafogo]." "Scorned" sent in to complain to Fluminense's Mano for not taking her telephone calls at work, while "A.C." wanted Botafogo's Leite to know that they would have the opportunity to "dance the night away" at the club's next party because "the other girl's not going."[77] Elsewhere, *Vida Sportiva* published a series of "Secrets," questionnaires wherein fans identified their favorite teams and interests and often alluded to their attraction to particular players.[78] And the social columnist Tá Visto, writing in *O Imparcial*, delivered a message on behalf of the capital's torcedoras, who asked that the city's sportsmen begin to wear lapel pins identifying the teams they supported, for many women were annoyed that they often found themselves flirting with men who belonged to the wrong clubs.[79]

Another woman to connect football to romance was Anna Amélia Queiroz, the well-known poet and feminist activist. In such poems as "A Medalha" and "O Salto," she alluded to the importance of football in building her relationship with her husband, Marcos de Mendonça, the model sportsman and one of the country's first sports idols. In Queiroz' poems, he was the protagonist, a "Greek warrior" whose football victory won him both sports glory and the heart of his muse:

Now I watch over your laurel with care,
Laying it close to my pulsating breast.
In it lies a conquered heart, which loves its conqueror.

So strong and bold, you won it in the contest,
Won it by force of will, and set it at my feet,
All to exalt the victory of love.[80]

Queiroz' poems, like the messages of "Indiscreet" and the others, reinforced the notion of the male athlete as the central actor in the world of sports. The laurel is the victor's, who is "strong and bold," while the speaker's heart is "conquered," and she is relegated to a passive role in the grandstand. This interpretation certainly resonates with Susan K. Besse's estimation of the limitations of Queiroz' feminism.[81]

However, it might also be said that the *player* was the muse and the object of the narrator's gaze, and that she was like Margarida in "As Torcedoras," who was so interested in watching the "dandies" on the football field. In a similar vein, a torcedora told *Sport Illustrado* about the various footballers she had loved, calling them "a volume of poems" she had collected, and "Mademoiselle Ventoinha [Weathervane]" reported to *Tricolor* about her interest in not one but four Fluminense players.[82] In the end, Ventoinha asserted that her romantic interests might waver but her real passion was not for any one player. It was for the sport itself, and, especially, "the glorious Fluminense."[83]

Pitch Invasions and Other Transgressions

Anna Amélia Queiroz, Margarida, Ventoinha, and other torcedoras personified the kind of spectatorship that the sportsmen hoped to cultivate among Brazilian football fans. Ideally, fans would dress well. They would speak properly and, when speaking about football, use English terms. They would become intensely interested in a club they would call their own, helping to promote and build Brazilian football as a sport and as more than a game. They would do all this while acknowledging the contributions of rival teams and the referee, and while allowing patrician male players the protagonists' roles.

However, spectators in Brazil did not always dress, speak, or cheer as sportsmen hoped they would. Instead, many among them dressed modestly and spoke only Portuguese, which is unsurprising given that Brazilian football could count only small minorities who personified the refined image preferred by elite organizers and ideologues. More disturbing, fans displayed intense partisanship, booed the opposing team, harried match officials, and even entered the playing area, sometimes violently. At times critics' attempts to train Brazilian fans in the proper ways to enjoy football matches seemed destined to fail, and calls for better behavior became more and more common over the years, as did more punitive measures designed to discipline fans.

There were many early indications that Brazilian fans did not accept the composed and secondary role sportsmen assigned them. The highlight of the 1903 São Paulo season was the August match between perennial champion São Paulo Athletic and the public's clear favorite, Paulistano. According to *O Estado de S. Paulo*, the "enormous" size of the crowd was matched only by its anxiety. And although, in the view of the paper, São Paulo Athletic merited its victory and the crowd's esteem, applause was generally not forthcoming. Instead, because the "multitude, almost completely and with limited exceptions, was fanatical for Paulistano," the "spectators' exit resembled a funeral cortège."[84] In other instances, fans were more assertive, such as when in 1907 a Botafogo supporter was heard to allege, "Even if Botafogo were to win the Championship, Fluminense would find a way to *rob* us of the trophy."[85] Also in 1907 the directors of Bangú had to remind the members of their club that better comportment was expected of them than they had lately displayed, for "families ought to be able to watch these *matches* without fear of hearing obscene or disagreeable remarks."[86] Ten years later, spectators palpably angry with the work of the referee in a match between Paulistano and Palmeiras in November 1917 shouted that he was a "thieving official" who had "robbed" Palmeiras in his favoritism for Paulistano.[87] In the view of their critics, all of these fans had forgotten themselves, forgotten the discipline expected of sportsmen.

While their would-be teachers held to the notion articulated by *O Imparcial* in 1921, that "Sport educates the soul and the spirit," many fans allowed their passions to rule, attending matches not because they wanted to see an edifying example of sporting and disciplined competition but simply because they wanted to see their team win.[88] Administrators demanded that fans accept that their role was important but that it was conditional and limited. Brazilian fans refused the lesson, and many took steps to become even more involved in the game.

Supporters unhappy with a referee's decision or the course of a match encroached on the touchlines and even "invaded" the pitch to confront the official or one of the athletes. The boy who ran onto the field and kicked one of the Corinthians during the team's 1910 tour was only one of many examples. The Englishmen remembered the incident as a picturesque example of Brazilians' passion for the game, but it was not an isolated one. For example, the writer Coelho Netto, who did much to legitimize football in Brazil and to articulate the tenets of the sportsman's ideal, was purported to have been the first spectator guilty of intervening in a match to complain to the referee about his decisions. That was in 1916.[89] Many sportsmen hoped that Brazilians would follow the example of Coelho Netto, whom they depicted as the country's leading fan and as a model of proper sportsmanship. In this manner, at least, many did. Writing, ironically enough, in Coelho Netto's own *Athletica*, one critic noted,

> These pitch invaders are known and named. They are of every class, every color, every shade: from the most elegant gentleman to the clumsiest bungler; from the most influential politician to the worthless ignoramus; from the most refined litterateur to the thickest illiterate; from the most belligerent rioter to the most coy *nolli me tangere* of the dandies; the most eager boys and fathers of the most respectable families.[90]

As was the case with Coelho Netto, many pitch invasions began with problems involving the match official, "a victim" who "invariably suffers attacks from all sides," according to *O Imparcial*.[91] In a 1920 match between Rio de Janeiro and São Paulo, the capital's Englishman, Harry Welfare, was injured while attempting to protect referee Carlos Santos from the aggression of Paulista supporters.[92] In an April 1931 match between the Fluminense and Brasil clubs, disagreements between the players and referee Moacyr Cravo became a general melee when spectators upset the barrier between themselves and the field. Neither club directors nor the police officers on duty at the match were able to calm the crowd, despite the latter's use of horses and swords. The match was suspended in an environment one reporter described as "hell," in which at least one player was struck in the head with a rock and several others were injured, and the referee was escorted off the field for his own protection. Unfortunately for Cravo, commentators in both *A Noite* and the *Jornal do Commercio* blamed him exclusively for the actions of the spectators.[93]

At other times, fans were more interested in confronting members of one of the sides. For example, at the conclusion of an August 1913 match, supporters of the Botafogo club tried to assault members of the Paysandú team; they were hindered, according to a reporter, only by the intervention of the members and directors of their own club.[94] In 1922 supporters of both Portuguesa-Mackenzie and Paulistano invaded the pitch in order to participate in a fight between the two sets of players. The fight began when Canhoto (João Pereira de Castro) of Portuguesa-Mackenzie kicked out at Paulistano's Formiga (Afrodisio Camargo Xavier). Before the referee could react, the Paulistano players were beating Canhoto, and fans of both sides joined the fight. Police intervention brought the fight to an end after fifteen minutes and the match resumed. Paulistano won, 2–0.[95]

Such incidents became more and more common as the years passed, and many matches were abandoned early because of fan intervention. Organizers took measures to counter the problem by appealing to the sportsmanship of the public, by raising higher and more solid barriers around playing fields, and by hiring police officers to maintain order. But they do not seem to have been able to discipline the football public to their satisfaction. "Exalted" fans continued to invade the field of play and, when unable to do so, followed referees and players into locker rooms or fought among themselves in the stands. For example, a match between the Carioca and Bonsuccesso teams ended with soldiers who were fans of Carioca following referee Waldemar Alves into Carioca's clubhouse and attempting to break down the door to the changing room. When one of the police officers assigned to protect Alves drew his pistol, one of the soldiers drew his saber and had to be disarmed. The referee was unharmed, but members of the visiting club were assaulted and injured when their changing room was overrun, and calm was restored only after members of the 3rd Infantry Regiment arrived on the scene.[96] While this was an extreme case, disorder and violence among fans was a regular feature of Brazilian football in the period from the late-1910s through the 1930s. Writing in 1918, one commentator complained that it was "rare" that football matches did not conclude with some form of "physical aggression" by fans, and injuries to spectators became common.[97]

Many sportsmen and journalists blamed working-class spectators for these problems although, as the *Athletica* writer quoted above said, they were not the only ones to blame. The difficulty of maintaining proper and sportsmanlike behavior was apparent just as well among the fans of big clubs like Fluminense and Paulistano, which struggled to discipline their own

FIGURE 4.3. Torcedores at a match between Fluminense and São Christovão de Futebol e Regatas, July 4, 1926. Note the presence of security personnel on the sideline. By permission of the Acervo Flu-Memória.

members. As early as 1907 Fluminense's directors were citing "some members' unacceptable behavior" and threatening to expel any member who insulted players, referees, linesmen, or other spectators.[98] This did not work.

According to a 1918 edition of the capital's *Vida Sportiva*, the problem was not that spectators did not know what was expected of them. The magazine said that "the majority of '*sportmen*' are familiar with this advice, and they don't follow it simply because they do not want to, and because they lack the sporting education necessary to calmly watch their favorite club lose or suffer difficulties."[99] The sports editor of *O Imparcial* agreed and refined the point further in 1921. He wrote that it was not usually the general public that caused trouble at football matches. Rather, it was "the '*clubmen*,' those passionate ones who think themselves knowledgeable of the game and who talk, shout, argue, and insult, disrespectful of the rest of the crowd and of the '*referee*.'" These fans "ought to be setting the example," giving lessons in good sportsmanship to other spectators, but they failed to do so, their partisanship and their emotion overcoming their knowledge of the ethics of the game.[100]

Sportsmen knew their responsibilities; they could hardly miss all of the many lessons aimed in their direction by writers and administrators. They simply chose to ignore them, and they were just as often indulged as disciplined, as long as they were the right color and members of the right class or the right club. The challenges faced by the Botafogo club during the 1910 decade illustrate the problem and demonstrate that some of these challenges were created as much by the clubs' own actions as by their members' missteps. During one match in mid-1913, two club members, Carlos Martins da Rocha and José Ribas, became involved in a fistfight with another spectator. Club directors at first severely reprimanded the two, but the punishments were afterward rescinded when the directors became convinced that the men had not initiated the assault and when the club received news that their antagonist had been arrested for his part in the scuffle. However, the next year the two men again troubled the directors and were, along with two other members, formally ousted from the club for unsportsmanlike behavior, what the directors called problems of "comportment."

Still, many refused to accept the possibility that wealthy white sportsmen could violate the sportsman's code without provocation, and clubs also made exceptions for their members when they did create trouble. So it was that Martins da Rocha continued to play for Botafogo's second team even after the directorate decided to expel him from the club in May 1914. This was probably due to the fact that he was brother to Pedro and Luiz Martins da Rocha, "whose services to the club," according to directors, "were not abundantly known, [or,] that is, recognized." Carlos Martins da Rocha seems to have escaped punishment because club directors did not wish to irritate his brothers, one of whom (Luiz) was an accomplished player.[101]

Club documents show that Botafogo continued to encounter problems in the ensuing years, ranging from fights between members and other spectators to the inability of club officers to collect admission from up to two thousand spectators who pushed their way into the ground to watch a match between the club team and Fluminense in 1919.[102] There is little doubt that some among these two thousand fit the idealized image of the sportsman, and Botafogo was only one of the many clubs that faced indiscipline from their own members, few of whom were ever really punished.

The career of Carlos Martins da Rocha attests to this. Despite his past offenses, he had become a club director by the time of a melee between supporters of Fluminense and Botafogo in August 1917. A majority of directors believed club members were responsible and ought to be punished for "attacks not only against the 'referee' but also against other people, the members of other Clubs." Martins da Rocha disagreed, and said the Botafoguenses should not be punished. In his view, the members of other clubs acted as badly as, "or even worse," than the members of Botafogo, "without having been subjected to punitive measures by their Directorates." Martins da Rocha could not convince his fellow directors to refrain completely from punishment, and one member was suspended for two games and another was censured for their parts in the Fluminense incident. Still, the punishments seem light and narrowly targeted for a series of offenses that motivated a special meeting of the club directorate and that club president Miguel de Pino Machado referred to as "lamentable and grave incidents."[103] In fact, Martins da Rocha's influence at the club only grew until, in 1948, he became club president, a far different outcome than had been imagined by the directors who had voted to expel him thirty-four years earlier.

Passionate, "Brazilian" Spectatorship

It is little wonder, then, that football's administrators and promoters sought out certain women to participate in their clubs and their game. The social engineers of the early twentieth century were particularly dedicated to teaching Brazilians to practice reserve and to resist their passions, an education they believed was especially important in Brazil, which was so fraught with obstacles of race, climate, and history. These engineers—legal theorists and prosecutors, writers and intellectuals, doctors and hygienists—carved out a special role for women, whose dangerous sexuality must be bridled but whose good example, once their passions were checked, could also guide men toward a gracious reserve. As Besse writes, "Women were expected to cultivate an outward appearance of modern sophistication while carefully preserving the 'eternal' female qualities of modesty and simplicity."[104] Resisting the corruptions of modern life, such as seeking their own independence and new temptations to moral vice, Brazilian women would help the country to realize its modern destiny. They had positivist jurists, conservative feminists, and other self-appointed teachers to help them become the kind of women Brazil required.

The torcedora, the genteel representative of football's "feminine element," was an iteration of this ideal modern woman, and there was no doubt that her example was needed in the football grandstands of Brazil. The sport's leaders hoped her participation would do more than attract new fans and stamp the sport as chic and cosmopolitan. They also hoped that it would attest to football's respectability and guide fans toward what they defined as the proper etiquette for spectators. The torcedora defined that etiquette as well as any could, for her dress, class, race, and comportment modeled sportsmen's notions of what football spectatorship should be. That she accepted a secondary role to her male social peers only reinforced that she represented the kind of Brazil the sportsmen and many other middle- and upper-class Brazilians hoped to create.

But the torcedoras were themselves passionate about football, and they did not accept every aspect of the roles assigned them. They might not fight or intervene directly by staging pitch invasions, but like many other football fans the torcedoras saw themselves as active participants in football, and they felt directly tied to the action on the field. For example, one fan told *Vida Sportiva* about her experience at an especially important match in 1919, when she and her friends were overtaken with the impulse "to cheer passionately, raising our arms up, yelling, frantically gesticulating." Upon leaving the ground, she said, "I noticed that I had lost my hat, my gloves, my fan, and everything else that I was carrying."[105] The writer Lellis Vieira described other well-dressed torcedoras who seemed to forget themselves at a 1920 match between Paulistano and Palestra Itália, reporting that one of them was so nervous that she bit through her fingernails until she was bleeding and required medical assistance. Another was so tied up in the action on the field that in the most tense moments "she contorted her body like a human cobra, and her movements were such that her corset burst open and her elegance was transformed into a doughy mess."[106] In 1928 a torcedora told Fluminense's club magazine that she rejected the idea that she should be reserved and that she engrossed herself in the football experience. When she attended a Fluminense match, she cheered "with all my soul, full of passion, joining a thousand and more shouts in the same triumphant song of praise!"[107]

Whatever football leaders and their counterparts in law and medicine hoped, these women did not check their passions when they entered the grandstands. Rather, the torcedoras embodied some of the fears traditionalists articulated about football, about modernity, and especially about the modern woman. Moreover, football seemed to affect Brazilian men in a similar manner, as is suggested by the cartoonist Leite's depiction of the typical fan in *Sport Illustrado* in 1922. For Leite, the torcedor was a respectable gentleman in a suit and hat, carrying a cane, who was transformed during the match into a tousled mess with a mismatched suit, a ripped jacket, tie and collar on the ground, hair standing straight on end, legs twisted together, carrying in one hand a club and in the other a pistol.[108] According to Vieira, all of these torcedores were suffering from "the neurosis, the collective insanity, the generalized degeneration" of football as it came to be experienced in Brazil during the twentieth century.[109] At best, this might lead to picturesquely disheveled spectators; at worst, respectable men and women mixed with the "thousand and more" fans Fluminense's torcedora mentioned, and violence and injury could ensue, ruining the game and destroying the deep meaning of the sport.

Organizers and commentators never stopped worrying about fan discord and violence, never tired of trying to convince spectators of the importance of good sportsmanship and self-discipline. However, beginning in the 1910s a few also began to accept the partisanship and passion of Brazilian football fans, depicting passion as defining a Brazilian way of football spectatorship, one that was intensely, directly active in helping to construct the particular culture of the game in Brazil. Fans expressed their enthusiasm in a variety of ways, from screaming themselves hoarse to invading the pitch. What they shared was that they took their lessons in good sportsmanship literally, and they saw themselves as important participants in making Brazilian football. For many fans and for commentators who grudgingly came to indulge, if not accept, their behavior, football spectatorship came to mean fans who were thoroughly involved in the game.

One mark of Brazilians' acceptance of passion among football fans was that, beginning in the 1910s, they began calling male and female fans "torcedores" and "torcedoras." This was one of the earliest examples of Brazilians' nationalization of football language.[110] The term is rooted in the verb "*torcer*," "to twist," and suggests the emotional contortions to which spectators subjected themselves in supporting their chosen sides. An individual fan was a "twisted one." The fans together were "twisted"—the torcida, contorted by their collective passion. Leite's depiction of the typical Brazilian fan, with his legs twisted together, gives a good sense of the idea. Even more distorted was the "torcedor" who witnessed nine goals at Palestra Itália's Antarctica stadium in São Paulo in 1920; a cartoonist in *S. Paulo Illustrado* depicted him as twisted nine times, from feet to neck, once for each goal.[111] These torcedores were not admirers or even fanatics but intimately connected to the play itself, physically involved in the football spectacle.

The involvement of passionate and partisan torcedoras, the welcome organizers extended to them, and their positive depiction in the sports press were crucial to changing Brazilian attitudes about football spectatorship. This is not to say that the participation of women fans made football a feminist space. Their participation always remained limited, and middle-class and wealthy sportsmen thought of their clubs as safe places where young, well-to-do women could indulge their passions under the protection of their families and other self-appointed guardians.[112] And much of the discourse on the passionate torcedora was patronizing and sexist, as male journalists fetishized women fans' partisanship: "expressive little shouts," a kiss promised an opposing goalkeeper should he agree to allow the home team to score, and a "satanically beautiful woman" joining one who was "as pure as a goddess" as they cheered on their teams were often framed as little more than charming examples of women fans' excitement.[113]

Still, football organizations and the sports press paid close attention to these women and acknowledged and even cultivated their passions. Administrators invited them to matches, editors afforded them space in the sports press, and playwrights like Iglesias and Paradella depicted them on stage. They depicted the torcedoras as intensely passionate and partisan, and often uninhibited, and almost always did so in an approving way. Further, even though their approval came freighted with condescension, it also came with the assertion that the torcedoras were as important to football as were the players themselves, as Ivan Ney suggested in a poem published in the short-lived *O Football* in 1914. He wrote,

> It's chic and it's elegant
> It's smart, and it's the best,
> To giggle, and almost faint . . .
> All for a game of *football*!
>
> She's blushing, how charming
> To hear her clapping her hands.
> Our delight so much,
> We've an unconscious glow.

We make perfect passes
We play with such zeal,
When her eyes, so brazen
With ardor drive us on!

In the midst of the struggle, how fine!
How matchless that delirium!
Look at her, so hoarse, she's crying out
To push us on, to win!

And the whole *TEAM* is stirred
By its chance to earn
The passionate praise
Of a watchful lady . . .

Hearts are beating,
Thousands of cries and much distress,
While some are dribbling
Others tumble down.

It's chic and it's elegant
It's smart and it's the best,
To bite and chew your lip . . .
At a *match* of *football*![114]

Football and its fans were elegant and chic, but because fans were fully part of the game, Ney said, they were also passionate and involved and could not be expected to maintain their reserve.

When they were given the chance to speak for themselves, women fans demonstrated their partisanship and their commitment to the sport. In *Vida Sportiva*'s "Secrets" series, women fans asserted their allegiances, voiced hostilities, and announced themselves as true torcedoras. "Mlle. Lyzette" told the periodical that her "characteristic passion" was "to love the glorious Botafogo," while her "principal defect" was an inability to "tolerate the 'dandies' of Fluminense." For her part, "Mlle. Jessy" said that it was not cheering for her team, Flamengo, that she most enjoyed but rather rooting against its main rival, and that her dream was "to see Fluminense lose the 1920 championship."[115]

In *Careta*, a fan of Fluminense returned the sentiment, indicating in a few exchanges with the magazine her intense commitment to "her" club.

—Miss, what is your principal character trait?
—That I am a great torcedora for Fluminense.
—And what is your dominant passion?
—Foot-ball.
—What traits do you prefer in men?
—Sporting ones.
—And what do you prefer in women?
—That they be passionate for their Club.
—What is your principal quality?
—That I am partisan.
—What is your principal defect?
—That I am the adversary to any *team* other than my Club.
—What is your preferred occupation?
—Fluminense.
—And your dream of happiness?
—Beating Flamengo.
—What would you count the worst misfortune?
—Watching Fluminense lose.
—What would you like to have been?
—A man, to defend my Club's standard.
—How would you like to die?
—For Fluminense, on a day of victory.
—What wrongs merit your indulgence?
—Those that are made against Fluminense's adversaries . . .

This torcedora went on, making it clear that her entire identity was wrapped up in her involvement in and passion for her club. Her favorite poets and writers, her favorite flowers, her favorite colors, her favorite music, her heroes and enemies—all flowed from her love for Fluminense. Trying to make sense of the torcedora's answer, the interviewer speculated that for its fans, football was as intoxicating as cachaça, and in closing he noted that his host at Fluminense assured him that, were he to ask these questions of any other torcedora, he would hear the same answers.[116]

Neither this woman nor the other passionate women fans who so interested contemporaries were criticized for their partiality; instead, they were depicted as true fans and true partners in building football, as their ubiquity in the sports press demonstrates. An advertisement published in 1918 for Rouxinol, evidently some sort of tonic, acknowledged women fans' passion when it suggested that every torcedora ought to drink two glasses of this "National Drink" each day in order to preserve her voice "for shouting."[117] Like the makers of Rouxinol, *Sport Illustrado*, *Vida Sportiva*, and *Careta* knew their audience and catered to it. Given that many contemporary experts were suspicious of passion as unmodern and unhygienic, the acceptability of excitement and partisanship here is remarkable, even if it was often patronizing.

While passion and partisanship were better tolerated among well-to-do women fans, they became increasingly acceptable and expected of other fans as well. In 1903 a writer in *O Estado de S. Paulo* wondered whether it was possible to be an "indifferent spectator" at a football match, but he went no further.[118] In 1917 another Paulista defender of the old ways suggested in *A Cigarra Sportiva* that it was "natural" to "make manifest one's enthusiasm and joy" as long as one did so with "composure."[119] By 1921 *S. Paulo Illustrado* was arguing that administrators needed to accept a certain amount of passion on the part of football fans, who felt a "paramount obligation" to attend every one of their teams' matches, for they were crucial to the teams' success.[120]

Similarly, even while critiquing the excesses of fans whose actions he found "embarrassing," another writer in 1920 still affirmed in *A Gazeta* that "cheers, shouts, hands clapping, cries of encouragement [and] all of the noise" of the grandstands "is the life, the beauty, the grace, the stimulus of the great football matches: this there will be, because it is essential, it is indispensable, and it is beautiful."[121] He acknowledged the fact of passion and celebrated it, and he argued that football could not exist without the passions of the torcedores. This was a far cry from the sensibility of earlier years, when sportsmen recommended impartiality, sober comportment, and the essentially passive behavior of an audience at a particularly gripping night at the opera.

The change that had been hinted at in the first two decades of the twentieth century became more obvious and widely accepted during the 1920s. During that decade, Brazilians came to expect and even to consider "essential" and "indispensable" to the football spectacle the partisanship, passion, and involvement of football fans. It was during this decade that some Brazilian fans began to think of organizing themselves according to their loyalties, to think in ways that have come to be associated with the modern torcidas organizadas. Not coincidentally, it was also in the 1920s when the torcedoras began to retreat from the grandstands and when they began to be forgotten,

FIGURE 4.4. Torcedores at a match between Fluminense and the Bangú Athletic Club, April 11, 1920. By permission of the Acervo Flu-Memória.

in part because it was male fans who organized clubs of supporters, through which they began to make football spectatorship their own domain.

Most historians trace the torcidas organizadas' roots to uniformed fan clubs that appeared in the 1940s, but Brazilians were already experimenting with similar ideas in the late-1920s.[122] In April 1927, in reporting on what it called "a winning idea," *Rio Sportivo* told of the activities of Fluminense member Carlos Burlamaqui, who had organized a group called the "Torcida Tricolor." The group would wear badges signifying their allegiance, they would sit together at matches, travel in "caravan" to away games, and they would "incentivize and animate our athletes" through coordinated cheers and songs. In his letter seeking the approval and support of Fluminense's directors, Burlamaqui demonstrated he understood what was expected of the gentleman sportsman, noting that "it is the torcedor's duty to applaud his club's athletes, whether they are victorious or defeated, and to applaud as well their adversaries, when they come out onto the field of play and when they accomplish some feat worthy of applause." The directors accepted his proposal, and the group was allowed to use the club grounds to practice its "songs and war cries."[123]

The Torcida Tricolor seems to have had a short life, and club directors do not seem to have been very interested in it judging by club records. Nor does it seem to have received much attention in the sports press. But Burlamaqui's story is significant. While he reiterated the ideal of the earlier years, he also saw a direct and active role for football fans, a role the editors of *Rio Sportivo* and the directors of Fluminense were happy to promote. Moreover, Burlamaqui helped point the way to two other phenomena that characterized Brazilian spectatorship in the 1930s and 1940s. First, the members of the Torcida Tricolor were men, all members of the club, contributing to the creation of a new kind of spectatorship that marginalized women. Second, Burlamaqui thought in terms of organization and hierarchy, conceiving of the directors of the club as natural and legitimate authorities to whom the group must appeal for permission to get involved. Burlamaqui and the Torcida Tricolor thus helped give shape to a version of spectatorship that was characterized by fans' passion and involvement, but it was also a kind of spectatorship that attempted to channel fan involvement to ends football authorities considered helpful, and one that left women less room than they had enjoyed in the past.

The ubiquitous Mário Filho picked up on the ideas Burlamaqui had been experimenting with. While editor of the short-lived *Mundo Esportivo* in the early-1930s, Filho organized a "Duel of Torcidas," a version of the Carnival competitions that he promoted through the paper. He brought the concept to the broadsheet *O Globo* and the *Jornal dos Sports*, which he took over in 1936. Thomaz Mazzoni and other leading journalists followed Filho's lead, and they helped amass the weight of the sports press behind the idea of organized fan clubs and in support of the clubs' view of themselves as vital participants in the football spectacle in their own right. Moreover, as Bernardo Borges Buarque de Holanda shows, they reimagined the passion and commitment of Brazilian football fans as masculine and as hierarchical, in line with the politics of the Vargas regime they supported. The fan clubs they promoted in the 1930s and 1940s were like the Torcida Tricolor organized by Carlos Burlamaqui in the late-1920s. They demanded fans' passion and commitment, they excluded women, and they were organized in a vertical manner, each one having its own "chief," a leader who directed fans' passions in useful directions.[124]

Thus, although the *Jornal dos Sports* did not mention Burlamaqui in its 1938 profile of Roberto Lugo, there was much in common between Burlamaqui and Lugo, whom the paper called "Fluminense fans' master of ceremonies."

Lugo orchestrated Fluminense's fans in support of the team and organized travel to away games. According to the paper, these fans contributed "in an undeniable way" to the club's victories. The paper also called Lugo's group Fluminense's "*hinchada*," employing a Spanish term for a group of organized and dedicated supporters. Hinchadas, all-male and famously passionate, were already active in Argentina by this time and were insisting that they were vital to the lives and fates of their chosen clubs. By adopting the term in its glowing coverage of Lugo's activities, the *Jornal dos Sports*, the single most influential sports publication in Brazil, seems to have been recommending that Brazilians follow the example of their neighbors. It accepted and promoted the claim made by Lugo, that he and the fans he organized played an important role in the Fluminense story. It mentioned neither Burlamaqui nor Burlamaqui's predecessors, the torcedoras, who had done so much to promote the claim Lugo was making. Instead it characterized the activities of fans like Lugo as novelties that emerged from a new and better kind of football in Brazil, a reformed football that the *Jornal dos Sports* fought for, and the meaning of which it took the lead in defining.[125]

Although the torcedoras were not part of the fan clubs of the 1930s and 1940s and were less and less visible in the press, the idea that they had done so much to promote—that spectators were passionate, involved, and crucially important to Brazilian football—persisted. This was never more clear than on the eve of and during the 1938 World Cup. Commentators had justified the partisanship of Brazilian fans in earlier instances of international competition. For example, writing about a match between Brazil and Uruguay in 1922 in São Paulo's *Vida Moderna*, K. Fico noticed that fans' patriotism could breed passion, even "frenzy," and that football could bring fans together as Brazilians. He wrote about "thousands of individuals of every category, of every age, of every color, owners and outcasts, lawyers and shoe shine boys, and, who knows, perhaps some elevated Excellence," who came together in support of Brazil. Expecting Brazil's victory, "all think with only one brain, all share one beating heart, all feel with the same nerves, all desire only one thing." In a passage of mixed metaphors, he suggested that football spectators were part of football, the "gears" of a football engine:

> *Yes, in order to be better understood*, if you will permit me the use of a futuristic image, I will say that the struggle was a bizarre electric battery, the size of Fluminense's *Stadium*, whose pedestrian discharges, faster than a six-cylinder Hudson going down Angelica Avenue in third,

regulated by 22 strong and brave ignition switches coming to excite the gears that are depending on them, which are all of us. Each one, a telephone without a number, cordless, without telephone operators, operators without the gas of love in the engine of their hearts, metallic, which don't connect, and only know how to say: Sorry, wrong number.

A direct and automatic connection. Running perfectly. What one feels, all feel; what one wants, all want. Equality and fraternity. Liberty we've had for one hundred years. We didn't have Football a hundred years ago. Today, we see its despotic dominance, from the modest farm lost in the virgin coastal forest to the most civilized capital.[126]

Football—and football spectatorship—revealed a powerful and modern Brazil, a Brazil unified and animated by patriotism, the country that Brazilians wanted it to be.

By 1938 the sports media was finding new ways to involve fans and to build community in Brazil by incorporating them into the game. For example, like *Sport Illustrado* had done in the 1920s when it printed messages from torcedoras, in the late-1930s the Transmissora Brasileira radio station (PRE-3) in Rio de Janeiro reserved space for fans' participation. Its *Palavra Sportiva* program set aside thirty minutes each day to take calls from torcedores, offering each caller the opportunity of "pointing out technical errors and frankly stating what he thinks about teams and clubs."[127] The *Jornal dos Sports* also solicited the direct participation of torcedores, for example, by organizing contests as sports publications had done in the past so that fans could interact with one another and with football as a whole. The paper held one of these, a 1937 contest for readers under fifteen years of age, in partnership with the Flamengo club; the contest and its results were especially revealing of Mário Filho's view of the relationship between fans, football, and the nation. The paper invited young readers to submit phrases that included both of the words "Brazil" and "Flamengo," and readers did not disappoint, sending in submissions that carried the kind of patriotic messages Filho and the club hoped for, such as "Flamengo, the future of Brazil's youth" and "Brazil! The daring of your people built a Flamengo." Marcio Lyra's winning entry, which could have just as well been composed by the Vargas regime, read, "Flamengo teaches: love Brazil above all things."[128]

In 1938, in partnership with *O Globo*, the *Jornal dos Sports* launched a "Stamp Campaign" to raise money to help defray the expenses of the seleção at the World Cup. The paper called participation in the campaign a "proof of Brazilianness" because Brazil's participation in the World Cup was a "national question," and the campaign was a success.[129] The two newspapers also ran a contest to name two ambassadors to represent Brazilian fans at the tournament. The ambassadors' expenses were paid, and they traveled with the team, reporting from France on their experiences and Brazil's progress through the tournament. Over the course of several weeks, hundreds of thousands of votes poured in, until Leonor Silva, a fan of Vasco da Gama, and Oswaldo Menezes, a Flamengo player who had not been called to the seleção, were named the female and male "Ambassadors of the Brazilian Torcida."[130]

Thousands could participate in these projects, many more than could participate in the paper's other 1938 venture, the organization of an expedition to take Brazilian fans to France to support the seleção during the tournament. Over the course of forty-seven days, torcedores would travel from Brazil to France and back again. The *Jornal dos Sports* organized travel arrangements and room, board, and tickets to the matches of the seleção. The total cost was almost nine contos de réis per person, a significant sum and far beyond the means of the vast majority of Brazilians, a reminder that neither in politics nor in football did populism mean equality.[131]

Like K. Fico and their other predecessors in football and in the football media, the journalists of the 1930s believed there could be no seleção without Brazilian football fans, just as there could be no Fluminense, no America, no São Paulo without their torcedores. That many Brazilians shared the feeling was made apparent throughout the 1920s and 1930s, and especially during such moments as Paulistano's 1925 tour of Europe and the seleção's participation in the 1930 and 1934 World Cups. The thousands and tens of thousands who turned out to cheer these teams as they practiced, when they embarked, and upon their return; those who carried Fausto dos Santos on their shoulders to the port; those who attacked the headquarters of Palestra Itália and Vasco da Gama when Brazil was eliminated from the World Cup—all asserted that football fans in Brazil were central to what football in Brazil had become, and that it was tied up in what it meant for Brazilian football to be Brazilian.

Once it began, the 1938 World Cup highlighted the transformation of attitudes about Brazilian football spectatorship plainly, even though the matches themselves were taking place across the Atlantic. Players, administrators, and journalists depicted referees as weak and even criminal, blaming them for the seleção's defeat in the semifinal, and fans spoke out as well, empowered do so by the press. The *Jornal dos Sports* said that the Hungarian referee of Brazil's match against Czechoslovakia had won "42 million personal enemies" because of his decisions, and that all manner of Cariocas took part in the spontaneous public protests against him and on behalf of the dignity of Brazil: "Sophisticated and important gentlemen, spiritual folks, wise men, shoeless kids, young ladies, mothers—everyone rooted frankly, openly, unabashed, loudly." Many telephoned the newspaper to complain about the referee. With "tears in her voice," one woman called to accuse the referee of being a thief, and promised to contact Getúlio Vargas to complain. Another fantasized about shooting the referee.[132]

When the team defeated Czechoslovakia in the replay match, fans in Rio de Janeiro, São Paulo, and throughout Brazil took to the sea and to the streets to celebrate.[133] When the players finally arrived in Rio de Janeiro after their third-place finish, up to five hundred thousand fans met them in what the *Jornal dos Sports* called a "delirium" of football enthusiasm.[134] Despite their evident joy, Brazilians were left bittersweet, happy to celebrate their "kings without crowns" but angry with what they perceived to be the unfairness of their team's treatment at the hands of European referees and administrators. While some contemplated Brazil's withdrawal from FIFA and its tournaments, Apoxy, writing in *O Estado de S. Paulo*, had a different suggestion. For him, the only way to guarantee fairness to Brazil would be to turn to those vital football actors who were not in France to support their countrymen. Next time, he wrote, Brazilians should "travel en masse to whichever European country [is hosting the tournament]. Only in that manner will we obtain the crushing victories that we well deserve."[135]

In the mass media of the 1930s, in the *Jornal dos Sports* and *O Globo*, in *O Estado de S. Paulo* and *A Gazeta Esportiva*, the torcedora was a rarer and rarer figure, and women—especially wealthy white women—were less likely to attend football matches every year. This does not mean that women withdrew completely from football, as the participation in the World Cup of Leonor Silva and the late-1930s experiments in women's football indicate. Reports and photographs of the massive crowds that protested and celebrated the seleção's progress through the 1938 tournament show women fans who were as eager, as passionate, and as involved as men were. And in the elite clubs, women continued to attend social events and pursue their own athletic interests, from swimming to volleyball.

The role of the torcedora was, however, eroded in the changing football of the 1930s. The Vargas movement attempted to revive older gender norms, marginalizing many of the modest advances feminists and "modern" women had made, including in football. Given that Vargas' policies and ideologies directly affected the organization and function of football for women and for men, there is no reason to doubt that the regime's paternalism did not also affect the torcedora, and it is clear that many within football shared the views of the regime. It seems likely that some women fans would have understood the formal prohibition of women's football as a suggestion that they ought not participate in the sport at all.

Wealthy and middle-class Brazilians also became less comfortable with participation in football by their young people, especially young women, in the 1930s, which meant that when the state officially barred women from playing football in 1941 and journalists paid less attention to them than to male fans, these circumstances only exacerbated women's growing distance from the game. Larger and larger stadiums hosted larger and larger numbers of working people and people of color, there to watch professionals who could no longer be relied upon to be upstanding sportsmen with whom apprehensive parents might encourage their daughters to interact. Where attendance at a football match had once been among the most respectable of pastimes, in part because of the participation of sportswomen, now it had become the pastime of the masses, and respectable Brazilians withdrew into their directors' boxes when they did not withdraw from football altogether.

This points to the limits of the figure of the torcedora and the limited nature of the opportunities participation in Brazilian football afforded her. She was a vital member of Brazil's football culture, helping to popularize the game and to convince Brazilians that it should be accepted by polite society. In return, she won breathing room, outlets for her opinions, venues for athletic pursuits, and the ability to affect football culture with her own tastes. It is impossible to understand the history of Brazilian football without understanding her participation and her influence, and it is telling of the choices made by the narrators of the futebol tradition, in the 1930s and since then, that they rarely mention her role. Part of the reason for this may be that the torcedora was never in complete control of her own participation in football. She was not a member of the sports clubs that dominated the game, she rarely spoke in the sports media without being filtered by male editors and interviewers, and she rarely played the game. Her opportunities and influence were considerable, but they were also constrained by the dominant position of male players, administrators, club members, and writers. Such actors could marginalize her from football and its story, especially if the story they wanted to tell did not leave room for a complicated figure who was wealthy, white, and female—and who was also unreserved and passionately involved in the football spectacle.

The most important lasting effect of the figure of the torcedora, then, was probably not what she accomplished for Brazilian women, though this was significant—after all, in football Brazilian women found a rare setting where they could pursue many passions and interests. It was rather that, in spite of sportsmen's expectations, and in spite of what popular history about Brazilian football has tended to remember, the torcedora practiced a kind of spectatorship that came to define what it meant to be a football fan in Brazil. Expected to display respectable reserve, her passionate involvement surprised many and became one of the most remarked-upon facets of Brazilian football in the crucial years of the 1910s and 1920s. She helped make football respectable and helped make the partisanship and intensity of football fans acceptable. Many commentators treated the torcedora's passion with patronizing indulgence, but because of her some Brazilians also began to indulge the passions of all fans and eventually to celebrate them as important characteristics of Brazilian spectatorship. Football fans—women and men—played a vital role in transforming ideas about what football in Brazil should be and in Brazilians' coming to see the game as something they had made their own. The torcedora is a tangential figure in the "soccer madness" that has come to dominate popular depictions of Brazilian football fans, but her stamp is upon it.

The Invention of the Beautiful Game

When the Club Athletico Paulistano toured Europe in 1925, the team surprised and impressed their hosts. They were called the "kings of football" because of their remarkable run of results, their wins often coming with outsized score lines, the most famous a 7–2 victory against the French national team. Like their Argentine and Uruguayan counterparts who were dazzling European audiences in the mid-1920s, Paulistano also impressed because the team won while playing in a very particular way. According to European writers, the Brazilians were highly skilled and exceptionally fast, both as individuals and as a team. They were agile and they moved constantly, and they controlled the ball with ease, dribbling with it remarkably well. This was very different from the more stationary, slower football that Europeans had come to expect, which relied mainly on precise passing and physical strength. Paulistano played what *Paris Soir* called a "Latin game," which some Europeans hoped to imitate.[1]

Commentators on both sides of the Atlantic had already begun to talk about regional differences by the mid-1920s, but those years were especially important in solidifying the idea that Old World football was something different from football in America. Because Paulistano and other South American teams won matches and praise in Europe—and because many South Americans continued to defer to European opinion—the 1925 European tours by Paulistano, Boca Juniors, and Nacional as well as Uruguay's victories in the 1924 and 1928 Olympics had as much of an impact in South America as the South Americans had made in Europe. Ever since then, in South America, in Europe, and everywhere else in the football world, what the Frenchman called the "Latin game" has informed popular understanding of how Brazilians and their neighbors along the River Plate play football and how they play it in comparison to their rivals elsewhere. It exists in a constellation of views that includes English football's purported directness and physicality, Germans' efficiency and regimentation, and Italians' elegant defensiveness. Meanwhile, elsewhere in the sports world, American and Cuban baseballs are said to embody strength and power, and dexterity and finesse, respectively, while commentators assert that West Indian cricket has traded traditional English might for Caribbean artistry.[2]

This is one reason that Paulistano's European adventure was such a highly significant moment: it contributed to a new discourse about Brazilian football that has come to dominate images and expectations of how Brazilians play the game. According to this view, Brazilians do not play English or European football. They play in their own way, which has come to be described as o jogo bonito, as futebol arte, and as samba soccer, a beautiful, artistic, and rhythmic style.[3] Brazilian footballers, especially the members of the seleção, are supposed to prefer attack to defense, to possess wonderful individual technique, and to play with flair, imagination, and joy. The idea is popular in Brazil as well, where it has evolved into a demand for the beautiful game and the rejection of the much-maligned futebol de resultados and futebol força, styles that seem to prioritize outcomes more than means, and in which strength marginalizes skill. José Miguel Wisnik, for example, has written of his regret that Brazilians have not always played o jogo bonito, a problem that he explains by pointing to the influence of globalization and administrators' quotidian pursuit of victory. He writes that these factors have cost modern Brazilian football some of its lyrical quality, and that now it balances between futebol arte and futebol força, "not poetry, but a type of essaystic prose that yearns toward poetry," with fans constantly hoping for a return to the beautiful.[4]

Together with their fans, Brazilian players are supposed to create Brazilian football as Brazilian. Importantly, as the term "Latin game" suggests, the idea of national styles insinuates that the way people play their sports springs from the distinctive features of their national and even ethnic characters. It is not only Brazilian football that is depicted as vibrant, joyous, and creative; it is Brazilians themselves. English stolidity, German efficiency, American strength, Caribbean flair—these describe popular depictions not only of national styles of play but of the nations that employ them. This is one reason to handle claims of national styles with care, for such claims can easily drift into essentialist allusions to ethnic and racial differences. Another is that the Frenchman did not see much difference between Argentine, Uruguayan, and Brazilian football, but that is not a widespread opinion today, suggesting the fluid nature of ideas about nation, ethnicity, and football style. Still, the idea of essential distinctions is extremely important because it was this idea that convinced many Brazilians in the 1920s and 1930s to accept and promote Brazilian futebol as intrinsically distinct and distinctive.

At least until 1914—when Brazilians were disappointed to learn from Exeter City that Englishmen had a variety of ways of playing football, not all of which were admirable—wealthy, white, cosmopolitan sportsmen hoped to mold Brazilian football according to their sense of how Europeans played the game. Playing a game invented by Europeans was not enough. This was the only correct and profitable way of playing the game—the best way for clubs to build winning sides, the only way athletes would learn the proper lessons from the game, and, most importantly, the means by which Brazil would most benefit from football's appearance on its shores. When sportsmen recruited European coaches and read European manuals, they were doing more than proving they were cosmopolitan and using their resources to learn from experts. They were also attempting to learn the tactics, strategies, and style of their European heroes.

However, despite the sportsmen's hopes and in part because of the limits they placed on participation in organized football, many Brazilians failed to learn to play football the "right" way. Often uncoached and ignorant of or neglecting to follow foreign advice, Brazilians discovered that there were as many football styles as there were footballers, and there was little that could staunch their innovations. The sportsmen could guard the gates of institutions like clubs and leagues, but they could not stop others from playing the game or playing in ways that did not correspond to European teaching. Nor was it only the marginalized who played their own ways. Charles Miller himself is alleged to have been the author of what Mário Filho called the "first Brazilianism in foot-ball," the "Charles," a backheel pass, and Paulistano was full of classically trained sportsmen when it amazed European audiences with its supposedly South American style in 1925.[5]

The fact is that football is an activity, not a finished product for consumption. It is necessarily impressed with each player's personality, and there was no way that Brazilians could play the game exactly as they imagined Europeans did. As Exeter City showed, there was no single European or even an English way of playing football, and, even if Brazilians could agree on one

European style, there was no way to enforce it on everyone who played football in Brazil, no matter how much some sportsmen hoped for the possibility.

At first, football's leaders and ideologues bristled when confronted with alternative styles, especially any version of the game which smacked of indiscipline or individualism. Despite the fact that Englishmen and wealthy, white Brazilians played in unexpected ways, critics in the 1910s and early 1920s blamed Brazil's social and ethnic character for the appearance of styles they did not like and complained about the influence of working people, people of African descent, and the country's Portuguese inheritance. Critics argued that new and unsettling styles grew out of multiethnic and working-class suburbs, not white, wealthy urban neighborhoods, and their conflation of innovation with undesirable characteristics of class, color, and ethnicity helped them justify their dissatisfaction with new styles of play.

But some of those who Brazilians perceived as playing differently were effective, prompting administrators, coaches, and writers to begin to reconsider. As early as 1919 the writer Americo Netto was reframing what some saw as undisciplined individualism both as "Brazilian" and as the approach Brazilians ought to take toward the game, one that promised great success.[6] It took a decade for Netto's view to become widely accepted, but the idea of a Brazilian style was the key to making the beautiful game. It offered nationalists a means by which to adapt football to their purposes, making difference—once considered a vice—into a virtue.

During the 1920s and 1930s, nationalists also began to invert critics' racial and ethnic characterizations, and they used the idea of a Brazilian style of football to contribute to a reassessment of Brazil's ethnic and racial heritage. They drew attention to what they saw as the Latin and African elements of Brazilian football and the idea that a national style could bring together the many streams that created Brazil, coalescing in a performance of national union. They were encouraged to do so by the Frenchmen and other Europeans who had been so impressed by Paulistano's "Latin game," while others, including, most famously, Mário Filho and Gilberto Freyre, advertised Brazilian football's "African" elements, which they said were especially important in making futebol an organic expression of the nation's particular mix of races and cultures. Whether a Brazilian style of football exists now or has ever existed, by the 1930s many Brazilians asserted that it did. They became convinced that Brazilians had discovered an authentically national, even racial, genius for the game, and they decided that this should be celebrated.

The beautiful game was not discovered but invented, and examining the invention and its consequences helps to illuminate how Brazilian ideas about race and national character changed during the early twentieth century. It was an idea that brought together a set of choices: by players on what to do with a ball, by coaches on what formations to adopt, by administrators on which players to sign for their clubs, and, especially, by journalists and other commentators on what stories to tell. But the idea of discovery was so attractive and became so popular that it obscured the choices that had been made and overshadowed disagreements among its promoters, such as whether it was a consequence of race and ethnicity or of coaching and practice. More than the previous chapters in this book, this chapter pays attention to Brazilian conversations, debates, and discourse about what happened on the field once the referee blew his whistle and the players kicked off. It shows that Brazilians invented the idea of the beautiful game as an authentic expression of Brazil's national character, and it demonstrates the consequences of the invention, on the field, in the grandstand and press box, and far beyond the game.

Playing the English Game the English Way

In August 1903 Charles Miller's São Paulo Athletic faced Paulistano in a match that went a long way in helping decide the city championship. São Paulo Athletic won, 4–0, and went on to win the competition, as it had the city's inaugural championship the year before. Paulistas viewed the match as an important opportunity to test the country's progress in the sport because, sportswriters said, it pitted the best of the local expatriate community against the best of the city's native population. Paulistano's popularity and the fact that São Paulo Athletic was often referred to as a team of Englishmen highlight the tension between nationalism and Eurocentrism in the thinking of many sportsmen; from an early date, some Brazilians looked to football to express their sense of national differences. Covering the 1903 match, *O Estado de S. Paulo* noted that the two teams, so differently constituted, also played the game differently. While Paulistano displayed "firmness in defense" and "intensity in attack," the Englishmen possessed an abundance of "discipline and calm." These were the qualities that explained São Paulo Athletic's continuing success, qualities the Brazilians "still" lacked.[7]

Hopeful that Paulistano would one day learn to play as the Englishmen did, the paper articulated the view that dominated Brazilian conversations about football styles during the first two decades after football's arrival in

Brazil. Calm and discipline and the Englishman's stereotypical phlegm in the face of adversity were the watchwords of the sportsmen.[8] Wealthy and middle-class sportsmen learned about the English style from a variety of places, most directly from coaches like John Hamilton and J. H. Quincey-Taylor, from players like Charles Miller and Harry Welfare, and from visiting teams like the Corinthian Football Club. But they were not the only Brazilians who learned about English football. The Brazilian members of the Bangú club, for example, worked and played with the Englishmen who were their fellow employees at the Companhia Industrial Progresso, and Welfare coached Afro-Brazilian and working-class players at Vasco da Gama in the 1920s. Working-class players also learned about football by watching and playing against teams trained to play like Englishmen did, and some of them read the periodicals and manuals that proliferated during the early twentieth century, which invariably promoted English tactics and teachings.

Sports periodicals and the regular press spilled much ink in describing the minutiae of the visits of foreign sides, going beyond their observation of visitors' moral qualities to notice, for example, the Corinthians' technical skill and the precision of their passes and shooting. The Brazilian media also filled many column inches, and entire volumes, with direct translations and local interpretations of English and other European teachings on how to play the game. Sportsmen's favorite writer, the Frenchman Ernest Weber, whose guide and rulebook was so popular in Brazil, was clear that there was a correct way to play football, and that was English.

Weber stressed the importance of the moral qualities of good players, especially "knowledge of the rules, skill, cold-bloodedness, [and] a spirit of discipline." Translating these qualities into the player's performance on the field, he argued that the proper way to approach the game was to understand it as "an exercise of science and skill," one in which neither passion nor the search for personal glory was helpful. He insisted that passion could only hurt the football player, and that "in many circumstances, a cold-blooded player is more useful than a skillful but impressionable one." And he took pains to emphasize that teamwork was of the utmost importance because, regardless of his other qualities, a player who could not be counted upon to "forget his individuality" could not contribute to his side's success. Rather than think of himself, the footballer ought "to consider himself merely one eleventh of an anonymous whole, a weak but useful piece of a machine, whose strength is clear but in which no part is more valuable than another."[9]

Weber's ideal football was characterized by intellectual and moral training, reason rather than feeling, and, above all, discipline and teamwork. As proof of his claims, he cited English experience and success not only in team sports but in physical education as well, and he recommended that all athletes pay close attention to English ways. They should play according to the example of "our masters, the English."[10] Directly and through local interpreters like Mário Cardim, Weber helped consolidate Brazilian sportsmen's sense that football was English in origin and in spirit, that the English way of playing the game was the only correct one. Other Brazilian admirers of English football helped carry the message of Weber and expatriate English coaches and players to their countrymen.

For example, C. Viveiros wrote in *Rio Sportivo* in 1909 that he learned his tactics from the English national team, which he had seen play against Australia in London. He marveled at the Englishmen's "well practiced *tricks*" and their "great courage," but he was especially impressed by their teamwork. "They do honor to their positions," he reported, and their game hinged on "cooperation, which is really the most important part of the beautiful *sport*." He emphasized that the forward line of attackers must work together and move upfield as a unit. It was also to function as the team's first line of defense. For their part, the side's midfielders and defenders must remain disciplined—"in the correct position"—alert to the possibility of the forwards' loss of possession. If all did their jobs, the team would use all of its parts intelligently, and it would never be surprised.

According to Viveiros, players concentrating on their own accomplishments were likely to neglect the roles assigned to them, to be found out of position, and to hurt the team when their services were most needed. He said that a "team of valiant foot-ballers, of strong men with impressive *kicks*, can do absolutely nothing against a *team* of boys who sustain among themselves a calm and precise combination." In his view, the essence of football was the "simple and precise *pass*" because, above all, football was "a conversation of positions." Echoing Weber, he insisted that football could be taught and it must be learned. It might seem easy, but it was "without any doubt one of the most complicated [sports] that young Brazilians practice today." It required commitment and persistence because "in neither one day nor one month of continuous practice can one acquire with justice the name of *good foot-baller!*"[11]

For at least a decade after Viveiros wrote, Brazilian tacticians echoed his advice. In 1915 Afranio Hiroz spoke of the example set by a team of visiting Englishmen, most likely the Corinthians, that defeated a Brazilian team, 4–0,

FIGURE 5.1. During a match between the Paysandú Cricket Club and the Botafogo Foot-ball Club, September 15, 1907. Note that some of the players are stationary, hands on hips, maintaining their positional "discipline." By permission of the Acervo Flu-Memória.

because the visitors showed that in football the individual "does not exist, except as part of a *team*." "Passes," he wrote, "the team game, of all for the group, the association of the parts, gave [the visitors] the victory." Meanwhile, the Brazilians playing them were "miracles of individualism," displaying "these *driblings* [sic] which we perform so well, while the *team* loses." He called on his readers to follow the model of the winning team, not the glory hunting of the losers.[12]

Brazilians' awareness of English football explains why Brazilian teams—all of them, it seems, from the wealthy to the working class—always used the formation favored by their English and European contemporaries. In the early years, this was the 2-3-5 formation, meaning that in front of the goalkeeper the team fielded two defenders, three midfielders, and five forwards, very different from the defensive-minded configurations that dominate football today. The 2-3-5 formation was popular throughout the football world as people new to the game followed British practice as closely as possible, and Brazilians were no exception. Changes did come with time, for example, with the "WM" formation (a more balanced 3-2-2-3 structure), which

Brazilians favored in the 1920s and 1930s. Even so, such changes usually came from Europe, and Brazilians' usage of the WM can be traced to their awareness of the designs of the English tactician and Arsenal manager Herbert Chapman.[13]

In 1918, five years after São Paulo Athletic, Brazil's great English team, had retired from competition, *Vida Sportiva* was still attempting to focus Brazilian attention on the English approach, dedicating twelve paragraphs to a discussion of "the role of '*forwards*'" in English football.[14] A month later the magazine's editor, the unapologetic elitist Alberto Silvares, reminded his readers that the best proof of the proper approach to football was "its results for the education of the English people." The English showed that football "places the cultivation of the moral sentiments of the true gentleman on par with physical development," and that, when played properly, it was a "team game, which brings to mind the noble sentiment of, all for one, one for all." Silvares therefore insisted that Brazilians follow what he believed was the English model, which for him meant not only the "team game" but also explicit social limitations on participation so that only the well-to-do would play at the highest levels.[15] *O Estado de S. Paulo* agreed with at least the first part of Silvares' advice, repeating the opinion in 1918 that it had offered fifteen years before, that "sporting power . . . resides in discipline."[16]

Football Arguments

Aiming to benefit from Brazilians' preoccupation with English football, and also promoting his view of what Brazilian football should be, in 1920 Alberto Silvares published a Brazilian edition of *Association Football and How to Play It*, a 1908 book by the English amateur and coach John Cameron.[17] The same year, *O Estado de S. Paulo* published Odilon Penteado do Amaral's *Cousas de "Football,"* in the preface of which influential sportswriter Leopoldo Sant'Anna described football as a game of refined gentlemen, "courteous and well-mannered." Speaking directly to players, whose social standing he communicated by addressing them formally, he wrote, "For every foul you involuntarily commit, even if it is punished by the '*referee*,' you ought to beg the pardon of the offended. If you do not do this, you will be fatally branded an egotist and poorly bred, which we do not believe you to be." Like Sant'Anna, Amaral warned against individualism, and he applied the lesson to football tactics—"not a shred of egotism" ought to enter into a player's thinking.[18]

This was a year after Brazilians had won their first international title, the South American Championship of 1919, which some depicted as the best proof that Brazilian footballers had been given a good education by Charles Miller and John Hamilton, by the Corinthians and Ernest Weber, by Viveiros, Hiroz, and Silvares. Writing in *Vida Sportiva*, Marcio Vidal explained that Brazil had won the 1919 championship because players like Marcos, Friedenreich, and Neco had learned their lessons well. They possessed the classic sportsman's values of valor, courage, perseverance, and intelligence. And, though Vidal acknowledged the importance of their physical attributes and their skills, he focused upon their teamwork and their "gallantry, which fills us with enthusiasm."[19]

The 1919 victory was indeed important, and not only because it was the first in what would become a long and storied history of Brazilian accomplishment in international competitions. Contrary to Vidal's assertions, the victory helped break the consensus among public commentators that there was only one proper way to play football. While Vidal focused on the seleção's teamwork, Americo R. Netto viewed the championship very differently. In the inaugural edition of *Sports* magazine, Netto argued that the championship had revealed that football as it was being played in Brazil contrasted with football as Englishmen played it and as Anglophile Brazilians recommended.

According to Netto, a "Brazilian school" had supplanted the "English school" in local football. In his telling, the English style, of course, was based upon teamwork and discipline, with the side playing "in complete and perfect harmony." Netto argued that this style had been rejected by Brazilian players, who evolved their own brand of attacking play despite the hard work of many Eurocentric sportsmen. The new style depended upon the skill and assertiveness of individual players who did not wait on their teammates to move forward or to shoot but instead launched attacks at every opportunity and from every angle. Netto claimed that this was the "Brazilian Innovation" that had allowed the seleção to win the South American Championship, and that Brazilians ought to cultivate. In his words, Brazilians had won "simply because we do not play like [the English], because it is very different, very much ours, very Brazilian, the school of *foot-ball* that we have adopted, or, better, that we have created for our own exclusive use." Given this, it would be short-sighted to attempt to force Brazilian footballers to play in the old way; in Netto's view, playing the Brazilian way Brazilians could "without vanity aim to be world champions."[20]

Americo Netto knew that he did not speak for all Brazilians interested in football. He knew that some would continue to preach the importance of teamwork and the disciplined approach. In fact, in the very next issue of *Sports*, one of Netto's colleagues called upon Brazilian players to understand that "Association *football* is, characteristically, a team game" and a "school of discipline." Even physical exercises should be performed collectively, the author argued, for this would build players' sense of teamwork and would "contribute decisively to the firmer discipline of the players who practice them." Once the match began, good players put aside their individual goals because football's "adepts know and want to sacrifice glory and personal vanity to the interests of the group, which is what it means to be part of a team."[21]

The difference in perspective between this writer and Marcio Vidal, on one hand, and Americo Netto, on the other, signaled that the 1920s would be a decade of debate and disagreement among those who thought and wrote about football tactics. For example, when in 1920 Paulistano traveled to Rio de Janeiro and came away with a victory over Fluminense that entitled its players to call themselves champions of Brazil, commentators were unable to agree on how to interpret the event. Rio de Janeiro's *O Imparcial* argued that Paulistano's victory owed to the fact that its players practiced "true *association*, which is nothing other than intelligent combination play." It called attention to the Paulistas' teamwork, their courage, and their commitment to the cause, framing the victory as a victory for classic standards and practices.[22] However, *O Estado de S. Paulo* saw the match very differently, calling it "a victory for the Brazilian school," which was based upon individualistic initiatives taken by light, quick players, who would "always have the advantage" over sturdier, more disciplined teams. Because of this, the outcome was entirely predictable, for Paulistano had adopted the approach of the new school while Fluminense continued to play in the old way.[23]

These commentators watched the same matches, the same players, the same football. But they understood them very differently, exposing the fact that comment on football styles involved choices, required interpretation, and communicated preferences. Viveiros, Hiroz, and Silvares conflated ethics, tactics, and styles in the service of their effort to make Brazilian football as much as possible correspond to their understanding of English practice. Sant'Anna, Amaral, Vidal, and others echoed their message without their predecessors' emphasis on the Englishness of the model. Conversely, Netto and the *Estado* specifically rejected the notion that Brazilians should play football like Englishmen were imagined to play. They identified distinctive

FIGURE 5.2. During a match between Botafogo and Fluminense, May 21, 1922. By permission of the Acervo Flu-Memória.

characteristics in the way Brazilians were playing, and they welcomed them as part of a nationalization of the sport. Informed by their own expectations and tastes, these commentators could watch the same match and come to very different conclusions about its outcome and its meaning.

These were debates about how to win football matches, but they were also ideological ones, which helps explain why the 1920s was a decade of criticism and nostalgia. Defenders of the old ways rejected Netto's advice, continuing to insist on the importance of moral and tactical discipline, which writers like Weber and Viveiros had asserted was the foundation of proper football. When they granted that Brazilian football was changing, they depicted it as fallen. In their telling, the football played in Brazil until the mid-1910s was an idyll played by gentlemen with the proper spirit and in the right way. The football of the 1920s was, at best, a bad dream of selfishness, and it was often a nightmare of indiscipline and violence.

The record is in fact littered with evidence that critics had reason to complain. It would be impossible to describe even a fraction of the instances of misconduct documented by critics, but the record of the Judicial Commission of the Associação Paulista de Esportes Athleticos, Paulista football's governing body, hints at the character and scope of the problem. In fewer than ten months in 1929, the commission suspended thirty-three players for violations that occurred during official matches, including violent play, "aggression" against players and referees, and teams abandoning their matches. The suspensions ranged from one to four games.[24] Other violations merited verbal or written warnings, expulsion from individual matches, and even an outright ban from the league, and there were plenty of other minor violations that never came to the attention of the league or were dealt with by referees, by club officers, or by no one at all but were highlighted in the complaints of sportswriters.[25] Such transgressions tested Brazilians' faith that football would provide an education in sportsmanship and, for some, undermined confidence in the entire football project.

Critics were especially concerned about violence on Brazilian football fields, with some justification. The perception that Brazilian football had become especially violent was common enough in 1918 that the Casa Stamp sporting goods store advertised in *Vida Sportiva* with a cartoon that featured a shockingly violent football match, including blood spatters, broken limbs, and one player who had had his head kicked clean off by another.[26] Clearly less amused, the magazine's Julio Roma wrote of his concern that football was becoming so violent that the game was in jeopardy of losing its fans, who would not want to watch if it became brutal. He called violent play the "most condemnable" tactic a footballer could adopt.[27] Elsewhere in the capital, Aduato de Assis, the editor of *Athletica*, complained in 1920 that players had lost the "proper respect and necessary courtesy" they owed their rivals, which their predecessors had demonstrated. Tension, argument, and violence were the predictable results.[28]

A Gazeta described Paulista football in similar terms in a pair of commentaries published in 1922. It depicted the football of the early twentieth century as genteel and decorous, characterized by "camaraderie" and games played "without incident, gentlemanly, correct." But the civility of the sportsmen had been lost. Teams entered the field with a "malicious exchange of looks between the two groups," and violent clashes followed kick-off. The paper renamed contemporary football "*futebriga*," or "foot-fighting," and said that the problem was not one of isolated offenses by individual players but a comprehensive breakdown that transformed football into "a game of life and death." This new game was played in São Paulo and also in Rio de Janeiro,

Buenos Aires, and Montevideo as South American footballers had found a "new system of playing the sport," which was becoming more and more common.[29]

Like these critics, Carlos Villaça, who had played for America and Botafogo between 1906 and 1917, suggested that these transgressions were a novelty of the late-1910s and the 1920s. Writing in the *Diario da Noite* in 1927, Villaça insisted that in his day "players respected each other" and "had the composure of true sportsmen," but contemporary "players view one another with hatred." He drew a connection between tactics and ethics, remembering his generation as having played with "discipline" and "harmony," traits that the athletes of the 1920s had lost, even if they were technically superior.[30] The next year, Paulistano's A. G. Filho published a piece in the club's magazine that carried the same message of change and decline. He said that for many years Brazilians had played football properly, but in the 1920s a new generation had abandoned the game's ethics and had transformed "football games into boxing matches ... [with] fractured shins, dislocated feet, broken heads, [and] players knocked unconscious." Filho was so dismissive of what the sport had become that it seems likely he meant the article to help prepare club members for Paulistano's withdrawal from competitive football, a step it took the year after its publication.[31]

These critics explained football's violence in several ways. Some, like Julio Roma and Aduato de Assis, blamed club administrators, who indulged in partisanship, ambition, and even corruption, most obviously and worryingly by engaging in the deceptions of masked professionalism. If football's leaders regularly violated the mores and tenets of sportsmanship, it was no wonder that players so often failed to live up to its ethical demands. Others blamed fans who were too partisan and passionate, who "go to watch a football match only in order to see the inevitable tumult," according to *A Gazeta*.[32] According to A. G. Filho, for some, "'to cheer' has the sense, the character of a punch," and these torcedores encouraged footballers to hurt one another. Filho explained that respectable fans, the "good part, the elite," were "horrified" at what football had become, and had "completely abandoned the grandstands of the stadiums" by 1928. They left behind their social inferiors, who liked the "innovation" of players who kicked one another as often as they kicked the ball.[33] Other critics agreed, pointing to social and racial undesirables in explaining the decline of the game. *Sport Illustrado* did not blame the Botafogo club and its supporters for disturbances at a home match in 1920 but instead pointed at "individuals of an inferior condition, lacking instruction and education, and therefore unable to discern what is inappropriate . . . and from there comes a series of insults and slurs against referees or opposing *players*, depending on how much they feel like fighting."[34]

These critics also looked to the game's popularization to explain problems in how players approached the game. Alberto Silvares explained in 1918 that the decline of Brazilian football was due to the participation of those who lacked the "moral education" to realize that football should be a venue "to cultivate the moral sentiments of the true gentleman." Instead, they "consider '*foot-ball*' an emotional spectacle," which led too many of them to play violently, and even to "specialize in this wrong and dishonest way of playing, cultivating brutality for the enjoyment of an audience whose education is so lacking as to desire it." Silvares admitted that "at times" and "in a few abnormal moments," wealthy fans and players were guilty. But, true to form, he saw the problem mostly as one of "lesser classes."[35] Cicero Brasileiro Meirelles reported in 1922 that he noticed similar problems when he visited Salvador, Bahia. Bahians seemed to be getting better at the game, he said, but two problems stood out. First, their football was far too violent. Second, "their biggest defect" was that Bahians lacked "harmony and cohesion, the most important characteristic of teams which are efficient and battle-tested." This was because Bahian players succumbed to the vice of "the individual game, the persistent and almost systematic abuse of tricks in a pernicious exhibitionism for the grandstand." In the capital of Afro-Brazil, fans and players joined in building a football that was violent and spectacular, which Meirelles explained as the result of their failing to learn the lessons of discipline and selflessness.[36]

A Gazeta asserted that similar problems had led to the "regression" of Paulista football. The paper described the cacophony as players yelled at one another for failing to pass the ball and for other mistakes, making a match a veritable "fish market!" Here was selfishness, and it threatened to ruin Brazilian football, and the paper explained the problem by pointing to football's social diffusion, saying that "in every way, official contemporary football strains to imitate so-called 'suburban' football."[37] That is, *A Gazeta* argued that the root of football's decline lay in suburban working-class neighborhoods, where residents had adopted the game but lacked the breeding of the middle-class and wealthy players of the city proper. Without the resources and training necessary to learn how the sport ought to be played, working-class athletes crafted a debased version of the game, which had overtaken what football should have been.

If a sportswriter in *O Imparcial* was correct, this was a common view among well-to-do fans by 1921. He reported overhearing the fans of a respectable Carioca club jeer an opposing player for rough play, yelling, "What a brute! Giddyap, you animal! Get the beast off the field! Go play with the blacks!" They saw a game reminiscent of boxing and stickfighting and said it belonged to black players rather than to players produced by polite white society, "in the elegance of their 'toilettes' and in the beauty of their sun-kissed faces."[38] As Carlos Villaça suggested in 1927, nostalgic critics conflated playing styles with class and racial identities, and the popularization of the game with its decline. He and his fellow players had demonstrated "discipline and absolute amateurism." With the failure of amateurism, and the social diffusion of the game that came with it, came the collapse of discipline, and football suffered tremendously for it.

A. G. Filho, Carlos Villaça, and other critics offered a coherent story of the rise and fall of Brazilian football. It began with wealthy and middle-class amateurs who loved the game and were willing to learn the right way to play it from Englishmen and other experts. Learning to play in the right manner, at their best these amateurs played with calm and discipline; they played as a team rather than a group of individuals, and, because they were unselfish, they treated their opponents as friendly rivals rather than enemies. Then, according to critics, social and racial inferiors had taken up the game. Lacking the moral and sporting training of their betters, they indulged their passions when they played, especially their egotistical desire for personal glory and their base compulsion to win at all costs. Their football was selfish, often individualistic, and sometimes violent. Allowed or, worse still, invited onto the playing fields of respectable people who had discarded the lessons of sportsmanship in the pursuit of victory, these outsiders had contaminated Brazilian football and transformed it into a grotesque of glory hunting and brutality.

The critics did have evidence of missteps by working-class players. In Rio de Janeiro in 1912, for example, Bangú expelled two of its members, Othelo de Medeiros and Ernesto de Farias, from the club for "poor behavior" on the field that the referee and other authorities could not prevent and that had led to disorder and "disagreeable incidents." At first Medeiros protested his innocence. But, cowed by the club's intransigence, he eventually apologized.

He was readmitted to the club, but not until eight months later.[39] Ten years later in São Paulo, a group of boys were playing a game on Álvaro de Carvalho Street when an argument between two of them ended with the hurling of rocks and Fernando Rodrigues de Conceição in a coma, his skull fractured. *O Estado de S. Paulo* explained the event as an example of the "stupid aggression" typical of working-class football.[40]

Nostalgic critics pointed to anecdotal evidence that working-class players had debased the game, but they were also remembering a past that may never have existed at all, and, as Americo Netto indicated, they were describing a present that could be interpreted in more than one way. As early as 1915 Afranio Hiroz described Brazilian footballers who were "miracles of individualism" who dribbled too much, and in 1918 both Alberto Silvares and Julio Roma admitted in *Vida Sportiva* that some wealthy players were guilty of rough tactics. They ought to have known better, according to Roma, "having received an excellent education."[41] He may have had in mind Botafogo and Fluminense, whose August 1917 match was characterized by confusion, conflict, and violence. In their conversations afterward, Botafogo's directors refused to accept that their players could be to blame. The club president pointed to the "unfortunate and absurd performance of the referee" to explain the players' behavior, and the directors considered requesting that the Liga Metropolitana annul Botafogo's 4–2 defeat.[42]

This was an ongoing problem. *O Estado de S. Paulo* described the 1915 championship as wonderful, "belissima," and said that "not one disagreeable incident occurred in any of the sixty matches." There were "neither fights, nor violent arguments, nor malicious booing, nor insults; in sum, nothing which could diminish the celebrations and the sporting traditions of São Paulo." But this was remarkable because it followed two seasons during which fans had "the displeasure of watching some pretty unedifying scenes," prompting pessimists to predict "the definitive decline of *foot-ball*" in the city. Club rivalries had made players "intransigent, implacable," making football matches into "true conflicts, with all of the risks of real battles." The paper was happy to report that the 1915 season had proved "the sporting education of this city has not completely withered," as some had feared.[43]

In fact, *A Cigarra Sportiva* asserted in 1917 that Paulista football had already entered into an era of "decadence" by 1905, only a little more than ten years after Charles Miller introduced the sport to the country. According to the magazine, by 1905 the era of "the fair and gentlemanly contests of the first championship organized in S. Paulo" and of "honesty and civility" was over. Instead, "the germ of Discord, of indiscipline, of intrigue began to infect the organisms of even the most perfect sporting societies."

> Shameful scenes were inevitable: fistfights in the middle of matches, disastrous decisions by referees, vulgar displays by fans in the bleachers, insulting exits by *teams* from the playing field, insults, threats, [and] punches! ...
>
> Clubs blinded by the winning of trophies have forgotten their noble mission, and have begun to act in a manner which provokes only distaste among their admirers. Upright organizations, with fine traditions, with histories full of glory and a record of the most noble activities, have abandoned their old ways and have entered with arms wide open upon a career of professionalism, corruption, and perfidy.[44]

This was not the football that Carlos Villaça and A. G. Filho remembered when they looked back from the 1920s. Most of the transgressors here were wealthy and middle-class Brazilians, not suburbanites, workers, or people of color, who had yet to be allowed into elite football by 1905 and were only beginning to participate in it when it seemed Paulista football was in terminal decline in 1913 and 1914. It took imagination for nostalgics to render such chaotic scenes as a dream of calm and discipline.

Warren Goldstein demonstrates that something similar characterized early American baseball. There, critics who objected to the commercialization and social diffusion of baseball in the 1870s remembered a past in which gentlemen amateurs played the game for the right reasons, and they objected to the businessmen and professionals who had transformed the sport into something unrecognizable and disagreeable. Goldstein shows that the critics imagined this past and that their critiques were as much generational and social as they were objections to substantive changes in the game itself. When they complained about what baseball had become, they were fighting a rearguard action in defense of their own privileges and their own preferences. With their "class snobbery" hindering their appeal, they largely failed.[45]

In Brazil, the inconsistencies, favoritism, and nostalgia of a Silvares or a Paulistano indicated their dissatisfaction with the characteristics of football in the late-1910s and 1920s, including false amateurism and violent and undisciplined play. But the problems they complained about knew no class, no race, and no generation, despite their claims. Infractions by Botafogo and not just Bangú were why the sports press published so many pieces on discipline; why even big clubs so often felt compelled to remind their members and guests of proper standards; why league bodies in Rio de Janeiro and São Paulo, at all levels, were kept busy with the transgressions of their athletes, who were fined, suspended, or censured, depending upon the gravity of their offenses. Such actions were necessary because administrators, players, and fans of all types violated the ethics set down by early-twentieth-century commentators like Ernest Weber and adopted and promulgated by their Brazilian disciples.

What many critics in the late-1910s and 1920s seem to have been most unhappy with was not changes in the way the game was played in Brazil but its popularization and the challenge to middle-class and wealthy privileges it brought with it. The middle class and wealthy found ways to defend their privileges, especially by reinforcing football's social order via professionalization. In professionalizing the game, middle-class and wealthy clubs marginalized their working-class rivals by using their financial resources to recruit the best players of smaller and poorer clubs. And they disciplined those players by binding them to formal contracts and the constraints of the workplace, much as the Vargas regime sought to discipline labor by coopting the message of worker empowerment and channeling worker action through government instruments.

The defenders of the old order faced a different challenge in protecting their ideal of how the game should be played, especially because respectable commentators like Americo Netto depicted instances of individual play as expressions of Brazilian invention rather than as signs of indiscipline or selfishness, and Brazilians inside and outside of football seized on the idea as a positive expression of national difference. However, the rhetoric of restraint and control survived the football arguments of the 1910s and 1920s. It survived because the most prominent champions of the idea that Brazilians played football in their own way continued to insist that individual invention be yoked to collective discipline, something obscured by a futebol tradition that asserts that in the 1930s the dribble, not the pass, became the symbol of how Brazilians ought to—even must—play the game.

A Brazilian Brand of Football

Among the champions of the futebol tradition, one of the most influential and best known was Gilberto Freyre, whose comments about football reinforced his argument that the authentic character of Brazil was rooted in ethnic and social miscegenation and exemplified in expressions of popular Afro-Brazilian culture, such as samba.⁴⁶ Freyre described what he perceived to be the game's evolution and transformation in Brazil, from the hobby of well-to-do expatriates to the pastime of the masses, and focused on the participation of blacks in making football the national sport. He called football as it was played in Brazil an "Anglo-Afro-Brazilian game," recognizing its English roots while depicting it as transformed into a local practice by Afro-Brazilians who played it in a distinctive manner. He wrote about the differences between "Apollonian" and "Dionysian" football and suggested that truly Brazilian football was a game in the spirit of the god of wine. Apollonian football was characteristic of the ways in which whites and Europeans played the game: organized, strategic, and serious. Opposed to it was the style of Afro-Brazilian footballers, who infused the European game with African-derived traditions, survivals of Africa shaped by the historical experience of Brazil. Their Dionysian football was spontaneous, creative, and festive, and it was unique. It was, Freyre argued, "authentically Brazilian" and a "Brazilianism."⁴⁷

The views of Freyre and other nationalists of the 1930s and 1940s who popularized the idea of futebol as a "Brazilianism," such as José Lins do Rego, Thomaz Mazzoni, Nelson Rodrigues, and, especially, Mário Filho, have remained influential, and their work has often been depicted as groundbreaking by scholars and commentators who have adopted their view of the story of Brazilian football.⁴⁸ However, these writers were building on a set of ideas that had existed for some time, not only among those who complained about Brazilian departures from English models but also among commentators who saw value in Brazilian innovation. The idea of Brazilian difference was advanced, for example, by one of the English Corinthians, who in 1910 complimented Brazilian players for "the nimble nature of their play and their quickness on the ball." He attributed the rapid development of Brazilian football to lessons well learned by Brazilians during residences in England and their passing their wisdom on to their countrymen. He said that those "who have been educated at home have proved very apt pupils," but he also said that they "have readily adopted the knowledge thus obtained to the conditions that exist in their own country."⁴⁹

Like the Corinthian and, later, Americo Netto, many of the Brazilians who promoted the idea of a Brazilian style defined it against what they depicted as the English version of the game. Writing in *Rio Sportivo* in 1927, for example, one Carioca argued that Brazilians had dispensed with "the phlegm and the stationary system of the English," preferring to allow the "impetuousness" of individual players to drive their teams forward.[50] In 1929 *A Gazeta* asserted that an "abyss" had opened up between Anglo-Saxon and Latin football, with "patience and Platonism" on one side and "spectacle and improvised juggling" on the other. The British and Central European footballer moved the ball like a chess player, according to the paper. The South American was a magician.[51] That same year, *O Estado de S. Paulo*, which had a long record of promoting disciplined, "English" football, republished Americo Netto's 1919 article under a new title, "A Training Error." The new title emphasized Netto's argument that it was a mistake to train Brazilians according to English standards and methods. Brazilians must be encouraged to be assertive, to dribble, to shoot, to abandon caution and disciplined teamwork in favor of expressions of their individual imaginations.[52]

In 1919 Netto was in the minority among commentators, many of whom did not even see the "innovation" he described. By the late-1920s and early-1930s, the terms he had employed were ubiquitous in the sporting press, as was his central idea. Even Leopoldo Sant'Anna, a critic of the new fetish for dribbling and invention over discipline and strength, wrote in 1930 of South American and European "schools" characterized by spontaneity and what he called "constructions of the moment," on one hand, and "calculation" and "meticulousness," on the other.[53] Three years later, Floriano Peixoto Corrêa, the soldier who enjoyed a stellar playing career in spite of his struggles against false amateurism and who later became a successful coach, showed that some Brazilians still looked to England to learn to play the game. In *Grandezas e Miserias do Nosso Futebol*, Floriano dedicated a full chapter to the teachings of an English manager, "The A.B.C. of Charles Griffith." He also mentioned that his Anglocentric tactical thinking was informed especially by the work of Max Valentim of the *Imparcial* newspaper. In his columns and his own 1941 book, *O Futebol e Sua Técnica*, Valentim repeatedly cited British coaches and players as models for Brazilian footballers. Valentim gave special attention to the teachings of Herbert Chapman, who Floriano called "the Napoleon of English football," and Harry Welfare, who had had an enormous impact on Carioca football in the 1910s and 1920s as a Fluminense player and Vasco da Gama coach and whose reliance on strength rather than guile was captured in his nickname as "The Tank." In their books Floriano and Valentim mentioned British tacticians and models much more often than they cited Brazilian ones, despite Brazilian football's growing international reputation.[54]

However, Floriano admitted that he and Valentim had become exceptions among Brazilian coaches and commentators by 1933. Although most tacticians were still using English-designed formations, by then Brazilians had embraced the possibility of a variety of approaches to the game, and, according to Floriano, most had reached the point of refusing to accept the idea that foreigners could offer any useful advice. They were "fools who twist their noses, alleging that, *soccer* having been popularized among Brazilians, a race especially chosen by the gods and goddesses of the leather ball, it was clear that Brazilians had automatically become the best in the world." They felt they had no more to learn from Englishmen, Europeans, or anyone else; the lessons of the Brazilian school had largely supplanted all other teachings, and Brazilians were even parodying what their predecessors had once revered.[55] For example, in 1931 A.C. wrote in the *Jornal dos Sports* of "a cold game, resembling a chessboard, a *made in England* style, without emotional individual moves, almost without movement," which Brazilians had once tried to play. They had abandoned this style, this "mechanical *football, standardized*," in favor of their own kinetic approach, centered on the skills and performances of individual, and individualistic, players.[56]

As A.C. indicated, one significant aspect of the attempt to distinguish Brazilian and English styles was writers' perspective on players' gender identities. The sportsmen hoped Brazilian footballers would be upstanding young men. As comfortable in uniform and on the playing field as in a tuxedo at a ball, they would play in a style that complemented the bearing of the women and men who watched them from the grandstands and who they met in formal dining rooms. They would be reserved and unexcitable, "cold" according to A.C., cast in a mold designed in Victorian and Edwardian England to produce sturdy leaders for society and government. Their football would be cultivated, thoughtful, and well-planned; in a word, it was disciplined.

A different notion of masculinity accompanied the idea of a new way of playing the game in Brazil, similar in character to the gendering of Argentine football as described by Eduardo Archetti. In Archetti's telling, Argentine football commentators in the 1920s promoted a new style, *lo criollo*, which excluded its British roots in favor of an Argentine hybrid of the country and the city, the rural gaucho and the urban *pibe*, the wily street urchin of Buenos Aires. Criollo masculinity demanded intense commitment and a will to win, even though it was "divested of force and courage." In their place was a special focus on invention and performance, of dribbling and cunning, "making the opponent believe the opposite of one's true intentions, turning deceit into victory."[57]

Archetti's description echoes a point commentators have frequently made about the role the *malandro* figure has played in the making of the Brazilian style.[58] The malandro is an antihero, a trickster and rogue, characterized by Roberto DaMatta as "one totally averse to work and highly attuned to spectacle, as seen in his typical way of walking, his seductive mode of speaking, and in his singular dressing."[59] He resides between the community and the margins, an "ambiguous midway world [where] popular creativity is fully exercised."[60] Gilberto Freyre believed that football served as a creative outlet for *malandragem*, without which, he feared, it would be "entirely a vice or a disadvantage."[61] Football provided the malandro a liminal space between order and chaos where he could bend the potentially destructive aspects of his character toward creativity and imagination. On the football field, joyful rather than toiling, the malandro could indulge the imaginative flair that defined the Brazilian football spectacle as Brazilian and as beautiful.

The parallel between the pibe and malandro is part of a larger correlation between the ideas of lo criollo and o jogo bonito. The correlation was especially apparent in the 1920s and 1930s, when European and South American commentators saw and emphasized the "Latin" similarities of the styles of Paulistano, Boca Juniors, and Nacional club teams and the styles of the Brazilian, Argentine, and Uruguayan national teams. It became less obvious over time as commentators began to insist upon the distinctiveness of the "national" styles of their countrymen, but the echoes persist in spite of claims of difference, hinting at the work of construction and invention that Freyre and other theorists performed and continue to perform in crafting South American football language and philosophies.[62]

In 1930 commentators tried to make sense of Brazil's failure at the World Cup, and as they did so they dealt explicitly with gender ideas in rejecting the sportsman's ideal and designing a new one. Fausto dos Santos called his wealthy teammates on Brazil's World Cup team "dandies," and critics who were annoyed by Brazil's poor performance latched onto the jibe. They attacked the organizers who had followed Marcos de Mendonça's call to choose players because of the gentlemanly image they broadcast rather than the skill they possessed, and they were especially irritated by Poly and other players who seemed more interested in nightclubs than football matches. *Rio Sportivo* said that Fausto was right about his teammates, and the paper cited a well-placed source who called Poly a "Useless Refrigerator"; Nilo, "Slow Motion"; Joel de Oliveira Monteiro, "the biggest 'poseur' in the world"; and Theophilo Bettencourt Pereira, "the Whiner."[63]

In this version of football masculinity, refinement read as affectation, cool reserve was useless, and the gentleman was emasculated. Class differences informed the critique, as did regionalism, with the São Paulo press adopting Fausto's taunt in order to attack the heavily Carioca side on behalf of the Paulista players who had been left out of the team. Cartoonist João Brito lampooned the pretense of the Cariocas in *A Gazeta*, depicting them as playing in top hats, tuxedo jackets, dress shirts, and ties while the goalkeeper smoked a cigarette through an elegant holder. A Paulista in football gear leaned against the post and laughed as the goals flew in.[64] In the same paper Leopoldo Sant'Anna endorsed Fausto's accusation, noting that to call the wealthy players dandies was to acknowledge that their problem was that they and their football were "effeminate."[65]

This was a reinterpretation of the roles of calm, restraint, and even violence in playing football and in defining Brazilian masculinity. Whereas Poly, Nilo, Joel, and Theophilo played according to an older style—slowly, deliberately, and as if they were "writing poetry"—Fausto and those willing to "fight" for the seleção and for Brazil were characterized as true footballers and authentic Brazilian men.[66] Those who adopted this view did not recommend the use of violence as a football tactic, but they did demand the kind of passionate commitment that critics like Alberto Silvares had blamed for Brazilian football violence.[67]

Race, Ethnicity, and the Beautiful Game

Argentine and Brazilian commentators have echoed one another in discussing football in their countries, but they have differed in one major respect. Since the 1930s, discussions of racial and ethnic issues have been more prevalent in Brazil than in Argentina, where issues of geography and class have dominated football discourse. According to many commentators, what has made Brazilian football Brazilian is the country's distinctive racial and ethnic constitution.[68]

Unlike Gilberto Freyre, most Brazilian commentators in the 1930s purposefully excluded the English influence as they identified the ethnic strands that led Brazilians like Fausto to the style they seemed to be employing. They saw their game not as an English-Brazilian hybrid but as diametrically opposed to the English version and detected instead mainly Latin and African influences as coming together to create Brazilian football. Thus, among the unflattering nicknames *Rio Sportivo* listed for the wealthy players of the 1930 World Cup squad was one for Fernando Giudicelli, called the "Mestizo Englishman." In former times such a name might have served as a compliment, but in 1930 it seems to have been meant as a way of criticizing the pretensions and the restrained playing style of another of the dandies, all of whom were light skinned. In contrast, the Afro-Brazilian Fausto was the leader of those "who have Brazilian blood," players who deserved to be praised.[69]

For this critic, Brazilians' performances of their gender and their nationality flowed naturally from their racial character onto the playing field. Truly Brazilian players did not cultivate imported ways but instead were guided by native instinct when they played football. Significantly, the writer was rejecting not only the ideas of Anglophile sportsmen but also the nationalist argument offered by Americo Netto in 1919. Netto had stated that Brazilians had "created" their own style of football. He called it an "innovation" and called on coaches and administrators to lead their players through the "Brazilian school." The style was not inborn; it could be taught, and Netto hoped Brazilian players would learn it and hone it to perfection in order to conquer the football world.[70]

There is no doubt that training was an important part of the emergence of Brazilian football in the 1920s and 1930s. For example, São Christovão's rise in the Carioca championship in the mid-1920s, which included winning the league in 1926, owed much to the coaching of Luiz Vinhais. Vinhais regularly brought his team from the north side of the city to Copacabana in the south, where the players ran the length of the beach in full uniform, cleats and all. Extremely fit and comfortable in the period's heavy gear, São Christovão's players were able to play the game of dribbling and speed that Vinhais demanded.[71] Vinhais brought these methods to many footballers in his long career in Carioca and national football, including when he served as coach of Bangú and of Brazil's 1934 World Cup team. And he was only one of Brazil's innovators. The 1938 seleção, which was at the time depicted as the embodiment of the national style and native Brazilian genius, owed part of its unprecedented success to the fact that organizers "concentrated" the team in the town of Caxambu, Minas Gerais, isolating the players for a period of intensive training.[72] This is now a common practice in Brazil.

In spite of this, many of the football ideologues who attempted to explain the character of the Brazilian style in the 1920s and, especially, in the 1930s were more interested in discussing the essential aspects of Brazil and Brazilians than athletes' hard work and coaches' inventive systems. Ten years before the Confederação Brasileira Desportos oversaw the seleção's concentration in Caxambu, it had insisted on the importance of training. In its yearly report for 1927, it said that the most important factor in a player's will to win was "to understand: virtues can be developed; they can be sought and they can be attained." But it also said that "the moral impulse depends on some hereditary capacities and can also depend on some specific instincts, like, for example, combativeness."[73]

The CBD seems to have been wrestling with the same kinds of problems that confronted Brazilian geneticists in the 1920s. Like the sportsmen who saw football as a school of improvement, in taking upon themselves the long-term task of building a better and stronger country, Brazilian scientists and policymakers in the late nineteenth and early twentieth centuries had rejected racial determinism and vested their faith in the power of ameliorating the local environment. Better hygiene, better medicine, and attacking public health problems like alcoholism, they argued, would lead to permanent advances for the nation. However, in the 1920s, some scientists became worried that such campaigns were not working, demonstrated, for example, by the truculence of the labor movement. They turned back to racial explanations for Brazilian reality and to Mendelian genetics, with its emphasis on nature over nurture. The eugenicist Renato Kehl responded to these challenges with pessimism and antiblack racism, but most others followed the problem-solving optimism of Octavio Domingues, who saw in race mixture the means to resolve the Brazilian dilemma. Domingues and his intellectual successors, like Gilberto Freyre, accepted the importance of race and heredity in the constitution of the nation. But they argued that fusion, accompanied by a renewed commitment to improving public health, would resolve racial and social tensions by producing Brazilians as a homogenous and therefore harmonious nation. In the 1930s, Nancy Leys Stepan says, this view became "the unofficial ideology of the national state."[74]

Freyre's idea of an Anglo-Afro-Brazilian game is an explicit demonstration that the notion could be applied to football. The CBD report shows that some in Brazilian sport were considering the same questions that worried scientists and policymakers in the 1920s. The CBD was considering the relationship between education and heredity, opening up the possibility that "Brazilian blood," not only Brazilian training, was responsible for the progress of national football. The same year, a *Rio Sportivo* writer answered his own question on these matters: "Is there a people predestined to practice a particular *sport*?" He stated that it would be "very difficult for an Anglo-Saxon or Scandinavian to imitate the elegant, delicate, classic movements and honest joy of the bullfighter Belmonte, but it would also be impossible for a Latin to employ the indifference that allows Saxons the physical force needed in rugby." The Latin was "made for" games that demanded "speed, intelligence, and intuition" but could not play those that required "detachment from oneself, excessive endurance or discomfort." In his view, the Latin was best suited for "individual *sports*," such as tennis and cycling; it was not surprising if Latin American football had become individualistic.[75] It also explains why the paper spoke in 1930 of Brazilians being a "predestined race" to succeed on the football field.[76]

Commentators promoted these ideas and employed these terms with increasing frequency in the late-1920s and the 1930s, so that in Brazilian discourse the divide between European and Brazilian football only grew, as it must, given that many writers were asserting that the way someone played football was written into their hereditary makeup. For example, when *A Gazeta* previewed a 1929 match between Corinthians and Chelsea, it said it expected the English team to perform a "classical dance" on the field. In comparison, their Brazilian opponents would employ "the delirium, the vertigo of a '*black botton*' [sic] adapted to the green carpet." Hinting at the idea that would later be called "samba soccer," the paper said that Corinthians' Andrade was the model of the Brazilian player and compared him to Josephine Baker. The Afro-Brazilian Andrade performed a football dance as exotic to the game's English roots as Baker's performances seemed to Europeans eager for provocative stage fare.[77]

In 1931 A.C. explained the disappearance of European players from Brazilian fields by comparing football to a foreign plant, which, he suggested, "acquires new virtues, new qualities" in a new climate. It was not Europeans' lack of interest or their ethnocentrism that explained why they no longer played on Brazilian teams but an essential change that made football in Brazil inhospitable to European players. The change was rooted, he argued, in "the virtues innate to the [Brazilian] race and its temperament," which Europeans simply could not possess.[78] Later *O Estado de S. Paulo* spoke of national "temperament" and "innate qualities" in explaining the differences between Brazilian and Spanish sides that would soon meet in the 1934 World Cup.[79] Spain's 3–1 victory, which meant Brazil's elimination from the tournament, would therefore have been cause for national concern if the seleção had not been compromised by the administrative dispute that meant many of Brazil's best players had been left at home.

The rhetoric of race and heredity was especially prevalent during the 1938 World Cup, the importance of which is impossible to overstate. In advance of the tournament, *Sport Illustrado* noted that most Brazilian players lacked strength and size, but, channeling the language of both nature and malandragem, it insisted that their "instinctive guile assures them an easy means by which to flee from the hard and heavy burden of massive European players." Moreover, it said that "other qualities inherent in the race lead toward individualistic, improvised moves," which would lead the seleção to victory.[80] Apoxy hedged on whether national distinctions were permanent, arguing in *O Estado de S. Paulo* that in 1938 no great difference existed between European and South American football styles. But this was, he said, only because Europeans had adopted the "improvisation, agility, [and] quickness" of South American football, and he spoke of the "inborn qualities" that had led Brazilians and their neighbors to that brand of football in the first place.[81]

Similarly, the *Jornal dos Sports* explained Italy's triumph in the tournament by calling attention to the presence of Brazilians and other South Americans in the Italian league, and in the 1934 Italian World Cup–winning side as well. It argued that these migrants had taught their Italian teammates their way of playing the game and asserted that "only the Latin inheritance made [the 1938 victory] possible."[82] In fact, the ideas and vocabulary of inherence had become ubiquitous in discourse about the way Brazilians played the game, appearing even in an advertisement for Radiotropina, "infallible eliminator of uric acid." Although Brazilian players were very well trained, and although they were intelligent enough to use Radiotropina, these were not the reasons that "we always win." The key to the success of the seleção was instead the fact that "the talent for football is an inborn quality in the absolute majority of Brazilians."[83]

These commentators insisted that Brazilians played football differently from others and that the difference was rooted in inherent national differences. However, they were also making clear choices in explaining the character of Brazilian football, choices that indicate the extent to which the divide they described was, in reality, a matter of rhetoric. First, before and during the 1934 World Cup, Brazilian writers had challenged the idea that footballers of Italian descent who had moved to the peninsula and played for the Italian national team had actually ever been Brazilian at all. They had largely ignored Filó's contributions to Italy's victory and had even used the episode to question the loyalty and Brazilianness of the larger Italian immigrant community. Now, according to the *Jornal dos Sports*, these players were "Latin," and the Italian victories of 1934 and 1938 were proof of the "superiority of South American *foot-ball*."[84] Second, commentators differed in their descriptions of the style of play they thought their countrymen employed. Some called it "South American," others "Latin," and others "uniquely Brazilian." The ease with which commentators moved between the terms suggests the flexibility of nationalists who could advertise the exceptional nature of their countrymen in one moment and emphasize the traits they shared with their (more successful) neighbors in another, in each moment claiming they were pointing out objective proof of Brazil's greatness.

Finally, and related to this, promoters of the notion of a Brazilian style differed in their statements about where in Brazil it emerged and about which players were most likely to embody it. Some nationalists argued that the Brazilian style required the participation of all of Brazil's constituents, as seen, for example, in José Lins do Rego's depiction of the 1932 seleção that defeated Uruguay in Montevideo as proof of Brazil's social and racial democracy. Lins do Rego argued the victory owed not only to who the players were but to how they played, asserting that the 1932 seleção won "in good Brazilian style, with the most entertaining improvisation." Echoing his contemporaries in science and government, he said that the accomplishment reinforced his faith in the country. "I believe in Brazil," he wrote, "in the eugenic qualities of our mestizos, in the energy and the intelligence of the men of the Brazilian land, forged from diverse bloodlines, giving them an originality which will one day shock the world."[85]

Others argued over regional differences, especially between Rio de Janeiro and São Paulo. Thomaz Mazzoni hoped that Brazilians would one day overcome their regional loyalties to improve national football, but as of 1932, he said, there were obvious differences between Carioca and Paulista football, the former faster and the latter more technically skilled.[86] Six years later, in O Estado de S. Paulo, Apoxy made a different version of the argument, saying that Paulistas had followed their instincts to become "first in 'technique and haste'" among Brazilians. They had created what he called "the 'productive game,' the game of unexpected and thrilling strikes," while other Brazilians were wasting their energies, straining to imitate European football.[87] This helps explain why he complained that France's *L'Auto* had called the members of the 1938 seleção "mestiços of the black race," saying the French must be "jealous" to use such racial terminology.[88] There were, after all, white players on the team, including one of its captains, Martim, along with Batatais (Algisto Lorenzato), Romeu Pellicciari, and Tim (Elba de Pádua Lima), all of whom were Paulistas and all of whom played in Brazilian victories.

In contrast, like the nationalists who adopted the samba of the capital and promoted it as typically Brazilian, Rio de Janeiro–based football commentators used the 1938 World Cup to brand the Brazilian style as Carioca and as Afro-Brazilian.[89] Gilberto Freyre, for example, highlighted the African contribution to the national style in *Diários Associados* in June 1938, when he said that "our passes, our catches, our misleads, our floridness with the ball" reminded him of dancing and capoeira, the Afro-Brazilian martial art. Tiago Maranhão shows that, although Freyre argued that he did not mean the "Mulatism" that he said characterized Brazilian football to allude to ethnicity, he did later state that he believed the Brazilian style to be most common among and exemplified by those whose blood or culture was "African."[90]

One of the players that Freyre had in mind was Leônidas da Silva, who Freyre later said played football as if he were dancing the samba, "the dance full of irrational surprises and Dionysian variations."[91] Leônidas' goals and incredible performances led Brazil to the semifinal of the tournament and earned the team the unofficial title of "kings without crowns." He was the "Rubber Man," able to twist his body into unlikely positions and perform spectacular tricks, like executing a successful bicycle kick. And he was the "Black Diamond," performing his brilliant Brazilian blackness to dazzle crowds, competitors, and journalists. Leônidas had achieved national renown when he scored both of Brazil's goals in the 1932 Copa Rio Branco, but before the tournament in France he was popular mainly in Rio de Janeiro. Denaldo Souza argues that Leônidas' popularity was rooted in the way he played the game, for even as a small man, he was able to deceive bigger opponents, "dribbling around them, as one dribbled around the difficulties of life." Working-class fans identified with Leônidas, Souza says, seeing in him the possibilities open to "a person humble, yet cunning and bold, against the powerful," and they were inspired by his success.[92] They were inspired, in other words, by his performance of malandragem.

Leônidas also understood football's transformation into a business and the role he could play in managing his own public image to benefit his career. In 1938 he was playing for Flamengo and, alongside several other Afro-Brazilian players, was helping administrators transform its image from a club

FIGURE 5.3. Leônidas da Silva in the colors of the Bonsuccesso Football Club, circa 1930. By permission of the Club Athletico Paulistano.

of the capital's sports aristocracy to the club of the masses. He made himself available to fans and journalists, unlike his Flamengo teammate Domingos da Guia, to whom he was often compared. In Mário Filho's view, one of the reasons Leônidas was popular was because fans "could get close to" him while, because of Domingos' reserve, fans were obligated to "admire Domingos from afar." Domingos was, Filho said, like "the cold, imperturbable Englishman" of innumerable Brazilian anecdotes.[93]

In early 1938 Leônidas demonstrated his understanding of the business of Brazilian football when he campaigned to win a contest sponsored by Magnolia cigarettes to find the capital's most popular player. During the contest he gave interviews encouraging his fans to vote, he delivered cigarettes to one of Rio de Janeiro's prisons, and he appeared in advertisements for the company. He announced he was a "Carioca da Gemma," reminding voters he was Rio de Janeiro–born and bred, from the embryo, or "yolk," according to the traditional and popular expression, staking a claim to fans' support because of who he was, not how he played. Leônidas won the contest and the grand prize, a Chevrolet automobile, collecting 249,080 votes, which was more than the combined number of votes received by Hercules de Miranda and Oscarino, who finished in second and third place, respectively.[94]

In the aftermath of the World Cup that year, fans, journalists, businessmen, and even Getúlio Vargas came together in support of the idea that Leônidas was the perfect example of the national style and that his style and his success were rooted in his true Brazilianness. Eager to associate themselves with Leônidas and appeal to his fan-consumers, the grocer Silva, Farias & Cia., Vencedor clothing, the federal government lottery, Luz flourmill, the Vulcain watch company, and the J. M. Mello dishware company all featured him in advertisements or invited him to visit their offices, where they presented him with gifts, making sure to alert the press.[95] In its advertisement, Recife's Peixe brand guava jam included a group photograph of the entire seleção, along with their autographs, beneath a larger photograph of director Manoel de Britto shaking hands with Leônidas, and next to a handwritten note from the great player. Including copy that claimed Britto was proud to have been "one of the first to embrace Leônidas upon his arrival on home soil," the advertisement was an overt statement that it was Leônidas more than any other player who really counted, especially when it came to appealing to the public; he was, it said, "the supreme Brazilian '*Crack*.'"[96]

Other businesses promoted themselves alongside Leônidas as well and drew attention to both the way he played the game and his race. The Broadway and Pathé Palacio theaters used Leônidas' image in their advertisements for films of Brazil's tournament matches, calling him "the human phenomenon!" The São Luiz theater used Leônidas to advertise the film *Alma e corpo de uma raça* (Body and soul of a race), about the storied history of Leônidas' club, Flamengo, which was directed by Mário Filho's brother, Milton Rodrigues.[97] Most famously, Lacta hired him to brand its "Black Diamond" chocolate bar, which is still available in Brazil, while Rio de Janeiro's Carlos Gomes theater presented a "burlesque-review" with the same name. In two acts and seventeen scenes, the review presented the "Story of the Glorious *Football 'Crack'*!" Leônidas also appeared on stage himself, in Rio de Janeiro and Belo Horizonte, where he told packed crowds about his performances in the World Cup and even demonstrated how he had scored against Poland after having lost his cleat, removing his shoe to reenact the event.[98] Not to be outdone, politicians, including Getúlio Vargas and the governor of Minas Gerais, Benedito Valadares Ribeiro, availed themselves of the opportunity to pay their own respects to Leônidas and bask in his reflected glory.[99] No other player received this kind of attention. Other members of the seleção, such as Domingos, Oscarino, and Walter de Sousa Goulart, appeared in advertisements for local businesses after the tournament, but the notice afforded them by media, advertisers, and fans was dwarfed by the image of the larger-than-life Leônidas, to the point that Domingos and other teammates became annoyed about the difference in treatment.[100]

The business most dedicated to promoting and benefiting from Leônidas' celebrity, the sports press, made many of the same points, often in a more explicit manner. For example, Thomaz Mazzoni mentioned that Leônidas was black when he described and explained his ability to "undo opponents' aggressive play" by dribbling around them. When they succeeded in fouling him, he courageously picked himself each and every time, "in order to impose respect."[101]

None were more eager to use Leônidas' image and none more important in promoting his image as the personification of national football as an Afro-Brazilian expression than Mário Filho and the *Jornal dos Sports*. Having published Leônidas' image on innumerable occasions and reported on any happening or even rumor related to the star, the paper explained the attraction in reporting on some of this extraordinary attention, stating that it was fueled by more than goals or victories. In a report on Leônidas' visit to the Mello dishware company, the paper said that he and his teammates had demonstrated "an artistic, elegant, and spectacular style" along with "the substance of authentic Brazilians, a ceaseless devotion, a will to win renewed with each move of the match." Among the members of the team, Leônidas "was one of those who most merited popular acclaim, and he has earned lasting popular affection." He was "an astonishing virtuoso on the ball, football's stylist, a sensation and spectacle on the field, in a word, the 'Black Diamond.'" Finally, the paper called him the "Malabarista," or Trickster.[102] For Mário Filho and many others, such as Mazzoni, who also wrote about his "disconcerting trickery," Leônidas' success at football had marked him as special, but it was the way he played that made him the best among "authentic Brazilians."[103] In him, nationalist admirers read lessons about courage and masculinity, authenticity and blackness, nature and magic. They located his style of football in essential aspects of the Brazilian environment and Brazilian race. It was a matter of innate national genius, a "phenomenon" that could be performed but could not be taught.

However, Leônidas' consecration in 1938 is also an indication that, when Brazilians discussed the national style, they did not always agree on what they were discussing and that the discourse of the Brazilian style obscured choices motivated by nationalism and by the market. Mário Filho was often critical of Leônidas, disappointed that he did not seem able to fulfill the role that nationalists designed for him. Black and working class, Leônidas had accomplished much, especially on behalf of the nation as a member of the seleção, and thus might potentially symbolize the state's success in raising workers' economic level and folding the marginalized into the national polity. Unfortunately, he clashed with coaches and administrators, broke contracts, and was reluctant to train. Mário Filho's doubts about Leônidas grew in the aftermath of the World Cup, when Filho became convinced that the accolades Leônidas had won convinced him he merited permanent special treatment. Like Fausto before him, Leônidas clashed with his coach at Flamengo, Dori Kürschner, as well as Kürschner's successor, Flávio Costa. And, like Fausto, Leônidas lost the struggle in spite of his celebrity. When Flamengo sold his contract to the São Paulo club in 1942, Filho approved; he had already called Leônidas "Flamengo's biggest adversary" on the eve of the club's 1939 game against Fluminense.[104]

Filho was already concerned about Leônidas' behavior before the World Cup, and his critique extended to his performances on the field. Filho believed Leônidas was either unable or unwilling to join his imagination and invention to a sense of purpose that would bring about productive ends, to dribble but also to score goals and win victories, and so he was surprised when Leônidas emerged as the hero of Brazil's tournament run.[105] Neither his misgivings nor his surprise prevented Filho from promoting Leônidas in *O Globo* and the *Jornal dos Sports*, though, because he understood how popular Leônidas was with the reading public, and he understood the benefits to be had in embracing Leônidas during the "apotheosis" of the World Cup. In July 1938 the *Jornal dos Sports* noted that Leônidas was so popular that businessmen knew that associating themselves with him ensured public notice, for "Leonidas' presence anywhere in the city is an enduring attraction," and Filho later said that during this period "journalists counted on Leonidas to finish a page," the most mundane item about him guaranteeing higher circulation.[106]

In 1938 the steady pull of the market was strengthened by an impulse to take advantage of the World Cup moment to build the nationalist story, and Mário Filho promoted Leônidas as the ideal Brazilian footballer. In fact, however, in spite of some of the items he published in *O Globo* and *Jornal dos Sports*, Filho did not believe that Leônidas was either the country's best player or the most exemplary of the ideal Brazilian style. In the first edition of *O negro no foot-ball brasileiro*, published in 1947, he claimed that Domingos da Guia had been "recognized, unanimously, as the best Brazilian player of all time," the perfect blend of imagination and tactical intelligence. Leônidas could inspire fans, but he did not seem able to engineer the triumph of his team the way Domingos could. Domingos was "The Divine Master," a player who was both exceptionally talented and a thoughtful leader.[107]

Filho believed, according to Souza, that "technique, ability, a Brazilian way of playing, swing [*ginga*], the dribble, all of this was indispensable if Brazilian football were to acquire its own style. However, these characteristics were not enough."[108] Also necessary were "tactical discipline [and] organization, in order to give rhythm to the game," traits that Filho said Domingos possessed and Leônidas did not. It was because of this that Filho and his collaborator, Gilberto Freyre, believed that it was Domingos who "best represented, not the real nation, but the nation they aimed to create." Like Leônidas, Domingos had the right social and racial profile to symbolize national integration and emergence. Like Leônidas, he was talented and played in the Brazilian way, as seen especially in his signature move, the "Domingada," in which he dribbled the ball out of defense, making defense into attack in a surprising, confident, and potentially risky way. But Domingos was disciplined off the field, in his dealings with coaches, administrators, and journalists, as well as on it, where he seemed to know how to translate imagination into advantage, which was why, Filho argued, Domingos won more often than Leônidas did before Leônidas' late-career move to São Paulo.[109]

Mário Filho, Gilberto Freyre, and other nationalists hoped that Brazilian football would become a hybrid of discipline and imagination, of "English" restraint and "Afro-Brazilian" creativity. Filho knew that it was imagination and creativity that inspired fans and sold papers because they satisfied the nationalist appetite for a distinctive Brazilian identity and pleased working-class torcedores who saw this as a display of the craft that humble people needed to make their way in the world. Filho and other promoters of the idea of a Brazilian brand of football therefore spoke mainly about natural, national genius and instinctive artistry. They did, though, also advocate for discipline, restraint, and teamwork in the hopes that popular and gratifying fantasy football could be combined with the unglamorous and yet necessary old principle of discipline. In fact, the influential Mazzoni, who was an unapologetically patriotic champion of Brazilian football in the 1930s, was also certain that indiscipline was one of the principal problems facing the

FIGURE 5.4. José Meurer Ripper and Domingos da Guia (*right*) during a match between Fluminense and Bangú, July 28, 1929. Mário Filho believed Domingos was "the best Brazilian player of all time." By permission of the Acervo Flu-Memória.

game in that decade.¹¹⁰ He dedicated many of his editorials in *A Gazeta* to the subject and demanded that football authorities take a stronger hand to promote order and restraint among the country's footballers.¹¹¹ Discourse about the way the game should be played was far from uncomplicated in the 1930s, far from describing an era of unbridled and optimistic celebration of Afro-Brazil.

In 1931, five years before Mário Filho took over the paper, the *Jornal dos Sports* was already celebrating "the superiority of Brazilian *football*" and stating that "the agility of Brazilians can overcome European technique."¹¹² But it also complained that the old problem of violence continued to plague Carioca playing fields. It pointed out that it was "rare, extremely rare, that there are matches played here in which various players do not leave the field injured" due to violent play. Frequently, the paper said, athletes were obligated to go directly to the hospital because of violence they suffered on the playing field. "*Football* is ceasing to be a *sport* one plays in order to improve his physical condition or amuse himself for a little while, becoming instead an extremely dangerous practice, in which life itself runs a grave risk."¹¹³

At the same time, the national style was leading Brazilians inexorably toward international dominance, and they were playing a game that, the paper said, "one cannot call a *sport* without doing grave offense to the truth." The problem was rooted in Brazilian notions of masculinity, with players and even referees believing in the "insidious and unacceptable excuse that 'football is a game for men.'" Especially troubling were those "whose specialty is violent play, who have the habit of aiming to incapacitate their opponents through kicks and other illicit means, a practice that degrades and demeans." It called on administrators to punish the offenders, protect the innocent, and moralize the sport, "not only because the laws of *sport* demand it, but because it is a duty of humanitarianism."¹¹⁴

The paper expected that professionalization would go a long way in resolving the game's problems, restoring it to its proper purpose by cutting away the immorality of false amateurism and raising players' sense of mutual respect as fellow professionals. But a particularly violent match between Fluminense and Palestra Itália during Brazilian football's first professional season demonstrated that problems persisted even after that reform came. In that August 1933 match, referee Argemiro Ballio controversially marked off a Fluminense goal at the beginning of the second half for what he saw as a foul on Palestra Itália's goalkeeper, Nascimento. Soon after, Palestra Itália scored from an "obviously off-side" position, according to J. T. de Carvalho in *Athletica*, but the goal stood.¹¹⁵ These incidents set the stage for the outbreak of violence among the players, Palestra Itália's João Lara Nascimento attacking Nariz (Álvaro Lopes Cançado), Chiquito (Francisco de Matos) defending his Fluminense teammate, and Sandro (Alessandro Bressani) coming to Lara's aid. Ballio attempted and failed to expel the players, and the police guarding the field failed to restrain angry fans who invaded the pitch. Fluminense fans, allegedly including a policeman, argued with Ballio and even attacked him, obligating club directors to save him from the crowd and usher him off the field.¹¹⁶ At that point, three minutes from time, the match was abandoned and Palestra Itália won, 4–1.

Carvalho asserted that the referee shared the blame and was unable to "exercise his authority" and "impotent" in his attempt to maintain order. *O Globo* agreed, calling his performance "very weak," though *A Noite* said the criticisms were "unjust" and that Ballio had demonstrated "impartiality" throughout the match.¹¹⁷ Regardless, all agreed that what resulted was a scandal. Both Carvalho and *O Globo* saw "savagery," and *A Noite* called the events "lamentable" and "most disturbing." It was troubling that the police did not perform their duty, and that Ballio missed the offside player in the buildup to Palestra Itália's goal, but the real problem lay in the lack of sportsmanship among players and fans and a reflexive aggression that appeared as soon as one's side began to struggle. Like the editor of the *Jornal dos Sports* in 1931, these commentators appealed to sports authorities to act to improve what Carvalho called the game's "disciplinary aspect," since players did not seem willing to control themselves.

In fact, all of these writers spoke in terms reminiscent of the rhetoric of Ernest Weber, C. Viveiros, and others from the earliest years of Brazilian football. *A Noite* spoke of fans' "misunderstanding" of the game. *O Globo* referred to Fluminense's "lack of control." And Carvalho spoke of the necessity of providing fans and players the "sporting education that will allow us to accept, in a gentlemanly fashion, our adversaries' victory."¹¹⁸ Carvalho had been writing on football since at least 1918 under the occasional pseudonym John Karr and had been discussing the necessity of educating the sports public for his entire career, including in the elitist *Vida Sportiva*. By 1933 he had become unsure whether the game could be saved, whether "at last, we will make football what it ought to be, a pastime." He left such "painful questions" unanswered.¹¹⁹

Carvalho therefore might be considered a holdover from the era of the Anglophile and elitist sportsmen. But *A Noite* served the popular classes, and

Mário Filho was sports editor *O Globo* in 1933, by which time he had been honing his populist message about the glories of working-class football, the importance of professionalization, and the value of passion and intensity to the Brazilian style for some time. In the face of the "scenes of true savagery" displayed by Fluminense, Palestra Itália, and their fans, *O Globo* reminded readers of passion's proper limits, and of the continuing importance of control and discipline to Brazilian football.

Finally, five years later, on the eve of the 1938 World Cup, concerns about discipline and teamwork led promoters of the Brazilian style to doubt the seleção's performance. In *O Estado de S. Paulo*, Apoxy said that "agility, intuition, [and] speed" had helped Brazilians to create a potentially successful national style, and he called on his countrymen to maintain and improve it. But he also argued that Brazil could not depend upon these qualities, for others could adapt to counter them. He echoed earlier tacticians' advice that "no matter how much it is boasted of, superior technique does the player no good if it is not conditioned by mental training," and, even after Brazil's famous victory against Poland he said he hoped the team's defense would not "worry themselves in impressing fans with useless moves." Instead, he reported the "hard truth" that "football is played with more than the feet." Clearly exasperated, he reminded his readers that "football—how many times will it be necessary to repeat it!—is essentially a collective sport, demanding teamwork and more or less perfect communication between all of the elements of the side." He cautioned against an overreliance on improvisation and lamented that the seleção had not trained enough to succeed. When Brazil lost in the semifinal against Italy, he joined other Brazilians in complaining about the referee, but he also pointed out that the team had come to rely too heavily on the solitary brilliance of individuals like Leônidas, who was hurt and missed the match, and Apoxy was therefore unsurprised at the result.[120]

Before the tournament began, Mário Filho explained in the *Jornal dos Sports* that he too doubted the teamwork and the discipline of the members of the seleção. He wrote,

> The ideal *team* shares an absolutely identical objective. The *crack* is part of a system, making himself one part of a machine which functions perfectly only if each part fulfills the role assigned him....
>
> To be part of a *scratch* team, for which it is not the supremacy of clubs which is in play but rather the prestige of Brazilian *foot-ball*, the *crack*

has to learn obedience—the basic requirement for discipline. Obedience means silence, in the sense of not arguing with orders, or even of thinking about them from the point of view of one's own interests.[121]

Once the matches began and Brazil began to win, Filho and his *Jornal* writers seem to have forgotten uniformity, systems, machinery, obedience, discipline, and silence, focusing instead on the seemingly organic and inspired artistry of the Brazilian style, especially that of the Trickster, Leônidas. Filho would remember these traditional values in the ensuing months and years, explaining Leônidas' surprising success as a function of the player's having temporarily accepted the value of discipline right before the tournament began.[122] During the heady days of the 1938 World Cup, Filho seems to have been willing to set aside his doubts and his concerns in the service of a satisfying and profitable celebration of national genius. Afterward he returned to the theme of discipline, and he was not alone; Thomaz Mazzoni, for example, argued that since sports authorities could not bring discipline to Brazilian football, the "authoritarian voice" of the Vargas regime must take the responsibility of doing so.[123]

Floriano had also doubted Brazil would perform very well in France and told the *Jornal dos Sports* that Brazilian players lost "at least fifty percent" of their effectiveness when playing abroad because they relied too heavily on the inspiration provided by home crowds.[124] In 1938 Floriano left Brazil to find work as a coach abroad, leaving behind the "fools" who believed Brazilians had been specially chosen by the gods of football and who refused to countenance the idea that foreigners could offer them useful advice. Mário Filho's doubts and Apoxy's exasperation indicate that Floriano was not alone in fearing that Brazilians had forgotten the lessons of discipline and teamwork; even promoters of the Brazilian style worried that Brazilian players and fans had been seduced by the heady and patriotic discourse of innate styles of play and natural national genius.

However, partnered by fans, players, administrators, and statesmen, these journalists and many of their colleagues were themselves vital in constructing this discourse. They participated in its construction because they believed in some of its principal tenets; because they saw the possibility of using it to build pride in Brazil and a distinctive, homogenous, and hopeful national identity; and because they wanted to sell newspapers. The tactical ideals of the sportsmen echoed in their writings—for example, in the "English" part of the hybrid football Filho and Gilberto Freyre hoped to promote and, especially, in persistent calls for discipline. But these were overwhelmed, Floriano said, by the temptation to believe that Brazilians possessed an exceptional and even innate talent for football that did not require training, planning, or structure. Even in the comments of its purveyors, the ideal of a hybrid was often marginalized by the notion of absolute differentiation, of a dichotomy between English and European football on one hand and Brazilian football on the other. As Simoni Guedes says in describing later iterations of this argument, this meant the exclusion of English influences and a preference for seeing the national football style as a realization of "the myth of the three races"—Indian, European, and African coming together in "a *mestiço* amalgam in which doubtlessly the place of the Black race is determinant"—so that, rather than a true amalgam, many influential writers over the years described Brazilian football as an Afro-Brazilian game.[125]

Filho, Freyre, and their contemporaries did not speak of a "Brazilian school" as Americo Netto did, or a Brazilian "adaptation," as Apoxy called the Brazilian style, both of which implied training and active intervention. Instead, they promoted the idea that the national style was innate to Brazil and Brazilians—Afro-Brazilians, especially—and that it was distinct from the game played outside Brazil's borders. They demanded practice and discipline not to create the style but to tame its basic characteristics and channel them to productive ends. This idea is challenged from many directions, especially from the past, when it was first articulated. In the 1910s, 1920s, and 1930s, Brazilian coaches worked to invent new ways of playing, and footballers practiced intensely and chose to play in a particular way, often because it pleased their fans. Far from particularly distinct, the discourse of the Brazilian style echoed commentary about football in Uruguay and Argentina and even about how others played very different sports, while Europeans strained to learn from what they often described as the South American way.[126] Commentators argued about whether the national style was Carioca or Paulista; about the extent of the influence of English and Latin and African elements; and about the relative importance of instinct and training. They sometimes contradicted themselves, revealing their own doubts and hinting at their choices.

During the 1930s those who promoted the idea of a Brazilian style wrestled with these inconvenient facts, but they also often ignored or minimized them in the service of a discourse of nationalism centered on the idea that a particular kind of football was a metaphor of Brazil's realization of its "lofty destiny." Setting aside their doubts, they traced their beautiful game to Brazil's cultural and racial roots. They asserted that Brazilians had not created, invented, or adapted this game but had discovered it within themselves when they set aside their compulsion to follow English and European teachings. It is this discourse that represented the real and most important invention of Brazilian football, for its triumph is as plain as the idea of an authentic and innate Brazilian style is questionable. After all, since Floriano's time, the conviction that Brazilians are naturally "the best in the world" at football because they play it in an inherently distinctive way—the beautiful game—has only become more popular in Brazil and far beyond.

Epilogue

The Life of the Beautiful Game

The idea of the beautiful game is a powerful one, and it has had a long and prosperous career since the 1930s. For eight decades, coaches and politicians, journalists and scholars have used it as a shorthand for describing Brazilians' authentic national identity, one that celebrates the creative promise of cultivating harmony from diverse roots. They have used it to communicate their ideas, to campaign for public support, and to tell their stories. Businesses have also used it to sell their products, for example, as FIFA and the Brazilian organizing committee did in marketing the 2014 World Cup held in Brazil with the slogan "All in one rhythm" and advertising materials that referenced Brazilian popular culture, such as Recife's traditional umbrella dance, the *frevo*, and Salvadoran women in hoop skirts, in the emblematic Bahian style associated with candomblé.[1] In the extraordinary number of works of every type released to coincide with the 2014 World Cup, the idea of the beautiful game was ubiquitous.[2]

Although its promoters asserted that the beautiful game was inherent to Brazil, the assertion was based on their selective narration of Brazilian football history and their particular interpretation of the character of Brazilian culture, just as footballers who seemed to be naturally disposed to play in a distinctive manner had in fact crafted the "Brazilian" style. Brazilians created the idea of the beautiful game, and succeeding generations of Brazilians have remade it according to their own perspectives about football and their country. Moreover, not every Brazilian has embraced the idea; among those who have, they have not always found it in their football when they looked for it. Whether they dislike what it purports to say about Brazil or whether they have worried about its absence, Brazilians have often debated the meaning and the value of the beautiful game, so it has been not only a shorthand used to speak about Brazil but also a lexicon for Brazilians' arguments about their country and a touchstone for their actions to make it correspond more closely to their hopes.

One way to consider the life of the beautiful game is to examine how Brazilians have used it to talk about the country in a few key moments, intervals marked by the quadrennial World Cup. The seleção did not win the tournament until 1958, coming closest with a second-place finish in 1950. However, the World Cup was already important to the Brazilians who built the futebol tradition; the 1938 tournament was their proof of the country's football genius, their players "kings without crowns" robbed of victory by biased referees. Once Brazil won the competition, many Brazilians began to expect victory in every World Cup, and the seleção often met their expectations, Brazil having won the tournament four more times since 1958. Brazilians and foreigners alike have argued that Brazil won so often because Brazilians played the beautiful game, which, beside its authenticity and aesthetic appeal, also had the advantage of being effective. It is no surprise, then, that some Brazilians have marked the life of the nation in four-year increments, each tournament an opportunity to revisit ideas about Brazil, and, as Édison Gastaldo puts it, to perform a "true ritual of celebrating nationality."[3]

In 1950 Brazil hosted the World Cup for the first time. It came at a moment of national optimism, five years after the fall of the Vargas regime and the restoration of electoral politics, during a period when the national economy was growing at a rapid pace. The tournament seemed a metaphor for Brazil's entry into the first rank of nations, not least because much of it took place in Rio de Janeiro's new and colossal Maracanã stadium, the concrete symbol of Brazil's great ambitions. Once the tournament began, expectations grew. The seleção won and kept winning, and it won in style, black men and whites playing with imagination and verve, cheered on by huge crowds that, in the words of José Sergio Leite Lopes, made the Maracanã into a carnival, "a collective dramatisation of a cultural and playful sentiment of nationality dissociated from politics and from the habitual military and patriotic context."[4] That is, it was not only hosting the competition but also Brazilians' way of playing and watching football that ought to have made the tournament the announcement of Brazil's greatness, the ultimate demonstration of the value of the beautiful game.

It was not to be. Due to the odd format of the tournament in that year, Brazil needed only a draw against Uruguay in the final match to win the World Cup. Many expected a landslide victory for the home team, with, for example, Rio de Janeiro's mayor Ângelo Mendes de Morais famously calling the members of the seleção world champions before the match, but Brazil lost 2–1 to a goal by Alcides Ghiggia late in the game.[5] The loss is often referred to as the Maracanaço, which one writer has called "Brazilian football's biggest tragedy," and it scarred Brazilians and Brazilian sport.[6] The journalist Paulo Perdigão called it "the Waterloo of the tropics" and the Maracanã "a type of mixed-race Titanic," and Nelson Rodrigues' oft-recorded comment that "every country has its Hiroshima" gives a sense of the scale of the loss' impact for some Brazilians.[7] Looking back, many Brazilians explain the defeat as a consequence of a combination of overconfidence and the weight of expectation felt by the players, the crowd chanting "One more! One more!" after Brazil scored an early goal and encouraging the seleção to attack, when a more pragmatic approach would have been to protect the lead. Few mention the possibility of Uruguay having been the better team.[8]

Some contemporaries went beyond identifying the flaws of the seleção's approach to the match. They suspected that Brazilians' trust in the effectiveness of the beautiful game was a sign of national naiveté, which they in turn explained by pointing to the country's racial constitution. Lopes points out that contemporaries rarely mentioned race or color in celebrating the seleção in its run to the final, but after the loss, "old stereotypes" returned, and critics attacked Brazilians' acceptance of purportedly unreconstructed Afro-Brazilian influences, alleging that immaturity was a characteristically African trait.[9] They assigned blame for the defeat to the Afro-Brazilian members of the team, especially the defender Bigode and the goalkeeper Moacyr Barbosa, who were beaten on Uruguay's second goal. Barbosa suffered a remarkable amount of abuse, so much so that he felt the burden of the defeat until his death almost fifty years later. As even Mário Filho was forced to admit, despite his earlier claims of futebol's racial democracy, Brazilians were not yet prepared to treat all of their players equally.[10] As long as they were successful, Afro-Brazilian players were accepted and could even be celebrated; when they failed, they faced fierce recrimination from those whose allegiance was always conditional.

The 1950 episode demonstrates that many Brazilians had become convinced of the central tenets of the futebol tradition invented during the 1920s and 1930s. They had become convinced that Brazilians, especially Afro-Brazilians, played football in a particular way because they must—because it was in their blood, in the country's environment and history, and it was the authentic expression of their national identity. Hence the scale of their sense of the "tragedy" of the Maracanã in July 1950. If the Brazilian style was an authentic expression of Brazil's national character, then the flaws it revealed might permanently inhibit Brazil's development. Some critics demanded football's complete renovation, arguing that Brazilian football and, they hinted, Brazil could only succeed by the reduction of "Afro-Brazilian" influences and the promotion of greater discipline and pragmatism. Others worried that this was impossible, and Brazilians might have to come to terms with permanent backwardness.

The administrator João Lyra Filho, for example, explained Brazil's failed 1954 World Cup campaign by arguing that Brazilians and Europeans were opposites, spontaneity and instinct on one side, experience and reason on the other. Lyra Filho was a director of the Botafogo club and had been a member of the Conselho Nacional de Desportos, through which he had worked to shape football as a school of discipline and to train Brazilians to combine natural talents and tutored order to create a productive playing style.[11] According to Lyra Filho, the seleção's failures in the early-1950s demonstrated that Brazilians still lacked self-control, which was Europeans' distinctive and most advantageous trait, and they lacked it because "the fundamental characteristics of the *Brazilian people (mestizo, mulatto)* are those of black people."[12] In a 1954 volume he argued that the project of combining European and Brazilian traits had faltered, and he worried about whether it could be revived; like many commentators in 1950, he blamed the country's African roots. Lyra Filho helped sustain the ideas of the Vargas years, and the dichotomy he described continued to inform Brazilian views of their football and their country for generations.[13]

Such pessimism seemed absurd when Brazil won the 1958 World Cup as well as two of the next three, in 1962 and 1970, eradicating many doubts about national football and the value of the Brazilian style. According to contemporary commentators and to popular memory, the seleção of the

1958–70 period played with joy and flair and imagination, its style personified by talented Afro-Brazilians who played the beautiful game, especially the mulatto Garrincha and the black Pelé. Many have overlooked administrators' unprecedented level of planning and the seleção's unusually intense training in favor of depicting this "Golden Age" as the natural result of Brazilians' instinctive genius for the game.[14] Those successes seemed to ratify the futebol tradition, making it an even more durable feature of Brazilian ideas about football, including the conviction that essential and racial characteristics directed the destiny of the nation. The difference between Brazilian responses to 1958–70 and 1950–54 was not a difference of the interpretation of the meaning of futebol. It was a difference between optimism and pessimism, and the confidence of the late 1930s came coursing back, renewed and deepened.

In 1964 Mário Filho published a revised edition of *O negro no futebol brasileiro* in which he celebrated the victories of 1958 and 1962 as the culmination of the transition from "foot-ball" to "futebol," from a game of Eurocentric whites and the wealthy to a game of authentic Brazilians of all colors and classes but played best by black men. The book included a new final part, "The Proving of the Black Man," whose protagonist was Pelé, and who was, as Denaldo Souza says, "the hero of which [Filho] always dreamed for Brazil." Filho argued that Pelé blended European and Brazilian football characteristics and therefore embodied the futebol hero. Pelé was black and working-class, a dribbler who played with flair and imagination, in a *Brazilian* way. Like Domingos da Guia before him, and unlike Leônidas da Silva and his own contemporary, the famously impetuous and, perhaps not coincidentally, more beloved Garrincha, Pelé also worked hard and was thought to be disciplined and sensible. According to Filho, Pelé showed that Brazilians could learn discipline and could channel natural instincts to productive ends without losing what made them Brazilian.[15] Gilberto Freyre found Pelé just as useful in making his argument that Brazilian football was a synthesis, an "Anglo-Afro-Brazilian game" that he tracked from the "aristocratic" Marcos de Mendonça to the "admirable" Pelé. According to Freyre, Pelé and other "dancers of the ball" demonstrated the possibility of reconciling English and Brazilian cultures that had seemed "apparently irreconcilable."[16]

However, as much as Filho and Freyre championed the idea that futebol could enact a synthesis of the dichotomy between Brazilian and English/European traits, both still promoted the idea that this dichotomy existed and that it was rooted in essential racial categories. The triumphs of 1958–70 seemed to ratify their views, and they helped sustain the influence of those authors and the influence of their partners in inventing the futebol tradition, such as José Lins do Rego and Nelson Rodrigues.[17] They depicted futebol as embodying Brazil's authentic national identity, and they argued that World Cup victories were the proof the Brazilian people required to accept their true identity and its value. Rodrigues, for example, asserted that the working-class and nonwhite Brazilians he met after the 1958 victory were more confident and more assertive than they had ever been. "After 1958," he wrote, "the Brazilian was no longer a stray dog [vira-lata] among men and Brazil was no longer a stray among nations."[18]

One demonstration of the futebol tradition's renewed influence on Brazilian thinking is its almost constant appearance in commentators' analysis of the 1958–70 period, including its emphasis both on the importance of Brazil's racial identity and on inborn talent over training. For example, in describing the way the Golden Generation played, José Miguel Wisnik has said that, through football, "mulattoes created a playful language—curving the straight line and squaring the circle—in which they wove the tangled threads of a barely abolished slavery and the chaos left in its wake into a splendid affirmation of power and, with it, the 'promise of happiness.'"[19] Similarly, Richard Follett has depicted Garrincha as embodying the malandro and playing "an authentically Afro-Brazilian footballing style," while Arlei S. Damo and Rubén G. Oliven describe futebol as "made in Brazil: white in its laws, black in its style," and coming of age in the 1958–70 period.[20]

Another indication of the tradition's influence was the perspective of the military rulers who governed Brazil from 1964 to 1985, especially their attempt in the 1970s to remake football by curbing what they saw as the disorderly aspects of the Brazilian style. The dictatorship took advantage of Brazil's World Cup victories for their propaganda potential, one of many interventions in the sports world. But it also sought to use football and the seleção to model a different Brazil than the one the Brazilian style described: a country, a sport, and a national team "in its own image," as Matthew Shirts says. This meant "an emphasis on discipline and obedience to the detriment of improvisation, on teamwork in place of individual expression, on physical force instead of art."[21] Thus, the military-appointed coach of the seleção, army captain Claudio Coutinho, called dribbling "a waste of time and proof of our weakness."[22] The military rulers accepted that the Brazilian style was an authentic expression of contemporary national identity. What they sought in confronting the style was to change that identity, to remake Brazil by remaking Brazilian football.

The military dictatorship changed football in important ways, for example, by creating the country's first true national championship for club teams (in 1971) and by annulling the Vargas-era ban on women's football. But it was unable to dislodge the futebol tradition, and critics of the regime challenged its legitimacy by defending the Brazilian style throughout the 1970s and early 1980s, especially because the 1974 and 1978 World Cup teams failed to turn the military's "modern" football into victory. The regime's critics depicted a return of the seleção to the beautiful game as a means of returning Brazil to itself, and it is therefore no surprise that the democracy movement cultivated the regime's football critics for their own campaign. The most famous of these was Sócrates, the outspoken midfielder who led the "Corinthian Democracy" movement of the early-1980s, which challenged the hierarchical structure of Brazilian club football. Sócrates insisted on "preserving the ludic, joyous and pleasurable nature" of football in the face of rationalization and bureaucracy.[23]

Sócrates was also one of the leading players on Brazil's 1982 World Cup team, a team formed amid the *abertura* or "opening" allowed by the military, which served as a prelude to democratization. Besides Sócrates, the team included other talented players regarded as football artists, such as Zico and Falcão, and was coached by Telê Santana, who was committed to attacking play and was willing to accept player input about training and tactics. Though it lost in the semifinal, the 1982 seleção remains one of the most beloved of Brazilian teams, in part, according to its admirers, because it restored the joy, the fantasy, and the allure of Brazil's beautiful game. Marcos Natali points out that Brazilians' fondness for that team has grown over the years because it seemed to symbolize the return of the Brazilian style and the genuine, democratic Brazil, and because many later commentators used it to criticize the 1994 World Cup team. The 1994 seleção won the tournament but, it seemed to critics like the journalist Armando Nogueira and the former player Tostão, it played to win rather than by playing the "Brazilian" way. According to Natali, in the 1990s "some fans and observers even disregarded the 1994 victory altogether, counting as legitimate only Brazil's previous three World Cup victories."[24]

The style of the 1994 seleção was cause for debate at the time both within and outside Brazil. Coach Carlos Alberto Parreira spoke of wanting Brazil to play attacking football, "to go back to our roots," but he also said, "We will play in the way today's football demands. Magic and dreams are finished in football. We have to combine technique and efficiency."[25] Critics objected, and complained that Parreira relied too much on defense, too much on brawn, and he encouraged Brazil to play a "European style," which they identified with the team's captain, the combative ball-winning midfielder Dunga, who was almost as unpopular as a seleção player as he later would be as its coach.[26] Fortunately the team had a handful of players who seemed to play futebol, the best of whom was Romário, depicted as "the country's savior" both for his goals and for how he scored them.[27] Many foreign commentators reacted in a similar manner, a German paper calling the seleção "disappointingly European, dominated by 'Nordic cool,'" and the Uruguayan novelist and critic Eduardo Galeano complaining that it "was stingy on poetry" and "much less Brazilian" than it should be.[28]

These critiques suggest the extent to which the futebol tradition has affected how Brazilians and others watch the seleção and what they think about Brazil. In 1982 and 1994 commentators expected joy and fantasy and magic, traits they asserted were inherent to Brazil and to Brazilian football, traits that showed that "Brazil is always Brazil," as Ronaldo Helal puts it.[29] When commentators thought they saw those traits, as in 1982, they asserted futebol's triumphant revival, despite the seleção's defeat. When they did not find what they were looking for, they argued that what they saw was European, not Brazilian. Looking for explanations, critics blamed Parreira and Dunga and a culture of rationalization that encouraged their futebol de resultados. And they pointed to the increasing numbers of Brazilian football migrants who played abroad, especially in Europe, and alleged that what Wisnik has called "the postcolonial transnationalization of soccer" meant they played more like Europeans than Brazilians.[30]

Linking their critique to a larger concern about development and globalization, they feared the loss of distinctiveness of Brazilian football and of Brazilian culture as a whole. Among the ways critics fought against this threat, one was their attack on a 1997 sponsorship contract between the Confederação Brasileira de Futebol (CBF) and the Nike company. The contract gave the American firm unusual influence over the activities of the seleção, including in decisions about when, where, and against whom the seleção would play, and some blamed it for Brazil's loss in the 1998 World Cup final. According to then-congressman Aldo Rebelo, who helped lead a congressional inquiry into the relationship between the company and the CBF, "My fight is the preservation of national identity in front of the pressure of globalization."³¹ Rebelo attacked Nike not only to defend Brazilian sovereignty but also to defend what he understood to be the character of Brazil, which he believed was made manifest in the seleção and which he feared the relationship with the American company would diminish.

Aldo Rebelo became minister of sport in 2011 and oversaw the national government's participation in the organization of the 2014 World Cup, which was clearly influenced by the futebol tradition. Organizers drew on Brazilian football history, recruiting former star players like Pelé and Ronaldo to help them depict the tournament as a homecoming—football returning to its spiritual roots in the country that had perfected the game by transforming it into futebol. It would be the "Cup of Cups," according to Brazilian president Dilma Rousseff, and it would be played "All in one rhythm," according to the official slogan, which played on both the idea of samba soccer and Brazilian football's purported capacity for promoting harmony.³² Organizers also employed the tradition's insistence that futebol served as a portmanteau of national culture by packaging Brazil's racial diversity, its genres of dance, its architecture, and its natural environment in the story they told about Brazilian football, for example, in the official posters created for the World Cup and its host cities.³³ And, like their predecessors in 1950, they depicted the World Cup as an announcement of Brazilian development and football as a key to the nation's progress.

The tournament came after a period of sustained and much-remarked-upon economic development, the fruits of which were more equitably distributed than the benefits of growth had been in the past, and it came with the promises of leaders outside and inside football, such as Rebelo and Rousseff and CBF president José Maria Marin, that through it football would advance Brazil in a literal sense because it would yield infrastructure development in the form of new stadiums as well as new roads and new airports. As if ensuring that the connection between the 2014 World Cup and the futebol tradition would not be missed, the Brazilian government republished pieces written by Nelson Rodrigues between 1950 and 1970 as part of its official media strategy for the tournament.³⁴

Brazilians began to articulate this discourse as soon as they learned in 2007 that they would host the World Cup. In accepting the invitation to host the tournament, then-president Luiz Inácio Lula da Silva announced that Brazil was more than ready to host the tournament again. In 2014, he said, the world would not only see Brazil's great footballers but would also see "the marvelous fruits of nature . . . our capacity for building good stadiums . . . [and] the thing that will impress the players, reporters, and administrators of world football, and even the fans . . . the extraordinary comportment of the Brazilian people." The world would see Brazilians embrace the tournament because, Lula said, "for us football is not just a sport, it is more, it is a national passion."[35] Many Brazilians seem to have agreed, with almost 80 percent of respondents telling the Datafolha service of their support for Brazil's hosting the tournament in late 2008.

However, this had changed by 2014, and on the eve of the tournament only 48 percent of those surveyed said they thought Brazil should host.[36] Between 2007 and 2014 Brazilian economic growth had slowed, preparations encountered a variety of obstacles, and the World Cup became increasingly controversial. Some Brazilians were uncomfortable with demands made by FIFA, which included alterations to Brazilian laws about ticket prices and the sale of alcohol in stadiums, and many objected to the tournament's expense. It ultimately required at least $13.5 billion in public money, in spite of organizers' assurances that they would not need tax funds, while infrastructure projects the organizers had promised were left incomplete or not even begun. When the games began, even some stadiums were unfinished, further angering critics who had already noted that construction had seen the displacement of working-class communities and fatal accidents and who had argued that some of the stadiums built for the competition would become white elephants.

There had been a few who objected to Brazil's hosting the tournament from the beginning, but these problems grew their number greatly until there were millions of protestors who took part in public demonstrations against the World Cup and its organizers during the 2013 Confederations Cup, the dress rehearsal for the World Cup. The demonstrations were about more than the World Cup, part of larger and longer-lived social and political movements aimed at improving living standards and against public corruption, but many critics argued that the problems that affected Brazil's World Cup preparations exemplified these larger challenges.[37] They also took on the futebol tradition directly, alleging that the World Cup showed that football did indeed reveal truths about Brazil, though uncomfortable ones. Pointing to evidence of corruption in the CBF and the organization and mismanagement of the World Cup, critics like Romário, the former star player who became a federal deputy, argued that Brazilian football was controlled by an undemocratic hierarchy of powerful men—the *cartolas* (top hats, a name recalling the era of aristocratic football)—who manipulated the rhetoric of the beautiful game to obscure football inequalities. They argued that the cartolas' corruption and those inequalities were football's true revelations about the country.[38]

There were protests during the World Cup itself, but they were much smaller than they had been in 2013, in part because many seem to have been swept up in the pageantry of the games and because authorities took proactive measures against protest leaders. But the challenge to the futebol tradition did not dissipate. Critics continued to speak out, for example, pointing out that, despite the tradition's assertion that futebol was inclusive, ticket costs meant Brazilian crowds were much more affluent and much less racially diverse than football crowds usually were, and they objected to what they saw as the marginalization of popular football celebrations in favor of official "fanfests" sponsored by international corporations and full of products branded with the vocabulary of the beautiful game.[39]

Worse, from the point of view of organizers and other defenders of the futebol tradition, the tournament ended with a revival of the kind of criticisms that had been aimed at the 1994 seleção. Although Brazil finished in fourth place and included players such as Neymar, Oscar, and Willian, who admirers said played the beautiful game, the 2014 seleção seemed more defense-minded than attacking, more reliant on strength than skill—it was a team playing for results. When its defense failed, and without the injured Neymar, the result was truly shocking. For the first time in almost forty years the seleção lost a competitive match in Brazil, defeated by Germany in the semifinal by the remarkable score of 7–1, which was followed by a 3–0 loss to the Netherlands in the third-place game. Torcedores booed the team off the field after each loss, and media responded by reviving the memory of 1950, some calling the defeat to Germany worse than the Maracanaço. A few critics argued that Brazil lost because it had not played the beautiful game but had instead played *um jogo feio*, an ugly game, and therefore argued that the tournament did not reveal a crisis but rather the need for Brazilians to return to futebol. But many worried that 2014 had seen the culmination of the process they had feared was unfolding in the 1990s. They worried that Brazilians had learned too much from Europe, where eighteen of the twenty-three members of the seleção played professionally as compared to the ten who played there in 1994, and they worried Brazilians could no longer play the beautiful game.[40] Meanwhile, in the protests of 2013 and 2014 many of their countrymen demonstrated they were willing to break from the futebol tradition in order to make a different kind of Brazil, one no longer defined or molded by the idea of the beautiful game.

The scale and intensity of those protests surprised many, including administrators, members of the government, and observers who assumed that Brazil was still the "Fatherland in football boots."[41] But Brazilian football has been confronting what some have described as a crisis for quite some time, at least since the 1970s, the symptoms of which have included the loss of more and more players to professional leagues in Europe; mismanagement and corruption, which have hindered effective football administration; and stadium violence and other problems faced by fans, which have led to declining attendance. Many of these problems were rooted in the way Brazilians organized their football in the late nineteenth and early twentieth centuries so that, for example, reformers adopted professionalization in 1933 but left administration largely as it had been in earlier decades—amateur and dominated by powerful figures like Arnaldo Guinle who were the forerunners of the modern cartola. Unsurprisingly, late-twentieth-century reformers recommended the modernization of football administration as a first step toward resolving the "crisis" faced by Brazilian football, and they focused on bureaucracy in the 1993 Zico Law and the 1998 Pelé Law, measures taken by the national government and named for the former players who served as minister of sport at the time.[42]

However, as Cesar Gordon and Ronaldo Helal suggest, in the twenty-first century, Brazilian football faces a challenge perhaps greater than anything to do with its administration, the behavior of its fans, or even Brazil's relative underdevelopment. They write, "One has the impression that the agents of the football world often fail to see that the [idea that Brazil is the] 'football country' is not a natural reality but rather a social construction which depended on an *ad hoc* connection between football and more unifying influences of social life" in the 1930s, such as the nationalist movement and Vargas-style populism. Without "a project which links [football] to these more inclusive instances," they say, "the metaphor loses its force and we end up feeling that something is lacking." They suggest that the "real crisis" of Brazilian football has to do with the way Brazilians think about the game rather than any specific aspect of the way the game is organized or the way it is played. Gordon and Helal suggest that by the late twentieth century, Brazilians had begun to reject the idea that their football culture embodied their nation, perhaps because they no longer believed in the idea of the nation in a globalizing world.[43] Seen from this perspective, the demonstrations of 2013 and 2014 can be understood as a consequence of a crisis for the futebol tradition made by the growing number of Brazilians who no longer accepted that football could or should serve as a tool for great national projects and who objected to leaders who insisted on doing so.

As this book demonstrates, football's connections to national "projects" is even older than those of the 1930s that Gordon and Helal mention. Almost from the very beginning, football was more than a game in Brazil; many of those who encouraged Brazilians to take up the game with Charles Miller did so because they linked it to other initiatives aimed at national improvement, such as education and public health campaigns. The sportsmen have often been depicted as exclusionary and elitist, dilettantes who played football because they saw it as a fashionable and cosmopolitan pastime through which they played at being European. There is some truth in this depiction, as many sportsmen were indeed elitist and certainly Eurocentric, but it misses much of what made football important in late-nineteenth- and early-twentieth-century Brazil.

Many sportsmen saw football as a tool for making Brazil a better country because they believed it would make Brazilians better soldiers, better workers, and better citizens. They hoped to expand interest in the sport among men and women; whites and people of color; the wealthy, the middle class, and the working class; urbanites and rural dwellers; northerners and southerners. This does not mean that they believed all Brazilians should participate in football in the same way, with most recommending, for example, that women attend matches as fans but not take to the field in their own right. But even the most elitist of football's promoters thought all Brazilians should participate, as was the case for the administrator and journalist Alberto Silvares, who argued that although working-class players should not be allowed to play in first-class leagues, they should have their own competitions. Adapting arguments made by professional educators like José Veríssimo, Silvares and the many who agreed with him asserted that most Brazilians required guidance to understand football and its lessons, but they also argued that these men and women could indeed benefit from what football offered if they played and watched it in the correct way.

The sportsmen defined what was correct by a careful and selective reading of the way they thought football was practiced in Europe, making critical choices about what kind of European football suited their plans to improve Brazil and insisting that fans and players follow this "European" football. This outlook also guided the way they organized the game, from the way they built their clubs and leagues to their insistence on amateurism, and it helps account for their eagerness to use football to advertise their view of Brazil in international competition. In short, the sportsmen played and watched football because they liked it, but what made it more than a game was not only that a handful of wealthy and middle-class urbanites thought it made them seem modern and cosmopolitan. What made football more than a game was that many sportsmen saw it as part of a larger movement to remake Brazil in the late nineteenth and early twentieth centuries. The football culture they created reflected not only their class and race and gender biases but also their commitment to using football to improve their country.

The way the sportsmen thought about and acted in football indicates the complexities that characterized the First Republic, despite its reputation for oligarchy and Eurocentrism. The actions the sportsmen took to limit Brazilians' participation in football suggest why the period should have earned that reputation. Just as important in building the sportsmen's reputation as mimic men, I argue, was the narrative crafted by critics and reformers in the 1920s and 1930s. They defined a dichotomy between foreign and Brazilian, between elite and popular, and between white and black. They staked a claim to nationalism, populism, and racial democracy and used these ideologies to justify their attacks on football as it had been organized in the late nineteenth and early twentieth centuries, which they portrayed as irredeemably un-Brazilian, unacceptably exclusionary, and baldly racist. This was the futebol tradition, the story that reformers told about the history of Brazilian football, one of steady progress and the discovery of a Brazilian version of the game that could be a venue wherein Brazilians found themselves and came together as a nation.

These reformers did alter the game, helping to usher more men of color onto the playing field, winning the fight for professionalization, and convincing the government to take a more active role in managing football. Most importantly, they changed the way Brazilians talked about the game, which helps explain why the popular history of Brazilian football has often missed the complexities of the sportsmen and all of the ways the reformers of the 1920s and 1930s did not change the game. Reformers said they fought for a fairer and more democratic football, but they worked closely with the wealthy white administrators who controlled the organizations of football and with the Vargas regime so that football administration became even more hierarchical in the 1930s than it had been in the past. They said they had made football more inclusive, but professionalization meant both curbing the freedom of players and the decline of clubs that could not compete financially with the big ones of the middle class and wealthy, and Brazilian women became less welcome in the 1940s than they had been in earlier decades. And the reformers said they cleared the field of outside influence so that the Brazil's beautiful game could flourish and be advertised on Brazilian and foreign pitches. Still, they insisted on "European" discipline, they worried about foreign opinions of Brazil and Brazilian football, and they explained "Brazilian" traits by reviving essentialist explanations that many sportsmen had rejected.

The futebol tradition helped obscure many of these complexities, and it contributed to the idea championed by the Vargas regime and its allies that the 1920s and, especially, the 1930s witnessed a successful challenge to the elitism of the First Republic and the discovery of Brazil's authentic identity. The futebol tradition, though, relied on a selective reading of the history of Brazilian football, and understanding the choices made by its narrators helps demonstrate what changed and what did not in the 1920s and 1930s in Brazilian football and beyond it. Mário Filho and other reformers invented the futebol tradition, and they used football in much the same way as the sportsmen they criticized and sometimes attacked. Like the sportsmen—and like many, many Brazilians since the 1930s and 1940s—the reformers who invented the idea of the beautiful game argued that the kind of football that they preferred was the only right way for their countrymen to play the game, and they argued that football was a vital way to make Brazil the country they wanted it to be. They told a powerful and attractive story about football and about Brazil, a story that for generations informed Brazilians' views of their country and their actions in shaping it. In the twenty-first century, many in Brazil have begun to challenge that story, while others have insisted that it continues to reveal basic truths about the country. Once again, Brazilians have turned to football to engage in debates about what Brazil is and should be, just as the sportsmen at the turn of the twentieth century and the populists of the 1920s and 1930s did before them.

Notes

Introduction

1. Hamilton, *An Entirely Different Game*, 9.
2. Full-back, "Foot-ball," *Kosmos*, August 8, 1904; and Veríssimo, *Educação Nacional*, 73–74.
3. Bruce, *Brazil and the Brazilians*, 258.
4. Barreto, "Como Reposta," in *Marginália*, 71.
5. Rodrigues, *A Pátria de Chuteiras*; and Lever, *Soccer Madness*.
6. Silva, "Discurso do Presidente da República."
7. See, for example, Wisnik, *Veneno Remédio*.
8. British sailors may have played the game during shore leave before 1894, and foreign educators may have incorporated it into Brazilian schools in the late nineteenth century. See, for example, Marinho, *Rui Barbosa*, 130–31 and 135. But the evidence of these episodes is fuzzy. For example, in *A Liberdade dos Índios*, J. M. Madureira claimed that football was played at the Colégio Anchieta as early as 1886, but that work was published only in 1929. Similarly, in a 1906 edition of *A Educação Nacional*, José Veríssimo stated that it was played at the Ginasio Nacional as early as 1890, but the book's 1890 first edition does not mention the sport. This seems to justify the preference for the watershed year of 1894. Before then, football was basically unknown in Brazil; after 1894, it never would be again.
9. Corrêa, *Grandezas e Miserias do Nosso Futebol*, 187.
10. Freyre, *Ingleses no Brasil*, xviii.
11. Hobsbawm and Ranger, *Invention of Tradition*.
12. Soares, "História e invenção de tradições no futebol brasileiro," 114.
13. Helal, Soares, and Lovisolo, *A invenção do país do futebol*; Souza, *O Brasil entra em campo!*; and Kittleson, *The Country of Football*.
14. See esp. Alabarces, *Fútbol y Patria*; Guedes, *O Brasil no campo do futebol*; and Panfichi, *Ese gol existe*.
15. Elsey, *Citizens and Sportsmen*; Melo, *Cidadesportiva*; and Pereira, *Footballmania*.
16. Barbara Weinstein points out the necessity of understanding the material consequences of discourse and tradition in her 2008 presidential address to the American Historical Association; Weinstein, "Presidential Address."
17. James, *Beyond a Boundary*.
18. See esp. Vianna, *O Mistério do Samba*; and Woodard, *A Place in Politics*.

19. Besse, *Restructuring Patriarchy*.
20. On heterosocial space, see Caulfield, *In Defense of Honor*.
21. Antunes, "Com brasileiro, não há quem possa!," 40.

Chapter 1. Playing for the Nation: The Ideology of Brazilian Sports

1. Decree-Law 3199 of April 14, 1941, Article 3(b), *Diário Oficial da União*, April 16, 1941.
2. Getúlio Vargas, quoted in Costa, *Nações em jogo*, 75.
3. Mazzoni, *O esporte a serviço da pátria*.
4. João Alberto Lins de Barros, Fernando de Azevedo, and Mario Ary Pires, quoted in Souza, *O Brasil entra em campo!* 84–85.
5. Decree-Law 3199, Article 3(a).
6. For a comparison of Perón and Vargas, see Costa, *Nações em jogo*. On Perón, see Duke and Crolley, "*Fútbol*, Politicians and the People"; and Rein, "'El primer deportista.'" On Mexico's postrevolutionary government, see Brewster, "Patriotic Pastimes"; and Brewster, "Redeeming the 'Indian.'"
7. Decree-Law 3199, Articles 32, 51, 52, and 54.
8. Washington Luís, quoted in "Em pról dos desportos," *O Imparcial (Supplemento Sportivo)*, April 9, 1921.
9. Marinho, *Rui Barbosa*, 156. See also O'Neil, "The Search for Order and Progress"; and Parada, "Corpos Físicos como Corpos Cívicos."
10. Davis, *Avoiding the Dark*, 122.
11. For example, Justice Minister Francisco Campos modeled his plan for a national youth organization on fascist practice. The scheme failed, but the Conselho Nacional de Desportos and other projects adapted its purpose of using sport to intervene in Brazilians' physical, moral, and civic orientation.
12. Besse, *Restructuring Patriarchy*.
13. Needell, *A Tropical* Belle Époque.
14. Carvalho, "Brazil 1870–1914," 156.
15. Stepan, *"The Hour of Eugenics"*; Schwarcz, *Spectacle of the Races*; and Peard, *Race, Place, and Medicine*. See also Comaroff and Comaroff (*Modernity and Its Malcontents*) on the ways in which postcolonial actors have used ritual to transform foreign notions of the "modern" into local customs; applying their argument to the present case, we can understand the act of playing football as a ritual by which Brazilians made "European" modernity their own.
16. A few historians have begun to examine the claims of Vargas-era sports ideologues more critically. See esp. Souza, *O Brasil entra em campo!*; and Helal, Soares, and Lovisolo, *A invenção do país do futebol*. For other reassessments of the Vargas regime and its claims, see Wolfe, *Working Women, Working Men*; Williams, *Culture Wars in Brazil*; and Corsi, *Estado Novo*, for examinations of the regime's labor, arts, and foreign policies, respectively.
17. Editorial, *Anglo-Brazilian Times*, April 7, 1865.
18. João do Rio, "O Foot-Ball," *Gazeta de Notícias*, June 26, 1905.

19. See esp. Assunção, *Capoeira*; and Talmon-Chvaicer, *Hidden History of Capoeira*.
20. Rio, "O Foot-Ball."
21. Verissímo, *Educação Nacional*, 73–74.
22. Ibid., 74.
23. Rio, "O Foot-Ball."
24. O., "A funcção social do 'Sport,'" *Brasil Sport*, March 16–31, 1907.
25. Besse, *Restructuring Patriarchy*, 29.
26. Caulfield, *In Defense of Honor*.
27. Sevcenko, *Orfeu extático na metrópole*, 52.
28. O., "A funcção social do 'Sport.'"
29. Greenfield, "Development of the Underdeveloped City"; Greenfield, "Dependency and the Urban Experience"; and Greenfield, "Challenge of Growth."
30. Blount, "The Public Health Movement in São Paulo, Brazil."
31. See esp. Benchimol, *Pereira Passos*; Meade, *"Civilizing" Rio*; and Boone, "Streetcars and Politics in Rio de Janeiro."
32. Owensby, *Intimate Ironies*, 88–91. See also Peixoto-Mehrtens, *Urban Space and National Identity in Early Twentieth Century São Paulo, Brazil*, 13–39.
33. Todd A. Diacon (*Stringing Together a Nation*, 14) asserts that the "incorporation of faraway lands and peoples was quite possibly the primary activity of the Brazilian central state during the Old Republic."
34. Carvalho, "Brazil 1870–1914," 145–62.
35. Costa, *A History of Ideas in Brazil*, esp. chap. 5, "The Advent of Positivism," 82–175; and chap. 7, "Ideas in the Twentieth Century," 205–71.
36. Velloso, *A cultura das ruas no Rio de Janeiro*, 28–29.
37. Carvalho, *Os Bestializados*, 143–45 and 163.
38. Meade, *"Civilizing" Rio*.
39. Rodrigues Filho, "Lima Barreto."
40. See Soares, *Educação Física*; O'Neil, "Search for Order and Progress"; and Hentschke, *Reconstructing the Brazilian Nation*.
41. For example, Antônio Marciano da Silva Pontes discussed physical education in his 1874 work *Compêndio de Pedagogia*. Soares, *Educação Física*, 102.
42. Rui Barbosa, quoted in Marinho, *Rui Barbosa*, 66 and 78.
43. Magalhães, *Gymnastica Infantil*, 1.
44. Soares Dias, "Educação Physica," *A Eschola*, August 1900.
45. Pereira, *Footballmania*, 43 and 209–10.
46. Marinho, *Rui Barbosa*, 134–52.
47. Gymnasio Anglo-Brazileiro, *Estatutos da Succursal Fluminense*, 8 and 26.
48. "Campeonato Collegial," *O Certamen*, May 1908.
49. Italics in original. "Gymnasio Anglo-Brazileiro," *A Illustração Brazileira*, February 17, 1910.
50. Brazil's basic unit of currency during the First Republic was the *mil-réis*, or one thousand *réis*; one U.S. dollar was worth about 3.65 mil-réis. Chazkel, *Laws of Chance*, 278n10. In 1910, beside an initiation fee, day students in the primary program paid 330 mil-réis annually, and those in the secondary course paid between 480 and 650 mil-réis

annually. Boarding students paid 1,250 mil-réis at the primary level, and between 1,400 and 1,550 mil-réis at the secondary level. Gymnasio Anglo-Brazileiro, *Estatutos da Succursal Fluminense*, 21.

51. Jorge de Souza, quoted in Soares, *Educação Física*, 122–23.
52. Mendonça, *O Sport está deseducando a mocidade brasileira*, 52.
53. There were also financial concerns in play because marching and calisthenics were less costly than team sports like football. O'Neil, "The Search for Order and Progress," 35–36; Soares, *Educação Física*, 159–61; and Pereira, *Footballmania*, 60.
54. X., "A Cidade," *Gazeta de Notícias*, republished in *A Canoagem*, July 4, 1903.
55. "Gymnastica Infantil," *O Imparcial*, May 20, 1913.
56. Captain John, "Fluminense Football Club," *Selecta*, July 21, 1915.
57. "Escola de Disciplina," *Sports*, January 1920; and "A educação physica moderna," *Rio Sportivo*, January 22, 1930.
58. Watermann, "Os Beneficios da Canoagem," republished in *A Canoagem*, July 18, 1903; and Magalhães, *Gymnastica Infantil*, 21.
59. X., "A Cidade."
60. Dr. Semana (Dr. Alfredo Redondo), "Chronica Estrangeira: De Genera," *Sportman*, September 1906.
61. Pereira, *Footballmania*, esp. 42–55.
62. Captain John, "Fluminense Football Club."
63. Yantok, "Plastica e esthetica," *Athletica*, October 23, 1920. The worry echoes a lampoon published by Arnaldo in *O Malho* in 1903 of runners with enormous feet, bow-legged cyclists, and rowers with laughably big arms and torsos held up by matchstick legs. Pereira, *Footballmania*, 48.
64. "O segredo da Marathona: Conferencia sobre athletica e eugenia realisada em S. Paulo, pelo Dr. Fernando de Azevedo sob os auspicios da Sociedade Eugenica de S. Paulo," *Athletica*, February 16, 1920.
65. "Ao que vimos," *Epoca Sportiva*, April 5, 1919.
66. "A Victoria dos brasileiros," *Brasil Illustrado*, August 1, 1919.
67. Dr. Athayde Pacheco, "'Brasil Eugenico' por Ulysses Freire," *A Gazeta Esportiva*, May 25, 1930.
68. For example, see Faustino Esposel, "Os exercicios physicos: Sua repercussão sobre os apparelhos e funcções da organização humana," *Rio Sportivo*, January 2, 1930.
69. "Uma attitude lamentavel do governo: Foi negado auxilio para a delegação brasileira que vae concorrer ao Campeonato Mundial!" *Rio Sportivo*, July 4, 1930.
70. Ibid.
71. Woodard, *A Place in Politics*, 12; and Love, "Political Participation in Brazil."
72. Paulo Lauret, "Educação physica," *Semana Sportiva*, June 1, 1901; and O., "A funcção social do 'Sport.'"
73. "Escola de Gymnastica e Educação Physica da Força Publica: Procurem ser fortes, educando o corpo," *Illustração de S. Paulo*, November 1917.
74. Italics in original. "A razão de ser dos esportes," *Athletica*, August 28, 1920.
75. Ibid.
76. "Foot-ball," *O Malho*, August 19, 1905.

77. Alberto Silvares, "Sporting," *Revista Sportiva*, December 26, 1908.
78. Weber, *Sports athleticos*, 153.
79. "O 'Stadium' do Fluminense: Uma obra patriotica e nacional que se tenta impugnar," *Correio da Manhã*, August 9, 1918.
80. "A Victoria dos brasileiros," *Brasil Illustrado*.
81. Coelho Netto, "Mandamentos Civicos," *Athletica*, April 17, 1920.
82. O'Neil, "The Search for Order and Progress," 115–16.
83. "Festa Sportiva," *O Estado de S. Paulo*, September 7, 1918.
84. For example, "A festa de hontem em beneficio da 'Cruz Vermelha,'" *Correio da Manhã*, November 30, 1915.
85. Confederação Brasileira de Desportos, *Relatorio da Directoria 1918*, n.p.
86. I have translated the French-derived epithet "boches" as "Huns" here. Pullen was born not in Brazil but in Southampton, England. "Sidney Pullen embarcou para a Europa," undated newspaper clipping, "Botafogo de Futebol e Regatas: Fotografias (II)," Archive of Botafogo de Futebol e Regatas.
87. "Escola de Gymnastica e Educação Physica da Força Publica." On the match to benefit the Italian war effort, see "Match em beneficio da Cruz Vermelha Italiana e do Comité Italiano Pró-Patria, Palestra v. Paulistano," *O Estado de S. Paulo*, June 30, 1915.
88. Anselmo Ribas, "A volta dos heroes," *Athletica*, March 20, 1920.
89. See, for example, Club de Regatas Vasco da Gama, *Relatorio da Directoria de 1930*, n.p.; and "Mobilisação Esportiva," *O Estado de S. Paulo*, August 10, 1932.
90. "Aspectos da Estada dos 'Scratchmen' em Terras Bahianas," *Jornal dos Sports*, May 4, 1938.
91. Soares Dias, "Educação physica."
92. Ibid.
93. Tell, "O 'sport' e a educação physica do homem," *Brasil Sport*, February 16–28, 1907.
94. Antunes, "O futebol nas fábricas."
95. Tristão, quoted in Negreiros, "Resistência e Rendição," 62–63.
96. Antunes, "O futebol nas fábricas," 107.
97. "A Victoria dos brasileiros," *Brasil Illustrado*.
98. Faustino Esposel, "As vantagens da educação physica," *Rio Sportivo*, January 3, 1930.
99. Azevedo, *A Evolução do Esporte no Brasil*, 26–29.
100. "Um Novo Sport Europeu," *O Imparcial*, March 14, 1913; and "Base Ball: A Technica do Baseball," *Sports*, July 1920.
101. Rictus, "Vida Sportiva," *Sportman*, November 14, 1912.
102. Flavio Vieira, "Water-Polo: O melhor dos esportes," *Athletica*, February 16, 1920.
103. Guttman, *From Ritual to Record*.
104. "Consulta de 29 de novembro de 1877, sobre os Estatutos do 'Club Tauromachico,'" Consultas do Conselho do Estado, Secção do Imperio, Codigo do Fundo 1R, Caixa 555, Pacote 2, Documento 24, Arquivo Nacional do Brasil. On similar developments elsewhere in Latin America, see Beezley, *Judas at the Jockey Club*; Pérez,

"Between Baseball and Bullfighting"; and Slatta, "The Demise of the Gaucho and the Rise of Equestrian Sport in Argentina."

105. On "the violent game," see, for example, Joffre, "A nossa Campanha," August 6, 1915. On "an exaggerated form," see Captain John, "Fluminense Football Club."

106. Garcez, *O Mackenzie*, 116.

107. "Liga Paulista de Hockey," *O Imparcial*, July 3, 1913. See also Besse, *Restructuring Patriarchy*, 126.

108. Tell, "O 'sport' e a educação physica do homem."

109. "Foot-ball," *O Malho*, August 19, 1905.

110. "De onde vem o football?" *Sportman*, August 1906.

111. "A famosa 'equipe' Corinthians está no Rio," *Correio da Manhã*, August 23, 1910.

112. "Criticas e Suggestões: Os Jogadores Requistados Não Podem Discutir Ordens," *Jornal dos Sports*, March 31, 1938.

113. Barreto, "Bendito futebol," in *Feiras e Mafuás*, 85.

114. Barreto, "Educação Física," in *Feiras e Mafuás*, 171; and Barreto, "O meu conselho," in *Feiras e Mafuás*, 104; Barreto, "Educação Física," in *Feiras e Mafuás*, 170.

115. "A Victoria dos brasileiros," *Brasil Illustrado*.

116. O Estado de S. Paulo, *Almanach para 1916*, 238–39.

117. The executives of the Canadian-owned São Paulo and Rio de Janeiro Tramway, Light & Power companies, collectively known as "Light," were unusually forthcoming about their rationales for patronizing employee sports. C. A. Barton claimed that "the Company is best served" by workers who enjoyed and succeeded in sports, and Gilbert Hearn claimed that "sport in indispensable in the formation of a man" because it made him healthier and more responsible. "O Que Nos Disse Mr. Gilbert Hearn," and "Porque Mr. C. A. Barton Quiz a Victória da Tracção," *Light*, December 23, 1929. See also Antunes, "Futebol na Light."

118. Afranio Hiroz, "Desporto e disciplina," *Sports*, August 6, 1915.

119. "O Domingo esportivo," *Athletica*, May 1, 1920.

120. Italics in original. Confederação Brasileira de Desportos, *Relatorio da Directoria 1918*, 6–7.

121. "Ao que vimos," *Epoca Sportiva*.

122. "Foot-ball," *Jornal do Brasil*, March 12 and 13, 1919.

123. "Chronica," *Athletica*, May 29, 1920.

124. "A Officialisação dos Esportes," *O Estado de S. Paulo*, May 28, 1921.

125. J. E. de Macedo Soares, "Material importado" and "doc. n. 5," in Confederação Brasileira de Desportos, *Relatorio apresentado pela Directoria 1920–1921*, n.p. A version of the proposal was adopted in Law 4440 of December 31, 1921.

126. Sans Peur, "O Governo e o Sport," *O Imparcial (Supplemento Sportivo)*, March 12, 1921.

127. "A festa de hontem em beneficio da 'Cruz Vermelha," *Correio da Manhã*; and Minutes of the Meeting of the Directorate of the Fluminense Football Club, August 28, 1916, "FFC Atas da Diretoria 03/01/1910 a 11/09/1916," Acervo Flu-Memória, hereafter FFC.

128. Minutes of the Meeting of the Directorate of the Fluminense Football Club, November 5, 1917, "F.F.C., Atas da Diretoria, 1916–1918," FFC.

129. Fluminense Football Club, *Relatorio*, n.p.

130. Fluminense Football Club, Appendix, *Regulamento da Secção de Escoteiros do Fluminense Foot-Ball Club*, n.p.; and Guinle and Pollo, *Manual do Escoteiro Brasileiro*.

131. "Escotismo," *O Echo*, February 1917; and Fluminense Football Club, "Controle de Escoteiros 1926," FFC.

132. "Um 'stadium' para 40.000 pessoas: Uma brilhante iniciativa do Fluminense," *A Notícia*, October 16, 1917.

133. For example, Marcio Vidal, "Salve Brazileiros!" *Vida Sportiva*, May 31, 1919.

134. "O Campeonato Sul Americano," *Revista de Theatro e Sport*, March 9, 1918.

135. About US$140,000 in 1917. The "conto de réis" was the term for one million réis. In 1917 one conto de réis was equivalent to US$273. Minutes of the Meeting of the Directorate of the Fluminense Football Club, October 22, 1917, "F.F.C., Actas da Directoria, 1917–1918," FFC; and *Relatorio do Fluminense Football Club*.

136. About US$550,000. Coelho, "Estádio das Laranjeiras," 34.

137. Gaffney, *Temples of the Earthbound Gods*, 24.

138. Minutes of the Meeting of the Directorate of the Fluminense Football Club, October 15, 1917, "F.F.C., Actas da Directoria, 1916 a 1918," FFC.

139. "Football: O 'Stadium' do Fluminense," *Correio da Manhã*, August 9, 1918; and Minutes of the Meeting of the Directorate of the Fluminense Football Club, September 16, 1918, "F.F.C., Actas da Directoria, 1918–1919," FFC.

140. Intruso, "Impugnar as Obras do Fluminense F.C.?" *O Imparcial*, August 8, 1918.

141. "As Cousas Absurdas: Um monstro que se ergue em plena rua!" *A Noite*, June 9, 1918.

142. Intruso, "Impugnar as Obras."

143. "Football: O 'Stadium' do Fluminense."

144. "As Obras do Fluminense," letter to the editor from "Um grupo de sportsmen," *A Noite*, August 8, 1918.

145. Intruso, "Impugnar as Obras."

146. "As Obras do Fluminense," letter to the editor from "Um grupo de sportsmen," *A Noite*, August 8, 1918.

147. "Football: O 'Stadium' do Fluminense."

148. "Campeonato Sul Americano," *Revista de Theatro e Sport*, March 23, 1918.

149. "Vamos ter o 'stadium' nacional," *Gazeta de Notícias*, April 5, 1918.

150. "Visita dos ministros da marinha e da viação ao Stadium do Fluminense," *O Paiz*, September 13, 1918.

151. "Football: O 'Stadium' do Fluminense."

152. Intruso, "Impugnar as Obras."

153. Minutes of the Meeting of the General Assembly of the Fluminense Football Club, May 29, 1918, "Actas de Assembleas Geraes no Fluminense Football Club, 21 Julho 1902 a 29 Maio de 1918," FFC.

154. Coelho, "Estádio das Laranjeiras," 70.

155. *Jornal do Brasil*, quoted in ibid., 47.

156. *Regras Officiaes de Todos os Sports*, 44–46.

157. *Relatorio do Fluminense Football Club*, 1919.

158. Mário Pollo, "Historico do Fluminense Football Club," FFC.

159. "A parada sportiva de domingo, no Stadium do Fluminense F.C.," *Sport Illustrado*, October 2, 1920.

160. Caulfield, *In Defense of Honor*, 53.

161. Eduardo Dale et al., Commissão Pro-Estadio, to "Exmo. Snr.," n.d., Arquivo da Liga Nacionalista, pacote 2, item 1, Instituto Histórico e Geográfico de São Paulo. The letter was probably addressed to Vergueiro Steidel, president of the Liga Nacionalista de São Paulo, and written between 1917 and 1924, the years of existence of the league. James P. Woodard located and identified the document.

162. "Ultimas Notas Sportivas," *O Jornal*, July 7, 1931.

163. "O majestoso espectaculo desta tarde no estadio do Fluminense: Cerca de cincoenta mil pessoas ouvindo quinze mil vozes a entoar o Hymno Nacional," *A Noite*, October 24, 1932; and Membership card, FFC.

164. Malhano and Malhano, *Memória social dos esportes*, esp. part 3, "O Espetáculo Sociopolítico e a Representação Cívica no Cenário de São Januário," 187–230.

Chapter 2. Building and Rebuilding the Society of Football

1. A.C., "A ausencia de elementos estrangeiros no nosso football: O ultimo abencerragem foi Harry Welfare," *Jornal dos Sports*, May 13, 1931.

2. "Renegados! Ingratos! Del Debbio, Amilcar, Ratto e Serafine declaram, em Roma, que são italianos e fazem questão de não ser brasileiros," *Jornal dos Sports*, August 26, 1931.

3. Lanfranchi and Taylor, *Moving with the Ball*, 83; "O Exodo dos jogadores," *O Estado de S. Paulo*, July 10, 1931; and "Tribuna oficial," *La Cancha*, January 24, 1931.

4. Alberto Arena, "A Independiente se le ha aflojado el corazon," *La Cancha*, September 15, 1928.

5. "O Exodo dos jogadores."

6. "Renegados! Ingratos!"

7. "Os Futebolistas brasileiros, contratados como profissionaes para a Italia, renegaram a sua patria," *Folha da Manhã*, August 27, 1931.

8. As Jeffrey Lesser says (in *Welcoming the Undesirables*, 66), in the early-1930s, "Nativism sold newspapers."

9. "Renegados! Ingratos!"; and "Criticas e suggestões: Renegados!" *Jornal dos Sports*, August 27, 1931.

10. "Amilcar e os demais companheiros desmentem as declarações que lhes foram attribuidas," *A Gazeta*, September 18, 1931.

11. "O presidente do Palestra e a victoria da Italia," *A Folha da Manhã*, June 6, 1934.

12. "Associação Paulista de Esportes Athleticos," *O Estado de S. Paulo*, July 18, 1931; "Ministrinho e sua eliminação da APEA," *A Gazeta*, September 10, 1931; "Como irá acabar a questão," *A Gazeta*, September 26, 1931; and Minutes of the Meeting of the

Joint Executive of the Societá Sportiva Palestra Itália, July 10, 1931, "Atas. Conselho Deliberativo," Archive of the Sociedade Esportiva Palmeiras.

13. Elsey, *Citizens and Sportsmen*, 127–64; and Rein, *Los bohemios de Villa Crespo*.
14. "O Exodo dos jogadores."
15. "Ultimas: A primeira colheira," *A Gazeta*, July 10, 1931.
16. See esp. Fischer, *A Poverty of Rights*, 125.
17. Veríssimo, *Educação Nacional*, 73–74.
18. Melo and Mangan, "A Web of the Wealthy."
19. Pereira, *Footballmania*, 61.
20. See esp. Levine, *Vale of Tears*; and Meade, *"Civilizing" Rio*.
21. On the labor movement, see Alexander and Parker, *A History of Organized Labor in Brazil*; and Azevedo, *A resistência anarquista*.
22. Costa, *Brazilian Empire*, esp. 196–98. On the urban middle classes, see Owensby, *Intimate Ironies*.
23. Pereira, *Footballmania*, 62.
24. See chapter 1, note 50.
25. For examples, see Agustinho Pereira da Cunha et al., "Apontamento para a Memoria Historico do Club de Regatas do Flamengo, 1–4 fasciculos: 1895–1935," Archive of the Club de Regatas do Flamengo; and *Germania de São Paulo: Estatutos Aprovados*, chap. 5, art. 19. For league costs, see Liga Metropolitana de Football, *Estatutos da Liga Metropolitana de Football*, art. 4; and Cardim, *O Guia de Football*, 10.
26. Liga Metropolitana de Sports Athleticos, *Estatutos da Liga Metropolitana de Sports Athleticos*, chap. 1, art. 1; Fluminense Football Club, *Estatutos do Fluminense Football Club*, chap. 1, art. 3; Botafogo Football Club, *Estatutos do Botafogo Football Club*, chapt. 2, art. 3; and Liga Metropolitana de Sports Athleticos, *Estatutos da Liga Metropolitana de Sports Athleticos*, chap. 1, art. 37; chap. 8, art. 44 and 45; and chap. 9, art. 49.
27. Botafogo Football Club, *Estatutos do Botafogo Foot-Ball Club*, chap. 2, art. 8 and art. 9, subsec. 1; and Fluminense Football Club, *Estatutos do Fluminense Football Club*, chap. 2, art. 3 and art. 5, subsec. 2.
28. Minutes of the Meeting of the Directorate of the Fluminense Football Club, April 25, 1905, "Actas da Directoria, 3 Julho 1902 a 25 Abril 1905," FFC; and "Os preços das entradas," *Jornal de Theatro e Sport*, September 3, 1921.
29. Ball, "Inequality in São Paulo's Old Republic," 88 and 178. On costs of living and price fluctuations, see Cardim, *Ensaio de Analyse de Factors Economicos e Financeiros do Estado de São Paulo e do Brasil*, esp. 24–26.
30. Advertisement for Mappin Stores, *Sports*, April 1921.
31. Fluminense Football Club, "Relatorio de 1902–1903: Relativo ao periodo de 21 de Julho de 1902 a 31 de dezembro de 1903," FFC.
32. "Relatorio apresentado pela Directoria em Assembléa Geral Ordinaria realizada em 20 de Dezembro de 1904"; and Minutes of the Meetings of the Directorate of the Fluminense Football Club, November 3, 1905, and March 23, 1906, "Actas da Directoria 5 de Maio 1905 a 23 de Maio 1911," FFC.
33. Minutes of the Meeting of the Directorate of the Bangú Athletic Club, May 6, 1907, "Atas da Assembléia Geral Ordinario, 20-12-05, Acta da Assemblea Geral

extraordinario, 6-12-07; Atas de Reunião de Diretoria 1906–1908," Archive of the Bangú Atlético Clube. Minutes of the Meeting of the Directorate of the Botafogo Football Club, May 18, 1908, "Atas da Directoria 23/01/1907 a 04/10/1909," Archive of Botafogo de Futebol e Regatas.

34. Report presented by Edmundo de Azurém Furtado to the General Assembly, November 8, 1912, quoted in Pereira da Cunha et al, "Apontamento para a Memoria."

35. Minutes of the Meeting of the Directorate of the Botafogo Football Club, June 4, 1917, "Atas da Directoria 09/10/1916 a 24/09/1917," Archive of Botafogo de Futebol e Regatas.

36. Advertisements, *Sportman*, June 1907; *Careta*, March 1, 1913; and *Sports*, April 1921.

37. Report presented by Azurém Furtado to the General Assembly.

38. Law 4440 of December 31, 1921, art. 29, *Diário Oficial da União*, January 1, 1922.

39. "Club Athletico Paulistano," *O Estado de S. Paulo*, February 28, 1907.

40. "Chronica," *O Jornal do Commercio*, April 2, 1911.

41. Minutes of the Meeting of the Directorate of the Fluminense Football Club, May 1, 1914, "Actas da Directoria, 21 de Outubro a 31 de Julho 1914," FFC.

42. Paulo Justo, "Harry-Welfare," *Sports*, August 6, 1915.

43. "As Figuras Impressionantes do Football: Harry Welfare conta-nos uma porção de coisas interessantes de sua carreira sportiva," *Rio Sportivo*, five parts, beginning March 20, 1930. See also Hamilton, *An Entirely Different Game*, 79–96.

44. "Fluminense Football Club: Diario do Trainer," FFC.

45. For example, Paulistano sold silver buttons and gold pins, English-made and available only to club members, in 1919. "Club Athletico Paulistano," *Sports*, November 1919.

46. "Fluminense Football Club: Registro dos Socios, (1920)," FFC.

47. Liga Metropolitana de Football, *Estatutos da Liga Metropolitana de Football*, art. 3; and "Regulamento de Foot-Ball," rules 3 and 9, Liga Metropolitana de Sports Athleticos, *Estatutos da Liga Metropolitana de Sports Athleticos*, 21–22.

48. Mangan, *Athleticism in the Victorian and Edwardian Public School*.

49. Corbett, *Annals of the Corinthian Football Club*, vi.

50. Minutes of the Meeting of the Directorate of the Botafogo Foot-ball Club, May 10, 1907, "Atas da Directoria 23/01/1907 a 04/10/1909," Archive of Botafogo de Futebol e Regatas; and Minutes of the Meetings of the Directorate of the Fluminense Football Club, May 7 and June 25, 1907, "Actas da Directoria 5 de Maio 1905 a 23 de Maio 1911," FFC.

51. Italics in original. M. Marcello, "Egualdade das classes: Operarios e Sport," *Sportman*, July, September, October, and December 1906.

52. Italics in original. Ibid.

53. Minutes of the Meeting of the Directorate of the Botafogo Foot-ball Club, May 10, 1907.

54. Minutes of the Meetings of the Directorate of the Bangú Athletic Club, April 2, 1906, September 14, 1909, and August 14, 1912, "Atas da Assembléia Geral Ordinario, 20-12-05, Acta da Assemblea Geral extraordinario, 6-12-07; Atas de Reunião de

Diretoria 1906–1908"; and "Atas de Reuniões da Directoria, 28-2-09 a 12-1-15," Archive of the Bangú Atlético Clube.

55. Minutes of the Meeting of the Directorate of the Fluminense Football Club, May 7, 1907.

56. Minutes of the Meeting of the Directorate of the Botafogo Foot-ball Club, May 10, 1907.

57. Nogueira, *Futebol Brasil memória*, 98.

58. Pereira, *Footballmania*, 116.

59. Joffre, "A nossa Campanha," *Sports*, August 6, 1915.

60. He wrote that the players believed "nós no campo somo iguá." Ibid.

61. Ibid.

62. Pereira, *Footballmania*, 116–18.

63. Liga Metropolitana de Sports Athleticos, quoted in Negreiros, "Resistência e Rendição," 76–77.

64. Confederação Brasileira de Desportos, "Lei de 29 de Janeiro de 1917," *Relatorio da Directoria 1918*, n.p.

65. More than 60 percent of Brazilians aged fifteen and older were illiterate as late as 1920. Ferraro, "Analfabetismo e Níveis de Letramento no Brasil," 34.

66. Confederação Brasileira de Desportos, "Lei de 29 de Janeiro de 1917," *Relatorio da Directoria 1918*, n.p.

67. Confederação Brasileira de Desportos, *Estatutos*, chap. 11, art. 35 and 36, 28–29.

68. In 1910, for example, *Sportman* cost 300 réis per issue, one mil-réis for special issues, eight mil-réis for an annual subscription in its home state of São Paulo, and ten mil-réis for subscribers in other states. Martins, "Quem conta um conto . . . aumenta, diminui, modifica," 13.

69. Ribeiro, *Os Donos do Espetáculo*, 19–55.

70. Cardim, *O Guia de Football*, 55–72.

71. Felippe Felix Fernando, "Coelho Netto e o foot-ball," *Epoca Sportiva*, April 19, 1919.

72. "Um benemerito do esporte," *Athletica*, May 15, 1920.

73. Ribeiro, *Os Donos do Espetáculo*, 27.

74. Weber, *Sports athleticos*, 154–207; and "Regras," *Guia Sportiva para 1912*, 12–45.

75. Oliveira, *Guia de Football (Association)*, 97.

76. *Guia Brasileiro de Foot-ball Associação*, 27.

77. João do Rio, "O Foot-ball," *Gazeta de Notícias*, June 26, 1905.

78. A common misspelling made "shoot" into "schoot." For examples, see "Chronica Sportiva," *Sportman*, October 2, 1913; and "Schootando . . . (Ás cariocas footballers)," *O Football*, May 23, 1914.

79. "Uma nova grammatica," *Careta*, November 14, 1908.

80. Bruce, *Brazil and the Brazilians*, 259.

81. Center-half, "Shootando . . ." *Jornal de Theatro e Sport*, April 8, 1916; *O Off Side*, July 1, 1916; and M.F., "Carta de um Sportman à Sua Filha Torcedora," republished in *Sport Illustrado*, July 9, 1921.

82. Ribeiro, *Os Donos do Espetáculo*, 40.

83. *O Comercio de S. Paulo*, quoted in Negreiros, "Resistência e Rendição," 136.
84. Negreiros, "Resistência e Rendição," esp. 135–63.
85. Ibid., 134.
86. Pereira, *Footballmania*, 112–13.
87. Letter from General Manager W. N. Walmsley to Vice-President F. A. Huntress, "The São Paulo Tramway, Light & Power Co. Ltd., Annual Report for 1919," 1–4, Fundação Património Histórico da Energia de São Paulo.
88. "Faculdade de Medicina," *O Estado de S. Paulo*, October 27, 1919.
89. "Foot-Ball: O Stadium Moderno," *Gazeta de Notícias*, quoted in *Regras Officiaes de Todos os Sports*, 44–46.
90. "Vamos ter o 'stadium' nacional," *Gazeta de Notícias*, April 5, 1918.
91. "A Ultima Sessão da Confederação Brasileira de Desportos," *O Imparcial*, June 8, 1918.
92. *Relatorio do Fluminense Football Club*, 1910–34.
93. João Manuel Casquinha Malaia Santos explores some of these issues in "Arnaldo Guinle, Fluminense Football Club, and the Economics of Early International Sport in Rio," esp. 396–98.
94. Pollo, "Historico do Fluminense Football Club."
95. Minutes of the Meeting of the Directorate of the Fluminense Football Club, April 25, 1905.
96. Minutes of the Meeting of the Directorate of the Fluminense Football Club, August 12, 1918, "F.F.C. Actas da Directoria, 1918 a 1919," FFC; and Coelho, "Estádio das Laranjeiras," 34.
97. Clube de Regatas do Flamengo, *Flamengo*, 19.
98. Vianna, *O Mistério do Samba*, 116n6.
99. Filho, *O negro no futebol brasileiro*, 138.
100. Soares, "O racismo no futebol do Rio de Janeiro nos anos 20," 106–8.
101. Ibid., 116.
102. Santos, "Uma Breve História Social do Esporte no Rio de Janeiro," 37–38.
103. The inquiry was undertaken by three men, members of Fluminense, Flamengo, and America. Mércio, *A História dos Campeonatos Cariocas de Futebol*, 47.
104. "Regulamento de Foot-Ball," rule 9, 22.
105. Associação Metropolitana de Esportes Athleticos, *Codigo Esportivo*, chap. 6, art. 1–6.
106. Filho, *O negro no futebol brasileiro*, 60.
107. Corrêa, *Grandezas e Miserias do Nosso Futebol*, 60.
108. Paulo Várzea, "Prefácio," in Corrêa, *Grandezas e Miserias*, 33. See also Ribeiro, *Os Donos do Espetáculo*, 66 and 83–85.
109. Confederação Brasileira de Desportos, *Lei de Transferencia de Amadores*.
110. "O profissionalismo no Rio," *O Estado de S. Paulo*, April 9, 1933. On the adoption of professionalization, see Caldas, *O Pontapé Inicial*, esp. chap. 5, "A Luta Política pelo Profissionalismo," 65–168.
111. Várzea, "Prefácio," 34. Waldenyr Caldas (in *O Pontapé Inicial*, 37) writes of a

"democratizing revolution of Brazilian football," of which professionalization was a major part.

112. R. Castello, "O futebol exportador," *Folha da Manhã*, July 10, 1931.

113. Souza, *O Brasil entra em campo!* 93.

114. Caldas, *O Pontapé Inicial*, 173–76. See also Costa, "Os Gramados do Catete."

115. "Ultimas," *A Gazeta*, July 10, 1931.

116. "Os jogadores paulistas passaram pelo Rio," *Folha da Manhã*, July 26, 1931.

117. "Criticas e Suggestões: E Kruschner [sic] Foi Chamado para Servir ao Football Brasileiro . . ." *Jornal dos Sports*, March 9, 1938.

118. "A derrota da nossa équipe em Genova e as manifestações que provocou," *Diario Popular*, May 28, 1934; and "O presidente do Palestra e a victoria da Italia."

119. "O povo apedrejou as sédes do Palestra Italia e da A.P.E.A.," *A Plateia*, May 28, 1934.

120. "A derrota da nossa équipe em Genova e as manifestações que provocou."

121. "O presidente do Palestra e a victoria da Italia."

122. Brazilian constitution of 16 July 1934, quoted in Lesser, *Welcoming the Undesirables*, 67; see also Lesser, *Welcoming the Undesirables*, 105.

123. Lesser, *Welcoming the Undesirables*, 10.

124. Araújo, *Imigração e Futebol*, 126–27.

125. Corrêa, *Grandezas e Miserias*, 13.

126. Ribeiro, *Os Donos do Espetáculo*, 83–85.

127. Soares, *Vendo o Jogo pelo Rádio*.

128. Ribeiro, *Os Donos do Espetáculo*, 22–25.

129. "Collaboração dos Leitores," *A Cigarra Sportiva*, June 16, 1917.

130. Such organizations also provided journalists with financial support, sponsoring events to raise funds for members, among other activities. "Associação dos Chronistas Sportivos," *O Estado de S. Paulo*, February 1, 1916.

131. Minutes of the Meeting of the Directorate of the Bangú Athletic Club, August 24, 1909, "Atas de Reuniões da Directoria, 28-2-09 a 12-1-15," Archive of the Bangú Atlético Clube.

132. "Uma victoria nacional," *Sports*, August 14, 1915.

133. Paulo de Magalhães, "Futibó," *Vida Sportiva*, September 21, 1918.

134. "Shootando," *O Imparcial*, July 3, 1916.

135. Arcy Tenorio D'Albuquerque, "Stadium ou Estadio?" and "Desporto, esporte ou sport?" *Athletica*, May 29 and August 21, 1920.

136. A. D'Arcanchy, "Foot-Ball Não! Ballipodo," *Vida Sportiva*, May 18, 1918.

137. "Ballipo: Uma Conferencia feliz," *Jornal de Theatro e Sport*, February 15, 1919.

138. João Silva Limeira, "O Vocabulario de football," *Vida Sportiva*, September 21, 1918; and Pauloma Gomes, "Pébol," *Vida Sportiva*, October 19, 1918.

139. "Neologismos versus Barbarismos," *Vida Sportiva*, February 8, 1919.

140. Raul Gomes credited Candido Figueiredo with coining the term in "O Vocabulario do Football," *Vida Sportiva*, August 24, 1918. See also *Sport Illustrado*, April 2, 1921, for an example of early adoption.

141. "Nacionalisemos!" and "Excesso do Futebol?" *Sports*, July 1920.

142. "Os Termos do Futeból Nacionalisados," *Sports*, December 1921.

143. *Guia Brasileiro de Foot-ball Associação*, 3–4.

144. Lopes, "A vitória do futebol que incorporou a *pelada*," 65–68.

145. Nelson Rodrigues, quoted in Antunes, *"Com brasileiro, não há quem possa!,"* 125.

146. José Lins do Rego, quoted in Holanda, *O descobrimento do futebol*, 138.

147. "A Voz do 'Fan' Carioca Atravez O Microphone De Pre-3," *Jornal dos Sports*, September 29, 1938. Bento Soares (in *Vendo o Jogo pelo Rádio*, 24 and 246) notes that Tuma's energetic style was representative of Paulista radio journalism while Carioca radio coverage was slower, "without the emotions and enthusiasm of São Paulo's announcers." For example, the influential Ary Barroso was "ironic, satirical, and spoke slowly."

148. Gordon and Helal, "The Crisis of Brazilian Football," 145.

149. Ribeiro, *Os Donos do Espetáculo*, 75.

150. Arbena, "Sports Language, Cultural Imperialism and the Anti-Imperialist Critique in Latin America."

151. For an alternative view, see Pardue, "Jogada Lingüística," 367–69.

152. Cardim's football guide was the basis for the *Guia Brasileira de Football Associação*, which adopted Brazilian terms in the mid-1920s, and Cardim was also involved in other nationalist projects, such as the Boy Scouts movement.

153. Ribeiro, *Os Donos do Espetáculo*, 40–54.

154. Corrêa, *Grandezas e Miserias*, 129.

155. Souza, *O Brasil entra em campo!*, 44.

156. Caldas, *O Pontapé Inicial*, 65–168.

157. Fausto dos Santos, quoted in Souza, *O Brasil entra em campo!*, 142.

158. See, esp., Williams, *Culture Wars in Brazil*; and Besse, *Restructuring Patriarchy*. Emilia Viotti da Costa (in *The Brazilian Empire*, 53–77) demonstrates that nineteenth-century liberals abandoned colonial paternalism while preserving traditional hierarchies.

159. Fischer, *A Poverty of Rights*, esp. 120–26.

160. Wolfe, "'Father of the Poor' or 'Mother of the Rich'?"

161. Agostino, *Vencer ou Morrer*, 142. See also Costa, "Os Gramados do Catete."

162. Silva, "Imprensa esportiva e o pensamento autoritário na obra de Thomaz Mazzoni." See also Soares, *Vendo o Jogo pelo Rádio*, 26 and 84.

163. Ribeiro, *Os Donos do Espetáculo*, 100.

164. Olimpicus, *Problemas e Aspectos do nosso Futebol*, 63–65.

165. Holanda, *O descobrimento do futebol*, 63.

166. Filho, *O negro no foot-ball brasileiro*, 293.

167. Matthew Karush (in "National Identity in the Sports Pages," 29) points out that populist sportswriters in 1920s Buenos Aires adopted a similar approach, depicting football as a game of the masses, who were "deserving yet untrustworthy."

168. Holanda, *O descobrimento do futebol*, 87 and 213–14.

169. Thomaz Mazzoni, quoted in Silva, "Imprensa esportiva e o pensamento autoritário na obra de Thomaz Mazzoni," 5.

170. Souza, *O Brasil entra em campo!*, 180–86.

Chapter 3. Students and Masters: National Identity and International Football

1. "Exeter versus Brazileiros," *A Leitura Para Todos*, July 1914.
2. "Foot-Ball: Grandes matchs [sic] internacionaes S. Paulo versus Campeões de amadores inglezes," *A Vida Moderna*, September 15, 1910.
3. See esp. Santos, *O Brasil entre a América e a Europa*; and Garcia, *Entre América e Europa*.
4. For example, "Match: Brazil–Inglaterra," *O Jockey*, September 23, 1911; and "Secção de Foot-ball," *Auto-Sport*, October 15, 1912.
5. Olimpicus, *História do Futebol no Brasil*, 44. See, for example, a report of a match between Fluminense and sailors from the English cruiser *Amethyst*; no title, *Revista Sportiva*, October 16, 1909.
6. Corbett, *Annals of the Corinthian Football Club*, vi.
7. "The Corinthians' Return," *Sporting Opinion* (Port-of-Spain, Trinidad), November 6, 1910.
8. "*Corinthians* versus Fluminense," *Campo e Sport*, August 27, 1910.
9. "Foot-ball," *Jornal do Commercio*, August 22, 1913.
10. A. Ford, "Sports," *A Leitura Para Todos*, August 1910.
11. Creek, *A History of the Corinthian Football Club*, 88.
12. On republicans' faith in expertise, see Costa, *A History of Ideas in Brazil*, 82–175. See also Stepan, *Beginnings of Brazilian Science*; and Diacon, *Stringing Together a Nation*, esp. chap. 4, "The Power of Positivism," 79–100.
13. "Programme of Entertainments, etc. Organized by The Fluminense F. C. during the Stay of The Corinthian Team in Rio de Janeiro, August 1910"; and "Banquet em honra dos Corinthians offerecido pelo Fluminense Football Club, Rio de Janeiro, 28 de Agosto de 1910," pamphlets, FFC.
14. Hamilton, *An Entirely Different Game*, 76.
15. "Banquete aos Corinthians," *Sportman*, September 4, 1913.
16. "Foot-Ball: Grandes matchs [sic] internacionaes S. Paulo versus Campeões de amadores inglezes."
17. "The Corinthians' Return."
18. The team's steam passage cost six contos and five hundred mil-réis. Minutes of the Meeting of the Directorate of the Fluminense Football Club, August 17, 1910, "Actas da Directoria: 5 de Maio 1905 a 23 de Maio 1911," FFC.
19. Creek, *A History of the Corinthians*, 84.
20. "Os Corinthians," *A Notícia*, August 25, 1910.
21. Hambloch, *British Consul*, 120.
22. "Foot-Ball," *Jornal do Commercio*, September 17, 1910. See also Hamilton, *An Entirely Different Game*, 77–78.
23. "Foot-Ball," *Jornal do Commercio*, September 19, 1910. The Corinthians did notice the crowd's partisanship but do not seem to have been offended. "The Corinthians' Return."
24. "Foot-ball," *A Leitura Para Todos*, October 1914.

25. "Um Grande Acontecimento Sportivo," *Correio da Manhã*, July 22, 1914; and "O memoravel match de 21," *O Jockey*, July 25, 1914.

26. Unknown title, *A Tribuna*, July 20, 1914, Yearly Album, FFC.

27. Unknown title, *O Paiz*, July 20, 1914, Yearly Album, FFC.

28. Unknown title, *O Imparcial*, July 21, 1914, Yearly Album, FFC.

29. "Foot-Ball: Grandes matchs internacionaes S. Paulo versus Campeões de amadores inglezes."

30. "Foot-ball," *A Leitura Para Todos*, July 1914.

31. "Um Grande Acontecimento Sportivo."

32. "A Equipe Nacional derrota os profissionaes inglezes por 2 × 0," *Jornal do Brasil*, July 22, 1914. See also Hamilton, *An Entirely Different Game*, 112.

33. Lima Filho, *O Campeonato Sul-Americano de Foot-Ball*, n.p.

34. "Foot-ball," *A Leitura Para Todos*, September 1914.

35. "Uma torcida negra," *O Imparcial*, May 7, 1919.

36. *O Imparcial*, quoted in Pereira, *Footballmania*, 171 and 174.

37. Epitácio Pessoa, quoted in ibid., 176.

38. Pereira, "Pelos Campos da Nação," 29–30.

39. Filho, *O negro no futebol brasileiro*, 119.

40. Dávila, *Diploma of Whiteness*, 6. See also Borges, "'Puffy, Ugly, Slothful and Inert.'"

41. Manchester, *British Preëminence in Brazil*.

42. Ibid., esp. 316–27.

43. Graham, *Britain and the Onset of Modernization in Brazil*, esp. 112–24 and 232–76. See also Munn, "Britain and Brazil." Munn is less convinced than some that British influence extended beyond the economic realm.

44. Garcia, *Entre América e Europa*, 579–80. See also Bueno, *Política Externa da Primeira República*, 484–86.

45. Garcia, *Entre América e Europa*, 149.

46. Hamilton Hamilton, quoted in Bethell, *The Abolition of the Brazilian Slave Trade*, 230.

47. See, for example, Rubim, *Os ingleses no Brasil*. This 1863 play is based upon the so-called Christie Affair, one of several controversies relating to British attempts to end the slave trade, and which threatened to bring the two nations to violence. See Forman, "Imperial Intersections," 292–306.

48. Santos, *O Brasil entre a América e a Europa*, 128.

49. Garcia, *Entre América e Europa*, 579; and Bueno, *Política Externa da Primeira República*, 135.

50. Garcia, *Entre América e Europa*, 374–424.

51. "Excursão do C. A. Paulistano á Europa," *O Estado de S. Paulo*, February 8, 1925.

52. Patusca, *Os reis do futebol*, 193–204.

53. Ibid.

54. *Austral*, Gabriel Hanot, and Gabriel Courtial, quoted in ibid., 88–89.

55. *Paris Soir* and *Le Journal*, quoted in ibid., 16 and 19.

56. "Jogos Internacionaes: O Brasil vence a França por 7 pontos a 2," *O Estado de S. Paulo*, March 16, 1925.
57. Patusca, *Os reis do futebol*, 24 and 27.
58. Mário Vespaziano Macedo, quoted in Patusca, *Os reis do futebol*, 42.
59. "Excursão do C. A. Paulistano á Europa."
60. "O Regresso do C. A. Paulistano," *O Estado de S. Paulo*, May 14, 1925. The comparison to São Paulo's legendary slave and fortune hunters was a common one.
61. Minutes of the Meeting of the Directorate of Club Athletico Paulistano, November 9, 1925, "Actas da Directoria do Club Athletico Paulistano, Livro 1," Archive of the Club Athletico Paulistano.
62. For example, "Jogos Internacionaes: O Brasil vence a França por 7 pontos a 2."
63. "O Regresso do C. A. Paulistano."
64. Coelho Netto, "Prefácio," and unknown Rio de Janeiro newspaper, quoted in Patusca, *Os reis do futebol*, 8 and 94.
65. "O Regresso do C. A. Paulistano."
66. "Jogos Internacionaes: O Brasil vence a França por 7 pontos a 2."
67. Letter from the São Christovão Athletico Club to the President of the Club Athletico Paulistano, March 25, 1925, Archive of the Club Athletico Paulistano.
68. Benjamin Costallat, "Os Brasileirinhos!" *Jornal do Commercio*, March 19, 1925.
69. For example, *S. Paulo Sportivo*'s Vespaziano de Macedo interviewed the French boxing champion Georges Carpentier, who obligingly praised the Brazilians' abilities. Patusca, *Os reis do futebol*, 103–4.
70. Carelli, *Culturas Cruzadas*, 199–210; and Amaral, "Stages in the Formation of Brazil's Cultural Profile." On European influence on Latin American opinions about tango and rumba, see Archetti, *Masculinities*, esp. 61; and Moore, *Nationalizing Blackness*, esp. 171–88.
71. "O 'Glorioso' partirá no dia 10 de Fevereiro, pelo Zeelandia," *S. Paulo Sportivo*, January 31, 1925.
72. "O internacional de hoje: Corinthians x Chelsea," *A Gazeta*, July 4, 1929.
73. "Football," *A Noite*, June 29, 1929; and "Football," *O Globo*, July 1, 1929. See also Hamilton, *An Entirely Different Game*, 130–47.
74. Annual Report for 1929, Christopher Steel to the Foreign Office, 10–11, enclosed in Confidential Dispatch 51 of April 10, 1930, National Archives (United Kingdom), FO 371/14207, File A3079/3079/6. See also Polley, "'No Business of Ours'?"; and Jones, "State Intervention in Sport and Leisure in Britain between the Wars."
75. "Quando os inglezes eram os unicos mestres, distribiuam tentos por atacado," *A Gazeta Esportiva*, February 9, 1930.
76. Mazzoni, *Almanach Esportivo 1932*, 26.
77. Frydenberg, "Boca Juniors en Europa."
78. See Giovannini, *La gira de Nacional por Europa en 1925*.
79. "Criticas e Suggestões: A superioridade do football brasileiro," *Jornal dos Sports*, July 11, 1931.
80. See, for example, "A temporada internacional encerrou-se sabbado com a victoria do seleccionado contra o Torino—6 a 1: O Lastimavel procedimento dos jogadores

italianos," *A Gazeta Esportiva*, September 16, 1929; and "Actuando pessimamente, os brasileiros venceram os norte-americanos por 4–3," *Jornal dos Sports*, August 18, 1930.

81. Olympicus, "Tempestade sobre o Vasco," *A Gazeta*, August 6, 1931.

82. Corrêa, *Grandezas e Miserias*, 58–61; see also Lopes, "Success and Contradictions in 'Multiracial' Brazilian Football," 65–67.

83. Minutes of the Meeting of the Directorate of the Fluminense Football Club, April 8, 1918, "Atas da Directoria 1/10/917–8/7/918," FFC.

84. "Foot-ball," *Jornal do Brasil*, March 12 and 13, 1919.

85. "O Sensacional Match de Hontem em S. Paulo," *Rio Jornal*, July 26, 1920.

86. "As Occorrencias do Jogo Cariocas x Paulistas: O que relata, na sua summula, o juiz do encontro," *A Noite*, November 17, 1927. Barbuy's words were italicized in the original.

87. Souza, *O Brasil entra em campo!*, 34–35.

88. "O Domingo Sportivo," *A Noite*, November 14, 1927.

89. Ibid.

90. "O Santos F. C. honra suas gloriosas tradições," *O Globo*, November 18, 1927.

91. "Amilcar, Tuffy, Fetiço e Pepe eliminados do sport nacional e Grané suspenso por um anno," *Rio Sportivo*, December 3, 1927.

92. The anecdote has been widely reproduced, for example, in Sérgio Augusto, "No reino do futebol, os negros têm sangue azul," *O Estado de S. Paulo*, April 17, 2005.

93. Letter from Tuffy Nejuen et al., "Melhorando seu proprio record!" *Rio Sportivo*, November 19, 1927.

94. Letter from Amílcar Barbuy et al., "Explicação necessaria," *Folha de Manhã*, November 20, 1927.

95. Instead of the select teams, the players who took the field for the match, to benefit the Associação dos Chronistas Esportivos, were "second-rate players" who had to be recruited because the Cariocas refused to participate and the Paulistas withdrew in response. Disappointed fans reacted violently and "reduced the sports field at the Parque Antarctica to a mountain of ruined fences, walls, and hoardings of all kinds, and was not far away from succeeding in its absolute destruction by fire!" "Até onde vamos?" *Folha da Manhã*, December 5, 1927.

96. João Brito, cartoon "A representação carioca em Montevideo," and "A segunda jornada do campeonato mundial de futebol," *A Gazeta*, June 28 and July 15, 1930.

97. "Uma attitude lamentavel do governo: Foi negado auxilio para a delegação brasileira que vae concorrer ao Campeonato Mundial!" *Rio Sportivo*, July 4, 1930.

98. Paulista interest did not mean they had put aside their annoyance; *A Gazeta* carried a series of pieces poking fun at the team's weaknesses, while supporters launched a coffin labeled "Carioca" into the Viaducto do Chá on the day of Brazil's first match. "Depois dos 2 a 1," *A Gazeta*, July 15, 1930.

99. "Envolta nas nossas maiores esperanças, partiu a delegação brasileira ao Campeonato Mundial," *Rio Sportivo*, July 3, 1930.

100. "As ultimas impressões dos nossos bravos," *Rio Sportivo*, July 3, 1930.

101. "Campeonato mundial de futebol," *A Gazeta*, July 15, 1930.

102. "Fausto tem razão!... Os 'Almofadinhas' em Montevideo formaram um bloco a parte," *Rio Sportivo*, July 22, 1930.

103. "Mais um..." *A Gazeta*, June 19, 1930.

104. "Fausto tem razão!..."; and Leop, "Elles-se bombardeam..." *A Gazeta*, July 22, 1930.

105. "Criticas e Suggestões: O valor das representações sportivas," *Jornal dos Sports*, December 25, 1932.

106. "Uma Consagração Aos Heróes Do Triplice Triumpho!" *Jornal dos Sports*, December 20, 1932.

107. Olympicus, "A Maior de Todas..."; and "O 'onze' revelação," *A Gazeta*, December 6 and 7, 1932.

108. José Lins do Rego, "Prefacio," in Filho, *Copa Rio Branco*, 5.

109. "Criticas e Suggestões: A actuação de Leônidas," *Jornal dos Sports*, December 6, 1932.

110. José Lins do Rego, quoted in Souza, *O Brasil entra em campo!*, 38.

111. Filho, *O negro no futebol brasileiro*, 214.

112. Olimpicus, *História do Futebol no Brasil*, 236. See also Filho, *O negro no futebol brasileiro*, 214.

113. Vianna points out that the promoters of samba as Brazil's national music were also promoting the idea that Brazilian culture was Carioca working-class culture. Vianna, *O Mistério da Samba*, 26.

114. "A Confederação e o campeonato mundial," *O Estado de S. Paulo*, May 9, 1934.

115. For example, "Campeonato Mundial," *O Estado de S. Paulo*, June 13, 1934; and "Regressam Hoje Os Players Patricios Ao Campeonato Do Mundo," *Jornal dos Sports*, August 7, 1934.

116. "A organização do seleccionado brasileiro de futebol," *O Estado de S. Paulo*, April 24, 1938.

117. "Tim Advertido!" *Jornal dos Sports*, May 7, 1938; and "Indisciplina no scratch!" *Jornal dos Sports*, May 31, 1938.

118. "Brasil e Argentina Provaveis Finalistas da Taça do Mundo? Assim Pensam Technicos e Chronistas Parisienses, Analysando as Possibilidades dos Sul-Americanos," *Jornal dos Sports*, March 8, 1938.

119. "O Brasil no Campeonato Mundial," *Sport Illustrado*, April 12, 1938.

120. "A Representação Brasileira no Campeonato Mundial de Futebol," *O Estado de S. Paulo*, April 23, 1938.

121. "Demonstrando uma fibra inquebrantavel e actuando com 9 e, durante algum tempo, com 8 elementos apenas, a selecção brasileira empatou domingo com o quadro da Tcheque-Slovania," *O Estado de S. Paulo*, June 14, 1938.

122. "O Destino conspirou contra o Brasil," *Sport Illustrado*, June 22, 1938.

123. Getúlio Vargas, quoted in Costa, *Nações em jogo*, 60.

124. "O 'Penalty' Do Jogo Contra a Italia," *Jornal dos Sports*, July 9, 1938.

125. "O regresso da delegação brasileira ao Campeonato do Mundo," *O Estado de S. Paulo*, July 9, 1938.

126. "Por effeito de uma pena maxima duvidosa assignalada pelo juiz, o seleccionado italiano levou vantagem sobre o quadro do Brasil por dois pontos a um," *O Estado de S. Paulo*, June 17, 1938.

127. "Criticas e Suggestões: Que os Juizes Europeus não Espoilem novamente o Brasil," *Jornal dos Sports*, June 19, 1938.

128. "Revoltados com o predominio Europeu! Os Delegados Brasileiros Sonham Agora com uma Liga Pan-Americana," *Jornal dos Sports*, June 19, 1938.

129. "O Destino conspirou contra o Brasil"; and Apoxy, "Com a realização do encontros Hungria versus Italia e Brasil versus Suecia, em Pariz e Bordeus, encerra-se hoje o Terceiro Campeonato do Mundo de Futebol," *O Estado de S. Paulo*, June 19, 1938.

130. Apoxy, "FIFA recusou-se a Alterar o resultado do Jogo Brasil versus Italia," *O Estado de S. Paulo*, June 17, 1938.

131. "Que Voltem os Reis do Football," *Jornal dos Sports*, June 17, 1938; "Criticas e Suggestões: Campeões Sem Coroa," *Jornal dos Sports*, June 21, 1938; and "A Consagração Definitiva dos 'Cracks!'" *Jornal dos Sports*, July 8, 1938.

132. Holanda, *O descobrimento do futebol*, 27; and Gilberto Freyre, quoted in Maranhão and Knijnik, "Futebol mulato," 59.

133. "Cuidado com Leonidas!" *Jornal dos Sports*, May 12, 1938.

134. "Leonidas!" *Sport Illustrado*, June 22, 1938; and Filho, *O negro no futebol brasileiro*, 246.

135. Lopes, "A vitoría do futebol que incorporou a *pelada*," 73.

136. Mário Filho, quoted in Souza, *O Brasil entra em campo!*, 184.

137. Maurício Drumond da Costa (in *Nações em jogo*, 97) notes the Vargas regime's interest in Brazil playing host to international sporting events and its disappointment that it was unable to do so during Vargas' time in power; the World Cup that might have taken place in Brazil in 1942 was delayed until 1950 because of the war.

138. Williams, *Culture Wars in Brazil*, esp. 192–251.

139. Corsi, *Estado Novo*.

Chapter 4. Respectability, Emotion, and Gender in Brazilian Spectatorship

1. See, for example, Carter, *Quality of Home Runs*, esp. 111–35; Alabarces, *Hinchadas*; and Panfichi, *Futbol*.

2. Caulfield, *In Defense of Honor*. See also Besse, *Restructuring Patriarchy*; and Esteves, *Meninas Perdidas*.

3. Lever, *Soccer Madness*, esp. 94–120.

4. For example, see Bellos, *Futebol*, esp. chap. 8, "Cars, Girls and Keeping It Up," 155–84.

5. "Disciplina, 'Torcedores!'" *Jornal dos Sports*, May 23, 1934.

6. Hamilton, *An Entirely Different Game*, photograph after 96; and Brandão, *Club Athletico Paulistano*, 19.

7. "Circular," June 26, 1907, "FFC (Recorte)," FFC.

8. Intruso, "Como se deve educar a assistencia nos campos de 'football,'" *Vida Sportiva*, August 3, 1918.

9. Marcio Vidal, "Nada de multas . . ." *O Imparcial (Supplemento Sportivo)*, May 27, 1922.

10. "Regimento Interno," art. 10 and 12, "Atas de Reunião da Directoria, 13-2-1919 a 24-11-1921," Archive of the Bangú Atlético Clube.

11. "Chronica Sportiva," *A Vida Moderna*, October 2, 1913.

12. Stuzenegger, "O publico 'torcedor' que frequenta os 'matches' de 'football,'" *Vida Sportiva*, January 18, 1919.

13. "Criticas e Suggestões: O Torcedor Deve Ser Mais Do Que Um Simples Torcedor: Um Sportista," *Jornal dos Sports*, April 23, 1938.

14. "Os Corinthians," *A Notícia*, August 25, 1910.

15. "Matches Internaciones: Portuguezes vs. Paulistano," *O Estado de S. Paulo*, July 28, 1913.

16. Lopes, "Class, Ethnicity, and Color in the Making of Brazilian Football," 243.

17. K. Fico, "Elegancias: Brazileiros x Uruguayos," *Vida Moderna*, October 20, 1922.

18. Franzini, "Futebol é coisa para macho?" 321.

19. Moura, "As Relações entre Lazer, Futebol, e Gênero," 26. See also Capraro and Chaves, "O futebol feminino."

20. Mourão and Morel, "As narrativas sobre o futebol feminino," 75–76.

21. Cover photograph, *Vida Sportiva*, March 20, 1920.

22. Maria Eugenia Celso, "O team de Eva," *Revista da Semana*, September 1, 1923. S. C. Feminino Vasco da Gama included "Nicia Barbosa, *goal-keeper*; Isolina and Isabel Teixeira, *full-backs*; Enriqueta and Isabel Puerta and Virginia Clement, *half-backs*; Luiza and Mary de Castro, Regina Adolphson, Maria José and Djanira Faria, *forwards*."

23. Toti, *Futebol*, 22.

24. Dr. S., "O football e as maes," *Sportman*, December 1906.

25. Marqueza de Ariana, "Femina (Uma Entrevista, graciosa, sobre a mulher no sport)," *O Imparcial (Supplemento Sportivo)*, March 26, 1921.

26. Magnolia, "Contra o feminismo," *Vida Sportiva*, January 12, 1918; Elza G. Do Nascimento, "Contra o Feminismo," *Vida Sportiva*, January 26, 1918; and Senhorita Bourrache, "As mulheres devem praticar a cultura physica," *Vida Sportiva*, March 23, 1918.

27. Besse, *Restructuring Patriarchy*, 187.

28. "A Mulher e os esportes," *Revista Feminina*, July 1923.

29. Magdala da Gama Oliveira, "A mulher e o Sport," *Tricolor*, December 1928–January 1929.

30. Magdala da Gama Oliveira, "A mulher moderna e cultura physica," *Tricolor*, April–May 1929.

31. "A Belleza Feminina e a Cultura Physica," *Revista Feminina*, April 1918.

32. E.P.D., "Não ha belleza feminina sem cultura physica," *Tricolor*, April–May 1929.

33. Goellner, *Bela, Maternal e Feminina*.

34. For an exception, see Gama Oliveira, "A mulher moderna e a cultura physica."

35. "O bello sexo e o sport," *Diario de Notícias*, June 30, 1911.

36. "A Mulher e os esportes."

37. Ibid.; and "A Mulher e o esporte," *Revista Feminina*, July 1925.

38. "Um grave problema," *Revista Feminina*, August 1921.

39. Among the few works on the early history of women's sports, see esp. Devide, *História das mulheres na natação brasileira no século XX*.

40. Bruce, *Brazil and the Brazilians*, 266.

41. Fluminense Football Club, *Relatorio*, 1916, FFC.

42. The founding of the *secção* is described in *'Excelsior' no Fluminense F.C.* The claim is made in Fluminense Football Club, *Relatorio* 1931, FFC.

43. *'Excelsior' no Fluminense F.C.*

44. Fluminense Football Club, *Relatorio*, 1921, 1927, 1929, 1931–35.

45. Ibid., 1927.

46. Ibid., 1931, 1935.

47. Ibid., 1927–28.

48. Ibid., 1934.

49. Gama Oliveira, "A mulher e o Sport."

50. Ibid.

51. Caulfield, *In Defense of Honor*, 73–74.

52. "Entrevista com João Hamilton na Inglaterra," *O Estado de S. Paulo*, September 20, 1907.

53. "O preço das entradas," *Jornal de Theatro e Sport*, September 3, 1921; and "Campeonato Municipal de S. Paulo," *Kosmos*, September 10, 1919.

54. Minutes of the Meeting of the Directorate of the Società Sportiva Palestra Itália, July 4, 1927, "Atas Diretoria 11/02/1927 à 8/02/1929, Livro 07," Archive of the Sociedade Esportiva Palmeiras.

55. Minutes of the Meeting of the Directorate of the Botafogo Football Club, November 26, 1919, "Atas da Directoria, 14/04/1919–12/04/1920," Archive of Botafogo de Futebol e Regatas.

56. "O bello sexo e o sport," *Diario de Notícias*, June 30, 1911.

57. "A educação physica da mulher," *Revista Feminina*, August 1923.

58. Gama Oliveira, "A mulher e o Sport."

59. Goellner, *Bela, Maternal e Feminina*, 60.

60. "Football: *Rio versus S. Paulo*," *Sportman*, August 31, 1907; and "A brilhante victoria do Fluminense F.C.," Unknown journal, May 28, 1917, Album for 1917 season, FFC.

61. "Football: O grande match de hontem," *O Imparcial*, May 14, 1916.

62. Goldstein, *Playing for Keeps*, 38–39.

63. Pérez, "Between Baseball and Bullfighting," 507.

64. "Nosso concurso photographico," *Tricolor*, March 1928.

65. "A Exma. Sra. D. Maria Prado Aranha é a rainha do C. A. Paulistano," *CAP*, October 1928.

66. "Qual é a torcedora mais renitente do C. R. do Flamengo," *Sport Illustrado*, November 20, 1920.

67. Besse, "Defining a 'National Type.'"

68. For example, "Mascottes," *Gazeta Esportiva*, April 19, 1934.
69. Rosenfeld, "O futebol no Brasil," 66–67.
70. "Collaboração dos Leitores," *A Cigarra Sportiva*, June 16, 1917.
71. A. G. Filho, "O Futebol de Hontem e o de Hoje," *C.A.P.*, March 1928.
72. Goldstein (in *Playing for Keeps*, 8) notes that in American baseball's early years, "The sporting press, in fact, was the theatrical press."
73. J. Brito, "Off-Side. Revista em 2 Actos," 1924; Bittencourt [and] Menezes, "FLÁ-FLU! . . . Revista em 2 actos e 26 quadros," 1925; Luiz Iglesias and M. Paradella, "As Torcedoras: Durleta em Um Acto e Dois Quadros," 1927; and Gino Roma, "America 'Versus' Fluminense, Burletta em I Acto e 5 Quadros," 1928, Arquivo Nacional do Brasil, Delegacia Auxiliara da Polícia do Rio de Janeiro, 2a, Código do Fundo 6E, Seção de guarda SDE, no. 518, Caixa 25, no. 1044, Caixa 45, and no. 1335, Caixa 57.
74. Bittencourt [and] Menezes, "FLÁ-FLU!"
75. Roma, "America 'Versus' Fluminense."
76. Moura, "As Relações entre Lazer, Futebol, e Gênero," 21.
77. "Carnet Mundano Sportivo: Recados," *Sport Illustrado*, January 8, 15, and 29, 1922.
78. For example, "Confidencias," *Vida Sportiva*, January 17, 1920.
79. Tá Visto, "A necessidade do uso á lapella de distinctivos 'chics' por parte dos nossos footballers e torcedores," *O Imparcial (Supplemento Sportivo)*, March 25, 1922.
80. Mendonça, "A Medalha," n.p.
81. Besse, *Restructuring Patriarchy*, 160.
82. "Carnet Mundano Sportivo," *Sport Illustrado*, October 30, 1920.
83. Cid, "Amor 'Eliminatorio,'" *Tricolor*, October–November, 1928.
84. "Campeonato de 1903 (Undecimo match) S. Paulo Athletic Club–Club Athletico Paulistano," *O Estado de S. Paulo*, August 3, 1903.
85. Italics in original. Minutes of the Meeting of the Directorate of the Fluminense Football Club, September 17, 1907, "Actas da Directoria 5 de Maio 1905 a 23 de Maio 1911," FFC.
86. Extraordinary General Assembly of the Bangú Athletic Club, December 6, 1907, "Atas da Assembléia Geral Ordinario, 20-12-05, Acta da Assemblea Geral extraordinario, 6-12-07; Atas de Reunião de Diretoria 1906–1908," Archive of the Bangú Atlético Clube.
87. Guilherme, "Chronicas de Sports—Paulistano 3–Palmeiras 0," *O Echo*, November 5, 1917.
88. "Publico," *O Imparcial (Supplemento Sportivo)*, August 13, 1921.
89. Netto, *Coelho Netto e os esportes*, 12–13.
90. "Torcedores," *Athletica*, February 27, 1920.
91. "Publico," *O Imparcial*.
92. "Uma aggressão covarde," *Vida Sportiva*, July 31, 1920.
93. "Um Conflicto entre jogadores e assistentes não permittiu terminasse o match Fluminense x Brasil," *A Noite*, April 13, 1931; and "Fluminense F.C. x S.C. Brasil: A Partida não terminou devido as occorrencias havidas em campo," *Jornal do Commercio*, April 13, 1931.

94. "Football: Liga Metropolitana: Botafogo Paysandu [0–3]," *O Jockey*, August 2, 1913.

95. "O Caso do Paulistano: Trechos do Relatorio do Juiz," *O Estado de S. Paulo*, May 28, 1922.

96. "As lamentaveis scenas de domingo no campo do Carioca," *Jornal dos Sports*, June 2, 1931.

97. Marcio Vidal, "Os disturbios nos campos de 'football,'" *Vida Sportiva*, July 20, 1918.

98. Minutes of the Meeting of the Directorate of the Fluminense Football Club, June 25, 1907, "Actas da Directoria 5 de Maio 1905 a 23 de Maio 1911," FFC.

99. Intruso, "Como se deve educar a assistencia nos campos de 'football.'"

100. "Publico," *O Imparcial*.

101. Minutes of the Meetings of the Directorate of the Botafogo Football Club, undated, probably late July or early August 1913; undated, August 1913; and 8 May 1914, "Atas da Directoria 03/-1/1910 a 11/09/1916," Archive of Botafogo de Futebol e Regatas.

102. Minutes of the Meeting of the Directorate of the Botafogo Football Club, November 26, 1919.

103. Minutes of the Meetings of the Directorate of the Botafogo Football Club, August 16 and 27, 1917, "Atas da Directoria 09/10/1916 a 24/09/1917," Archive of Botafogo de Futebol e Regatas.

104. Besse, *Restructuring Patriarchy*, 37.

105. J. Roma, "A torcedora alvi-negra," *Vida Sportiva*, February 15, 1919.

106. Lellis Vieira, "A nevrose do foot-ball," *A Vida Moderna*, December 30, 1920.

107. "Nosso concurso photographico," *Tricolor*, March 1928.

108. Leite, "Torcida," *Sport Illustrado*, March 5, 1922.

109. Vieira, "A nevrose do foot-ball."

110. The invention of the term is widely attributed to Coelho Netto, who is said to have noted women fans twirling their handkerchiefs or gloves in the air as they willed on their teams. However, the earliest reference I have located for the term is in J. Semana, "Foot-ball," *A Vida Moderna*, June 13, 1912. For an example of the popular version of the term's etymology, see Holanda, "The Fan as Actor," 12.

111. "Na Antarctica," *S. Paulo Illustrado*, August 20, 1920.

112. Caulfield, *In Defense of Honor*, 73–74.

113. "Os Corinthians em S. Paulo: O match de hontem," *O Estado de S. Paulo*, August 29, 1913; "Uma interessante entrevista com o grande 'keeper' Hugo Moraes," *Vida Sportiva*, June 22, 1918; and Vieira, "A nevrose do foot-ball."

114. Ivan Ney, "Schootando . . . (Ás cariocas footballers), *O Football*, May 23, 1914.

115. "Confidencias," *Vida Sportiva*, January 17, 1920, and March 13, 1920.

116. "Uma entrevista," *Careta*, November 4, 1916.

117. Advertisement, *Vida Sportiva*, August 3, 1918.

118. "Campeonato de 1903 (Undecimo match) S. Paulo Athletic Club–Club Athletico Paulistano," *O Estado de S. Paulo*, 3 August 3, 1903.

119. "Associação Paulista de Sports Athleticos: Palestra vs Mackenzie," *A Cigarra Sportiva*, June 16, 1917.

120. "A Chronica dos Esportes," *S. Paulo Illustrado*, January 22, 1921. See also J. Roma, "A torcedora alvi-negra," *Vida Sportiva*, February 15, 1919.

121. "Termina amanhã o grande campeonato paulista de 1920: Paulistano contra Palestra," *A Gazeta*, December 18, 1920.

122. Toledo, *Torcidas Organizadas de Futebol*, 21.

123. "Torcida Tricolor," *Rio Sportivo*, April 11, 1927; and "Torcida Tricolor: Uma idea victoriosa," *Rio Sportivo*, April 21, 1927.

124. Holanda, *O Clube Como Vontade e Representação*, 103–7.

125. "Torcida, Força Que Conduz ás Arrancada Triumphaes," *Jornal dos Sports*, September 13, 1938.

126. Fico, "Elegancias."

127. "A Voz do 'Fan' Carioca Atravez O Microphone De Pre-3," *Jornal dos Sports*, September 29, 1938.

128. Marcio Lyra and others, quoted in Costa, *Nações em jogo*, 68.

129. "Criticas e Suggestões: A Participação do Brasil no Campeonato do Mundo É Uma Questão Nacional," *Jornal dos Sports*, April 8, 1938; and "Criticas e Suggestões: Todos os Brasileiros de Pé, pela Victoria do Brasil!" *Jornal dos Sports*, May 25 and 27, 1938.

130. "Leonor Silva e Oswaldo Menezes: Embaixadores Da Torcida Brasileira em Paris! O Desfecho Empolgante De Uma Campanha Sensacional," *Jornal dos Sports*, April 17, 1938. Silva received 215,669 votes, and Menezes received 314,372 votes.

131. "As Emprehendimentos Sensacionaes de Jornal dos Sports," *Jornal dos Sports*, March 30, 1938.

132. "42 milhões e tanto de inimigos pessoaes! Eis o que o Juiz Hungaro Arranjou no Brasil," *Jornal dos Sports*, June 13, 1938.

133. "A Alegria da cidade pelo Grande triumpho dos Brasileiros!" *Jornal dos Sports*, June 15, 1938; and untitled photographs, *O Estado de S. Paulo*, June 15, 1938.

134. "Criticas e Suggestões: A Formidavel Apotheose de Hontem," *Jornal dos Sports*, July 12, 1938.

135. Apoxy, "FIFA recusou-se a Alterar o resultado do Jogo Brasil versus Italia," *O Estado de S. Paulo*, June 18, 1938.

Chapter 5. The Invention of the Beautiful Game

1. *Paris Soir*, quoted in Patusca, *Os reis do futebol*, 16. See also "Opinião da Imprensa Franceza," *S. Paulo Sportivo*, Edição Extra Illustrada, April 1925.

2. See, for example, Milby, "Stylin'!"; Carter, *Quality of Home Runs*; and Beckles and Stoddart, *Liberation Cricket*.

3. Heloisa Turini Bruhns makes the connection between futebol and samba explicit in *Futebol, carnival e capoeira*, 55–90.

4. Wisnik, "The Riddle of Brazilian Soccer," 209.

5. Filho, *O negro no futebol brasileiro*, 243.

6. Americo R. Netto, "Innovação Brasileira," *Sports*, November 1919.

7. "Campeonato de 1903 (Undecimo match) S. Paulo Athletic Club–Club Athletico Paulistano," *O Estado de S. Paulo*, 3 August 3, 1903.

8. See, for example, P., "Cortezia ingleza," *Careta*, January 3, 1914; and "Os inglezes," *Careta*, January 24, 1914.

9. Weber, *Sports athleticos*, 190–91, and 199–200.

10. Ibid., 190, 26.

11. Italics in original. C. Viveiros, "Foot-ball e suas artes!" *Rio Sportivo*, August 7, 1909.

12. Afranio Hiroz, "Desporto e disciplina," *Sports* (Rio de Janeiro), August 6, 1915.

13. On the history of football formations, see Wilson, *Inverting the Pyramid*.

14. "O papel dos 'forwards,'" *Vida Sportiva*, July 7, 1918.

15. Joffre, "Moral e Football," *Vida Sportiva*, August 31, 1918.

16. "A Disciplina," *O Estado de S. Paulo*, May 11, 1918.

17. Advertisement for Papeleria Confiança, Alberto Silvares & C., *Vida Sportiva*, May 15, 1920.

18. Leopoldo Sant'Anna, "'Footballers'!!," in Amaral, *Cousas de "Football,"* 15; and Amaral, *Cousas de "Football,"* 18.

19. Marcio Vidal, "Salve Brazileiros!" *Vida Sportiva*, May 31, 1919.

20. Netto, "Innovação Brasileira."

21. "Escola de Disciplina," *Sports*, January 1920.

22. "A Quinzena Nacional de Football," *O Imparcial*, 29 March 29, 1920.

23. "A Recepção do Paulistano," *O Estado de S. Paulo*, March 29, 1920.

24. Official correspondence, collected in "Associação Paulista de Esportes Athleticos 7-1-29 to 28-12-29," Archive of the Sport Club Corinthians Paulista.

25. "Codigo de Penalidades, Approvado em sessão da Directoria, do 22 do Agosto do 1929," in ibid.

26. Advertisement for Casa Stamp, *Vida Sportiva*, June 1, 1918.

27. Julio Roma, "Jogo Violento," *Vida Sportiva*, November 9, 1918.

28. Advertisement, "Chronica," *Athletica*, September 11, 1920.

29. "O football de hoje . . . ," *A Gazeta*, April 29, 1922; and "O Futebriga," *A Gazeta*, May 25, 1922.

30. Carlos Villaça, "O Futebol de Hontem e o de Hoje," *Diario da Noite*, June 16, 1927.

31. A. G. Filho, "O Futebol de Hontem e o de Hoje," *C.A.P.*, March 1928.

32. "O Futebriga," *A Gazeta*, May 25, 1922.

33. Filho, "O Futebol de Hontem e o de Hoje."

34. C., "Chronica da Semana," *Sport Illustrado*, November 27, 1920.

35. Joffre, "Moral e Football."

36. Cicero Brasileiro Mereilles, "Como os Bahianos Jogam o Futebol," *A Gazeta*, January 5, 1922.

37. "O Retrocesso do Nosso Futebol," *A Gazeta*, May 10, 1922.

38. "Publico," *O Imparcial (Supplemento Sportivo)*, August 13, 1921.

39. Minutes of the Meetings of the Directorate of the Bangú Athletic Club, July 26,

August 2, September 13, 1911; and March 21, 1912, "Atas de Reuniões da Directoria, 28-2-09 a 12-1-15," Archive of the Bangú Atlético Clube.

40. "Aggressão Estupida," *O Estado de S. Paulo*, September 9, 1922.

41. Roma, "Jogo Violento."

42. Minutes of the Meeting of the Directorate of the Botafogo Foot-ball Club, August 16, 1917, "Atas da Directoria 09/10/1916 a 24/09/1917," Archive of Botafogo de Futebol e Regatas.

43. *O Estado de S. Paulo, Almanach para 1916*, 238–39.

44. "O Foot-Ball em S. Paulo," *A Cigarra Sportiva*, June 9, 1917.

45. Goldstein, *Playing for Keeps*, 129.

46. Vianna, *O Mistério da Samba*, 19–20.

47. Freyre, *Ingleses no Brasil*, xvii–xviii; and "Prefacio," in Filho, *O negro no futebol brasileiro*, ix–xii.

48. See, for example, Rosenfeld, "O futebol no Brasil," 61–85; and Damo and Oliven, "Fútbol made in Brasil." Richard Follett (in "'The Spirit of Brazil,'" 71–72 and 82) agrees with Freyre, Filho, and others that there has been "an authentically Afro-Brazilian footballing style," but he sees it as a challenge by black athletes to the discipline and hierarchy that characterized Brazil in the mid-twentieth century, serving as "an embodied script that challenged the culture of racial power and the discourse of harmonic nationhood."

49. "The Corinthians' Return," *Sporting Opinion*, November 6, 1910.

50. "A technica do Foot-ball: Methodos francezes contra outra methodos," *Rio Sportivo*, June 6, 1927.

51. "O internacional de hoje: Corinthians x Chelsea," *A Gazeta*, July 4, 1929.

52. "Um Erro de Orientação," *O Estado de S. Paulo*, August 15 and 16, 1929.

53. Leop, "Illusão que se evola . . . ," *A Gazeta*, July 26, 1930.

54. Corrêa, *Grandezas e Miserias*, 187; and Valentim, *O Futebol e Sua Técnica*, 27–28, and section entitled "Thank you!" n.p.

55. Corrêa, *Grandezas e Miserias*, 187.

56. A.C., "A ausencia de elementos estrangeiros no nosso football: O ultimo abencerragem foi Harry Welfare," *Jornal dos Sports*, May 13, 1931.

57. Archetti, *Masculinities*, 70.

58. For example, Soares, *Futebol, Malandragem e Identidade*. See also Follett, "'The Spirit of Brazil,'" 83.

59. DaMatta, *Carnivals, Rogues, and Heroes*, 132.

60. Ibid., 209.

61. Freyre, "Prefacio," in Filho, *O negro no futebol brasileiro*, x.

62. A few scholars have compared the rhetorics of Argentine and Brazilian football styles. For example, see Guedes, "On *Criollos* and Capoeiras"; Alabarces, "Tropicalismos y europeísmos en el fútbol"; and Helal, "'Jogo Bonito' y Fútbol Criollo."

63. "Fausto tem razão! . . . Os 'Almofadinhas' em Montevideo formaram um bloco a parte," *Rio Sportivo*, July 22, 1930.

64. João Brito, "A representação carioca em Montevideo," *A Gazeta*, June 19, 1930.

65. Leop, "Elles-se bombardeam," *A Gazeta*, July 22, 1930.

66. "Fausto tem razão!" and "As ultimas impressões dos nossos bravos," *Rio Sportivo*, July 3, 1930.

67. Nowadays flair and creativity are the watchwords of many Brazilian commentators, especially in comparing Brazilian football to football as it is played abroad. But they also regularly insist, especially in reference to domestic football, that players display the kind of passion that characterizes stereotypes of Brazilian torcedores, arguing that the best footballer is the one who combines imagination with *garra*, literally, claw or talon, which, translated to football, means commitment and intensity. See Helal and Soares, "The Decline of the 'Soccer-Nation,'" 139. Alabarces (in "Tropicalismos y europeísmos en el fútbol," 78) describes a similar theme in Argentine discourse, an allowance for a certain amount of violence that reveals the game as "full of subtle masculine signals."

68. Simoni Guedes (in "On *Criollos* and Capoeiras," 152) and Eduardo Archetti (in *Masculinities*, 61 and 193) both note that Argentine and Brazilian commentators have traditionally viewed their neighbor as an important "other" against which to measure national football, with race and ethnicity the defining difference they have focused on. See also Alabarces, "Tropicalismos y europeísmos en el fútbol" and Helal, "'Jogo Bonito' y Fútbol Criollo." Ricardo Pinto dos Santos (in *Entre 'rivais,'* 79–98) points out that the difference in Argentine and Brazilian football commentary may not be as large as it seems, showing that early-twentieth-century critics of football violence tended to blame working-class people of color, blacks in Brazil and mestizos in Argentina.

69. "Fausto tem razão!"

70. Netto, "Innovação Brasileira."

71. Mércio, *A História dos Campeonatos Cariocas de Futebol*, 50.

72. Ribeiro, *Os Donos do Espetáculo*, 98.

73. Confederação Brasileira Desportos, quoted in "A Moral desportiva," *C.A.P.*, May 5, 1928.

74. Stepan, *"The Hour of Eugenics,"* 164.

75. "Raça e sport: Haverá um povo predestinado á pratica de um sport determinado?" *Rio Sportivo*, January 8, 1927.

76. Untitled article, *Rio Sportivo*, July 3, 1930.

77. "O internacional de hoje."

78. A.C., "A ausencia de elementos estrangeiros no nosso football."

79. "Campeonato Mundial: Brasileiros contra Hespanhoes," *O Estado de S. Paulo*, May 27, 1934.

80. "O Brasil no Campeonato Mundial," *Sport Illustrado*, April 12, 1938.

81. Apoxy, "Campeonato Mundial: Sul-americanos e europeus," *O Estado de S. Paulo*, May 31, 1938.

82. "Criticas e Suggestões: Os Brasileiros, Campeões Sem Coroa," *Jornal dos Sports*, June 21, 1938.

83. "Porque Vencemos Sempre," advertisement for Radiotropina, *Jornal dos Sports*, June 13, 1938.

84. "Criticas e Suggestões: Os Brasileiros, Campeões Sem Coroa."

85. José Lins do Rego, quoted in Souza, *O Brasil entra em campo!*, 38.

86. Olympicus, "Depois das duas ultimas victorias contra os uruguayos," *A Gazeta*, December 7, 1932.

87. Apoxy, "Campeonato Mundial: Sul-americanos e europeus."

88. Apoxy, "Campeonato Mundial," *O Estado de S. Paulo*, June 14, 1938.

89. Vianna, *O Mistério da Samba*, 61–62.

90. Gilberto Freyre, quoted in Maranhão, "Apollonians and Dionysians," 514 and 516.

91. Freyre, "Prefácio," in Filho, *O negro no futebol brasileiro*, xi.

92. Souza, *O Brasil entra em campo!*, 136–37.

93. Filho, *O negro no futebol brasileiro*, 240 and 243.

94. Advertisement for Magnolia cigarettes, "Candidato dos 'fans' Cariocas!" "Cigarros Para Os Detentos," and "Leonidas O Conquistador Do Chevrolet 'Magnolia'!" *Jornal dos Sports*, January 9; February 2 and 3; and March 3, 1938.

95. Advertisements for Silva, Farias, & Cia. Ltda., Vencedor, Loteria Federal, "Recebido Pelo Sr. Mario De Oliveira O 'Diamante Negro' A Visita Do Grande Artilheiro Ao Conhecido Sportman E Industrial," "Um Relogio 'Vulcain' Para O Maior 'Crack,'" and "Leonidas Homenageado Pela Firma J. M. Mello & Cia.," *Jornal dos Sports*, June 12 and 14; July 15 and 17; and August 17, 1938.

96. Advertisement for Goiabada Marca Peixe, *Jornal dos Sports*, July 12, 1938.

97. Advertisements for Broadway e Pathé Pacifico and São Luiz theaters, *Jornal dos Sports*, June 21, and November 12, 1938.

98. Advertisement for Theatro Carlos Gomes, *Jornal dos Sports*, August 23, 1938.

99. "Leonidas! Leonidas! O Governador de Minas Quer Conhecer O Grande 'Crack' Rubro-Negro" and untitled photograph, *Jornal dos Sports*, July 5 and 20, 1938.

100. Souza, *O Brasil entra em campo!*, 118.

101. Thomaz Mazzoni, quoted in ibid., 140.

102. "Leonidas Homenageado Pela Firma J. M. Mello & Cia."

103. Thomaz Mazzoni, quoted in Holanda, *O descobrimento do futebol*, 272n50.

104. *O Globo Sportivo*, quoted in Souza, *O Brasil entra em campo!*, 146.

105. Souza, *O Brasil entra em campo!*, 182.

106. "Recebido Pelo Sr. Mario De Oliveira O 'Diamante Negro' A Visita Do Grande Artilheiro Ao Conhecido Sportman E Industrial," and Filho, *O negro no futebol brasileiro*, 275.

107. Filho, *O negro no foot-ball brasileiro*, caption to photograph after 240 and 275.

108. Bruhns (in *Futebol, carnival e capoeira*) argues that "ginga" and the "jogo de cintura," the swivel of the hips, best seen in Brazilian football, samba, and capoeira, are the essence of Brazilian popular culture.

109. Souza, *O Brasil entra em campo!*, 186, 191, and 194. While Domingos won four Rio de Janeiro titles to go along with championships in Montevideo and Buenos Aires, Leônidas won three Carioca championships and was relatively unsuccessful abroad. He did not become a serial winner until his move to São Paulo, with which he won five city championships.

110. Ribeiro, *Os Donos do Espetáculo*, 100. See also Silva, "O esporte a serviço da pátria."

111. Olimpicus, *Problemas e Aspectos do nosso Futebol*, 49–50.

112. "Fluminense x Ferencvaros," *Jornal dos Sports*, June 23, 1931; and "Criticas e Suggestões: A superioridade do football brasileiro," *Jornal dos Sports*, July 11, 1931.

113. "Criticas e Suggestões: A violencia nos jogos de football," *Jornal dos Sports*, October 28, 1931.

114. Ibid.

115. J. T. de Carvalho, "O Jogo Palestra x Fluminense foi encerrado com o score de 4 × 1 a favor do quadro paulista," *Athletica*, August 11, 1933.

116. "Scenas de selvageria," *O Globo*, August 7, 1933.

117. "O Encontro Fluminense Palestra foi suspenso quando faltavam tres minutos para o seu termino: Vencia o Palestra, 4 × 1," *A Noite*, August 7, 1933.

118. "O Encontro Fluminense Palestra"; "Scenas de selvageria"; and Carvalho, "O Jogo Palestra x Fluminense."

119. Carvalho, "O Jogo Palestra x Fluminense."

120. Apoxy, "Campeonato Mundial," "Comentarios e noticias a proposito do campeonato mundial de futebol," "Verdades cruas," and "Por effeito de uma pena maxima duvidosa assignalada pelo juiz, o seleccionado italiano levou vantagem sobre o quadro do Brasil por dois pontos a um," *O Estado de S. Paulo*, May 31; and June 8, 10, and 17, 1938.

121. "Criticas e Suggestões: Os Jogadores Requistados Não Podem Discutir Ordens," *Jornal dos Sports*, March 31, 1938.

122. Souza, *O Brasil entra em campo!*, 183.

123. Thomaz Mazzoni, quoted in Silva, "Imprensa esportiva e o pensamento autoritário na obra de Thomaz Mazzoni," 5.

124. "Floriano duvida que o Brasil levante o campeonato do mundo!" *Jornal dos Sports*, May 15, 1938.

125. Guedes, "On *Criollos* and Capoeiras," 154.

126. See, for example, Carter, *Quality of Home Runs*, esp. 63–88; and Beckles and Stoddart, *Liberation Cricket*.

Epilogue: The Life of the Beautiful Game

1. Fédération Internationale de Football Association (FIFA), "2014 FIFA World Cup Brazil," 5–6.

2. There were far too many of these works to mention here. For an example of the ways in which the futebol tradition has shaped popular depictions of Brazil, see esp. Zirin, *Brazil's Dance with the Devil*. In their 2014 works, scholars Roger Kittleson (*The Country of Football*) and Joshua H. Nadel (*Fútbol!*) offered important examinations of the tradition and its claims.

3. Gastaldo, *Pátria, Chuteiras e Propaganda*, 22. See also Gastaldo and Guedes, eds., *Nações em Campo*, an interdisciplinary examination of how Brazilians perform and negotiate Brazilianness during the World Cup.

4. Lopes, "Transformations in National Identity through Football in Brazil," 78.

5. Filho, *O negro no futebol brasileiro*, 331–33.

6. Neto, *Dossie 50*.

7. Paulo Perdigão and Nelson Rodrigues, quoted in Wisnik, "The Riddle of Brazilian Soccer," 204.

8. Bellos (in *Futebol*, 43–76) surveys popular memory of the match.

9. Lopes, "Transformations in National Identity through Football in Brazil," 80.

10. Filho, *O negro no futebol brasileiro*, 335.

11. Souza, *O Brasil entra em campo!*, 81–99.

12. Italics in original. João Lyra Filho, quoted in Guedes, *O Brasil no campo do futebol*, 32.

13. Guedes, *O Brasil no campo do futebol*, 19–38.

14. See esp. Soares, Salvador, and Bartholo, "Copa de 70," on commentators' tendency to ignore the rigorous training that contributed to these successes.

15. Souza, *O Brasil entra em campo!*, 193–94.

16. Freyre, *Ingleses no Brasil*, xvii–xviii.

17. Soares, "História e a invenção de tradições no futebol brasileiro," 114; Maranhão and Knijnik, "Futebol mulato," 69; and Zanin, "Nelson Rodrigues e o Mito do Futebol."

18. Nelson Rodrigues, quoted in Natali, "The Realm of the Possible," 280.

19. Wisnik, "The Riddle of Brazilian Soccer," 202.

20. Follett, "'The Spirit of Brazil,'" 71 and 87; and Damo and Oliven, "Fútbol made in Brasil."

21. Shirts, "Sócrates, Corinthians, and Questions of Democracy and Citizenship," 104.

22. Claudio Coutinho, quoted in ibid., 104.

23. Sócrates, quoted in ibid., 100. On the movement, see esp. Florenzano, *A Democracia Corinthiana*.

24. Natali, "The Realm of the Possible," 268.

25. Carlos Alberto Parreira, quoted in Milby, "Stylin'!" 68 and 228.

26. Maranhão and Knijnik, "Futebol mulato," 68–69.

27. Guedes, "O Salvador da Pátria."

28. *Hannoversche Allgemeine Zeitung* and Eduardo Galeano, quoted in Milby, "Stylin'!" 304–5.

29. Helal, "'Jogo Bonito' y Fútbol Criollo," 4.

30. José Miguel Wisnik (in "The Riddle of Brazilian Soccer," 209) suggests that globalization has meant the decline of distinctive football traditions but also that football can help protect national difference, calling it "a space in which the substratum of these traditions, and their residue, is most clearly legible."

31. Aldo Rebelo, quoted in Bellos, *Futebol*, 324.

32. Rousseff, "A Copa das Copas."

33. FIFA, "2014 FIFA World Cup Brazil," 5–6.

34. Aldo Rebelo introduced the volume (*A Pátria de Chuteiras*), and the pieces were serialized by federal government on its "Portal da Copa" website.

35. Silva, "Discurso do Presidente da República."

36. Datafolha Instituto de Pesquisas, Project PO813739, "Copa do Mundo, 02 e 03/04/2014."

37. Even coverage of the protests became controversial in Brazil, with protestors alleging a lack of objectivity in the traditional media, much of which cast the protestors and their demands in a negative fashion. For an example of the dissonance between reporters and protestors, see João Batista Jr. and Juliana Deodoro, "Um protesto por dia, quem aguenta?" *Veja São Paulo*, June 14, 2013. Like many media outlets, the *Folha de São Paulo* at first criticized the protestors and defended police action to break up demonstrations. It later softened its tone, and accused authorities of mishandling the protests. See esp. Juan Arias, "Editorial: Retomar a Paulista," and "Contra tarifa, manifestantes vandalizam centro e Paulista," and "Agentes do caos," *Folha de São Paulo*, June 12, 13, and 15, 2013. For an English-language overview of the demonstrations, see Goldblatt, *Futebol Nation*, 222–44.

38. On Romário, see, for example, Sam Borden, "Romário, a World Cup Champion, Is Now a World Cup Dissenter," *New York Times*, October 15, 2013.

39. For example, see Bruno Amorim, "Protesto contra a Copa do Mundo termina com bombas e feridos na Tijuca," *O Globo*, July 13, 2014; and Guilherme Boulos, "A Copa das Tropas," *Folha de São Paulo*, July 17, 2014.

40. For example, Carlos Heitor Cony commented on the problem of globalization in "Uma estreia medíocre" and "O futebol é assim," *Folha de São Paulo*, June 15 and 24, 2014. Economist Samuel Pessôa pointed to lingering administrative issues in "Tragédia no Mineirão e a Lei Pelé," *Folha de São Paulo*, July 13, 2014. In English, see Sam Borden, "For Brazil, Winning Trumps Aesthetics," *New York Times*, July 7, 2014; and Zico, "Brazil Capitulated to the First Strong Team They Encountered. I'm livid," *Guardian*, July 9, 2014.

41. See, for example, Simon Romero, "Brazil's Leftist Ruling Party, Born of Protests, Is Perplexed by Revolt," *New York Times*, June 19, 2013.

42. Martin, "Pelé's Law and the Commercialization of Brazilian Soccer"; and Helal, "The Brazilian Soccer Crisis as a Sociological Problem."

43. Gordon and Helal, "The Crisis of Brazilian Football," 154. See also Helal and Soares, "The Decline of the 'Soccer-Nation,'" which extends the argument.

Bibliography

PRIMARY SOURCES

ARCHIVES

Acervo Flu-Memória, Fluminense Football Club
Archive of the America Football Club
Archive of the Associação Portuguesa Desportos
Archive of the Bangú Atlético Clube
Archive of Botafogo de Futebol e Regatas
Archive of the Clube de Regatas do Flamengo
Archive of the Clube de Regatas Vasco da Gama
Archive of the Confederação Brasileira de Futebol
Archive of the Sociedade Esportiva Palmeiras
Archive of the Sport Club Corinthians Paulista
Archive of the Instituto Histórico e Geográfico de São Paulo
Archive of the Instituto Presbiteriano Mackenzie
Arquivo Nacional do Brasil
Centro Cultural Light
Centro Pró-Memória, Club Athletico Paulistano
Centro Pró-Memória Hans Nobiling, Esporte Clube Pinheiros
Fundação Património Histórico da Energia de São Paulo
National Archives (London, England)

PUBLISHED PRIMARY SOURCES

Amaral, Odilon Penteado do. *Cousas de "Football": Conselhos, Maximas e Observações.* São Paulo: O Estado de S. Paulo, 1920.
America Foot-ball Club. *Estatutos do America Foot-Ball Club, 1912,* n.p.
Associação Metropolitana de Esportes Athleticos. *Codigo Esportivo.* Rio de Janeiro: Typographia do Annuario do Brasil, 1929.
Associação Portuguesa de Esportes. *Estatutos da Associação Portuguesa de Esportes—A.A. Mackenzie.* São Paulo: Julio Costa & C., n.d.

———. *Relatorio* [title varies], n.p., 1928–31.
Azevedo, Fernando de. *A Evolução do Esporte no Brasil: A Evolução do Esporte no Brasil, Praças de Jogos para Crianças, Congresso de Educação Physica.* São Paulo: Companhia Melhoramentos de S. Paulo, 1930.
Barbosa. Directed by Ana Luiza Azevedo and Jorge Furtado. 1988; Porto Alegre: Casa de Cinema PoA.
Barreto, Afonso Henriques de Lima. *Feiras e Mafuás.* São Paulo: Editôra Mérito S.A., 1953.
———. *Marginália: Artigos e Crônicas.* São Paulo: Editôra Brasiliense, 1956.
Botafogo Football Club. *Estatutos do Club de Regatas do Botafogo* [title and publisher vary], 1914–27.
Bruce, G. J. *Brazil and the Brazilians,* 2nd ed. London: Methuen & Co., 1915.
Cardim, Mário. *O Guia de Football.* São Paulo: n.p., 1906.
Casa Colombo. *Guia Sportiva para 1912.* Porto Alegre: n.p., 1912.
Club Athletico Paulistano. *Relatorio dos Trabalhos Sociaes* [title and publisher vary], 1920–23.
Club de Natação e Regatas "Alvares Cabral." *Estatutos do Club de Natação e Regatas "Alvares Cabral" fundado no dia 6 de Julho de 1902.* Victoria, Espirito Santo: Typ. Modelo, 1909.
Club de Regatas do Flamengo. *Estatutos do Club de Regatas do Flamengo* [title and publisher vary], 1916, 1923.
Club de Regatas Paquetaense. *Estatutos do Club de Regatas Paquetaense.* Rio de Janeiro: Typ. G. Leuzinger & Filhos, 1883.
Club de Regatas Vasco da Gama. *Projecto de reforma dos Estatutos do Club de Regatas Vasco da Gama.* n.p., n.d.
———. *Relatorio da Directoria* [title and publisher vary], 1928–32.
Confederação Brasileira de Desportos. *Estatutos.* Rio de Janeiro: Typ. do *Jornal do Commercio,* 1929.
———. *Lei de Transferencia de Amadores.* Rio de Janeiro: Typ. do *Jornal do Commercio,* 1930.
———. *Relatorio* [title and publisher vary], 1918–32.
Corbett, B. O., ed. *Annals of the Corinthian Football Club.* New York: Longmans, Green, and Co., 1906.
Corrêa, Floriano Peixoto. *Grandezas e Miserias do Nosso Futebol.* Rio de Janeiro: Flores & Mano, 1933.
Creek, F.N.S. *A History of the Corinthian Football Club.* London: Longmans, Green and Co., 1933.
Datafolha Instituto de Pesquisas. Project PO813739, "Copa do Mundo, 02 e 03/04 /2014." datafolha.com.br
Edmundo, Luiz. *Recordações do Rio Antigo.* Rio de Janeiro: Editôra A Noite, 1950.
———. *O Rio de Janeiro do meu tempo.* Rio de Janeiro: Xenon Editora, 1987.
O Estado de São Paulo. *Almanach para 1916.* São Paulo: O Estado de S. Paulo, 1916.
Faria, Benito de. *A criminalidade nos esportes.* Rio de Janeiro: Pap. Velho, 1929.
Fédération Internationale de Football Association. "2014 FIFA World Cup Brazil:

FIFA Public Guidelines for use of FIFA's Official Marks," no. 7 (May 2013), 5–6, FIFA.com.

Filho, Mário [Rodrigues]. *Copa Rio Branco*, 32. Rio de Janeiro: Irmãos Pongetti, 1943.

———. *O negro no foot-ball brasileiro*. Rio de Janeiro: Irmãos Pongetti Editores, 1947.

———. *O negro no futebol brasileiro*. 2nd ed. Rio de Janeiro: Editôra Civilização Brasileira S.A., 1964.

Fluminense Football Club. *Estatutos* [title and publisher vary], 1912–35.

———. *Regulamento da Secção de Escoteiros do Fluminense Foot-Ball Club*. Rio de Janeiro: Typ. do Jornal do Commercio, de Rodrigues & C., 1916.

———. *Relatorio* [title and publisher vary], 1914–34.

Freyre, Gilberto. *Ingleses no Brasil: Aspectos da inflûenica britântica sobre a vida, a paisagem e a cultura do Brasil*, 2nd ed. Rio de Janeiro: Livraria José Olympio Editôra, 1977.

Guia Brasileiro de Foot-ball Associação. São Paulo: [publisher varies], 1916 and n.d. [1926].

Guinle, Arnaldo, and Mario Pollo. *Guia Pratico de Educação Physica: Calcado no methodo adoptado no Centro de Instrucção Physica de Joinville-le-Pont*. Rio de Janeiro: Pap.- Typ. Gomes Brandão, 1920.

———. *Manual do Escoteiro Brasileiro: Adaptação de obras congeneres inglezes, francezas e portuguezas*. Rio de Janeiro: Imprensa Nacional, 1922.

Gymnasio Anglo-Brazileiro. *Estatutos da Succursal Fluminense, Gymnasio Anglo-Brazileiro (Collegio Modelo Inglez) Fundado em 1899 e Equiparado ao Gymnasio Nacional Pelo Decreto N. 6.206 de 5 de Novembro de 1906*. Rio de Janeiro: Typ. Leuzinger, n.d.

Hambloch, Ernest. *British Consul: Memories of Thirty Years' Service in Europe and Brazil*. London: George G. Harrap & Company, Limited, 1938.

Higgins, Arthur. *Compendio de gymnastica escolar: Methodo Sueco—Belga—Brasileiro / gymnastica systematica livre e gymnastica recreativa ou jogos gymnasticos*. 3rd ed. Rio de Janeiro: n.p., 1934.

———. *Manual de gymnastica hygienica: Para uso, sem necessidade de professor, das pessoas de vida sedentaria, de constituição debil, fraca, anemica, de sangue impuro, obesas, dyspepticas, nervosas etc., etc. de Um e Outro sexo de Oito a Cincoenta Annos de Idade*. Rio de Janeiro: Typ. do Jornal do Commercio, 1902.

Jockey-Club. *Estatutos do Jockey-Club*. Rio de Janeiro: Typ. do Jornal do Commercio, 1895.

Liga Metropolitana de Football. *Estatutos da Liga Metropolitana de Football*. Rio de Janeiro: Typographia Leuzinger, 1905.

Liga Metropolitana de Sports Athleticos. *Estatutos da Liga Metropolitana de Sports Athleticos* [title and publisher vary]. 1907, 1908, 1913.

Lima Filho, Francisco Pereira. *O Campeonato Sul-Americano de Foot-Ball*. n.p., 1916.

Madureira, J. M. *A Liberdade dos Índios—A Companhia de Jesus—Sua Pedagogia e seus Resultados*, vol. 2. Rio de Janeiro: Imprensa Nacional, 1929.

Magalhães, Eduardo de. *Gymnastica Infantil*. Rio de Janeiro: Laemmert, 1900.

Mazzoni, Thomaz. *Almanach Esportivo 1932 (5.0 Anno)*. São Paulo: Agencia Soave, 1932.

———. *O esporte a serviço da pátria*. São Paulo: Olimpicus, 1941.

———. "A evolução dos esportes no Brasil." In *Heróis, deuses, super-homens: As*

Grandes Proezas Físicas do homem num apanhado histórico-cultural, edited by Walter Umminger, translated by Trude von Laschan Solstein, 199–207. São Paulo: Edições Melhoramentos, 1968.

Mazzoni, Thomaz, supervisor, and Nelson Martins de Almeida, coordinator. *Álbum Futebolístico de São Paulo*, Vol. I. São Paulo: Editôra Documentários Nacionais, Ltda., 1957.

Mendonça, Anna Amélia Queiroz de. "A Medalha." In *II Salão do Futebol*, n.p. Belo Horizonte: Fundação Clóvis Salgado, 1982.

Mendonça, Carlos Sussekind de. *O Sport está deseducando a mocidade brasileira: Carta aberta a Lima Barreto*. Rio de Janeiro: Empreza Brasil Editora, 1921.

Nascimento, Domingos. *Homem Forte: Gymnastica Domestica—Natação—Esgrima—Tiro ao Alvo*. Curitiba: Typ. e lith. a vapor 'Impr. Paranaense,' 1905.

Olimpicus. *História do Futebol no Brasil, 1894–1950*. São Paulo: Edições Leia, 1950.

———. *Problemas e Aspectos do nosso Futebol*. São Paulo: A Gazeta, 1939.

Oliveira, O. T. de. *Guia de Football (Association)*. Pelotas: Officinas da Livraria Universal, 1912.

Regras Officiaes de Todos os Sports. Rio de Janeiro: Edição da Casa Sportman, 1916.

Rodrigues, Nelson. *A Pátria de Chuteiras*. Rio de Janeiro: Editora Nova Fronteira, 2013.

———. *Somos o Brasil*. Rio de Janeiro: Editora Nova Fronteira, 2014.

Rousseff, Dilma. "A Copa das Copas." Blog do Planalto: Presidência da República. blog.planalto.gov.br/a-copa-das-copas-por-dilma-rousseff/.

Rubim, Frederico Kiappe da Costa. *Os ingleses no Brasil: Comedia em um prologo e um acto*. Rio de Janeiro: Typ. Portugal e Brazil, 1863.

Silva, Luiz Inácio Lula da. "Discurso do Presidente da República, Luiz Inácio Lula da Silva, na cerimônia do Brasil como sede da Copa do Mundo de 2014," October 30, 2007. Biblioteca da Presidência da República. biblioteca.presidencia.gov.br.

Sport Club Germania. *Germania de São Paulo: Estatutos Aprovados*. São Paulo: Typographia Brazil de Carlos Gerke, 1905.

———. *Sport-Club "Germania" São Paulo (Gegründet den 7. September 1899) Satzungen Angenommen in de General-Versammlung vom 10. Dezember 1904*. São Paulo: Typographia Brazil de Carlos Gerke, 1905.

Toti, Paschoal Totisone Jr. *Futebol: Entrevistas e Commentarios (Em S. Paulo)*. n.p.: Uberaba, 1921.

Valentim, Max. *O Futebol e Sua Técnica: A doutrina dos mais competentes treinadores aliada à pratica dos mais completos jogadores do mundo, com 90 desenhos e fotografias*. Rio de Janeiro: Alba Editora, 1941.

Veríssimo, José. *A Educação Nacional*, 2nd ed. Rio de Janeiro: Livraria Francisco Alves, 1906.

Weber, Ernest. *Sports athleticos*. Rio de Janeiro: H. Garnier, 1907.

SECONDARY SOURCES

Agostino, Gilberto. *Vencer ou Morrer: Futebol, Geopolítica, e Identidade Nacional*. Rio de Janeiro: Mauad, 2002.

Alabarces, Pablo. *Fútbol y Patria: El fútbol y las narrativas de la nación en la Argentina.* Buenos Aires: Prometeo, 2001.

———, ed. *Peligro de gol: Estudios sobre deporte y sociedad en América Latina.* Buenos Aires: CLASCO, 2010.

———. "Tropicalismos y europeísmos en el fútbol: La narración de la diferencia entre Brasil y Argentina." *Revista Internacional de Sociología* 64, no. 45 (2006): 67–82.

Alabarces, Pablo, et al. *Hinchadas.* Buenos Aires: Prometeo Libros, 2005.

Alexander, Robert J., and Eldon M. Parker. *A History of Organized Labor in Brazil.* Westport, Conn.: Praeger, 2003.

Alvito, Marcos. "Our Piece of the Pie: Brazilian Football and Globalization," *Soccer & Society* 8, no. 4 (2007): 524–44.

Amaral, Aracy. "Stages in the Formation of Brazil's Cultural Profile." *Journal of Decorative and Propaganda Arts* 21 (1995): 9–25.

Antunes, Fatima Martin Rodrigues Ferreira. *"Com brasileiro, não há quem possa!" Futebol e identidade nacional em José Lins do Rego, Mário Filho e Nelson Rodrigues.* São Paulo, SP: Editora UNESP, 2004.

———. "O futebol nas fábricas." *Revista USP*, no. 22 (1994): 102–9.

———. "Futebol na Light." *Memória* 6, no. 20 (1994): 62–66.

Araújo, José Renato de Campos. *Imigração e Futebol: O Caso Palestra Itália.* São Paulo: Editora Sumaré, 2000.

Arbena, Joseph L. "Dimensions of International Talent Migration in Latin American Sports." In *The Global Sports Arena: Athletic Talent Migration in an Interdependent World*, edited by John Bale, 99–111. London: Frank Cass & Co., 1994.

———. "Nationalism and Sport in Latin America: The Paradox of Promoting and Performing 'European' Sports." *International Journal of the History of Sport* 12, no. 2 (1995): 220–38.

———. "Sports Language, Cultural Imperialism and the Anti-Imperialist Critique in Latin America." *Studies in Latin American Popular Culture* 14 (1995): 129–41.

———. "Sport and the Promotion of Nationalism in Latin America." *Studies in Latin American Popular Culture* 11 (1992): 143–55.

———. "Sport and Social Change in Latin America." In *Sport in Social Development*, edited by Alan G. Ingham and John W. Loy, 97–117. Champaign, Ill.: Human Kinetics Publishers, 1993.

———, ed. *Sport and Society in Latin America.* New York: Greenwood Press, 1988.

Arbena, Joseph L., and David G. LaFrance, eds. *Sport in Latin America and the Caribbean.* Wilmington, Del.: Jaguar Books, 2002.

Archetti, Eduardo P. *Masculinities: Football, Polo and the Tango in Argentina.* Oxford: Berg, 1999.

Assunção, Matthias Röhrig. *Capoeira: The History of an Afro-Brazilian Martial Art.* London: Routledge, 2005.

Augusto, Gilberto de Palma, ed. *Álbum do Centenário do Esporte Clube Pinheiros.* São Paulo: Editora Alameda Projeitos e Pesquisa em Patrimônio Histórico, 1999.

Azevedo, Raquel de. *A resistência anarquista: uma questão de identidade, 1927–1937.* São Paulo: Arquivo do Estado, 2002.

Azevedo, Tânia Maria Cordeiro de. "A Mulher e a Atividade Desportiva: Preconceitos e estereótipos (Analize de periódicos especializados em Educação Física 1932–1987)." Master's thesis, Universidade Federal Fluminense, 1988.

Ball, Molly. "Inequality in São Paulo's Old Republic: A Wage Perspective, 1891–1930." Ph.D. diss., University of California, Los Angeles, 2013.

Barbosa, Claudemir M. *Album Historico da Sociedade Esportiva Palmeiras Oficializada pela Diretoria sob a presidência do Sr. Mario Frugiuele em homenagem á conquista da "Copa Rio."* São Paulo: n.p., 1951.

Beckles, Hilary McD., and Brian Stoddart, eds. *Liberation Cricket: West Indies Cricket Culture*. Manchester: Manchester University Press, 1995.

Beezley, William H. *Judas at the Jockey Club and Other Episodes of Porfirian Mexico*. Lincoln: University of Nebraska Press, 1987.

Bellos, Alex. *Futebol: Soccer, the Brazilian Way*. New York: Bloomsbury, 2002.

Benchimol, Jaime Larry. *Pereira Passos: Um Haussmann Tropical: A renovação urbana da cidade do Rio de Janeiro no início do século XX*. Rio de Janeiro: Biblioteca Carioca, 1990.

Besse, Susan K. "Defining a 'National Type': Brazilian Beauty Contests in the 1920s." *Estudios Interdisciplinarios de América Latina y el Caribe* 16, no. 1 (2005). http://www1.tau.ac.il/eial/index.php?option=com_content&task=view&id=361&Itemid=188.

———. *Restructuring Patriarchy: The Modernization of Gender Inequality in Brazil, 1914–1940*. Chapel Hill: University of North Carolina Press, 1996.

Bethell, Leslie. *The Abolition of the Brazilian Slave Trade: Britain, Brazil, and the Slave Trade Question, 1807–1869*. Cambridge: Cambridge University Press, 1970.

Blount, John Allen. "The Public Health Movement in São Paulo, Brazil: A History of the Sanitary Service, 1892–1918." Ph.D. diss., Tulane University, 1971.

Bocketti, Gregg. "Italian Immigrants, Brazilian Football, and the Dilemma of National Identity." *Journal of Latin American Studies* 40, no. 2 (2008): 275–302."

———. "Narratives of Loyalty and Disloyalty in the Migration of Professional Footballers: Argentina, Brazil, and Italy in the 1920s and 1930s." In *Global Play: Football between Region, Nation, and the World in Latin American, African, and European History*, edited by Stefan Ranke and Christina Peters, 277–304. Stuttgart: Verlag Hans-Dieter Heinz, 2014.

———. "Playing with National Identity: Brazil in International Football, 1900–1925." In *Negotiating Identities in Modern Latin America*, edited by Hendrik Kraay, 71–89. Calgary: University of Calgary Press, 2007.

Boone, Christopher G. "The Rio de Janeiro Tramway, Light and Power Company and the 'modernization' of Rio de Janeiro during the old republic." Ph.D. thesis, University of Toronto, 1994.

———. "Streetcars and Politics in Rio de Janeiro: Private Enterprise versus Municipal Government in the Provision of Mass Transit, 1903–1920." *Journal of Latin American Studies* 27, no. 2 (1995): 343–65.

Borges, Dain. "'Puffy, Ugly, Slothful and Inert': Degeneration in Brazilian Social Thought, 1880–1940." *Journal of Latin American Studies* 25, no. 2 (1993): 235–56.

———. "The Recognition of Afro-Brazilian Symbols and Ideas, 1890–1940." *Luso-Brazilian Review* 32, no. 2 (1995): 59–78.
Borges, Vavy Pachecho. *Tenetismo e revolução brasileira*. São Paulo: Brasiliense, 1992.
Botelho, André Ricardo Maciel. "Da geral à tribuna, da redação ao espetáculo: A imprensa esportiva e a popularização do futebol (1900–1920)." In *Memória social dos esportes. Futebol e política: A construção de uma identidade nacional*, edited by Francisco Carlos Teixeira Da Silva and Ricardo Pinto dos Santos, 313–35. Rio de Janeiro: Mauad X, 2002.
Brandão, Ignacio de Loyola. *Club Athletico Paulistano: Corpo e Alma de um Clube Centenario*. São Paulo: DBA, 2000.
Brewster, Keith. "Patriotic Pastimes: The Role of Sport in Post-Revolutionary Mexico." *International Journal of the History of Sport* 22, no. 2 (2005): 139–57.
———. "Redeeming the 'Indian': Sport and Ethnicity in Revolutionary Mexico." *Patterns of Prejudice* 38, no. 3 (2004): 213–31.
Bruhns, Heloisa Turini. *Futebol, carnival, e capoeira: Entre as gingas do corpo brasileiro*. Campinas: Papirus Editora, 2000.
Bueno, Clodoaldo. *Política Externa da Primeira República: Os anos de apogeu (de 1902 a 1918)*. São Paulo: Paz e Terra, 2003.
Burns, E. Bradford. *Nationalism in Brazil: A Historical Survey*. New York: Frederick A. Praeger, Publishers, 1968.
———. "Tradition and Variation in Brazilian Foreign Policy." *Journal of Inter-American Studies* 9, no. 2 (1967), 195–212.
Caldas, Waldenyr. "Aspectos sociopolíticos do futebol brasileiro." *Revista USP*, no. 22 (1994): 45–49.
———. *O Pontapé Inicial: Memória do Futebol Brasileiro (1894–1933)*. São Paulo: Instituição Brasileira de Difusão Cultural, 1990.
Capraro, André Mendes, and Alex Sandro Chaves. "O futebol feminino: Uma história de luta pelo reconhecimento social." efdeportes.com 12, no. 111 (2007).
Cardim, Mário. *Ensaio de Analyse de Factores Econômicos e Financeiros do Estado de São Paulo e do Brasil no periodo 1913–1934*. São Paulo: Secretaria da Agricultura, Industria e Commercio, Estado de São Paulo, Directoria de Publicidade Agricola, 1936.
Carelli, Mário. *Carcamanos e Comendadores: Os italianos de São Paulo: da realidade à ficção (1919–1930)*, translated by Ligia Maria Pondé Vassallo. São Paulo: Ática, 1985.
———. *Culturas Cruzadas: Intercâmbios culturais entre França e Brasil*. Campinas: Papirus Editora, 1994.
Carter, Thomas. *The Quality of Home Runs: The Passion, Politics, and Language of Cuban Baseball*. Durham, N.C.: Duke University Press, 2008.
Carvalho, Candido Fernandes de, org. *Club de Regatas Vasco da Gama, Memória do Cinquentenário 1898–1938*. Rio de Janeiro: Est. de Artes Graficas C. Mendes Junior, 1948.
Carvalho, José Murilo de. *Os Bestializados: O Rio de Janeiro e a República Que Não Foi*. 3rd ed. São Paulo: Companhia das Letras, 1998.
———. "Brazil 1870–1914—The Force of Tradition." *Journal of Latin American Studies* 24, no. S1 (1992): 145–62.

Caulfield, Sueann. *In Defense of Honor: Sexual Morality, Modernity, and Nation in Early-Twentieth-Century Brazil.* Durham, N.C.: Duke University Press, 2000.

Chazkel, Amy. *Laws of Chance: Brazil's Clandestine Lottery and the Making of Urban Public Life.* Durham, N.C.: Duke University Press, 2011.

Clube de Regatas do Flamengo. *Flamengo: um século de paixão.* Brasil: BR Communição, 1995.

———. *Glória ao Campeoníssimo Clube de Regatas do Flamengo: Album Rubro Negro.* Rio de Janeiro: Editôra Brasilidade, 1954.

Coelho, Andrea. *Jornalismo esportivo: Os craques da emoção.* Rio de Janeiro, RJ: Secretaria Especial de Comunicação Social, Prefeitura da Cidade do Rio de Janeiro, 2004.

Coelho, Eduardo. "Estádio das Laranjeiras: Monumento Nacional." http://www.cidadaofluminense.blogspot.com.

Comaroff, Jean, and John Comaroff, eds. *Modernity and Its Malcontents: Ritual and Power in Postcolonial Africa.* Chicago: University of Chicago Press, 1993.

Corsi, Francisco Luiz. *Estado Novo: Política Externa e Projeto Nacional.* São Paulo: Editora UNESP, 1999.

Costa, Alexandre da. *O tigre do futebol: Uma viagem nos tempos de Arthur Friedenreich.* São Paulo: Dórea Books and Art, 1999.

Costa, Emilia Viotti da. *The Brazilian Empire: Myths and Histories,* rev. ed. Chapel Hill: University of North Carolina Press, 2000.

Costa, Francisco. "O futebol na ponta da caneta," *Revista USP* no. 22 (1994): 84–91.

Costa, João Cruz. *A History of Ideas in Brazil: The Development of Philosophy in Brazil and the Evolution of National History,* translated by Suzette Macedo. Berkeley: University of California Press, 1964.

Costa, Leda Maria da. "Beauty, Effort, and Talent: A Brief History of Brazilian Women's Soccer in Press Discourse." *Soccer & Society* 15, no. 1 (2014): 81–92.

Costa, Maurício da Silva Drumond. *Nações em jogo: Esporte e propaganda política em Vargas e Perón.* Rio de Janeiro: Apicuri, 2008.

———. "Os Gramados do Catete: Futebol e Política na Era Vargas (1930–1945)." In *Memória social dos esportes. Futebol e política: A Construção de uma Identidade Nacional,* edited by Francisco Carlos Teixeira Da Silva and Ricardo Pinto dos Santos, 107–32. Rio de Janeiro: Mauad X, 2002.

Couto, Euclides de Freitas. "Football, Control and Resistance in the Brazilian Military Dictatorship," *International Journal of the History of Sport* 31, no. 10 (2014): 1267–77.

Cunha, Orlando Rocha da, and Therezinha de Castro. *O América na história da cidade.* Rio de Janeiro: Real Rio Gráfica e Editora Ltda., 1990.

Curi, Martin. "Arthur Friedenreich (1892–1969): A Brazilian Biography." *Soccer & Society* 15, no. 1 (2014): 19–28.

DaMatta, Roberto. "Antropologia do óbvio: Notas em torno do significado social do futebol brasileiro." *Revista USP,* no. 22 (1994): 10–17.

———. *Carnivals, Rogues, and Heroes: An Interpretation of the Brazilian Dilemma,* translated by John Drury. Notre Dame, Ind.: University of Notre Dame Press, 1991.

———. *Universo do Futebol: Esporte e sociedade brasileira.* Rio de Janeiro: Pinakotheke, 1982.

Damo, Arlei S., and Rubén G. Oliven. "Fútbol Made in Brasil: Blanco en las reglas, negro en el estilo." In *Fútbol postnacional: Transformaciones sociales y culturales del 'deporte global' en Europa y América Latina*, edited by Ramón Llopis Goig, 107–27. Barcelona: Anthropos, 2009.

Da Silva, Ana Paula. "Pelé, racial discourse and the 1958 World Cup," *Soccer & Society* 15, no. 1 (2014): 36–47.

Da Silva, Francisco Carlos Teixeira, and Ricardo Pinto dos Santos. *Memória social dos esportes: Futebol e política: A construção de uma identidade nacional*, vol. 2. Rio de Janeiro: Mauad X, 2002.

Dávila, Jerry. *Diploma of Whiteness: Race and Social Policy in Brazil, 1917–1945*. Durham, N.C.: Duke University Press, 2003.

Davis, Darién J. *Avoiding the Dark: Race and the Forging of National Culture in Brazil*. Aldershot, U.K.: Ashgate, 1999.

———. "British Football with a Brazilian Beat: The Early History of a National Pastime (1894–1933)." In *English-Speaking Communities in Latin America*, edited by Oliver Marshall, 261–84. New York: St. Martin's Press, 2000.

De Fiore, Elizabeth, and Ottaviano De Fiore, eds. *Presença Britânica no Brasil (1808–1914)/The British Presence in Brazil (1808–1914)*. 2nd ed. São Paulo: Editora Paubrasil, 1987.

Devide, Fabiano Pries. *História das mulheres na natação brasileira no século XX*. São Paulo: Hucitec Editora, 2012.

Diacon, Todd A. *Stringing Together a Nation: Cândido Mariano da Silva Rondon and the Construction of a Modern Brazil, 1906–1930*. Durham, N.C.: Duke University Press, 2004.

———. "Peasants, Prophets, and the Power of a Millenarian Vision in Twentieth-Century Brazil." *Comparative Studies in Society and History* 32, no. 3 (1990): 488–514.

Dias, Luiz Sergio. *Quem tem medo de capoeira? Rio de Janeiro, 1890–1904*. Rio de Janeiro: Secretaria Municipal das Culturas, Departamento Geral de Documentação e Informação Cultural, Arquivo Geral da Cidade do Rio de Janeiro, Divisão de Pesquisa, 2001.

Duarte, Luiz Carlos. *Friedenreich: A saga de um craque nos primeiros tempos do futebol*. São Paulo: Casa Maior, 2012.

Duke, Vic, and Liz Crolley, "*Fútbol*, Politicians and the People: Populism and Politics in Argentina." *International Journal of the History of Sport* 18, no. 3 (2001): 93–116.

Eakin, Marshall C. *British Enterprise in Brazil: The St. John d'el Rey Mining Company and the Morro Velho Gold Mine, 1830–1960*. Durham, N.C.: Duke University Press, 1990.

Elsey, Brenda. *Citizens and Sportsmen: Fútbol and Politics in Twentieth-Century Chile*. Austin: University of Texas Press, 2011.

Esteves, Martha de Abreu. *Meninas Perdidas: Os populares e o cotidiano do amor no Rio de Janeiro da Belle Époque*. Rio de Janeiro: Paz e Terra, 1989.

Feijó, Luiz Cesar Saraiva. *A linguagem dos esportes de massa e a giria no futebol*. Rio de Janeiro: UERJ, Tempo Brasileiro, 1994.

Fendt, Roberto, Jr. *Investimentos Ingleses no Brasil, 1870–1913: Uma avaliação da política Brasileira*. Rio de Janeiro: Série Separatas, 4, 1980.

Ferraro, Alceu Ravanello. "Analfabetismo e níveis de letramento no Brasil: O que dizem os censos?" *Educação e Sociedade* 23, no. 81 (2002): 21–47.
Ferreira, Izabel. *A Capoeira no Rio de Janeiro, 1890–1950*. Rio de Janeiro: Novas Idéias, 2007.
Fischer, Brodwyn. *A Poverty of Rights: Citizenship and Inequality in Twentieth-Century Rio de Janeiro*. Stanford, Calif.: Stanford University Press, 2008.
Florenzano, José Paulo. *A Democracia Corinthiana: Práticas de Libertade no Futebol Brasileiro*. São Paulo: FAPESP/EDUC, 2009.
Follett, Richard. "'The Spirit of Brazil': Football and the Politics of Afro-Brazilian Cultural Identity." In *Recharting the Black Atlantic*, edited by Annalisa Oboe and Anna Scacchi, 71–92. New York: Routledge, 2008.
Forman, Ross Geoffrey. "Imperial Intersections: Imperial Visions in Collision and Collapse in the Late Nineteenth and Early Twentieth Centuries." Ph.D. diss., Stanford University, 1998.
Franzini, Fábio. "Futebol é coisa para macho? Pequeno esboço para uma história das mulheres no país do futebol." *Revista Brasileira de História* 25, no. 50 (2005): 315–27.
Frydenberg, Julio D. "Boca Juniors en Europa: El Diario *Crítica* y el Primer Nacionalismo Deportivo Argentino." *História: Questões & Debates*, no. 39 (2003): 91–120.
———. *Historia Social del Fútbol: Del Amateurismo a la Profesionalización*. Buenos Aires: Siglo Veintiuno, 2011.
Gaffney, Christopher. *Temples of the Earthbound Gods: Stadiums in the Cultural Landscapes of Rio de Janeiro and Buenos Aires*. Austin: University of Texas Press, 2008.
Garcez, Benedicto Novaes. *O Mackenzie*. São Paulo: Casa Editôra Presbiteriana, 1970.
Garcia, Eugênio Vargas. "Antirevolutionary Diplomacy in Oligarchic Brazil, 1919–30." *Journal of Latin American Studies* 36, no. 4 (2004): 771–96.
———. *Entre América e Europa: A política externa brasileira na década de 1920*. Brasília: Editora Universidade de Brasília, 2006.
Gastaldo, Édison. *Pátria, chuteiras e propaganda: O brasileiro na publicidade da Copa do Mundo*. São Paulo: Annablume, 2002.
Gastaldo, Édison Luis, and Simoni Lahud Guedes, eds. *Nações em Campo: Copa do Mundo e identidade nacional*. Niterói: Intertexto, 2006.
Giovannini, Eduardo. *La gira de Nacional por Europa en 1925*. Montevideo: Nacional-Digital.com, 2003.
Goellner, Silvana Vilodre. *Bela, Maternal e Feminina: Imagens da Mulher na Revista Educação Physica*. Ijuí: Editora Unijuí, 2003.
———. "O Método Francês e Militarização da Educação Física na Escola Brasileira." In *Pesquisa Histórica na Educação Física Brasileira*, edited by Amarilio Fereira Neto, 123–43. Vitória: Universidade Federal do Espirito Santo, 1996.
———. "Mulheres e futebol no Brasil: Entre sombras e visibilidades." *Revista Brasileira de Educação Física y Esporte* 19, no. 2 (2005): 143–51.
Góis Junior, Edivaldo. "Gymnastics, Hygiene and Eugenics in Brazil at the Turn of the Twentieth Century." *International Journal of the History of Sport* 31, no. 10 (2014): 1219–31.

Goldblatt, David. *Futebol Nation: The Story of Brazil through Soccer.* New York: Nation Books, 2014.

Goldstein, Warren. *Playing for Keeps: A History of Early Baseball.* Ithaca, N.Y.: Cornell University Press, 2009.

Gordon, Cesar, and Ronaldo Helal. "The Crisis of Brazilian Football: Perspectives for the Twenty-First Century." In *Sport in Latin American Society: Past and Present,* edited by J. A. Mangan and Lamartine P. DaCosta, 139–58. London: Frank Cass, 2002.

Graham, Richard. *Britain and the Onset of Modernization in Brazil, 1850–1914.* Cambridge: Cambridge University Press, 1972.

Greenfield, Gerald Michael. "The Challenge of Growth: The Growth of Urban Public Services in Sao Paulo, 1885–1913." Ph.D. diss., Indiana University, 1975.

———. "Dependency and the Urban Experience: São Paulo's Public Service Sector, 1885–1913." *Journal of Latin American Studies* 10, no. 1 (1978): 37–59.

———. "The Development of the Underdeveloped City: Public Sanitation in São Paulo, Brazil, 1885–1913." *Luso-Brazilian Review* 17, no. 1 (1980): 107–18.

Guedes, Simoni. *O Brasil no campo do futebol: Estudos antropológicos sobre os significados do futebol brasileiro.* Niterói: Editora da Universidade Federal Fluminense, 1998.

———. "On *Criollos* and Capoeiras: Notes on Soccer and National Identity in Argentina and Brazil." *Soccer & Society* 15, no. 1 (2014): 147–61.

———. "O Salvador da Pátria: Considerações em Torno da Imagem do Jogador Romário na Copa do Mundo de 1994." *Pesquisa de Campo,* no. 1 (1995): 23–41.

Guenther, Louise H. *British Merchants in Nineteenth-Century Brazil: Business, Culture, and Identity in Bahia, 1808–1850.* Oxford: Centre for Brazilian Studies, 2004.

Guttman, Allen. *From Ritual to Record: The Nature of Modern Sports.* New York: Columbia University Press, 2004.

———. *Games and Empires: Modern Sports and Cultural Imperialism.* New York: Columbia University Press, 1994.

———. "Our Former Colonial Masters: The Diffusion of Sports and the Question of Cultural Imperialism." *Stadion* 14 (1988): 49–63.

Hamilton, Aidan. *Domingos da Guia: O divino mestre.* Rio de Janeiro: Griphus, 2005.

———. *An Entirely Different Game: The British Influence on Brazilian Football.* Edinburgh: Mainstream Publishing, 1998.

Helal, Ronaldo. "The Brazilian Soccer Crisis as a Sociological Problem." Ph.D. diss., New York University, 1994.

———. "'Jogo Bonito' y Fútbol Criollo: La relación futbolística Brasil-Argentina en los medios de comunicación." In *Pasiones Nacionales: Política y cultura en Brasil y Argentina,* edited by Alejandro Grimson, 349–85. Barcelona: Edhasa, 2007.

Helal, Ronaldo, and Antonio Jorge Soares, "The Decline of the 'Soccer-Nation': Journalism, Soccer and National Identity in the 2002 World Cup." *Soccer & Society* 15, no. 1 (2014): 132–46.

Helal, Ronaldo, Antonio J. Soares, and Hugo Lovisolo, eds. *A invenção do país do futebol—mídia, raça e idolotría.* Rio de Janeiro: Mauad, 2001.

Hentschke, Jens R. *Reconstructing the Brazilian Nation: Public Schooling in the Vargas Era.* Baden-Baden: Nomos Verlagsgesellschaft, 2007.

Hilton, Stanley. "Brazil and the post-Versailles World: Elite Images and Foreign Policy Strategy," *Journal of Latin American Studies* 12, no. 2 (1980): 341–64.

A história ilustrada do futebol brasileiro, 4 vols. n.p.: Editôra documentação brasileira, n.d.

Hobsbawm, Eric, and Terence Ranger, eds. *The Invention of Tradition*. New York: Cambridge University Press, 1983.

Holanda, Bernardo Borges Buarque de. *O Clube Como Vontade e Representação: O Jornalismo Esportivo e a Formação das Torcidas Organizadas de Futebol do Rio de Janeiro*. Rio de Janeiro: 7 Letras, 2010.

———. *O descobrimento do futebol: Modernismo, regionalismo e paixão esportiva em José Lins do Rego*. Rio de Janeiro: Edições Biblioteca Nacional, 2004.

———. "The Fan as Actor: The Popularization of Soccer and Brazil's Sports Audience." *Soccer & Society* 15, no. 1 (2014): 8–18.

Holzmeister, Antonio. "A Brief History of Soccer Stadiums in Brazil." *Soccer & Society* 15, no. 1 (2014): 65–80.

James, C.L.R. *Beyond a Boundary*. Durham, N.C.: Duke University Press, 1983.

Jones, Stephen G. "State Intervention in Sport and Leisure in Britain between the Wars." *Journal of Contemporary History* 22, no. 1 (1987): 163–82.

Karush, Matthew. "National Identity in the Sports Pages: Football and the Mass Media in 1920s Buenos Aires." *Americas* 60, no. 1 (2003): 11–32.

Kittleson, Roger. *The Country of Football: Soccer and the Making of Modern Brazil*. Berkeley: University of California Press, 2014.

Knight, Alan. "When Was Latin America Modern? A Historian's Response." In *When Was Latin America Modern?*, edited by Nicola Miller and Stephen Hart, 91–117. New York: Palgrave MacMillan, 2007.

Knijnik, Jorge. "Playing for Freedom: Sócrates, *futebol-arte* and Democratic Struggle in Brazil." *Soccer & Society* 15, no. 5 (2014): 635–54.

Lafer, Celso. "Brazilian International Identity and Foreign Policy: Past, Present, and Future." *Daedalus* 129, no. 2 (2000): 207–38.

Lanfranchi, Pierre, and Matthew Taylor. *Moving with the Ball: The Migration of Professional Footballers*. Oxford: Berg, 2001.

Lauerhass, Ludwig, Jr. . "Getúlio Vargas and the Triumph of Brazilian Nationalism: A Study on the Rise of the Nationalist Generation of 1930." Ph.D. diss., University of California, Los Angeles, 1972.

Lesser, Jeffrey. "Immigration and Shifting Concepts of National Identity in Brazil during the Vargas Era." *Luso-Brazilian Review* 31, no. 2 (1994): 27–48.

———. *Negotiating National Identity: Immigrants, Minorities, and the Struggle for Ethnicity in Brazil*. Durham: Duke University Press, 1999.

———. *Welcoming the Undesirables: Brazil and the Jewish Question*. Berkeley: University of California Press, 1995.

Lever, Janet. "Soccer as a Brazilian Way of Life." In *Games, Sport and Power*, edited by Gregory Stone, 138–59. New Brunswick, N.J.: Transaction Books, 1972.

———. *Soccer Madness: Brazil's Passion for the World's Most Popular Sport*. Prospect Heights, Ill.: Waveland Press, 1995.

Levi, Darrell E. *The Prados of São Paulo, Brazil: An Elite Family and Social Change, 1840–1930*. Athens: The University of Georgia Press, 1987.

Levine, Robert M. "The Burden of Success: Futebol and Brazilian Society through the 1970s." *Journal of Popular Culture* 14, no. 3 (1980): 453–64.

———. "Soccer and Society: The Case of Brazilian Futebol." *Luso-Brazilian Review* 17, no. 2 (1980): 233–52.

———. *Vale of Tears: Revisiting the Canudos Massacre in Northeastern Brazil, 1893–1897*. Berkeley: University of California Press, 1992.

Lopes, José Sergio Leite. "Class, Ethnicity, and Color in the Making of Brazilian Football." *Daedalus* 129, no. 2 (2000): 239–70.

———. "Success and Contradictions in 'Multiracial' Brazilian Football." In *Entering the Field: New Perspectives on World Football*, edited by Gary Armstrong and Richard Giulianotti, 53–86. Oxford: Berg, 1997.

———. "Transformations in National Identity through Football in Brazil: Lessons from Two Historical Defeats." In *Football in the Americas: Fútbol, Futebol, Soccer*, edited by Rory Miller and Liz Crolley, 75–93. London: Institute for the Study of the Americas, 2007.

———. "A vitória do futebol que incorporou a *pelada*: A invenção do jornalismo esportivo e a entrada dos negros no futebol brasileiro." *Revista USP*, no. 22 (1994): 64–83.

Love, Joseph L. "Political Participation in Brazil, 1881–1969." *Luso-Brazilian Review* 7, no. 2 (1970): 3–24.

Malhano, Clara E.S.M.B., and Hamilton Botelho Malhano, eds. *Memória social dos esportes: São Januário—Arquitetura e história*. Rio de Janeiro: Mauad X, 2002.

Manchester, Alan K. *British Preëminence in Brazil: Its Rise and Decline*. New York: Octagon Books, 1964.

Mangan, J. A. *Athleticism in the Victorian and Edwardian Public School: The Emergence and Consolidation of an Educational Ideology*. Cambridge: Cambridge University Press, 1981.

———. *The Games Ethic and Imperialism: Aspects of the Diffusion of an Ideal*. New York: Viking, 1986.

Maranhão, Tiago. "Apollonians and Dionysians: The Role of Football in Gilberto Freyre's Vision of Brazilian People." *Soccer & Society* 8, no. 4 (2007): 510–23.

Maranhão, Tiago Fernandes, and Jorge Knijnik. "Futebol mulato: Racial constructs in Brazilian football." *Cosmopolitan Civil Societies Journal* 3, no. 2 (2011): 55–71.

Marinho, Inezil Penna. *Rui Barbosa: Paladino da educação física no Brasil*. Brasília: Horizonte, 1980.

Marrero, Adriana, and Ricardo Piñeyrúa. "'Ora pro nobis': Fútbol, mística e identidad nacional en el Uruguay moderno." In *Fútbol postnacional: Transformaciones sociales y culturales del "deporte global" en Europa y América Latina*, edited by in Ramón Llopis Goig, 129–39. Barcelona: Anthropos, 2009.

Martin, Matthew C. "Pelé's Law and the Commercialization of Brazilian Soccer." Master's thesis, University of California, San Diego, 1999.

Martin, Simon. *Football and Fascism: The National Game under Mussolini*. Oxford: Berg, 2004.

Martins, Milena Ribeiro. "Quem conta um conto . . . aumenta, diminui, modifica: O processo de escrita do conto lobatiano." Master's thesis, Universidade Estadual de Campinas, 1998.

Mascarenhas, Gilmar. "The Adoption of Soccer in Southern Brazil: The Influences of International Boundaries Immigrants." *Soccer & Society* 15, no. 1 (2014): 29–35.

Mason, Tony. *Passion of the People? Football in South America*. London: Verso, 1995.

Máximo, João. "Memórias do Futebol Brasileiro." *Estudos Avançados* 13, no. 37 (1999): 179–88.

McDowall, Duncan. *The Light: Brazilian Traction, Light and Power Company Limited, 1899–1945*. Toronto: University of Toronto Press, 1988.

Meade, Teresa A. *"Civilizing" Rio: Reform and Resistance in a Brazilian City, 1889–1930*. University Park: Pennsylvania State University Press, 1997.

———. "'Living Worse and Costing More': Resistance and Riot in Rio de Janeiro, 1890–1917." *Journal of Latin American Studies* 21, no. 2 (1989): 241–66.

Meihy, José Carlos Sebe Bom, and José Sebastião Witter, eds. *Futebol e Cultura: Coletânea de estudos*. São Paulo: Convênio IMESP/DAESP, 1982.

Melo, Luiz Martins de. "Brazilian Football: Technical Success and Economic Failure." In *Football in the Americas: Fútbol, Futebol, Soccer*, edited by in Rory Miller and Liz Crolley, 193–208. London: Institute for the Study of the Americas, 2007.

Melo, Victor, and J. A. Mangan. "A Web of the Wealthy: Modern Sports in the Nineteenth Century Culture of Rio de Janeiro." *International Journal of the History of Sport* 14, no. 1 (1997): 168–73.

Melo, Victor Andrade de. *Cidadesportiva: Primórdios do esporte no Rio de Janeiro*. Rio de Janeiro: Relume Dumará: FAPERJ, 2001.

Mércio, Roberto. *A História dos Campeonatos Cariocas de Futebol*. Rio de Janeiro: Studio Alfa, 1985.

Milby, Susan P. "Stylin'! Samba Joy versus Structural Precision: The Soccer Case Studies of Brazil and Germany." Ph.D. diss., Ohio State University, 2006.

Miller, Nicola, and Stephen Hart, eds. *When Was Latin America Modern?* New York: Palgrave MacMillan, 2007.

Miller, Rory, and Liz Crolley, eds. *Football in the Americas: Fútbol, Futebol, Soccer*. London: Institute for the Study of the Americas, 2007.

Mills, John R. *Charles William Miller, 1894–1994*. São Paulo: Price Waterhouse, 1996.

Morgan, Zachary. *Legacy of the Lash: Race and Corporal Punishment in the Brazilian Navy*. Bloomington: Indiana University Press, 2014.

Moura, Eriberto José Lessa de. "As Relações entre Lazer, Futebol, e Gênero." Master's thesis, Universidade Estadual de Campinas, 2003.

Moura, Gerson. *Autonomia na Dependencia: A Política Externa Brasileira de 1935 a 1942*. Rio de Janeiro: Editora Nova Fronteira, 1980.

Moura, Roberto Marchon Lemos de. "O negro e o futebol Brasileiro." Master's thesis, Universidade Federal do Rio de Janeiro, 1978.

Mourão, Ludmila, and Marcia Morel. "As narrativas sobre o futebol feminino: O discurso da mídia impressa em campo." *Revista Brasileira de Ciências do Esporte* 26, no. 2 (2005): 73–86.

Munn, Barry Walter. "Britain and Brazil, 1900–1920," Ph.D. thesis, University of British Columbia, 1971.

Nadel, Joshua. *Fútbol! Why Soccer Matters in Latin America*. Gainesville: University Press of Florida, 2014.

Natali, Marcos. "The Realm of the Possible: Remembering Brazilian *Futebol*." *Soccer & Society* 8, no. 2/3 (2007): 267–82.

Needell, Jeffrey. "The Domestic Civilizing Mission: The Cultural Role of the State in Brazil, 1808–1930." *Luso-Brazilian Review* 36, no. 1 (1999): 1–18.

——. *A Tropical Belle Epoque: Elite Culture and Society in Turn-of-the-Century Rio de Janeiro*. Cambridge: Cambridge University Press, 1987.

——. "The Revolta Contra Vacina of 1904: The Revolt against 'Modernization' in Belle-Époque Rio de Janeiro." *Hispanic American Historical Review* 67, no. 2 (1987): 233–69.

——. "Rio de Janeiro at the Turn of the Century: Modernization and the Parisian Ideal." *Journal of Interamerican Studies and World Affairs* 25, no. 1 (1983): 83–103.

Negreiros, Plínio José Labriola de Campos. "Resistência e Rendição: A Gênese do Sport Club Corinthians Paulista e o Futebol Oficial em São Paulo, 1910–1916." Master's thesis, Pontifícia Universedade Católica de São Paulo, 1992.

Neto, Geneton Moraes. *Dossie 50: Os onze jogadores revelem os segredos da maior tragédia do futebol brasileiro*. Rio de Janeiro: Objetiva, 2000.

Netto, Paulo Coelho. *Coelho Netto e os esportes*. Rio de Janeiro: Editôra Minerva Ltda., 1964.

——. *O Fluminense na Intimidade*. 3 vols. Rio de Janeiro: n.p., 1955–75.

Nogueira, Claudio. *Futebol Brasil memória: De Oscar Cox a Leonidas da Silva, 1897–1937*. Rio de Janeiro: Editora Senac Rio, 2006.

Oliveira, Lúcia Lippi. *A Questão Nacional na Primeira República*. São Paulo: Editora Brasiliense, 1990.

O'Neil, Charles Francis. "The Search for Order and Progress: Brazilian Mass Education, 1915–1935." Ph.D. diss., University of Texas at Austin, 1975.

Owensby, Brian. *Intimate Ironies: Modernity and the Making of Middle-Class Lives in Brazil*. Stanford, Calif.: Stanford University Press, 1999.

Panfichi, Aldo, ed. *Ese gol existe: Una mirada al Perú a través del fútbol*. Lima: Pontificia Universidad Católica del Perú, 2008.

——, ed. *Futbol: Identidad, violencia y racionalidad*. Lima: Facultad de Ciencias Sociales, Pontificia Universidad Católica del Perú, 1994.

Panfichi, Aldo, and Jorge Thieroldt, "Barras Bravas: Representation and Crowd Violence in Peruvian Football." In *Fighting Fans: Football Hooliganism as a World Phenomenon*, edited by Eric Dunning, Patrick Murphy, Ivan Waddington, and Antonios Astrinakis, 143–57. Dublin: University College Dublin Press, 2002.

Parada, Maurício. "Corpos Físicos como Corpos Cívicos: Práticas Deportivas e Educação Física no Brasil sob o Estado Novo." In *Memória social dos esportes. Futebol e política: A Construção de uma Identidade Nacional*, edited by Francisco Carlos Teixeira Da Silva and Ricardo Pinto dos Santos, 155–83. Rio de Janeiro: Mauad X, 2002.

Pardue, Derek. "Jogada Lingüística. Discursive Play and the Hegemonic Force of Soccer in Brazil." *Journal of Sport & Social Issues* 26, no. 4 (2002): 360–80.

Patusca, Araken. *Os Reis do Futebol*. São Paulo: Industria Gráfica Bentivegna Editôra, Ltda, 1976.

Peard, Julyan G. *Race, Place, and Medicine: The Idea of the Tropics in Nineteenth-Century Brazilian Medicine*. Durham, N.C.: Duke University Press, 1999.

Pêgas, Luiz C. *Assim Nasceu o Foot-Ball no Rio Grande do Sul: Resumo Histórico do Sport Club Rio Grande*. n.p., 1973.

Peixoto-Mehrtens, Cristina. *Urban Space and National Identity in Early Twentieth Century São Paulo, Brazil: Crafting Modernity*. New York: Palgrave Macmillan, 2010.

Perdigão, Paulo. *Anatomia de uma derrota: 16 de julho de 1950—Brasil X Uruguai*. Porto Alegre: L&PM, 2001.

Pereira, Leonardo Affonso de Miranda. "Domingos da Guia: A Mestizo Hero on and off the Soccer Field." In *The Human Tradition in Modern Brazil*, edited by Peter Beattie, 147–64. Wilmington, Del.: SR Books, 2004.

———. *Footballmania: Uma história social do futebol no Rio de Janeiro, 1902–1938*. Rio de Janeiro: Editôra Nova Fronteira, 2000.

———. "Pelos Campos da Nação: Um *Goal-Keeper* nos Primeiros Anos do Futebol Brasileiro." *Estudos Históricos* 10, no. 19 (1997): 23–40.

Pérez, Louis A., Jr. "Between Baseball and Bullfighting: The Quest for Nationality in Cuba, 1868–1898." *Journal of American History* 81, no. 2 (1994): 493–517.

Polley, Martin. "'No Business of Ours'? The Foreign Office and the Olympic Games, 1896–1914." *International Journal of the History of Sport* 13, no. 2 (1996): 96–113.

Proença, Ivan Cavalcanti. *Futebol E Palavra*. Rio de Janeiro: Livraria José Olympio Editora, 1981.

Proni, Marcelo Weishaupt, and Felipe Henrique Zaia, "Financial Condition of Brazilian Soccer Clubs: An Overview." *Soccer & Society* 15, no. 1 (2014): 108–22.

Rachum, Ilan. "Futebol: The Growth of a Brazilian National Institution." *New Scholar* 7, nos. 1–2 (1978): 183–200.

Ramos, Roberto. *Futebol: Ideologia do Poder*. Petrópolis: Vozes Editora Ltda., 1984.

Rein, Raanan. *Los bohemios de Villa Crespo: Judíos y fútbol en la Argentina*. Buenos Aires: Sudamericana, 2012.

———. "'El primer deportista': The Political Use and Abuse of Sport in Peronist Argentina." *International Journal of the History of Sport* 15, no. 2 (1998): 54–76.

Ribas, Mário Graco. *História do Esporte Clube Pinheiros*. São Paulo: Papelaria Ancora, 1968.

Ribeiro, André. *O diamante eterno: Biografia de Leônidas da Silva*. Rio Janeiro: Gryphus, 1999.

———. *Os Donos Do Espetáculo: Histórias Da Imprensa Esportiva Do Brasil*. São Paulo: Editora Terceiro Nome, 2007.

Ribeiro, Gladys Sabina. *Mata Galegos: Os portugueses e os conflitos de trabalho na República Velha*. São Paulo: Editora Brasiliense, 1990.

Ribeiro, Rubens. *Caminhos da Bola: 100 anos de história da FPF*. São Paulo: CNB Comunicação e Marketing, 2000.
Rippy, J. Fred. *British Investments in Latin America, 1822–1949: A Case Study in the Operations of Private Enterprise in Retarded Regions*. Minneapolis: University of Minnesota, 1959.
Rocha Filho, Zaldo Antônio Barbosa. "A Narração de Futebol no Brasil: Um Estudo Fonoestilístico." Master's thesis, Universidade Estadual de Campinas, 1989.
Rodrigues Filho, Nelson. "Lima Barreto: Jogando contra o Futebol." *Pesquisa de Campo*, no. 1 (1995): 43–53.
Rosenfeld, Anatol. "O futebol no Brasil." Translated by Modesto Carone. *Argumento: Revista Mensal de Cultura* 1, no. 4 (1974): 61–85.
Rowe, William, and Vivian Schelling. *Memory and Modernity. Popular Culture in Latin America*. New York: Verso, 1991.
Santos, Afonso Carlos Marques dos, coordinator. *O Rio de Janeiro de Lima Barreto*, vol. 2. Rio de Janeiro: Prefeitura da Cidade do Rio de Janeiro, 1983.
Santos, Luís Cláudio Villafañe G. *O Brasil entre a América e a Europa: O Império e o interamericanismo (do Congresso do Panamá à Conferência de Washington)*. São Paulo: Editora UNESP, 2003.
Santos, João Manuel Casquinha Malaia. "Arnaldo Guinle, Fluminense Football Club, and the Economics of Early International Sport in Rio." *Journal of Sport History* 40, no. 3 (2013): 393–401.
Santos, Ricardo Pinto dos. *Entre 'rivais': Futebol, racismo e modernidade no Rio de Janeiro e em Buenos Aires (1897–1924)*. Rio de Janeiro: Mauad X, 2012.
———. "Uma Breve História Social do Esporte no Rio de Janeiro." In *Memória social dos esportes: Futebol e política: A construção de uma identidade nacional*, vol. 2, edited by Francisco Carlos Teixeira Da Silva and Ricardo Pinto dos Santos, 33–53. Rio de Janeiro: Mauad X, 2002.
Schwarcz, Lilia Moritz. *The Spectacle of the Races: Scientists, Institutions, and the Race Question in Brazil, 1870–1930*. New York: Hill and Wang, 1999.
Sevcenko, Nicolau. *Orfeu extático na metrópole: São Paulo, sociedade e cultura nos frementes anos 20*. São Paulo: Companhia das Letras, 1992.
Shirts, Matthew. "Sócrates, Corinthians, and Questions of Democracy and Citizenship." In *Sport and Society in Latin America*, edited by Joseph L. Arbena, 97–112. New York: Greenwood Press, 1988.
Silva, Carlos Leonardo Bahiense da. "Sobre *O Negro no Futebol Brasileiro*, de Mário Filho." In *Memória social dos esportes. Futebol e política: A Construção de uma Identidade Nacional*, edited by Francisco Carlos Teixeira Da Silva and Ricardo Pinto dos Santos, 287–312. Rio de Janeiro: Mauad X, 2002.
Silva, Rafael. "O esporte a serviço da pátria: por Thomaz Mazzoni." Paper presented at the XIV Encontro Regional de História da Associação Nacional de História-Rio. July 2010.
———. "Imprensa esportiva e o pensamento autoritário na obra de Thomaz Mazzoni." Paper presented at the XV Encontro Regional de História da Associação Nacional de História-Rio. July 2012.

Skidmore, Thomas E. *Black into White: Race and Nationality in Brazilian Thought*. Durham, N.C.: Duke University Press, 1993.

———. "Brazil's Search for Identity in the Old Republic." In *Portugal and Brazil in Transition*, edited by Raymond S. Sayers, 127–44. Minneapolis: University of Minnesota Press, 1968.

Slatta, Richard W. "The Demise of the Gaucho and the Rise of Equestrian Sport in Argentina." *Journal of Sport History* 13, no. 2 (1986): 97–110.

Soares, Antonio J. *Futebol, Malandragem e Identidade*. Vitória: Secretaria de Difusão e Produção Cultural/Universidade Federal do Espírito Santo, 1994.

———. "História e a invenção de tradições no futebol brasileiro." In *A invenção do país do futebol: Mídia, raça e idolatria*, edited by Ronaldo Helal, Antonio Jorge Soares, and Hugo Lovisolo, 13–50. Rio de Janeiro: Mauad, 2001.

———. "O racismo no futebol do Rio de Janeiro nos anos 20: Uma história de identidade." In *A invenção do país do futebol: Mídia, raça e idolatria*, edited by Ronaldo Helal, Antonio Jorge Soares, and Hugo Lovisolo, 101–22. Rio de Janeiro: Mauad, 2001.

Soares, Antonio Jorge Gonçalves, Marco Antonio Santoro Salvador, and Tiago Lisboa Bartholo. "Copa de 70: O planejamento México." In *Nações em Campo: Copa do Mundo e identidade nacional*, edited by Édison Luis Gastaldo and Simoni Lahud Guedes, 103–23. Niterói: Intertexto, 2006.

Soares, Bento. *Vendo o Jogo pelo Rádio: Memórias da Imprensa Esportiva Brasileira*. João Pessoa: Idéia, 2006.

Soares, Carmen. *Educação Física: Raízes Européias e Brasil*. São Paulo: Editora Autores Associados, 1994.

Sodré, Nelson Werneck. *O tenetismo*. Porto Alegre: Mercado Aberto, 1985.

Souza, Denaldo Alchorne de. *O Brasil entra em campo! Construções e reconstruções da identidade nacional (1930–1947)*. São Paulo: Annablume, 2008.

Souza, Edgard de. *História da Light: Primeiros 50 Anos*. São Paulo: Eletricidade de São Paulo, S.A., 1982.

Souza, Marcos Alves de. "A Naçao em Chuteiras: Raça e Masculinidade no Futebol Brasileiro." Master's thesis, Universidade de Brasilia, 1996.

Sport Club Mackenzie. *Esta é a nossa história*. Rio de Janeiro: Cia. Oscar Rudge de Papéis, 1964.

Stepan, Nancy Leys. *Beginnings of Brazilian Science: Oswaldo Cruz, Medical Research, and Policy, 1890–1920*. New York: Science History Publications, 1976.

———. *"The Hour of Eugenics": Race, Gender, and Nation in Latin America*. Ithaca, N.Y.: Cornell University Press, 1991.

Stone, Irving. "British Direct and Portfolio Investment in Latin America before 1914." *Journal of Economic History* 37, no. 3 (1977): 690–722.

Talmon-Chvaicer, Maya. *The Hidden History of Capoeira: A Collision of Cultures in the Brazilian Battle Dance*. Austin: University of Texas Press, 2008.

Toledo, Luiz Henrique de. *Torcidas Organizadas de Futebol*. Campinas, São Paulo: Autores Associados/Anpocs, 1996.

Tosta, Antonio Luciano de A. "Exchanging Glances: The Streetcar, Modernity, and the Metropolis in Brazilian Literature." *Chasqui* 32, no. 2 (2003): 35–52.

Urbina Gaitán, Chester. *Costa Rica y el Deporte (1873–1921): Un estudio acerca del origen del fútbol y la construcción de un deporte nacional.* Heredia: EUNA, 2001.

Velloso, Monica Pimenta. *A cultura das ruas no Rio de Janeiro (1900–1930): Mediações, Linguagens e Espaço.* Rio de Janeiro: Edições Casa de Rui Barbosa, 2004.

Vianna, Hermano. *O Mistério do Samba.* Rio de Janeiro: Jorge Zahar Editor, 1995.

Votre, Sebastião, and Ludmila Mourão. "Women's Football in Brazil: Progress and Problems." In *Soccer, Women, Sexual Liberation: Kicking off a New Era*, edited by Fan Fong and J. A. Mangan, 254–67. London: Frank Cass, 2004.

Wade, Peter. "Modernity and Tradition: Shifting Boundaries, Shifting Contexts." In *When Was Latin America Modern?*, edited by Nicola Miller and Stephen Hart, 49–68. New York: Palgrave MacMillan, 2007.

Weinstein, Barbara. "Presidential Address: Developing Inequality," *American Historical Review* 113, no. 1 (2008), 1–18.

Williams, Daryle. *Culture Wars in Brazil: The First Vargas Regime, 1930–1945.* Durham, N.C.: Duke University Press, 2001.

Wilson, Jonathan. *Inverting the Pyramid: The History of Football Tactics.* London: Orion, 2008.

Wisnik, José Miguel. "The Riddle of Brazilian Soccer: Reflections on the Emancipatory Dimensions of Culture." *Review. Literature and Arts of the Americas* 39, no. 2 (2006): 198–209.

———. *Veneno Remédio: O Futebol e o Brasil.* São Paulo: Companhia das Letras, 2008.

Wolfe, Joel. "'Father of the Poor' or 'Mother of the Rich'? Getúlio Vargas, Industrial Workers, and Constructions of Class, Gender, and Populism in São Paulo, 1930–1954." *Radical History Review* 58 (1994): 80–111.

———. *Working Women, Working Men: São Paulo and the Rise of Brazil's Industrial Working Class, 1900–1955.* Durham, N.C.: Duke University Press, 1993.

Woodard, James P. *A Place in Politics: São Paulo, Brazil, from Seigneurial Republicanism to Regionalist Revolt.* Durham, N.C.: Duke University Press, 2009.

Zanin, Luiz. "Nelson Rodrigues e o Mito do Futebol." *Revista USP*, no. 96 (2012–13): 136–44.

Zirin, Dave. *Brazil's Dance with the Devil: The World Cup, the Olympics, and the Fight for Democracy.* Chicago: Haymarket Books, 2014.

Index

Page numbers in *italics* refer to illustrations.

ABC Football Club, 167
Amateurism: class and, 5, 67, 77–82, 84, 216, 218; English model of, 75–76, 121, 123–24, 131; football administration and, 254; government and, 17–18, 101, 219; ideology of, 8, 63–65, 76, 118, 126, 214, 216, 256; race and, 78, 155, 216, 218; rules of, 66, 77–82, 99, 142; violations of rules, 95–96, 98–100, 135, 149, 167. *See also* Professional football
America Football Club, 72, 97, 128, 214; amateurism and, 98–99; character of, 68, 95, 177–78; professionalization and, 111
Andarahy Athletic Club, 88–89, 95, 97
Argentina: fans in, 160, 195; football style in, 201, 203, 222–24, 241, 286nn67,68; government of, 19, 54; in international football, 51, 125, 128, 130, 133, 142–43; migration and, 60–61, 64, 143
Associação Athletica das Palmeiras, 82, 87, 181
Associação Athletica São Bento, 88, 111
Associação de Chronistas Esportivas, 84, 137, 276n95; language and terminology and, 108, 110; role of, 106, 271n130
Associação Metropolitana de Esportes Athleticos, 82, 95–96, 98, 225
Associação Paulista de Esportes Athleticos, 87–88, 100, 103, 123, 146–47, 172, 213
Associação Portuguesa de Desportos, 90, 99, 183
Azevedo, Fernando de, 19, 21, 35, 43–44

Bangú Athletic Club, 68, 71, 112, *193*, 216–18, 225, 236; class and, 95, 163; Companhia Progresso Industrial do Brasil and, 42, 206; fans and, 163–64, 181; language and terminology and, 107; professionalization and, 111; race and, 78
Barbosa, Moacyr, 245
Barbosa, Rui, 30
Barbuy, Amílcar, 61–65, 143, 146–47
Barreto, Afonso Henriques de Lima, 1–2, 29, 32, 46–47
Bigode (João Ferreira), 245
Bilac, Olavo, 51, 177
Bonsuccesso Football Club, 99, 183, 231
Botafogo de Futebol e Regatas. *See* Botafogo Football Club
Botafogo Football Club, 74, 82, 89, 149, 152, *208*, 212, 217; class and, 68, 70–72, 95; fans and, 172, 179, 181, 183, 185–86, 190; professionalization and, 111–12; race and, 78–79, 101, 246
Boy Scouts, 50–51, 272n152
Britannia Athletic Club, 100
Burlamaqui, Carlos, 193–95

Campeonato Brasileiro de Football, 145–47
Capoeira, 23–24, 44–45, 66, 145, 230, 287n108
Cardim, Mário, 83–85, 104, 110–11, 114, 135, 207, 272n152
Carioca Football Club, 183
Carlos Alberto, 97
Carvalho, João de, 163, 237–38
Castelli, José, 61–65, 101

Chelsea Football Club, 141–42, 227
Citizenship, 37–39, 50–51, 63–64, 103–4, 114, 173, 260n11
Club Athletico Paulistano, 70, 72, 164–65, 205, 211; amateurism and, 100, 218; class and, 82, 87, 90–92, 130, 218; fans and, 172, 175, 181, 183, 187; foundation of, 83; 1925 tour by, 5, 134–41, 143, 157, 201–4, 223, 275n60; regionalism and, 144–45
Club Athletico Ypiranga, 88, 135
Club Atlético Boca Juniors, 142, 201, 223
Club Atlético Peñarol, 150
Club de Regatas do Flamengo, 39–40, 61, 63, 102, 114, 135, 151; class and, 70–72, 93, 95, 115, 144; fans and, 159, 175, 177, 190–91, 196–97; foundation of, 66; professionalization and, 112–13, 116; race and, 101, 230–34
Club de Regatas Vasco da Gama, 61, 167, 197, 206, 221; class and, 95–97, 99; foundation of, 95; migration and, 6, 63, 90, 102–3, 151; 1931 tour, 143–44; professionalization and, 95–97, 101–2, 111–12; race and, 95–97; São Januário stadium, 40, 58–59
Club Feminino Vasco da Gama, 167, 279n22
Club Nacional de Football, 142, 150, 201, 223
Confederação Brasileira de Desportos, 20, 48–49, 68, 91–94, 115, 145–46; amateurism and, 81–82, 96, 98–100, 111, 113–14; government and, 71–72, 128, 156–57; race and, 226–27; seleção (national team), 6, 36, 102–3, 128, 144, 147–57
Confederação Brasileira de Futebol, 250–52. *See also* Confederação Brasileira de Desportos
Conselho Nacional de Desportos, 17–19, 33, 101, 103–4, 113–16, 156, 246, 260n11
Copa Rio Branco, 133, 141, 149–50, 230
Copa Roca, 128, 133, 140–41
Corinthian Football Club, 128, 131, 206–8, 210; amateurism and, 75–76; fans and,

165, 182, 273n23; visits to Brazil, 120–26, 273n18
Corrêa, Floriano Peixoto, 3–4, 97–99, 104, 111, 144, 155, 221–22, 240–42
Costa, Flávio, 155, 234
Costa, Oscar, 96, 111–12

Del Debbio, Armando, 61–65, 101, 144
Democracy, 3–4, 13, 37–38, 67, 249, 252, 256–57; amateurism and, 78–79; professionalization and, 8, 11, 65, 92, 111–14, 270–71n111; race and, 115, 150, 229; Vargas state and, 114, 156–57
Discipline, 143, 145–47; fans and, 162–65, 181–85, 188; football style and, 3, 13, 155, 208, 210–12, 214–19, 221, 235, 237–41, 246–48 (English, 205–9, 222); ideology of, 10–11, 24, 33, 38, 41–43, 115–16, 257, 285n48; race and, 204–5, 215, 246; Vargas state and, 17–19, 116, 151
Dunga (Carlos Caetano Bledorn Verri), 250

Estado Novo, 17–19, 166
Eugenics, 19, 28; physical education and, 30–31, 33–36, 41; race and, 130, 225–26, 229; women and, 168–69, 173, 186
Exeter City Football Club, 120, 125–26, 128, 130, 203

Fan clubs. *See* Torcidas organizadas
Federação Brasileira de Football, 68, 81, 110, 144
Feitiço. *See* Mattoso, Luiz
Femininity, 25, 160, 166, 169, 173–75, 180, 186–92, 199
Filho, Mário, 97, 104, 156, 220, 231–32; fans and, 162, 194–96; football style and, 46, 155, 203–4, 233–37, 239–41; nationalism and, 5, 65, 114, 154; race and, 3–4, 115–16, 130, 149–50, 233–37, 245, 247–48, 285n48; writing style of, 109–10. See also *O negro no futebol brasileiro*
Filó. *See* Guarisi, Amphilogio

Fluminense Football Club, 27, 41, 70, 81, 84–85, 105, 114, 221, 234; class and, 68, 70–74, 97, 123–24, 128; fans and, 163, 174–75, 177–84, 187–88, 190–91, 193–95; football administration and, 82, 95–96, 157; matches of, 121–22, 144–45, 186, 217, 237–39, 273nn5,18; nationalism and, 50–51; professionalization and, 97–99, 101, 111–12; regionalism and, 15, 211–12; stadium, 51–58, 92–94, 265nn135,136; Vargas state and, 20, 40, 59; women's sports and, 168, 170–71, 173

Freyre, Gilberto, 7; football style and, 6, 156, 223, 235; race and, 154, 204, 219–20, 224, 226, 230, 235, 241, 247, 285n48

Friedenreich, Arthur, 51, 100, 128–30, 134–36, 145, 155, 210

Gambini, Bianco Spartaco, 88, 146
Garrincha, 247–48
Gradín, Isabelino, 127–28
Guarisi, Amphilogio, 61, 136, 144, 229
Guia, Domingos da, 3, 110, 231, 233, 236, 247, 286n109; playing style of, 235; professional career of, 102, 150
Guinle, Arnaldo, 3, 51, 82–83, 92, 94–95, 114, 254
Gymnasio Anglo-Brasileiro, 31, 66, 73, 76, 261–62n50

Hamilton, John, 61, 72–73, 172, 206, 210

Italy: in international football, 127, 136, 164, 202; migration and, 40, 62, 88, 102–3; professionalization and, 61, 63–64, 99, 101, 111; World Cup, 114, 117, 143–44, 151–54, 228–29, 239. *See also* Societá Sportiva Palestra Itália

Journalism, 2–3, 55, 104–6, 194, 206, 209, 231–34, 281n72, 290n37; class and, 14, 83–86, 91, 164–65, 269n68, 272n167; nationalism and, 62, 65, 106–8, 110–11, 116; women and, 172–73, 179; writing styles, 65, 85–86, 109–10. *See also* Associação de Chronistas Esportivas; Radio

Kürschner, Dori, 61, 102, 112–13, 151, 234

Labor movement, 42, 67, 90–91, 101, 219, 226

Language and terminology, 6, 33, 188, 223, 282n110; English, 75, 83, 85–86, 269n78; nationalism and, 65, 106–10, 271n140; race and, 80, 227–29, 269n60. *See also* Associação de Chronistas Esportivas; Bangú Athletic Club; Journalism

League of Nations, 119, 134
Liga Carioca de Basketball, 163
Liga Carioca de Football, 103
Liga Contra Foot-ball, 2, 32
Liga da Defesa Nacional, 39
Liga de Amadores de Futebol, 100
Liga Metropolitana de Football, 68, 75, 77–82, 95–96, 107, 163, 217
Liga Nacionalista de São Paulo, 39
Liga Paulista de Football, 68, 86–87, 111, 123, 181, 205, 217–18
Lugo, Roberto, 194–95
Luís, Washington, 19, 21, 36, 39, 91, 146, 148, 155
Lula da Silva, Luiz Inácio, 2, 251–52
Lyra Filho, João, 246

Mackenzie College, 68, 76, 87, 135, 183
Masculinity, 23–25, 37, 118, 166, 174–75, 178; fans and, 161, 182, 194; football style and, 215, 222–25, 233, 237, 286n68
Mattoso, Luiz, 146–47
Mazzoni, Thomaz, 3–5, 104; fans and, 162, 194; football style and, 220, 229, 235, 237; nationalism and, 65, 115, 142–44; race and, 149–50, 233; Vargas state and, 18, 116, 156, 240; writing style of, 110, 114–15
Mendonça, Marcos Carneiro de, 179, 210; class and, 81, 155, 223; race and, 128, 155, 223, 247; seleção (national team), 52, 145

Index · 313

Migration, 28, 60, 95, 119, 169, 250; Italian, 61–65, 103–4, 143–44, 150–51, 228–29. *See also* Societá Sportiva Palestra Itália

Miller, Charles, 1–3, 76, 203, 205, 255; national identity, 60–61, 63, 123, 206, 210

Motherwell Football Club, 141–42

Nationalism, 9, 39, 61–63, 119; football style and, 204, 220–21, 225, 233–35 (race, 229–30); history and, 4–5, 114–16, 241–42, 256; international football and, 140, 142–43, 150–51, 154–55, 157, 195–97; language and terminology and, 107–8, 110–11; professionalization and, 101–4; promotion of sports and, 21–22, 48–51, 53–55, 57–59, 173; regionalism and, 137, 150; Vargas state and, 17–19, 155–56

Neco. *See* Nunes, Manuel

Netto, Americo, 204, 210–12, 217, 219–21, 225, 241

Netto, Coelho, 8, 39, 49, 51, 138, 145; children, 84, 148; journalism, 34; spectatorship, 182

Nike, 250–51

Nunes, Manuel, 52, 210

O negro no futebol brasileiro, 4-5, 115-16, 235-36, 247

Parreira, Carlos Alberto, 249–50

Passos, Francisco Pereira, 26

Patusca, Araken, 147–48

Paysandú Athletic Club, 60, 63, 68, 88–89, 92, 97, 183, 208

Pelé (Edson Arantes do Nascimento), 247, 251, 254

Pepe. *See* Rizzetti, Pedro

Perón, Juan, 19

Pessoa, Epitácio, 128

Physical education, 17–19, 21, 39, 41–44, 66, 114, 261n41; class and, 24, 29–33, 47, 76–77; English, 30–31, 207; gender and, 168–71, 173

nta, Adhemar, 102, 151

Platero, Ramón, 95

Pollo, Mário, 51, 57, 94

Populism, 112, 150, 157, 194, 197, 256–57; journalism and, 109, 239, 272n167; professionalization and, 65, 101–2, 104; Vargas state and, 9, 19, 113–14, 156, 254

Prado, Antônio da Silva, 26, 91

Prado Júnior, Antônio, 3, 21, 83, 91, 135, 138, 140

Professional football, 50; class and, 5, 8, 11, 109, 112–13, 199, 218–19; England and, 75–76, 123, 126, 141–42; migration and, 61–65, 143–44, 249–50, 253–54, 256; professionalization, 95–104, 111–12, 149–51, 214, 237–39, 256–57, 270–71n111; Vargas state and, 17–18, 113–14. *See also* Amateurism

Public health, 26–29, 122, 160, 226; critiques of football and, 34; Vargas state and, 18, 114, 166, 226

Pullen, Sidney, 39–40, 63, 72, 263n86

Queiroz, Anna Amélia, 179–80

Quincey-Taylor, J. H., 72–73, 206

Radio, 105, 109, 196, 272n147

Rato. *See* Castelli, José

Rebelo, Aldo, 250–51, 289n34

Regionalism, 10, 68, 90, 144–47, 276n95, 277n113; international football and, 36, 49, 137, 147–50, 157, 224, 276n98; race and, 229–30, 149; Vargas state and, 17–18, 21

Rego, José Lins do, 109–10, 115, 220, 229, 248

Rio, João do, 23–25, 44, 85, 149–50, 154

Rio Cricket and Athletic Association, 60, 68, 88–89, 97, 105

Rizzetti, Pedro, 146

Rocha, Carlos Martins da, 185–86

Rodrigues, Nelson, 2, 109, 220, 245, 248, 251

Rodrigues Filho, Mário. *See* Filho, Mário

Romário (de Souza Faria), 250, 252–53

Rousseff, Dilma, 250–51

Sant'Anna, Leopoldo, 209–11, 221, 224
Santos, Fausto dos, 197; class and, 148; professional career of, 102, 112–13, 234; race and, 115–16, 148–49, 155, 157, 223–25
Santos Football Club, 88, 98–99, 135, 146–47
São Christovão Athletic Club, 92–95, 139, 184, 225
São Paulo Athletic Club, 68, 72, 76, 82, 181; British identity of, 1, 60, 63, 205–6, 209; withdrawal from competition, 86–87, 89
São Paulo Futebol Clube, 100, 111, 116, 157, 197, 234–35
São Paulo Tramway, Light & Power Company, 90–91, 264n117
Scottish Wanderers Football Club, 60, 88
Serafini, Henrique, 61–65, 101, 144
Silva, Leônidas da: class and, 3, 110, 155, 234, 247; playing style of, 116, 233–35, 247; professional career of, 102, 150, 231–32, 234, 286n109; race and, 3, 110, 150, 155–56, 230, 233–35, 247; seleção (national team), 154–55, 231–35, 239–40
Silva, Oscarino Costa, 150, 232–33
Silvares, Alberto, 38, 209–11, 224; class and, 79–80, 84–85, 215, 217–18, 255; as a football administrator, 82–83, 92
Silveira, Martim Mércio da, 150, 152, 230
Social Darwinism, 28, 30, 33, 168, 173, 186
Sociedade Esportiva Palmeiras. See Società Sportiva Palestra Itália
Società Sportiva Lazio, 143
Società Sportiva Palestra Itália, 40, 88–89, 111–12, 144, 146, 237–39; fans and, 187–89; nationalist criticism of, 6, 62–63, 102–4, 151, 197
Sócrates (Brasileiro Sampaio de Souza Vieira de Oliveira), 249
Sousa, Washington Luís Pereira de. See Luís, Washington
South American Championship, 120, 133–34; of 1916, 126–27; of 1919, 35, 43, 51–52, 56, 84, 93, 127–28, 145, 210–11

Sport Club Brasil, 182
Sport Club Corinthians Paulista, 14, 52, 72, 95, 111–12, 146, 227; class and, 87–89, 144, 164; Corinthians Democracy, 249; fans and, 159; foundation of, 87, 122
Sport Club Germania, 60, 68, 82, 89, 100, 130
Sport Club Internacional, 68, 82, 83

Taça Ioduran, 144–45
Torcidas organizadas, 159–62, 192–93

Uruguay, 95, 131; football style in, 201-03, 223, 241; government of, 54; in international football, 51-52, 117, 127–28, 130, 133, 142–43, 148-149, 195, 229, 245; migration and, 61, 102, 143, 150

Valentim, Max, 104, 221–22
Vargas, Getúlio, 40, 59, 103, 149, 152, 198, 219, 232; ideology of, 115–16, 194, 196, 254, 257; sports administration and, 9, 12, 101, 113–14, 151, 155–56, 240, 246, 278n137; women's football and, 162, 166, 199. See also Conselho Nacional de Desportos
Várzea, Paulo, 99–100, 111
Vasconcelos, Jaguaré Bezerra de, 101
Veríssimo, José, 1, 24–26, 66, 255, 259n8
Villa Isabel Football Club, 79, 92–93
Vinhais, Luiz, 225

Weber, Ernest, 38, 84–85, 206–7, 210, 212, 219, 238
Welfare, Harry, 61, 72–73, 81, 182, 206, 221
Williams, Charles, 61, 73
Women's sports, 45, 66, 118, 166–71, 173, 249
Women's World Cup, 161
World Cup, 13, 120, 159-60, 244; of 1930, 17-18, 36, 142, 147–49, 223–25; of 1934, 18, 61, 102, 114, 143, 150-51, 225, 227-28; of 1938, 40, 102, 151–56, 195–98, 228-30, 232–34, 239–40; of 1950, 157, 244–46,

World Cup—*continued*
    278n137; of 1954, 246; of 1958 and 1962 and 1970, 246-48, 289n14; of 1974 and 1978, 248-49; of 1982, 249; of 1994, 249-50; of 1998, 250-51; of 2014, 2, 117, 243, 251-54, 289n34, 290n37
World War I, 38–40, 50, 58, 63, 71, 88, 121, 134
World War II, 103–4, 156–57, 278n137

Gregg Bocketti is professor of history at Transylvania University in Lexington, Kentucky.

od-product-compliance